Visual and Plastic Poetics From Brazilian Concretism to the Chilean Neo-Avant-Garde

LEGENDA

LEGENDA is the Modern Humanities Research Association's book imprint for new research in the Humanities. Founded in 1995 by Malcolm Bowie and others within the University of Oxford, Legenda has always been a collaborative publishing enterprise, directly governed by scholars. The Modern Humanities Research Association (MHRA) joined this collaboration in 1998, became half-owner in 2004, in partnership with Maney Publishing and then Routledge, and has since 2016 been sole owner. Titles range from medieval texts to contemporary cinema and form a widely comparative view of the modern humanities, including works on Arabic, Catalan, English, French, German, Greek, Italian, Portuguese, Russian, Spanish, and Yiddish literature. Editorial boards and committees of more than 60 leading academic specialists work in collaboration with bodies such as the Society for French Studies, the British Comparative Literature Association and the Association of Hispanists of Great Britain & Ireland.

The MHRA encourages and promotes advanced study and research in the field of the modern humanities, especially modern European languages and literature, including English, and also cinema. It aims to break down the barriers between scholars working in different disciplines and to maintain the unity of humanistic scholarship. The Association fulfils this purpose through the publication of journals, bibliographies, monographs, critical editions, and the MHRA Style Guide, and by making grants in support of research. Membership is open to all who work in the Humanities, whether independent or in a University post, and the participation of younger colleagues entering the field is especially welcomed.

ALSO PUBLISHED BY THE ASSOCIATION

Critical Texts
Tudor and Stuart Translations • *New Translations* • *European Translations*
MHRA Library of Medieval Welsh Literature

MHRA Bibliographies
Publications of the Modern Humanities Research Association

The Annual Bibliography of English Language & Literature
Austrian Studies
Modern Language Review
Portuguese Studies
The Slavonic and East European Review
Working Papers in the Humanities
The Yearbook of English Studies

www.mhra.org.uk
www.legendabooks.com

STUDIES IN HISPANIC AND LUSOPHONE CULTURES

Studies in Hispanic and Lusophone Cultures are selected and edited by the Association of Hispanists of Great Britain & Ireland. The series seeks to publish the best new research in all areas of the literature, thought, history, culture, film, and languages of Spain, Spanish America, and the Portuguese-speaking world.

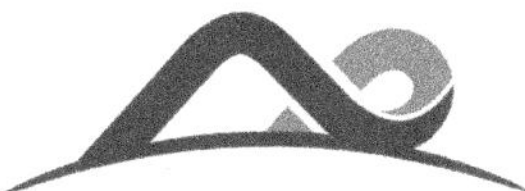

The Association of Hispanists of Great Britain & Ireland is a professional association which represents a very diverse discipline, in terms of both geographical coverage and objects of study. Its website showcases new work by members, and publicises jobs, conferences and grants in the field.

www.legendabooks.com/series/shlc

STUDIES IN HISPANIC AND LUSOPHONE CULTURES

20. *(Un)veiling Bodies: A Trajectory of Chilean Post-Dictatorship Documentary*, by Elizabeth Ramírez-Soto
21. *Photographing the Unseen Mexico: Maya Goded's Socially Engaged Documentaries*, by Dominika Gasiorowski
22. *The Rise of Spanish American Poetry 1500-1700*, edited by Rodrigo Cacho Casal and Imogen Choi
23. *José Saramago: History, Utopia, and the Necessity of Error*, by Mark Sabine
24. *The Cultural Legacy of María Zambrano*, edited by Xon de Ros and Daniela Omlor
25. *Cortázar and Music*, by Nicholas Roberts
26. *Bodies of Disorder: Gender and Degeneration in Baroja and Blasco Ibáñez*, by Katharine Murphy
27. *The Art of Cervantes in Don Quixote: Critical Essays*, edited by Stephen Boyd, Trudi L. Darby and Terence O'Reilly
28. *The Modern Spanish Canon: Visibility, Cultural Capital and the Academy*, edited by Stuart Davis and Maite Usoz de la Fuente
29. *The Novels of Carmen Laforet: An Aesthetics of Relief*, by Caragh Wells
30. *Humanizing Childhood in Early Twentieth-Century Spain*, by Anna Kathryn Kendrick
31. *Gómez Manrique, Statesman and Poet*, by Gisèle Earle
32. *No Country for Nonconforming Women: Feminine Conceptions of Lusophone Africa*, by Maria Tavares
33. *Form and Reform in Eighteenth-Century Spain*, by Carla Almanza-Gálvez
34. *Women and Nationhood in Restoration Spain 1874–1931*, by Rocío Rødtjer
35. *Francisca Wood and Nineteenth-Century Periodical Culture*, by Cláudia Pazos Alonso
36. *Pepetela and the MPLA: The Ethical Evolution of a Revolutionary Writer*, by Phillip Rothwell
37. *Queer Genealogies in Transnational Barcelona*, by Natasha Tanna
38. *Hispanic Baroque Ekphrasis: Góngora, Camargo, Sor Juana*, by Luis Castellví Laukamp
39. *Contemporary Galician Women Writers*, by Catherine Barbour
40. *The Marvellous and the Miraculous in María de Zayas*, by Sander Berg
41. *Twentieth-Century Sephardic Authors from the Former Yugoslavia*, by Željko Jovanović
42. *From Doubt to Unbelief: Forms of Scepticism in the Iberian World*, edited by Mercedes García-Arenal and Stefania Pastore
43. *Franco's Female Prisoners: Writing No / Bodies*, by Holly J. Foss
44. *Memory and Utopia: The Poetry of José Ángel Valente*, by Manus O'Dwyer
45. *Quim Monzó and Contemporary Catalan Culture (1975–2018)*, by Guillem Colom-Montero
46. *Horizontalism and Historicity in Argentina: Cultural Dialogues of the Post-Crisis Era*, by Brigid Lynch
47. *The Visualization of a Nation: Tàpies and Catalonia*, by Emily Jenkins
48. *Naturalism Against Nature: Kinship and Degeneracy in Fin-de-siècle Portugal and Brazil*, by David J. Bailey
49. *Queering Lorca's Duende: Desire, Death, Intermediality*, by Miguel García

Visual and Plastic Poetics

From Brazilian Concretism to the Chilean Neo-Avant-Garde

Rachel Elizabeth Robinson

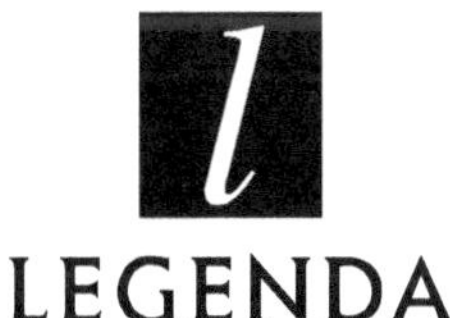

LEGENDA
Studies in Hispanic and Lusophone Cultures 53
Modern Humanities Research Association
2022

Published by Legenda
an imprint of the Modern Humanities Research Association
Salisbury House, Station Road, Cambridge CB1 2LA

ISBN 978-1-83954-028-8

First published 2022

Copy-Editor: Dr Ellen Jones

CONTENTS

ACKNOWLEDGEMENTS

First and foremost I would like to thank my DPhil supervisor, Ben Bollig. I am grateful for his intellectual and academic support from the beginning of my master's up until now. I also would especially like to thank my parents, Elizabeth Robertson and Jeffrey Robinson, not only for their emotional support, but also for teaching me how to read poetry and how to write. I would not have been able to do it without them.

I am extremely appreciative of Cecilia Vicuña for warmly sharing her poetry and art with me. I am grateful to Magda Sepúlveda and Hugo Herrera for introducing me, with open hearts, to the works of most of the poets I discuss in this book. I would also like to thank Claire Taylor, Xon de Ros, Claire Williams and Maria del Pilar Blanco for their thorough comments and suggestions, as well as for their academic and emotional support.

I am also very grateful to Diniz Pignatari, Eduardo Carvalho, Ivan de Campos, María Amélia Mello and Ferreira Gullar's relatives, Luiz Angelo Pinto, Marcelo Azeredo, Augusto de Campos, Alita Martínez and the Fundación de Juan Luis Martínez and Elisa Lira for their generosity in allowing me to use images of their works or the works of their relatives in this book.

I'd like to thank Alexander Aston for helping me work through my insecurities and making me feel like my insights are intelligent and important. I am grateful to Marzia D'Amico for reminding me of the social and emotional power of poetry and for sharing the excitement it brings. I'd also like to thank Matthew Kruger for helping me find my confidence (and for teaching me ALL of philosophy).

I could not have made it through the last five years without my best friends. I'd especially like to thank Ross Curello and Gregorio Drummond for crafting and puzzling our way through from the beginning, Achim Wolf for being such a delivery, Rachel Lamb, mi media naranja, and Dana Stepleton for giving up on the water fountain with me and for every moment since.

I'd like to thank my incredible siblings, Miriam Robinson and Sam Robinson for always believing in their little sister.

I am grateful to Carlos Fonseca Grigsby, Annabel Rowntree and Denisse Lazo for w(h)ining with me about our work and field.

The friends I have made in Oxford have been hugely supportive, intellectually and emotionally. I'd particularly like to thank Adele Bardazzi, Danielle Bishop, Kirsty Duffy, Zac Gross, Jean Hyun, Marten Krijgsman, Graham Long, Ketan Ramakrishnan, Jacob Reynolds, Hannah Ringheim, Julie Sachschal and Liana Semchuk.

Lastly, I am grateful to Nico, Ringo, Goose, Jeoffry and Barley for all the walks and cuddles.

R.R., August 2021

INTRODUCTION

It is well known that Chile has fostered and produced radical and experimental poets during the twentieth century, including Pablo Neruda, Vicente Huidobro, Gabriela Mistral and Nicanor Parra, but there are many who have yet to receive the global recognition that they deserve. This book aims to show how three lesser-known and more recent Chilean neo-avant-garde poets, Juan Luis Martínez (1942–1993), Rodrigo Lira (1949–1981) and Cecilia Vicuña (1947–), make use of and develop Brazilian concretism in order to articulate a poetics uniquely expressive of life in an oppressive society. By bringing together these poets in this study, I hope to illuminate the works of these understudied Chilean writers and to increase our understanding of Latin American experimental poetry. Despite observing concretist features in the poems of these Chilean writers, I do not argue that they are concrete poets or that their works are concretist. Instead, I propose that they have absorbed into their own later works features of concrete poetry that they develop as part of their own unique poetics with diverse motivations.

Visual and concretist practices have redefined (and continue to redefine) the limits of poetry and literature on a global scale. Visual poetry has existed for centuries, dating as far back as Ancient Greece, and became a fundamental practice in the poetic experiments of the early twentieth century, not only in European and American modernism, but also in the Latin American avant garde. While as a movement it had its roots in Brazil and Switzerland, concrete poetry quickly became an international phenomenon that spread throughout Europe and Latin America and expanded to literary centres all over the world, from Japan to South Africa to the United States. As things in-and-of themselves separate from their contexts (at least in theory), concrete poems appealed to readers and authors across cultures and continue to appeal to them today. My study of the instances of such poetry that this book addresses contributes to this global literary history of experimental poetry, and the comparison made here between Brazilian and Chilean poetry illuminates how the international visual poetry movements attracted so many readers and writers world-wide and how and when it became necessary or productive to modify its poetics. Conversely, the comparison is intended to convince the international poetry-reading community that Martínez, Lira and Vicuña belong with the major European and American experimentalists of the late twentieth-century.

Several key characteristics of concrete poetry are manifest in the works of these Chilean poets. In particular, they share 1) a focus on the word decoupled from syntax, 2) an emphasis on the space of page (and at times beyond the limits of the page) instead of the line and 3) a destabilisation of the authority of a poem which in turn facilitates the reader's entry into the creation of it. Making use of these strategies, all three Chilean poets uniquely develop and then significantly bend to their own purposes concretist poetics as a political gesture against authoritarian and capitalist ideals. My first example, Martínez, like the Brazilian concretists, undercuts the authoritative role the poet plays in many conventional works. However, recognising the inevitability of the authorial presence, he questions, without completely erasing (as the concrete poets attempt to do), his particular role as author in the creation of the text and makes room for the reader's participation. Lira's concretist critique of authorship and text takes a different form through his direct *détournement* of previous poetry and of quotidian materials. Unlike the concretists, however, he draws from literary and non-literary material that is particular to his Chilean context in his critique of the capitalist and authoritarian regime under which he wrote. Vicuña shares the concretist preoccupations above, but develops them as 'plastic' poetry (that is, poetry that invites the reader to enter into the creation of the work in its ideal state) at the level of the word, page and book that encourages active readerly participation and ultimately expresses a democratic and feminist vision.

In the opening chapter of this book, I situate the Brazilian and Chilean poets in a long line of experimental poetry within and outside of Latin America. Firstly, I argue that both the Chilean poets and the Brazilian concretists can be categorised generally as Latin American neo-avant-garde poets because they respond to the successes and failures of the historical avant-garde by experimenting with new forms of poetry from a particular context of the 'space between', that is, Latin America. Secondly, the Brazilian and Chilean poets can be placed in relation to one another because of their overtly 'anthropophagic writing', a defining designation that has been given to many Latin American writers; they perform a 'cannibalisation' of European, African, Asian and indigenous American cultures and literature. As both Latin American 'cannibalistic' and neo-avant-garde writers, they all contribute to the literary history of visual poetry that has its (known) origins in Ancient Greece, but flourished in the 1920s with the historical avant-garde. We can define visual poetry broadly as poetry that is *made* to be seen.

After thus characterising the points of contact between the earlier movements and later poets, I end the opening chapter with a detailed description of Brazilian concrete poetry. In the 1950s, the Brazilian concrete poets synthesised visual and experimental techniques, especially those seen in the poetic experiments of the early twentieth century, into object-like poems that both utilised the forms and techniques of, as well as criticised, the consumerist and capitalist societies that were beginning to thrive in Latin America and the world in general. Characteristics of concrete poetry include: an emphasis on the materiality of language (through the use of the ideogrammatic method, an emphasis on the page as the poetic unit and a rejection of traditional syntax, for example), an emphasis on verbal, vocal and visual aspects of language, the creation of a poem as an object, the rejection of the traditional lyric subject, the activation of the reader and a critical engagement with the techniques and materials of consumer society.

The second chapter of this book will show how, in *La nueva novela* (1977), the poet Juan Luis Martínez adapts the tenets of concrete poetry to his own particular needs as an experimental Chilean poet. Originally dismissed as a 'mad man' by many of his contemporaries, Martínez has recently been admired for his poetic innovations that question the supposed boundary between poetry and the visual arts.[1] In this book, Martínez breaks down traditional notions of the book and of writing in general by moulding language and other materials into (usually humorous) metaphysical and metapoetic discussions. Martínez uses object-poems to criticise seriously — although not directly — the dictatorship under which he wrote. What critics have not fully explored is the fact that these innovative techniques resemble the formal techniques and goals of the Brazilian concrete poets, who wrote only a generation before Martínez.[2]

This poet, I shall show, shares with the concrete poets many aims and characteristics. Like the concretists, he rejects conventional language by focusing on the page and blank space, rather than on the written line, as the primary units of poetry, and by mixing art and non-art (that is, everything that exists outside the traditional domain of pre-modernist art). Like these poets, he also creates a work of art to be perceived as an object rather than as a representation of other things. Such a shift in focus involves the dismantlement of the unified lyric subject and the encouragement of the reader to participate actively and creatively in the work. While Martínez makes use of these features to destabilise conventional ways of writing, he ultimately redirects them to political ends in a critique of Augusto Pinochet's dictatorship.

Martínez develops concrete poetics, I argue, by creating a playful tension between presence and absence in relation to the sign, the author, and the nation. By investigating the nature of the sign, he questions the relationship between word and silence; language, as he presents it, can only exist in relation to silence. This relationship is manifest on the page: language materialises as marks on the page, and silence as white space on the page.[3] He humorously challenges former engagements (such as those of Stéphane Mallarmé, John Cage and Eugen Gomringer) with the relationship between word and silence through various adapted experiments (including an attempt to convert a 'blank page' into a poem and to include musical scores as poetry). Martínez, like the concrete poets, attempts to rid their works of all subjectivity (and with it, authority) by creating doubt about the role of the author throughout his works. While he attempts to erase his name in a variety of ways and plays games with the reader that lead her/him to participate in the creation of the text, Martínez ultimately fails (perhaps consciously) to deny himself all authority.

1 *The Oxford Book of Latin American Poetry: A Bilingual Anthology*, ed. by Ernesto Livon Grosman and Cecilia Vicuña (Oxford: Oxford University Press, 2009), p. 452.

2 Although some critics have recognised the connection between Martínez and concretist poetics, to my knowledge none have explored this relationship. See, for example, Oscar Galindo, 'El Alfabestiario universal de "La nueva novela" de Juan Luis Martínez', *Revista Chilena de Literatura*, 57 (November 2000), 21–40 (p. 21), and Valeria de los Ríos, 'La fotografía como clave de lectura de *La nueva novela*', *Estudios Filológicos*, 44 (2009), 53–65 (p. 55).

3 As Martínez himself says, he, unlike other poets of the time (such as Raúl Zurita), works with (in Saussurean terms) signifiers, rather than solely with signifieds. In other words, the material of the word itself on the page is the focus of Martínez's work. See Martínez, *Poemas del otro: Poemas y diálogos dispersos* (Santiago: Universidad Diego Portales, 2003), p. 68.

Because a subjective text could easily lend itself to a local, and potentially national, expression, Martínez's struggle to rid the text of all subjectivity demonstrates a tension he sees between creating an international and a national text; his attempted creation of an international poetic text that transcends particular national concerns, or at least one that only comments on society through formal experiments, like those of the concrete poets, is ultimately not realised because his poetry seems unable to avoid commentary on Pinochet's authoritarian regime.

While Martínez experimented graphically and linguistically with poetics, the poet Rodrigo Lira 'manipulated' language through critical reworkings of both literary and non-literary materials.[4] In the third chapter, I will explore the ways in which Lira develops and transforms concretist poetics, especially drawing on their emphasis on the materiality of language, their focus on destroying the authorial position and their adoption of advertising techniques and other non-literary forms. Lira transforms the universality of the concretist 'object-poem' into an exploration of the material properties of a localised, colloquial language and history. In this way, Lira ultimately rejects the concretist effort for the erasure of subjectivity (a rejection which all the Chilean poets studied here share, albeit to different degrees). Although he draws on particularly Chilean materials, Lira, like the concrete poets, interlaces the verbal, visual and vocal aspects of poetry.

Because of his schizophrenia, diagnosed at the age of twenty-two, and his suicide at the age of thirty-two, Lira in many ways has been seen as a mythical figure in Chilean literary history. While this poignant biography has distracted many from exploring his works, it nonetheless has been recognised that he was an integral member of the literary scene of the time. He took to an extreme Chilean antipoetics (poetry against conventional poetic practices), reacting to the poetry of Nicanor Parra and Enrique Lihn (as well as many other Chilean poets) through his use of, for example, colloquial language, biting humour and intertextual combinations.[5] While Lira's poetry was only published in journals or distributed hand to hand during his lifetime, after his death in 1981, the majority of his works were compiled into a collection entitled *Rodrigo Lira: Proyecto de obras completas* for the first time in 1984.[6]

Lira creates *verbivocovisual* texts, to use James Joyce's term, through a synthesis of a variety of materials. Just as concretist poetics has been described as a synthesis of the European historical avant-garde's practices, Lira's poetry could be seen as a synthesis of specifically Chilean and Latin American avant- and neo-avant-garde ones. This literary 'cannibalism', however, emerges from a deeply critical stance from Lira himself towards the poets of his nation. This critique, furthermore, manifests itself through dark humour, direct and piercing criticisms of particular poets, and

4 In a conversation with Enrique Lihn, Lira referred to himself as a 'manipulator of language' rather than a poet. Lira, *Rodrigo Lira*, p. 157.

5 Jesús Sepúlveda, 'Sólo tendrás piedras: Rodrigo Lira' *Memoria Chilena* <http://www.memoriachilena.cl/602/w3-article-3693.html> [accessed 20 September 2017].

6 The collection was republished in 2003 and later in 2013. I shall refer to the later edition throughout this book. *Rodrigo Lira: Proyecto de obras completas* (Santiago: Ediciones Universidad Diego Portales, 2013 [1984]).

antipoetic practices. Not only does he appropriate and distort the language of his predecessors in a practice I call 'literary *détournement*' (a term I shall explain), he also, like the antipoets Nicanor Parra and Enrique Lihn, integrates materials and structures from sources typically not related to poetry, performing what I call 'non-literary *détournement*'. What emerges from this practice has been called 'anti-poetry'. His intertextual range, from weather reports and advertisements to collaged photographs and magazine clippings, reinforces his anti-poetic texts and furthers the concretist concern for the materiality of language.[7] However, although Lira engages antipoetry, at the same time he seriously criticises it. Ultimately, where the concrete poets, through their formal experiments, commented generally on capitalist and consumerist society, Lira, in reworking the materials and techniques of his predecessors, created politically 'committed' texts that directly engage with Chilean society at the time.

In the fourth chapter, I illustrate the ways in which the poet and artist Cecilia Vicuña transforms concretist poetics into a visionary 'plastic' poetics. By viewing her work in terms of plasticity, we can see how Vicuña draws on particular ideas and aspects of concrete poetics yet ultimately forms new and unique poetic experiments. With plastic poetics, Vicuña aims to create an egalitarian work that involves both reader and author equally. Such plasticity, as a development of concretist poetics, ultimately leads to a political engagement with language on the part of both reader and author.

Vicuña aims to create poems that are 'easily shaped or moulded' (the common definition of 'plastic'), just as objects in the plastic arts are. Furthermore, by emphasising the process of that moulding, her poems include a meta-discourse on their plasticity. Vicuña does not mould objects out of clay, wax, or stone, but instead utilises poetic, performative and visual art techniques to transform what seems flat on the page into artistic creations that evoke three dimensions or become three dimensional. Plasticity requires both spatial and verbal manipulation that allows a reader/viewer to participate in the creation of the poem. Such readerly participation in plastic art, however, involves a preliminary disruption of the reader's expectations of the space that s/he ordinarily occupies. While the concrete poets focused on materiality in order to illuminate their poems as product-objects, Vicuña emphasises particularly the *process* of art through the materiality of language. Her disruption of the reader's expectations and defamiliarisation of his/her sense of time and space produces, as I argue through a Deleuzean lens (one with which she explicitly engages), a political and indeed feminist art. Her goal is to redefine and strengthen the relationships one has not only with others, but also with the fragile environment of our Earth.

Vicuña expresses the plasticity of language through the rhizomatic creation of weavings, which allow her to adapt concretist practices to suit her own poetics. She takes the concretist preoccupation with the materiality of words and the importance

7 While he steals direct material from other poems and materials, he does not go as far as Kenneth Goldsmith, for example, with his explicit appropriations. See Goldsmith, *Uncreative Writing: Managing Language in the Digital Age* (New York: Columbia University Press, 2011).

of their physical positions on the page to develop a woven 'text' of words and parts of words presented as threads. While concrete poets aimed to rid their poetry of all subjectivity, I would argue that, in fact, they have displaced the subjectivity from author to reader. Similarly, weaving in Vicuña's work moves subjectivity from the author to the reader, allowing the reader to become an active participant in the creation of the text.

Vicuña develops these concretist characteristics, as I shall show, at the level of the word, the page and finally the book. Like the concrete poets and other visual poets, Vicuña allows the reader to engage with an object-like text not solely semantically, but also explicitly through its visual characteristics. As we shall see in PALABRAR*mas*, she allows the reader to do so at the level of the word. The spatial arrangement of the words on the page in *Instan* at times requires the reader to read, or engage, the text both visually and kinetically. Her politics, moreover, do not exist as a message to be received by her audience, but come into being in the experience of reading her work. Vicuña encourages the reader, in one way or another, to join with the other readers in a performance; her work becomes communally 'performative in its own right'.[8] The project *cloud-net* allows the participant to connect to others literally in performances and installations, and forces the reader of the book to be aware of the bonds woven in those events and to continue to weave the connections virtually.

In each chapter, I use distinct theoretical frameworks, not as defining structures, but as support for my arguments. In the Martínez chapter, I mostly draw on the twentieth-century Swiss and French theorists Ferdinand de Saussure, Michel Foucault, Jacques Derrida and Roland Barthes to help illuminate Martínez's questions of the nature of the sign and the author. While each of these theorists is distinct, I have chosen them not only for their usefulness, but also because Martínez explicitly refers to them throughout his work and complicates each of their theories. In the third chapter, the concepts of antipoetry and *détournement* help illuminate Lira's explicit and often parodic reworkings of the Chilean canon, which includes the antipoets themselves. In addition, Theodor Adorno's notion of 'committed' art as one that engages the social formally, rather than thematically, here helps illustrate the particular ways Lira manipulates form in order to criticise Chilean society. To better understand the weavings Vicuña makes and promotes and to highlight her expression and development of 'in-between space', I use two principal theories, respectively: Deleuzean rhizomatics, in which the structure of being is always in a process of *becoming* and unattached to specific roots, and Marc Augé's notion of the non-place, in which one exists *between* cultures. Vicuña directly engages with both of these concepts.

These chapters will show how all three of these Chilean poets share many poetic principles with the Brazilian concretists, yet expand and develop them into distinctly Chilean poetic experiments. Looking at the Chilean poets through a concretist lens will situate them within a Latin American literary context and within the wider

8 Kelly Gordon, 'Weaving Sight-Weaving Life: Threading the Sacred and Seeking the Meaning of Photography in Cecilia Vicuña's Works', *Hipertexto*, 11 (2010), 93–102 (94).

context of visual poetry and the neo-avant-garde. The Chilean and Brazilian poets share a concern for the visual aspects of poetry and respond to and engage with European, North American and Latin American avant-garde practices, yet do so from a particularly Latin American position (that which is expressed through 'antropofagia'). The European, North American and Latin American avant-garde poets were the first major poets of the Western world to attack and tear apart literary traditions, but after the peak of their writing, the Brazilian concrete poets, in response to their achievements and failures, aimed to synthesise the avant-gardist experiments into literary objects. The Brazilian concrete poets created their objects as general criticisms of the consumer and capitalist society that had emerged and flourished from the early twentieth century. At the same time, the poets recognised that the 'cannibalistic' consumption of earlier practices was a particularly Latin American approach. Martínez, Lira and Vicuña also 'cannibalise' avant-garde practices, but, in response to the oppressive regime under which they wrote in Chile, ultimately engage directly with their local context. Martínez moves towards a universal text, but inserts several poems and pages that situate his poems in Chile; Lira brings many concrete poetry principles and techniques to engage directly with Chilean literary and quotidian material in his antipoetic *détournements*; and Vicuña, as an exile, creates a space *between* cultures that allows for the exilic state to be a creative one.

CHAPTER 1

From the Neo-Avant-Garde to the Concrete

By analysing the overlap between the poetics of the Brazilian concretists and the Chilean poets, Juan Luis Martínez, Rodrigo Lira and Cecilia Vicuña, the aim of this book is to further a conversation between Brazil and Spanish America, a conversation that has yet to be fully opened.[1] This chapter will attempt to justify their comparison.

These three Chilean poets and the Brazilian concretists can be viewed in relation to one another for a number of reasons. First, the fact that they had direct and indirect personal relationships with each other suggests a loose influence they had on each other. Second, we can categorise both the concretists and Chilean poets under the broad name 'neo-avant-garde' because they can be understood as generally reflecting and expanding upon formal features of the historical avant-garde. Third, they all fit into Haroldo de Campos's categorisation of Latin American literature as 'anthropophagic', that is, they 'cannibalistically' consume other literature and literary techniques.[2] Fourth, within the broader definition of neo-avant-garde, the works of both the Brazilian concretists and Chilean poets belong to a long tradition of visual poetry.

1 There have been surveys of the Latin American avant-garde that have begun to develop a literary history that includes Brazil, such as Vicky Unruh and Merlin Forster and David Jackson's works, but there still are few focused comparisons. See Vicky Unruh, *Latin American Vanguards: The Art of Contentious Encounters* (Berkley: University of California Press, 1994); and Merlin Forster and David Jackson, *Vanguardism in Latin American Literature: An Annotated Bibiliographical Guide* (New York: Greenwood, 1990). In a review of Jorge Schwartz's *Vanguarda e cosmopolitanismo na década de 20,* the Argentine poet Néstor Perlongher (as Ben Bollig points out) 'call[s] for increased links between Argentina and Brazil'. Ben Bollig, 'Exiles and Nomads: Perlongher in Brazil', *Hispanic Research Journal,* 7.4 (2006), 337–51 (p. 339). Perlongher states: 'Há uma barreira entre as escrituras rioplatenses (e hispano-americanas em geral) e a brasileira, transposta apenas quando, em honra ao "boom", alguma obra de certo "sabor local" dá a volta ao mundo europeu e encosta nestas margens'. Néstor Perlongher, 'As Viagens da Vanguarda', *Leia Livros,* 62 (1983), 21. Just as Perlongher comments on the relationship between River Plate writers and Brazilian writers, I attempt to draw a bridge between Brazil and Chile. Interestingly, Augusto de Campos was the first Brazilian to win the Chilean Premio Iberoamericano de Pablo Neruda in 2015. This prize indicates that the literary conversation between the two countries is beginning to expand.

2 Haroldo de Campos takes this term from the poet Oswald de Andrade. See the section titled 'Anthropophagic Poetry'.

Direct and Indirect Relationships

Despite the fact that there is little evidence that the Chilean poets were directly influenced by Brazilian concrete poetry and poetics, there are nonetheless suggestions of a connection with the Brazilian concretists. Although she does not claim that they directly influenced her works, Vicuña has stated that she is aware of the Brazilian concrete poets and their formulation of concretist poetics and admits that her project PALABRAR*mas* could be identified as concretist.[3] The fact that she published a version of this book that includes translations by the well-known Scottish concrete poet and translator, Edwin Morgan, also implies that she recognises connections to concretism in some of her poetry.[4] Morgan, along with the other major late twentieth-century Scottish concrete poet, Ian Hamilton Finlay, was in direct contact with the Brazilian Noigandres group during the 1950s and 1960s and was dedicated to bringing these concretist experiments to the attention of readers in the United Kingdom.[5] Given her close relationship to Morgan, it is likely Vicuña shared with him an interest in the Brazilian concrete poets. Nonetheless, she is not known as, and indeed does not consider herself to be, a concrete poet.[6]

Although there is little evidence of such a personal connection between either Martínez or Lira and the Brazilian concrete poets, a strong personal and professional relationship exists among the three Chilean poets, which suggests their shared poetic interests. It is evident that Martínez and Vicuña had a professional and personal relationship. For example, celebrating their exchange of ideas in a tribute to Martínez, Vicuña indicates that she and Martínez were friends.[7] Vicuña explains that, in a conversation with Martínez, she discovered 'la existencia de una comunidad fantasmal que no se había llegado a congregar en Con-Cón, donde vivían al mismo tiempo y sin conocerse tres núcleos equidistantes de poetas: Zurita y Martínez, Bertoni y Vicuña y la futura Soledad Fariña.'[8] Even though they had not yet met each other, Vicuña believes these poets had a 'spiritual connection' in Con-Cón, a town north of Valparaíso. While there is also no evidence of a personal relationship between Lira and the other Chilean poets, it is clear that he was aware of Martínez as he directly engages with Martínez's *La nueva novela* in a version of his poem 'Nil Novi' by cutting and pasting particular pages of Martínez's work into his own.[9]

3 Cecilia Vicuña, 'Re: cloud-net and other questions', email to Rachel Robinson, 30 March 2015.

4 See Edwin Morgan and Vicuña, PALABRAR*mas*/WURDWAPPIN*schaw* (Edinburgh: Morning Star Publications, 1994).

5 John Coyle and others, *The Midnight Letterbox: Selected Correspondence, 1950–2010* (Manchester: Carcanet Press, 2015).

6 Vicuña, 'Re: cloud-net'.

7 Vicuña, 'Xuan // Luis', in *Merodeos en torno a la obra poética de Juan Luis Martínez*, ed. by Soledad Fariña and Elvira Hernández (Santiago: RIL Editores, 2001), pp. 63–66 (p. 64).

8 Ibid., p. 65.

9 Rodrigo Lira, *Cartapacio* (Santiago: Biblioteca Nacional de Chile), <http://www.memoriachilena.cl/602/w3-article-72711.html> [accessed 26 April 2018]. In addition, both Martínez and Lira were 'discovered' by the critic and poet Enrique Lihn. See Lira, *Rodrigo Lira: Proyecto de obras completas*, and Pedro Lastra and Enrique Lihn, *Señales de Ruta* (Santiago: Ediciones Archivo, 1987).

The Neo-Avant-Garde

Even though their personal and professional ties are somewhat tenuous, we can understand the commonalities between the Brazilian concrete poets and the Chileans when we place them within the larger frame of 'neo-avant-garde poetics'. The Brazilian concretists and the Chilean poets in question can be connected through their shared poetic responses to the historical avant-garde.

The avant-garde, according to Peter Bürger, was a European bourgeois artistic movement thriving during the 1920s.[10] It consisted of artists who not only questioned and stretched the limits of their media (a trait that, according to Jochen Schulte-Sasse, could be applied to all avant-garde art and literature[11]), but who also criticised and attempted to break away from the institution of art as well as to reconnect art with society.[12] Ultimately, as Bürger argues, the avant-garde failed in its attempt to destroy the institution because it soon became part of that very institution.[13] Thus, because the artists who followed those of the historical avant-garde attempted to criticise an institution that had integrated those who had failed to destroy it, the neo-avant-garde, according Bürger and others, could only be, in Anna Katharina Schaffner's terms, 'an inauthentic repetition, a reprise, even fraud' because it 'recuperates, incorporates and assimilates techniques of the forerunners and thus de-radicalises them'.[14]

However, the position and cultural development of Latin America, as other critics have argued, allows one to disregard some of the problems that Bürger and others point to as causing the avant- and neo-avant-garde movements to fail.[15] Forster and Jackson, for example, explain that the primary features of the European avant-garde — the search for newness and modernity, an iconoclastic stance against logic and reason, and the quest for artistic modernity amidst rapid

10 Peter Bürger, *Theory of the Avant-Garde* (Manchester: Manchester University Press, 1984).

11 Jochen Schulte-Sasse, in Bürger, pp. vii–xv.

12 See Bürger.

13 Ibid. This is clearly a simple summary of Bürger's argument. Other critics have also claimed that the avant-garde failed, but for a variety of reasons, such as for not successfully 'expressing the times' (Hobsbawm) or for not bringing art to the masses without falling into the category of 'kitsch' (Greenberg). See Eric Hobsbawm, *Behind the Times: The Decline and Fall of the Twentieth-Century Avant-Gardes* (London: Thames and Hudson, 1998), pp. 7–18; and Clement Greenberg, *Art and Culture* (London: Thames and Hudson, 1961), pp. 3–21.

14 Anna Katharina Schaffner, 'Inheriting the Avant-Garde: On the Reconciliation of Tradition and Invention in Concrete Poetry', in *Neo-Avant-Garde*, ed. by David Hopkins (Amsterdam: Rodopi, 2006), pp. 97–117 (pp. 109–10). If one considers integration into the 'institution' as a failure of the avant-garde and the neo-avant-garde, then Vicuña becomes the least successful of the three Chileans, as she is the one who has been most accepted into the 'institution' of art. Martínez (although to an extent he is becoming recognised as an important figure of the Chilean avant-garde) and Lira both actively distanced themselves from public recognition or canonisation. One could consider Lira's lack of publications (at least during his lifetime) a way (whether intentional or not) to resist this integration.

15 Moreover, Bürger only applies his criticism of the neo-avant-garde to a select few 'Western' artists and writers, thus ignoring other contexts in which neo-avant-garde works have emerged. See Bürger.

technological development — apply to Latin American vanguardism.[16] But, as they point out, two distinctive tensions in Latin America make its position unique: its involvement in a process of assimilation and change since colonisation and its search for modernity while engaging with its American roots.[17] The critics Vicky Unruh and Jean Franco both claim that, because the institution of art itself was a relatively recent phenomenon in the early twentieth century in Latin America, one rarely encounters in Latin American vanguardism an absolute stance against art that one would find in movements such as Dada.[18] In their view, Latin American vanguardism in some instances was an important player in establishing national and regional art and literature and was primarily concerned with bringing together life and art, or, in Unruh's terms, with actively 'rehumanising' art.'[19] In this light, Latin American vanguardism can be seen as an active movement essential to the development of Latin American culture as a whole rather than the failure it was seen to be in Europe.[20]

Therefore, when defined as a response to and an expansion of Latin American and European avant-garde formal strategies and techniques, the term Latin American neo-avant-garde applies to the poets studied here. Neo-avant-garde practices, as the critic Anna Katharina Schaffner writes, include:

> certain techniques and formal strategies, such as the exploration of the material, the abandonment of narrative and representation, the dissection of established linguistic and pictorial orders and conventions, and the thematisation of aesthetic qualities and conventions of usage of the signs and symbols deployed.[21]

Because they share these characteristics as responses to avant-garde experiments, the Brazilian concrete poets and Martínez, Lira and Vicuña all fall under the designation of 'neo-avant-garde'.[22] All of these poets, as I will illustrate throughout this book,

16 Forster and Jackson, pp. 5–6.

17 Ibid. These and other critics emphasise that, while there were geographical and national tensions within Latin American vanguardism, there was a general sense of a particularly Latin American, as opposed to European, vanguardism.

18 Unruh, p. 7 and Jean Franco, *An Introduction to Spanish-American Literature*, 3rd edn (Cambridge: Cambridge University Press, 1994), p. 260.

19 Unruh, pp. 7–26. A result of this 'rehumanisation' was an attempt to bring poetry into public spaces and, therefore, poetry that could be consumed at once, or, visual poetry (which I will define below).

20 Some of the examples of Latin American visual poetry below can be considered examples of this success.

21 Schaffner in Hopkins, *Neo-Avant-Garde*, pp. 111–12.

22 While this book only focuses on three Chilean neo-avant-gardists, there were many others of the same generation who drew from the Brazilian concretists. For example, it is pertinent to mention Guillermo Deisler (1940–1995), whose link to the Brazilian concretists is clear. Deisler himself explains that he developed his poetry by looking towards the Brazilian concretists (the founders and then those who practiced the 'poema proceso' (see Bianchi, *La memoria: Modelo para armar*, p. 94. In addition, Gonzalo Millán (who himself has poetry that has concretist tendencies) explains that Deisler was a promotor of concrete poetry within Chile, although primarily through the second generation (that is, the River Plate poets such as Edgardo Antonio Vigo and Clemente Padín). See María Inés Zaldívar, 'El contexto de Guillermo Desiler en Chile y la generación poética de los 60', Taller de Letras, 41 (2007), p. 117. The poet/musician Fernando García rewrote poems

emphasise the materiality of language, dismantle linear narrative, confuse traditional verbal and pictorial conventions and engage in a meta-discourse on art. Although the Noigandres group and other Brazilian concrete poets did not themselves use the term 'neo-avant-garde' to describe their works, they have characterised concrete poetry in terms that are suggestive of the neo-avant-garde, that is, as a radicalisation of historical avant-garde practices due to their synthesis of and response to them.[23] Similarly, the Chilean poets respond to, develop and expand upon the experiments of early twentieth-century European and North American avant-garde artists and writers (see 'Visual Poetry' section below for a more detailed explanation of direct influences). Various critics have also defined Martínez, Lira and Vicuña as part of the Chilean Neo-Avant-Garde for similar reasons. For instance, Marcelo Rioseco includes all three poets under this designation, defining the movement as one that responds to the historical avant-garde.[24] The term 'neo-avant-garde' is apt, then, as a general term to describe how both the Brazilian concretists and the Chilean poets respond to similar texts and experiments, that is, those of the historical avant-garde.

Anthropophagic Poetry

By looking at the concretist aspects of Martínez, Lira and Vicuña's works, this book delineates a certain literary genealogy within the Latin American neo-avant-garde (in this case between Brazil and Chile specifically). Instead of attempting to group together these poets under one limiting definition, however, it aims to illustrate

by Feirrera Gullar, José Lino Grünewald, Décio Pignatari and Augusto de Campos to music in *Los cuatro poemas concretos* (1966). Another Chilean neo-avant-garde poet and artist whose experiments could be linked to Brazilian concrete poetry is Gregorio Berchenko. Although he is primarily known for his sculptures, he could be compared to the concretists in his piece *Knock-Out* (1973) as well as his experiments with mail art. Nonetheless, the number of poets who experimented with concretist techniques during the second half of the twentieth century is, as the poet and critic Andrés Anwandter points out, nothing compared to that of Argentina, Uruguay and, of course, Brazil (Anwandter, 'Nota sobre Guillermo Deisler', *Cyber Humanitatis*, 21 (2002)).

23 See, for example, Haroldo de Campos, 'Evolucão de formas: Poesia concreta', in *Teoria da Poesia Concreta: Textos, Críticos e Manifestos, 1950–1960*, ed. by Haroldo de Campos and others (São Paulo: Invenção, 1965), pp. 47–53. Many critics have also described concrete poetry as neo-avant-garde. For instance, Schaffner argues that the term is appropriate to describe the works of Eugen Gomringer and the Brazilian concrete poets (Schaffner in Hopkins, *Neo-Avant-Garde*, pp. 97–118), and Dietrich Scheunemann found it appropriate to include Keith Aspley's discussion of surrealism and concrete poetry in his book on the avant-garde and the neo-avant-garde. See Keith Aspley, 'Verbal Chemistry and Concrete Poetry', in *Avant-Garde/Neo-Avant-Garde*, ed. by Dietrich Scheunemann (Amsterdam: Rodopi, 2005), pp. 131–48.

24 What makes the Chilean Neo-Avant-Garde unique, for Rioseco, is their additional responses to the Chilean avant-garde and antipoetic movement initiated by Nicanor Parra as well as their responses to Pinochet's oppressive dictatorship. For a thorough definition of the movement, see Marcelo Rioseco, *Maquinarias reconstructivas: Poesía y juego en Juan Luis Martínez, Diego Maquieira y Rodrigo Lira* (Santiago: Editorial Cuarto Propio, 2013), pp. 30–60. In addition, while she does not develop the comparison between Martínez and Vicuña, the critic Rebecca Kosick explains that both poets are examples of practitioners of 'material poetics of relation', therefore bringing their aesthetics into conversation with one another. Rebecca Kosick, 'Assembling *La nueva novela*: Juan Luis Martínez and a Material Poetics of Relation', *Latin American Research Review*, 52.5 (2017), 854–73 (p. 856).

the developments and transformations of Brazilian concretist poetics achieved by Chilean writing in the late twentieth century. Specifically, it brings the Chilean and Brazilian poets into conversation with one another within the frame of the (initially) Brazilian literary concept of 'antropofagia'.

In 1928, the Brazilian poet Oswald de Andrade published his 'Manifesto Antropófago', in which, as a response to the Parnassian and classical tendencies in Brazilian literature, he calls for a particularly Brazilian, 'cannibalistic' literature. He rejects both a colonial negation of an indigenous history of the country as well as their imposition of European (especially Christian) values upon Brazil: 'Nunca fomos catequizados [...] Fizemos Cristo nascer na Bahia [...] Fizemos foi Carnaval. O índio vestido de senador do Impêrio'.[25] Instead, he promotes a literature that consumes the 'inimigo sacro', absorbing its strength; just as the cannibal devours (and therefore destroys and sublates) its enemies to absorb its nutrients, the anthropophagic writer assumes the forms and ideas of the colonisers and reworks them into something stronger.[26] In other words, as Haroldo de Campos explains, the universal cultural heritage the Brazilian writer creates does not come from the perspective of the submissive 'bom selvagem', but from the view of the '"mau selvagem" [...] Ele não envolve uma submissão (uma catequese), mas uma transculturação; melhor ainda, uma "transvaloração"'.[27] The Brazilian writer therefore is not solely indigenous and does not solely appropriate or imitate the trends of the coloniser, but, through the act of cannibalism, asserts his Brazilian-ness. As the following line demonstrates, the Brazilian writer in*corpo*rates Shakespeare's famous line into his Brazilian context: 'Tupi or not tupi that is the question'.[28]

Although Oswald de Andrade applied 'antropofagia' only to Brazilian literature, Haroldo de Campos, in his essay 'Da Razão Antropofágica: Diálogo e Diferença na Cultura Brasileira', suggests that it applies to most of Latin America and proposes a specifically Latin American genealogy that builds upon de Andrade's theory.[29] This categorisation creates, as de Campos argues, a nationalism that is not based on the biological pattern of a plant's development, but one that is a 'movimento dialógico da diferença'.[30] He argues that the Latin American baroque

25 Oswald de Andrade, 'Manifesto Antropófago', *Nuevo Texto Critico*, 7.23 (1999), 25–31 (p. 28).

26 Ibid., pp. 27–31.

27 Haroldo de Campos, 'Da Razão Antopofágica: Diálogo e Diferença na Cultura Brasileira', in *Metalinguagem e outras Metas: Ensaios de Teoria e Crítica Literaria*, 4th edn (São Paulo: Editora Perspectiva, 1992), pp. 231–57 (p. 234). For the definition and discussion of 'transculturation' as not solely acculturation or deculturation, but a combination, see Fernando Ortiz, *Contrapunteo cubano del tabaco y el azúcar* (Havana: Consejo Nacional de Cultura, 1963), pp. 98–104.

28 de Andrade, 'Manifesto Antropófago', p. 27. Moreover, de Andrade uses philosophical and psychoanalytical language throughout his manifesto, connecting cannibalism to, as Mike Gonzalez and David Treece explain, the 'urge to dissolve the barriers between the self and the world, between subject and object', an urge which, as we will see, both the concrete poets and the Chilean poets discussed in this book address. Mike Gonzalez and David Treece, *The Gathering of Voices: The Twentieth-Century Poetry of Latin America* (London: Verso, 1992), p. 98.

29 When discussing the baroque and anthropophagous reason, de Campos claims that the term could apply to other Latin American cultures with the exception of the pre-Columbian cultures. Haroldo de Campos, *Metalinguagem e Outras Metas*, p. 239.

30 Ibid., pp. 235–39.

included the first anthropophagic writers, describing the baroque as 'Não...uma antitradição por derivação direta, que isto seria substituir uma linearidade por outra, mas do reconhecimento de certos desenhos ou percursos marginais.'[31] Another manifestation, or 'constellation' as de Campos calls it, of anthropophagic reasoning was concrete poetry.[32] He explains that concrete poetry: 'pode também reclamar essa tradição "antinormativa", por uma outra e peculiar redistribuição dos elementos configuradores disponíveis [...] Ela não apenas pôde falar a diferença num código universal [...] autores de uma literatura supostamente periférica subitamente se apropriavam do total do código, reivindicavam-no como patrimônio seu.'[33] In its cannibalisation of a universal poetics, Brazilian concrete poetry simultaneously maintained its national and regional identity while reaching beyond it to the universal: 'A poesia concreta, brasileiramente, pensou uma nova poética, nacional e universal.'[34] Even though it eventually expanded into an international movement and drew on universal poetics, concrete poetry, in its 'cannibalisation' of poetics, was a particularly Latin American one. The three Chilean poets of this study, I shall show, belong within de Campos' literary genealogy. By looking at their use and development of (Brazilian) concretist poetics as a synthesis and reworking of Latin American and European avant-garde poetics, the anthropophagic character of these Chilean poets comes to the fore.

Visual Poetry

The concretists and Chilean poets not only belong to the 'neo-avant-garde' and to an anthropophagic lineage, but also to a long tradition of visual poetry. Here, after providing a definition of visual poetry, I will survey some major strands of European and Latin American visual poetry. Given that today most poems appear on a page and require that the reader read them with his or her eyes, one could argue that all written poetry is visual. However, there are poems in which the visual elements are foregrounded and in which the boundaries between the visual arts and writing are blurred. Traditionally, the visual arts and literature were viewed as irrevocably distinct; as Gotthold Ephraim Lessing famously argued, because the visual arts were consumed simultaneously and poetry temporally (or, in structuralist terms, synchronically and diachronically), they could not be combined.[35] However, as the critic Willard Bohn explains, visual poetry seeks to overcome the dichotomy by offering simultaneous and temporal readings.[36]

How do we further distinguish the latter from other poems in which the visual patterns are subservient to or solely supportive of other formal aspects of the poem

31 Ibid., p. 243.
32 Ibid., p. 244.
33 Ibid., pp. 245–46.
34 Ibid., p. 247.
35 See Gotthold Ephraim Lessing, *Laocoön: An Essay on the Limits of Painting and Poetry* (London: Longman, 1853).
36 Willard Bohn, *The Aesthetics of Visual Poetry, 1914–1928* (Cambridge: Cambridge University Press, 1986), p. 1.

or its meanings? Bohn defines visual poetry as 'poetry that is meant to be seen'.[37] This definition emphasises that visual poetry aims not just to be read, but to be seen, as are the works of visual artists. Bohn implies that the intention of the author is crucial in understanding visual poetry. However, given that visual poets tend to diminish the significance of the author's intention, Bohn's definition needs some modification to shift the focus from the author to the text itself. I define visual poetry, then, as 'poetry that is *made* to be seen'. The making that is essential to visual poetry could be the author's doing, but it also could be the result of the reader's involvement in the poem's creation. My definition does not require that the poem be reduced to its author's intention, and emphasises the *poietic* characteristic of visual poetry, that is, the ways in which it foregrounds its *making*. Moreover, much visual poetry, in one way or another, demonstrates its own materiality; it becomes (or attempts to become) a *thing*.[38] Rather than mimic or represent some referent, a poem whose materiality is emphasised *presents* itself.[39] In this regard, visual poetry tends to reject mimetic traditions. Thus, through its visual elements, visual poetry, unlike other poetry, foregrounds the act of making and seeing.

Visual poetry has existed for thousands of years. The first known visual poems were the Greek *technopaigneia* and later the Roman *carmina figurata*,[40] such as Simmias of Rhodes' 'Egg', 'Axe' and 'Wings', each shaped like the object after which they are titled. After that, up until the nineteenth century, visual poems mainly followed this Greek and Roman technique and existed as what are called pattern poems (poems in which the shape resembles some object or figure). Many of these, such as George Herbert's 'Easter Wings' (1633), in the shape of wings, were religious texts.[41] Apart from acknowledging pattern poems and a few individual poems here and there, most historians of visual poetry have tended to skip ahead to catalogue poetry of the early twentieth century associated with modernism.[42]

In doing so, many, surprisingly, overlook the work of William Blake, whose place in the history of visual poetry should be acknowledged. Blake distinctively fills the white spaces of the page with engraved drawings, thereby creating a particular relationship between word and image. In many of his engravings, images and words interact with one another; sometimes the images border and surround the words, and at other times the letters themselves grow into images. Furthermore, he produces a dialectic between word and image in which one explains or contradicts

37 Bohn, *Reading Visual Poetry* (Madison: Fairleigh Dickinson University Press, 2011), p. 13.

38 Johanna Drucker defines materiality as 'the self-conscious attention to formal means of production in literature and the visual arts'. Johanna Drucker, *The Visible Word: Experimental Typography and Modern Art, 1909–1923* (Chicago: University of Chicago Press, 1994), p. 10.

39 Drucker explains that many of the twentieth century poets attempted to 'present' rather than 'represent'. Ibid., pp. 10–19.

40 Bohn, *The Aesthetics of Visual Poetry*, p. 1.

41 In 'Easter Wings', the wing-like shape enhances its Christian discussion of death and sin. George Herbert, 'Easter Wings', in *The Temple* (London: Penguin Classics, 2017), p. 54. Pattern poems, however, have received much criticism for their potentially closed forms; that is, for the fact that the figural form of the poem can limit the meaning of the poem instead of opening the poem up to multiple interpretations.

42 For instance, Bohn claims that visual poetry went through a long lull from a brief revival in the renaissance until the twentieth century. Bohn, *Reading Visual Poetry*, p. 13.

the other. While some have described the images as interpretations or translations of the poems, it is crucial, as the critic Irene Tayler explains, to understand the work as made up of both words and images:

> [Blake's works exist as] English words in something like the form of poetry [...] printed from hand-drawn plates as part of a larger nonverbal design, thus combining words and pictures into a new and unique whole.[43]

In order to understand Blake's poetry, one must consider the multiplicity of meanings that unfold from the relationship between image and word.

Along with the relationship he creates between image and word, the particular processes Blake used to engrave his poems also emphasise the materiality of the poem. The fact that the 'white space,' rather than the words, is what has been corroded by the acid used in his engraving process (the acid corrodes not the words but the surrounding material to create the engraving), accentuates the poem's object-like character; like a sculptor who moulds and chips away at a material to produce a sculpture, Blake 'finds' the poem through his application of corroding acid on the engraving.

Although there have been in the past scattered instances of such poetry including those above, visual poetry did not systematically flourish until the early twentieth century, in which many forms of visual poetry appeared within the avant-garde. Unlike what one sees in Blake's works, the visual elements in most of these modern works are produced through the manipulation of words and letters on the page rather than through the use of images. Credit for beginning this movement is given first and foremost to Stéphane Mallarmé (1842–1898) for his poem *Un coup de dés jamais n'abolira le hassard* (1897; a poem to which the concrete poets directly respond, as will be discussed in the section titled 'Concrete Poetry').[44] Mallarmé's poem, in representing syntax spatially rather than grammatically, draws the reader away from the word and the line as the primary poetic units and towards the page; the words in this poem are arranged not solely to follow linear, grammatical order, but are organised throughout the page in patterns.[45] At first, it seems as though Mallarmé attempts, as Giorgio Agamben argues, to emancipate the poetic text from its roots in oral tradition as purely visual.[46] However, while Mallarmé's poem emphasises 'that part of speech which is not spoken',[47] the white spaces take on importance as they do in music.[48] In other words, Mallarmé relates white space to silence and ink to sound.[49] His poem, moreover, is visually similar to a musical score, which takes the analogy between white space and silence further to connect the written work to vocal patterns. The emphasis on the relationship between the words and the

43 Irene Tayler, *Blake's Illustrations to the Poems of Gray* (Princeton: Princeton University Press, 1971), p. 6.

44 Martínez also directly refers to Mallarmé in several poems of *La nueva novela*. See Chapter 2.

45 Stéphane Mallarmé, 'Préface', in *Un Coup de dés jamais n'abolira le hazard* (Paris: Éditions Gallimard, 1914).

46 Giorgio Agamben, *The End of the Poem* (Stanford: Stanford University Press, 1999), p. 33.

47 Ibid., p. 46.

48 Mallarmé himself describes this relationship to music in his preface to *Un Coup de dés.*

49 Carole Anne Taylor, *A Poetics of Seeing: The Implications of Visual Form in Modern Poetry* (New York: Garland, 1985), p. 91.

white space on the page allows the physical layout of the poem to assume meaning and creates a new spatial syntax. The poem consists of what Mallarmé called 'constellations', which are formed as the reader connects the variously spaced words into a meaningful arrangement. Unlike in a conventional pattern poem (see above), the spatial organisation of *Un coup de dés* does not close down the meaning of the poem. Rather, the typography opens the poem up to multiple readings. Because of its typeface and size, the readings are especially multidirectional.[50]

Although the poet Guillaume Apollinaire (1880–1918)[51] did not see Mallarmé's *Un coup de dés* before he began to produce his own visual poems, which he eventually named 'calligrammes',[52] the similarities between his and Mallarmé's poem are clearly apparent.[53] Like Mallarmé, Apollinaire reconfigures syntax (particularly punctuation conventions) through spatial arrangements and typographical experiments. He also challenges the authority of the author through his appropriation of language from '"random" sources in "chance" combination'.[54]

In his calligrammes, Apollinaire attempted to 'figure the vernacular'.[55] He also spatially juxtaposed language from a variety of quotidian sources, such as newspapers and advertisements, and used informal language, in, for example, the poems 'Arbre' or 'Le musicien de Saint-Merry'. Apollinaire explains what his collaged juxtapositions bring to the poem: 'the relations between the juxtaposed figures in one of my poems are as expressive as the words that compose it. And this at least, I think, is a new invention.'[56] The relationships *between* words, not solely the words by themselves, make the poem. The integration of collage techniques into poetry connects his work with Cubism and other avant-garde movements in the visual arts, further illustrating Apollinaire's attempt to bring the visual arts into the realm of poetry.[57] He intended to shatter the divide Lessing asserts exists between language and image, claiming that his poems are to be consumed simultaneously (that is, that both the textual and the visual elements are to be taken in at once).[58]

Despite Apollinaire's popularity, few critics have taken his calligrammes seriously. Critical dismissal, from, for example, the critic Roger Shattuck and the concrete

50 Ultimately, however, the text lends itself to an overall linear reading (i.e. left to right, beginning to end, top to bottom). The concrete poets take Mallarmé's spacing a step further and rid their poems completely of a singular linear reading (see the section titled 'Concrete Poetry').

51 Another major French visual poet during the period was Pierre Albert-Birot. Very much influenced by Apollinaire (as seen in the various poems dedicated to him), Albert-Birot wrote similarly calligrammatic poems that he called 'Poèma imagé' ('imaged poems'), poèmes-affiches' ('poster poems') or 'poèmes-pancartes' ('placard-poems').

52 In fact, one of the initial terms he used was 'ideogram,' the term that Pound appropriated for some of his experiments (although it is uncertain who decided to use the term first, or if each came up with it separately). Taylor, p. 188.

53 Michael Webster, *Reading Visual Poetry After Futurism: Marinetti, Apollinaire, Schwitters, Cummings* (New York: Lang, 1995), p. 63.

54 Drucker, pp. 149–50.

55 Ibid., pp. 146–68.

56 Apollinaire, quoted by Bohn, *The Aesthetics of Visual Poetry*, p. 48.

57 For Apollinaire, typography can synthesise music, painting and literature. Drucker, p. 155.

58 Bohn, *The Aesthetics of Visual Poetry*, p. 66. However, one still has to read the majority of his poems in succession, so perhaps 'bringing together Lessing's dichotomy' is more fitting.

poet Augusto de Campos, may be due to the ultimately figural characteristic of most of the calligrammes.[59] Unlike *Un coup de dés*, some of Apollinaire's calligrammes take on the ultimately closed form of the pattern poem, and thus have been seen by many as basic, limited works.[60] The concrete poets attempt to avoid such figural constriction and open up the pattern of the poem to multiple interpretations; the spatial form of the calligramme, for the concrete poets, purely emphasises the semantic meaning, rather than opening the semantic meaning up to multiple readings.

Johanna Drucker also concludes that Apollinaire's calligrammes are essentially mimetic (as opposed to being objects in and of themselves),[61] but still recognises that, while most of his calligrammes have 'simple, evident, even banal forms', Apollinaire still manages 'to charge these [poems] with profundity, and to make them function through their structural integration of visual and verbal activities'.[62] As opposed to an ordinary pattern poem, the calligramme, according to Drucker, becomes a material object with its 'words as sonoric and colored and as presence [...] yet very clearly not at the expense of content or subject matter.'[63] One could argue that the 'profundity' of the calligrammes actually comes from the ways in which they highlight and allow for processes of construction (that is, by creating patterns on the page, the poet emphasises the act of making). This process of construction is, as it is in many concrete poems, seen most clearly in Apollinaire's use of collage techniques, but also can be found in the work's promotion of invention in the experience of the reader/viewer.[64] In particular, the reader can begin to read at multiple points in a poem and jump around among the words in different ways, even though the form of the poem is still subservient to its semantic content.

At the same time that Apollinaire was creating his calligrammes, the Italian Futurists (1909–1944) were similarly experimenting with typography and visual innovations in poetry. Led by Filippo Tommaso Marinetti, the artists of the Futurist movement promoted poetry that allowed the word to exist publicly and freely ('parole in libertà') from conventional syntax and form.[65] Also described as 'wireless imagination,' the Futurists strove to create 'absolute freedom of images or analogies, expressed in words which are untied and without the connecting wires of syntax'.[66] Like Apollinaire and other French avant-garde poets, the Futurists,

59 Roger Shattuck, 'Introduction', in *Guillaume Apollinaire: Selected Writings* (New York: New Directions, 1950), pp. 3–54 (p. 20), and Augusto de Campos, 'Pontos-Periferia-Poesia Concreta', in *Teoria da Poesia* (1965), pp. 31–45 (p. 31).

60 Drucker, p. 141.

61 Drucker, 'Experimental, Visual, and Concrete Poetry: Context and Concepts', in *Experimental-Visual-Concrete: Avant-Garde Poetry Since the 1960s*, ed. by Drucker and others (Amsterdam: Rodopi, 1996), pp. 39–61 (pp. 40–41).

62 Drucker, p. 141.

63 Ibid., p. 148.

64 Ibid., p. 151. In fact, Bohn describes Apollinare's calligrammes as '*plastic* imagination' (my emphasis), a term I will use to describe Vicuña's work that encourages readerly participation. Bohn, *The Aesthetics of Visual Poetry*, pp. 46–68.

65 Other visual poets of the Futurist movement included Carlo Carrà and Ardengo Soffici.

66 Bohn, *The Aesthetics of Visual Poetry*, p. 15.

with their deconstruction of syntax, also questioned the role of the lyric 'I' as one of self-expression and wrote poetry that emphasised the materiality of language. Looking forward to the future and eliminating any nostalgia for the past, the Futurists wanted their works to embody modernity.[67] They thus used a number of typographical and rhetorical techniques to indicate their engagement with technological progress.

Marinetti, for example, used a variety of visual elements to 'modernise' poetry. As Apollinaire attempted to counter Symbolist language by using colloquial material, Marinetti used aggressive and explosive language to do the same. In addition, he 'modernised' his poems with sophisticated typography that included reductive notation, mathematical symbols and structures (not unlike some used by the concrete poets), as well as onomatopoeic words and their physical representation.[68] Through these visual techniques, Marinetti emphasised the physical aspects of language as a means of modern transmission technology.[69] For instance, his famous 'FUMARE', in which the letters of the word for 'to smoke' imitate the motion and growth of smoke, illustrates the movement and growth of modernity heading towards an explosive end.[70]

Another major group of artists and poets that experimented with the materiality of language during the early twentieth century was the group known as Dada. Dada, according to Eric Hobsbawm, wanted to destroy all art completely.[71] In particular, Tristan Tzara stretched the boundaries of art genres and the boundaries between art and the public realm of commerce the public realm in his visual poems.[72] As Drucker describes the poet, he, like other Dadaists, was concerned 'at every level with the production of language within the sites and rhetorical structures of commodity culture', and wrote with a 'dependence on conventions and habits which were sufficiently familiar that their subversive use could be immediately recognized'.[73] Replete with obvious contradictions, such as in the poem 'Bilan', his visual poetry questions any sort of systematic position. Like Apollinaire, Tzara appropriated language from a variety of public media, such as newspapers and advertisements through which, as Drucker explains, 'the visual form of language [...] reveals the context, history, or origin of the phrases within the public sphere of printed matter'.[74] His appropriation and use of collage, like that of the majority of

67 Ibid., p. 29. This is one of many ways the Futurists rejected Symbolism, which, like Apollinaire, many of the Futurist poets had studied profoundly. See Bohn, *The Aesthetics of Visual Poetry* and Drucker.

68 Drucker, pp. 116–40.

69 Ibid.

70 The emphasis on modern progress and explosive, violent language might explain the futurists' tendencies towards fascism.

71 Hobsbawm, pp. 32–36.

72 Both Martínez and Vicuña allude to Tzara and Dada in their poems. See Chapters 2 and 3.

73 Ibid., p. 193 and p. 196. In the meantime, the Russian Futurists (1910s–1920s), including Velimir Khlebnikov, Alexei Kruchenykh and Ira Zdanevich, were also developing a visual poetics in which their focus was on the 'factura' (making) of their works, that is, the material and physical *production* of their work. Drucker, pp. 172–83.

74 Ibid., p. 193. Similarly, the concrete and Chilean poets use collage techniques in their works.

the poets mentioned above, challenges the role of the poet of mimesis by presenting materials rather than describing them.[75]

An American poet (to whom the concrete poets directly allude in their theoretical works) during this period created a different style of visual poetry from the poems mentioned above: e. e. cummings.[76] According to Webster, cummings, playing with the relation between language and image, expanded upon the idea that the basic material of poetry is the letter, as opposed to the line or word (see, for example, 'Poem 42').[77] As Taylor explains, cummings, unlike Apollinaire who wavered between the symbol and the figure, 'began by using visual form imagistically and moved toward a metaphoric sense of the relation between language and a poem's picturing'.[78] His imagistic form is apparent in his use of punctuation as patterns as well as syntactical tools, which 'undermines the role of punctuation as an indication of orally expressed junctures'.[79]

Many Latin American poets brought European visual poetic experiments to or engaged with them in their respective countries. As a result of travelling in Europe during this avant-garde period, the Chilean poet Vicente Huidobro, a visual poet at times, drew on the experiments of the French avant-garde, Dada poets and Italian Futurists to develop his movement of 'creacionismo' and to enhance his break from Spanish-American *modernismo.*[80] Huidobro, like these other poets, wanted to create a new poem that would be something *in and of* itself, not as something *for* anything else, whether for a reader or as a reference to some outside object; the poem, for Huidobro, should not reflect the world, but exist as a new world. He, as the creator of new things, hence received the title 'el pequeño dios' (a phrase he uses himself to describe the poet in his 'Arte poética') from many of his contemporaries. Especially influenced by Apollinaire, Huidobro created a handful of visual poems titled 'caligramas'. Like those of his French contemporary, most of Huidobro's calligrammes are figural, or pattern poems, and therefore the shape of the poem can constrict its meaning.

Huidobro brought the experimental visual poetics of the French avant-garde, Dada and the Italian Futurists not only to South America, but also to Spain, where he especially influenced the *ultraísta* group.[81] Mostly characterised as a collection of poets who appropriated aesthetics (including concepts and techniques taken from the Italian Futurists and the French avant-garde), the *ultraístas* from 1919–1923 produced many visual poems. Like Huidobro and the *creacionistas,* the *ultraístas* reacted to the ornate works of *modernismo.* The *ultraístas* included the poets Rafael

75 While the juxtapositions of these collaged languages are visually impressive, his typographical experiments were relatively simple.

76 Marius de Zayas and Agnes Ernst Meyer's 'Mental Reactions' (1915), according to Bohn, marks the birth of visual poetry in the United States of America. See Bohn, *The Aesthetics of Visual Poetry,* p. 185.

77 Webster, p. 129.

78 Taylor, p. 203.

79 Taylor, p. 206. For instance, a parenthetical mark may represent a waning or waxing moon.

80 Lira directly engages (and reworks) Huidobro's lines. See Chapter 3.

81 Catalonia also produced many visual poets during the period (1910s–1920s), such as Josep-Maria Junoy, Joaquim Folguera and Joan Salvat-Papasseit.

Cansinos-Asséns, Guillermo de Torre, Juan Bautista, Isaac del Vando-Villar, Pedro Raida, Andrés Nimero Francisco Vighi, Eliodoro Puche and a young Jorge Luis Borges. These poets characteristically used free verse and striking metaphors, and aimed to transform, rather than represent images, which sometimes resulted in visual poems.[82] De Torre, for example, experiments with visual effects, such as isolated words or phrases produced in bold face type and/or capital letters, which are clearly influenced by the movements mentioned above.[83]

Borges brought *ultraísmo* to Buenos Aires. With the magazine *Prisma*, followed by *Proa* and *Martín Fierro*, he advocated a prismatic, rather than mimetic, approach to poetry that the Spanish *ultraístas* promoted, but crafted it to engage with a particularly Latin American context. In *Prisma* in particular, contributors plastered poems onto the city walls as a means to 'democratise' the movement.[84] Other poets in Argentina contributed visual poems to the poetic scene in the early twentieth century. Alberto Hidalgo wrote calligrammes that are clearly influenced by Apollinaire, but tended to make abstract (as opposed to figural or patterned) images that for the most part are to be read in a traditionally linear way, from the top to the bottom of the page.

The principle visual poet in Argentina during the beginning of the twentieth century was Oliverio Girondo. In most of his works (just as in concrete poetry, as we will see), as the critics Jorge Schwartz and Francine Masiello explain, Girondo was preoccupied with language's representative function, showed a distrust in the process of signification, and celebrated the object.[85] These elements exist in a variety of forms in his work, from figural calligrammes (such as 'Espantapájaros') to Cubist and Surrealist prose and verse poems (in which juxtapositions are highlighted) accompanied by his own illustrations (such as the poems of *Calcomanías* and *Veinte poemas para ser leídos en el tranvía*).[86]

Mexico also saw a surge in visual poetry in the beginning of the twentieth century. The *contemporáneos* and the *estridentistas* (competing avant-garde groups of the 1920s) included poets who experimented with visual poetry.[87] For example, Salvador Novo, who was part of the *contemporáneos* group, wrote three calligrammatic poems composed of 'solid forms' (in which the words are blocked together to form a single shape), and Luis Quintailla, who was part of the *estridentistas* group and who was clearly inspired by Apollinaire, wrote multiple Cubist calligrammes in the early

82 They criticised works that acted like mirrors (such as those of the Futurists) and wanted their works to resemble prisms that instead transformed images. See, for example, Jorge Luis Borges, 'Anatomía de mi "ultra"', in *Textos recobrados 1919–1929* (Buenos Aires: Emecé, 1997), p. 95.

83 According to Bohn, these visual characteristics are purely emphatic, and the poems are typically oriented by the left or right-hand margin. Bohn, *The Aesthetics of Visual Poetry*, p. 172.

84 Borges, *Textos recobrados*, pp. 126–28. One major result of visual poetry was an exhaustion of the medium of the book and a movement of poetry to public spaces, as will be discussed in the Concrete Poetry section of this chapter.

85 Jorge Schwartz, 'The Moremarrow Trajectory of Oliverio Girondo,' in Drucker and others, pp. 73–90; and Francine Masiello, 'Oliverio Girondo: El carnaval del lenguaje', *Hispamérica*, 6.16 (1977), 3–17.

86 Masiello, pp. 3–17.

87 Bohn, *Reading Visual Poetry*, p. 50; and Franco, pp. 263–66.

1920s. Other visual poets of this period in Mexico included José Juan Tablada, José María González de Mendoza and José D. Frías.

In Peru, while there was no visual poetry movement or group *per se*, there were a couple of notable instances of visual experiments. For example, although his work as a whole might not be considered especially visual, César Vallejo experimented with typography and highlighted the material status of the signifier. One instance of this experimentation occurs in his poem 'Tiempo, tiempo' (in the collection *Trilce*), when he capitalises 'E' at the end of a list of the repeated word 'nombre' in order to emphasise, as Franco argues, that names are not necessarily identical with experience.[88] Another visual poet from Peru is Carlos Oquendo de Amat, who, in *5 metros de poesía* uses typographical and cinematographical techniques in eighteen poems that unfold into one long poem, questioning accepted notions of what constitutes poems or even books.

In sum, while examples of visual poems can be found as far back as the ancient period, the form exploded in the early twentieth century as a violent reaction against traditional verse. Visual poets rejected the lyric 'I', the concept of the line as the poetic unit and poetry's separation from the visual arts. These rejections resulted in poems that blended the temporal with simultaneous perception and the oral and aural with the visual. After the 1920s in Europe and late 1930s in Latin America,[89] the predominant avant-garde groups seemed to move away from visual poetry (with the exception of certain groups here and there).[90] However, it was not until the 1950s that the next surge of visual experiments in poetry occurred with the emergence of concrete poetry as a synthesis and development of the early twentieth century practices.[91]

Concrete Poetry

As a form of visual poetry, concrete poetry is, as I stated above, '*made* to be seen'. As I will illustrate, it draws on many of these visual poetic experiments that foreground language's physical characteristics. However, as a synthesis of many different (and not solely visual) avant-garde practices, concrete poetry attempts to avoid the figural restriction that many pattern poems have and instead to integrate the visual with the aural and the semantic so that the reader can engage with physical, yet malleable, *objects*.

Although I use this broad definition of concrete poetry, there has been much debate over its stricter definition, and indeed over whether or not concrete poetry can in fact be defined. On the one hand, a number of critics and poets, such as

88 Franco, pp. 274–75.

89 For general dates of the avant-garde movements, see Forster and Jackson, pp. 1–11.

90 For example, the French Lettrists in the 1940s proposed the general theory that poetry should be devoid of any semantic value and remain purely formal, and Ouvrior de Littérature Potentielle (OuLiPo), wrote with constraining designs or concepts.

91 Visual works that occur after the 1950s, especially those from Latin America (such as Pablo Neruda's *Estravagario* and Nicanor Parra's *Artefactos*) will be discussed when relevant throughout the book.

Stephen Bann and Eduardo Kac, have argued that concrete poetry was a specific movement that occurred in the 1950s–1970s, and a movement that did not extend beyond this period.[92] Even though many poems written before the movement came close to looking like concrete poems, according to these critics, they did not fully realise all the requirements that the movement outlined. In their view, concretist poetics had exhausted its medium at the latest by the end of the twentieth century, if not before.

On the other hand, other critics conceptualise the term ahistorically and expand the definition to include any poem that has a concern for its own materiality. Mary Ellen Solt, for example, does not acknowledge the historical specificity of the concrete poets of the 1950s and 1960s and argues that concrete poetry can appear anytime when the defining characteristics occur. She claims that a fundamental requirement for concrete poetry is a 'concentration upon the physical material from which the poem or text is made', and this material is generally but not limited to language.[93] Peter Mayer and Bob Cobbing also recognise the difficulty in defining concrete poetry and therefore bring their definition back to its basic characterisation in the visual arts:

> One clear distinction can be made i.e. *CONCRETE IS A NON-MIMETIC ABSTRACT* = abstract minus mimesis = *CONCRETE*. This arises from studying the titles of the paintings of Kandinsky as well as those of Malevich and Mondrian. Take a hypothetical example of two 'identical' paintings composed of a red circle on a blue ground which differed only in the respect that one of them was entitled *SUNSET* and the other *RED CIRCLE ON BLUE*. The first of these paintings would then be abstract and the second concrete.[94]

This definition allows Solt's concern for the materiality of the work to come forward: the focus of the poem is on what exists on the page (or other medium) itself, rather than on a referent.[95] In other words, according to these critics, concrete poets dwell upon the possibilities of language as material.

Although the answers to the questions of who wrote the first concrete poems and who first developed the concept of concrete poetry are debatable,[96] it is generally

92 See, for instance, Bohn, *Reading Visual Poetry*, pp. 142–62 and *Concerning Concrete Poetry*, ed. by Bob Cobbing and Peter Mayer (London: Writers Forum, 1978).

93 *Concrete Poetry: A World View*, ed. by Mary Ellen Solt (Bloomington: Indiana University Press, 1968), p. 7.

94 Cobbing and Mayer, p. 9. This analogy sparks the question of the title's role and relationship to the work of art. It seems that if there were no title, it would be up to the reader to interpret the painting as abstract or concrete. However, if we look at these concrete works as poems, we can consider the title a paratextual element that is part of the work as a whole. See Gerard Genette, *Paratexts*, trans. by Jane E. Lewin (Cambridge: Cambridge University Press, 1997), pp. 55–104.

95 Some critics believe that the material of concrete poetry was exhausted after twenty to thirty years, but others find that new mediums have allowed for a rejuvenation of the concrete poem. Kenneth Goldsmith, for example, believes that the new medium of the Internet allows for a rebirth of concretism. Kenneth Goldsmith, *From (Command) Line to (Iconic) Constellation*, (UbuWeb) <http://www.ubu.com/papers/goldsmith_command.html> [accessed 30 March 2016]. In addition, while he does not consider himself a concrete poet because he has moved from the medium of the page, concretist principles are apparent in his works. See Bohn, *Reading Visual Poetry*, pp. 142–62.

96 For instance, the Swedish poet and artist Öyvind Fahlström first used the term in his 'Manifesto

agreed that the Brazilian group 'Noigandres' (initially including Haroldo de Campos, Augusto de Campos and Décio Pignatari), in conversation with the Bolivian-born Swiss poet Eugen Gomringer, began the official concretist 'movement' in the early 1950s.[97] I would like to define concrete poetics as a convergence of the definitions found at the two poles of the debate (that is, whether or not concrete poetry is limited to a historical period): while there are many experimental poems from before 1950 that resemble or share certain characteristics with the experiments of the 1950s, the full realisation of concrete poetry as a movement properly began in the 1950s when the Noigandres group and Gomringer defined it as a poetics. However, instead of constraining it to a defined period, I argue that the 'movement' did not have a finite end. As the title of this book implies, concretist poetics can be a useful tool for description, if not as a complete definition, of some more recent poetry. Just as concrete poetry questioned the limits of conventional poetry, the supposed limits of the concrete poetry of the 1950s and 1960s have been expanded upon and stretched into new, fascinating experiments. While some claim that the medium of the page has been exhausted, new possibilities have been explored digitally, on the Internet, or in musical and other media. Furthermore, as Ernst Jandl asserts, concrete poets must continue to experiment with concrete poetry:

> I think concrete is just starting [...] at least I am trying all the time [...] to write some concrete poem that is really a concrete poem, and a sound poem that really is a sound poem. Declaring concrete and sound poetry dead is just a way of admitting one's own defeat (and, particularly, death), whereas declaring one's own defeat is at least a way of proving, to oneself and maybe to those who care, that one is still alive, and trying.[98]

Just as concrete poetry began as a movement that stretched the boundaries of what poetry can be, concrete poets should continue to try to do the same with their own poetry. I will thus include examples from subgenres of later Brazilian concrete poetry in my explanation of the poetry.[99] These developments, along with the Chilean poems that are studied in this book, embody what Jandl argues should happen: a continuation of attempts to question and reform the definitions of poetry.

The Noigandres group formed in the early 1950s (their first publication as a group was in 1952).[100] At the time, the dominant poetic group was the 'generation of '45,' which included the Brazilian poets João Cabral de Melo Neto, Mario Quintana, and

for Concrete Poetry' in 1953. Cobbing, *Concerning Concrete Poetry*, pp 51–62.

97 The group formed and published their first journal in 1952. They chose the name 'Noigandres' from Pound's Canto XX: 'duas palavras enigmáticas para designar talvez aquela flor cujo perfume... afasta — gandres, de gandir — o tédio, noia, lennui fonemas telismanicos que nos serviram o emblemas de busca e de persquisa poéticas'. Haroldo de Campos, *Depoimentos de Oficina* (São Paulo: Unimarco Editora, 2002), p. 19. They first used the term 'concrete poetry' after Pignatari's meeting with Eugen Gomringer in 1956. *An Anthology of Concrete Poetry*, ed. by Emmett Williams (Brooklyn: Primary Information, 2013), p. vi.

98 Cobbing and Meyer, p. 51.

99 Nonetheless, although this broad definition of concrete poetry should call for an expansive conversation about global concrete poetry, I will narrow my discussion to the Brazilian poets who first articulated the movement and those who joined later.

100 Haroldo de Campos, *Depoimentos de Oficina*, p. 19.

Ariano Suassuna.[101] Although it had no coherent ideological programme, this group reacted against the experimentalism and popular and socio-political commitment associated with the Brazilian modernists.[102] With the exception of Melo Neto, the Noigandres group (especially Haroldo de Campos, as he explains in *Depoimentos de Oficina*) was not attracted to the generation's supposedly reductive notions of form, nostalgia for classicism and their support of the neo-parnassian revival.[103] Instead, the Noigandres poets wanted to create a minimalist poetry that exalted form. They thus turned away from the generation of '45 poets towards early twentieth-century European and North American poets, artists and musicians (from Ezra Pound and Stéphane Mallarmé to Max Bill and Anton Webern) and towards the Brazilian modernists (such as the poet Oswald de Andrade and the musicians Gilberto Gil and Caetano Veloso) for inspiration for their work.[104] The Noigandres group claim that their poetry was an attempt to synthesise some of the modernist experiments of the early twentieth century.[105] In their 'Plano-Piloto para Poesia Concreta,' they define their poetry as a: 'producto de uma evolução crítica de formas'.[106] For them, concrete poetry is the next evolutionary step from avant-garde works that brought into question the limitations of artistic expression. Throughout their poetics, the group emphasises that the combination of avant-garde works that have influenced them are integral to their poetry.[107] Characteristics of concrete poetry include the combination of: an emphasis on the materiality of language (through the use of, for example, the ideogrammatic method, an emphasis on the page as the poetic unit and a rejection of linear syntax), an emphasis on verbal, vocal and visual aspects of language, the creation of an object, the rejection of the lyric subject, the

101 Paulo Franchetti, 'Poetry and Technique: Concrete Poetry in Brazil', *Portuguese Studies*, 24 (2008), 56–66.

102 Gonzalez and Treece, pp. 232–33. For detailed surveys of the Brazilian modernist movement, see, for example, Erico Verissimo, *Brazilian Literature: An Outline* (New York: The Macmillan Company, 1945) and Gonzalez and Treece.

103 Franchetti, pp. 56–66, and Haroldo de Campos, *Depoimentos de Oficina*, pp. 15–18.

104 While they allude to European, North American and Brazilian poets and artists, the Noigandres group initially only rarely mentioned other Latin American poets in passing. In more recent essays, however, they have recognised the works of some Latin American poets, such as Severo Sarduy, Oliverio Girondo and Jorge Luis Borges. See, for example, Haroldo de Campos, *Depoimentos de oficina*.

105 Haroldo de Campos, 'Evolucão de Formas: Poesia Concreta', *Teoria da Poesia Concreta* (1965), pp. 47–53.

106 Augusto de Campos and others, 'Plano-Piloto para Poesia Concreta', *Teoria da Poesia Concreta*, p. 154. Later, Augusto de Campos has stated that 'technically, concrete poets can be distinguished from their antecedents by the radicalization and condensation of the means of structuring a poem, on the horizon of the means of communication of the second half of the century'. Augusto de Campos in *Experimental-Visual-Concrete* (1996), p. 385.

107 Although their 'cannibalisation' usually involves the *chewing up* of previous poetic techniques and principles (as I will discuss shortly), some of the poems are direct reworkings of specific poems. For example, Augusto de Campos reworks William Blake's 'The Sick Rose' (1794) into a spiral shape and 'The Tyger' (1794) into the shape of two tigers mirroring each other (Figures 3.1–3.2). In other words, he takes the romantic poet's work and re*forms* them into poems that emphasise the spatial arrangement of the words on the page. In doing so, Augusto de Campos emphasises that the material used to construct a concrete poem can be literary.

activation of the reader, and a critical engagement with the techniques and materials of consumer society. These features, as this book will illustrate, are developed in unique ways in the works of Martínez, Lira and Vicuña.

For the Brazilian concretists, concrete poetry was an attempt to find and flesh out the possibilities of the materiality of language. As Augusto de Campos states, concrete poetry 'começa por assumir uma responsabilidade total perante a linguagem'.[108] The subject of a concrete poem is its language in and of itself. In particular, the concrete poets were specifically preoccupied with the word and its relationship with other words and the white space that surrounds it. They found that the physical structure of the word and its relationship to other words can 'mean' something, asserting that the semantic meaning of the line and its conventional syntax is not the only way language can communicate.[109] They thus decided to reject linear syntax for the sake of a concentration on the word itself. In some cases, influenced by e. e. cummings's phonetic minimalism, they broke down the word in order to explore the possibilities of its phonemes.[110] For example, Ronaldo Azeredo[111] illustrates the movement of the letters of the word 'velocidade' by repeating the letter 'v' for a line, adding one more letter of the word each line (of equal length), and arriving at the full word in 'Velocidade' (Figure 1.1).[112]

To emphasise the materiality of language, a concrete poem, like 'Velocidade', would not only include the semantic meanings of words, but also appeal to the visual and aural senses. The group therefore drew upon Ezra Pound's ideogrammatic method as a means to excite the eyes. The concrete poem is 'a estrutura dinâmica. O ideograma como idéia básica'.[113] Pound attempts to represent verbally the visual elements that form an ideogram; instead of lines in a character that form a picture, Pound uses words to evoke a picture.[114] The Noigandres group uses this method in

108 Augusto de Campos, 'Poesia Concreta', *Teoria da Poesia Concreta*, p. 42.

109 While they do not specifically state it, the Noigandres group and other Brazilian concretists seem to have been influenced by structuralism. Evidence of this influence is, for instance, Haroldo de Campos's essay on Saussure's journals (although written after his concretist phase): Haroldo de Campos, 'Diábolos no texto: Saussure e os anagramas', in *A ReOperação do Texto*, 2nd edn (São Paulo: Perspectiva, 2013), pp. 109–24.

110 They explicitly write: 'cummings: atomização de palabras, tipografia fisiognômica'. Augusto de Campos and others, 'Plano-Piloto para Poesia Concreta,' in Augusto de Campos and others, *Teoria da Poesia Concreta*, p. 154.

111 Azeredo joined the broader group of 'Semiotic' poets in the 1960s, along with Pignatari and Luiz Ángelo Pinto.

112 This poem has also been presented in video format. See Christian Caselli, *Cinco Poemas Concretos* (Rio de Janeiro, 2007), <https://www.youtube.com/watch?v=yC3e7rmSYM4> [accessed 20 May 2015]. The concretists even go as far as to replace words for images, such as in Augusto de Campos' 'Ôlho por Ôlho' (Figure 1.7), in which photographs of eyes replace words.

113 Pignatari, 'Nova Poesia: Concreta', Augusto de Campos and others, *Teoria da Poesia Concreta*, p. 40.

114 Pound developed the concept of an ideogram from Ernest Fenollosa's discussion of Chinese characters as pictorial representations of concepts and as non-arbitrary mimetic abstractions. Fenollosa's discussion, however, has been adamantly rejected as an accurate description of how Chinese characters function. The Noigandres group was aware of this inaccuracy but maintained that the Poundian method was an integral part of the making of a concrete poem. Augusto de Campos, 'Pontos-Periferia-Poesia Concreta', Augusto de Campos and others, *Teoria da Poesia Concreta*, pp. 20–21.

VVVVVVVVVV
VVVVVVVVVE
VVVVVVVVEL
VVVVVVVELO
VVVVVVELOC
VVVVVELOCI
VVVVELOCID
VVVELOCIDA
VVELOCIDAD
VELOCIDADE

FIG. 1.1. Ronaldo Azeredo, 'Velocidade' (1957).
Courtesy of Marcelo Azeredo.

order to create poems as visual objects in and of themselves. While still maintaining their semantic meanings, words interact with one another as physical *things* that take up space (just as lines do in an artwork), and their physical relationships become integral to the meaning of the poem.[115]

Drawing on the form of the ideogram, the concrete poets aim to transform the words themselves into opaque objects. As Rosmarie Waldrop explains, 'we do not usually see words, we read them, which is to say we look through them at their significance, their contents. Concrete Poetry is first of all a revolt against this transparency of the word.'[116] The concrete poets extract the essence of 'mere' (supposedly) arbitrary signs by drawing the reader's attention to the spatial and aural relationships between the words and thus to the sign's materiality. Many (if not all) of the Noigandres group's concrete poems are poetic ideograms, but some overtly embody the characteristics of ideograms and some even include Chinese characters.[117] As the critic Marjorie Perloff explains, concrete poets, rather than solely describing ideograms, 'in fact create new meanings by [the poem's] visual placement on the page and its particular context.'[118]

Pound's ideogrammatic method was not the only visual technique upon which the Noigandres drew: Mallarmé's *Un coup de dés* (see the section titled 'Visual Poetry' above) also influenced the Noigandres group's commitment to highlighting the visual in concrete poems. In order to signal the importance of space, just as Mallarmé did,[119] the concrete poets saw the page, instead of the line, as the poetic unit.[120] In *Un coup de dés*, the space that has been shaped by the placement of the words on the page (which form the constellation Ursa Major) ultimately moves the reader through the text in many directions at once. Because Mallarmé uses different typefaces throughout the poem, one's eyes, although reading somewhat linearly through the poem (a reading that the concrete poets attempt to avoid), move across the page connecting the words and phrases together that are in similar typeface, just as one moves one's eyes connecting the lines between stars to form constellations. With reference to Mallarmé's poem, the Noigandres group (along with Gomringer) claim that a poem is like a constellation, a drawn map created by the spatial relationships between the words on the page: 'A concepção da estrutura pluridividida ou capilarizada que caracteriça o poema-constelação mallarmeano'.[121]

115 The Noigandres group also recognised and appreciated Apollinaire's calligrammes, but criticised him for reducing the ideogram to mere figuration: 'condena, assim, Apollinaire o ideograma poético à mera representação figurativa do tema.' Ibid., p. 19.

116 Rosmarie Waldrop, as quoted by Marjorie Perloff, '"Concrete Prose" in the Nineties: Haroldo de Campos' "Galáxias" and After,' *Contemporary Literature*, 42 (2001), 270–93 (p. 271).

117 See, for instance, Haroldo de Campos's 'Poemandala'. Martínez also plays with the ideogrammatic method and directly includes Chinese characters in his text. See Chapter 2.

118 Perloff, 'Refiguring the Poundian Ideogram: from Octavio Paz's Blanco/Branco to Haroldo de Campos' Galáxias', *Modernist Cultures*, 7.1 (2012), 40–55 (p. 40).

119 Mallarmé, *Un Coup de dés*.

120 Perloff, '"Concrete Prose" in the Nineties', p. 272. One also has to look at the connection between the pages in *Un coup de dés*.

121 Haroldo de Campos, 'La Obra de Arte Aberta,' Augusto de Campos and others, *Teoria da Poesia Concreta*, p. 28.

It is not only the words that form the poem, but the spaces that connect them. The reader must look at the page in its entirety. By shifting the poetic unit from the line to the page, the concrete poets allow for communication not just through the semantic meaning of a word, but through the spatial relationships of words.

In concrete poetry, the poems, like Mallarmé's poem, use space in order to bring the visual and the aural together. To both Mallarmé and the concrete poets, space represents silence. Mallarmé writes: 'Les "blancs", en effet, assument l'importance, frappent d'abord; la versification en exigea, comme silence alentour.'[122] Just as written words represent sound on the page, the white space conveys a silence that in fact gives meaning to the words. Following Mallarmé's poetics, Gomringer's poem 'Silencio' exemplifies the idea that silence is an absence of something and that the poem best communicates where words are not present.[123] Gomringer ultimately recognises, however, that one cannot fully represent a 'pure' silence on the page, for silence paradoxically only exists in relation to sounds.[124] Both *Un coup de dés* and 'Silencio' are analogous to music: just as music ultimately consists of patterns of sound and silence, so these poems are made up of visual patterns of words and white space. The concrete poets (and Mallarmé) use the visual in order to express the aural.

One could take Mallarmé's musical analogy one step further and claim that *Un coup de dés*, and in turn concrete poetry, is not simply analogous to, but is in fact a musical score.[125] As Bob Cobbing explains, 'visual poetry is the plan, sound poetry the impulse; visual poetry the score and sound poetry your actual music for dancing'.[126] In addition, concrete poetry has its equivalent in music. Instead of dismantling syntax and words and including non-linguistic material in poetry, in 'musique concrète', a genre that began in the late 1920s and was theorised in 1940, compositional tools such as melody, harmony, rhythm and even compositions are rejected and non-instrumental sounds are incorporated.[127] The seeds of these ideas in Mallarmé are developed in concrete poetry, which, at least theoretically, draws on sight and sound: the poem offers both a score on the page and a song when recited. At the very least, the concrete poets attempt to incorporate musical technique and theory into their poems. The Noigandres group often allude to musicians from many different genres, such as Anton Webern, Arnold Schoenberg and Gilberto Gil, as influences on their poetics and poetry. In particular, they attempt to apply to the page Webern's technique of splitting the musical line or melody between several instruments (as opposed to one instrument or one set of instruments), known as 'klangfarbenmelodie' ('sound-colour-melody'); Schoenberg's serial

122 Mallarmé, *Un Coup de dés.*

123 While Gomringer is not Brazilian, 'Silencio' directly engages the concretist approach to silence and white space, and therefore I have included it as an example here.

124 Similarly, John Cage, another influence on the Noigandres group, concluded from his musical experiments that there is no such thing as an absolute silence. Peter Gutman, 'The Sounds of Silence,' *Classical Notes* (1999) <http://www.classicalnotes.net/columns/silence.html> [accessed 10 May 2015].

125 Martínez, as we will see in Chapter 2, includes a musical score in *La nueva novela.*

126 Cobbing and Meyer, p. 44.

127 See, for example, Daniel Teruggi, 'Musique Concrète Today: Its Reach, Evolution of Conception and Role in Musical Thought', *Organised Sound*, 20.1 (2015), pp. 51–59.

se
nasce
morre nasce
morre nasce morre
renasce remorre renasce
remorre renasce
remorre
re
re
desnasce
desmorre desnasce
desmorre desnasce desmorre
nascemorrenasce
morrenasce
morre
se

Fig. 1.2. Haroldo de Campos, 'Nascemorre' (1965). Courtesy of Ivan de Campos.

compositions; and Gil's modern experimentalism and *antropofagia* with his *tropicalista* music.[128] Furthermore, some of the concrete poems of the Noigandres group come to their full vocal realisation when they are performed. For example, Haroldo de Campos' 'Nascemorre' (Figure 1.2) was put to choral music conducted by Gilberto Mendes.[129] Thus, music is not only an analogy, but also a key element of concrete poetry, and, as I will discuss in the following chapters, of the works of Martínez, Lira and Vicuña.

A major characteristic of concrete poetry emerged from its relationship to music: its preoccupation with pattern. All music has a basic pattern (sound-no sound); similarly, concrete poetry explicitly deals with the pattern of word-white space. The emphasis on musical patterns in turn can lead to mathematical, non-subjective and rational poems. Haroldo de Campos' poem that begins 'mais mais' (1958, Figure 1.3), for instance, resembles a mathematical equation, as one can move through the poem adding ('mais' or 'e') or subtracting ('menos' or 'sem').[130] Just as music can be seen as based on mathematical patterns of 1 (sound) and 0 (silence), this poem creates multiple lines of music, depending on the way in which you read it.

While the Noigandres group explain that their objectives are to *construct* objects, or even products, they claim that the (musical) patterns used are in fact natural ones and thus make the objects come 'alive'. Augusto de Campos states: 'como um objeto dinâmico, uma célula viva, un organismo completo, com propiedades psico-

128 Augusto de Campos, 'Poetamenos', Augusto de Campos and others, *Teoria da Poesia Concreta*, p. 13.
129 Gilberto Mendes, 'Nascemorre' (2010), <https://www.youtube.com/watch?v=O6JrRwuY7Kk> [accessed 10 May 2015].
130 Martínez also uses mathematical structures, such as equations (although the symbols are photographs and words) in *La nueva novela*. See Chapter 2.

físicoquímicas, tacto antenas circulação coração: viva.'[131] Many other poets have described concrete poetry in 'natural' terms. The concrete poet Öyvind Fahlström compares the poetic pattern to bodily patterns: 'Not only in music is rhythm the most elementary, directly physically grasping means for effect; which is the joy of recognising something known before, the importance of repetition which has a connection with the pulsation of breathing, the blood, ejaculation.'[132] Pignatari's poem 'Organismo' (Figure 1.4), for example, exemplifies their preoccupation with the life-like qualities of the material used, that is, language.[133] Thus, concrete poems are objects and/or products in and of themselves that arise from natural, musical rhythms.

Whether as a musical score or a 'song' fulfilled in performance, the concrete poem takes on both visual and aural qualities. Members of the Noigandres group often refer to James Joyce's montage word (from *Finnegan's Wake*) 'verbivocovisual' to describe the multi-sensorial characteristic of the concrete poem.[134] Concrete poetry aims to communicate verbally, visually and vocally all in one instant. Just as Joyce combines the words 'verbal', vocal', and 'visual' together into one word (to be read all at once), concrete poetry aims to overcome Lessing's distinction between poetry as temporal and painting as simultaneous by allowing the words to be read synchronically as well as diachronically. As the Noigandres group states, a concrete poem, like a painting, is a: 'estrutura espácio-temporal, em vez de desenvolvimento meramente temporístico-linear.'[135]

The emphasis on the three basic elements of poetry of all kinds — shape, meaning, and sound — brings us to another essential preoccupation of concrete poetry, that is, its rejection of a traditional, temporal syntax and progression.[136] Because the poetic unit is, for the concrete poets, the page (or beyond), the concrete poem does not require or at times even allow for linear reading. This disruption of linear syntax contributes to the poem's dismantlement of the temporality of conventional literature. As Haroldo de Campos states, concrete poetry is 'A concepção da estrutura pluridividida [...] liquidando a noção de desenvolvimento linear seccionado em princípio-meio-fim, em prol de uma organização circular da material poética.'[137] Without linear syntax to guide the reader to move chronologically from one word to the next, the reader is encouraged to find new ways of connecting words together. The concrete poem thus communicates through its spatial arrangement and through its visual and vocal patterns. Without linear syntax, there is no beginning or end to a concrete poem and the reader can

131 Augusto de Campos, 'Poesia Concreta', Augusto de Campos and others, *Teoria da Poesia Concreta*, p. 42.

132 Cobbing and Meyer, p. 18.

133 For an exciting version of Pignatari's 'Organismo', see Christian Caselli.

134 See, for example, Augusto de Campos and others, 'Plano-Piloto para Poesia Concreta', in Augusto de Campos and others, *Teoria da Poesia Czoncreta*, pp. 154–55.

135 Ibid., p. 154.

136 The concrete poet Max Bense specifically discusses these three elements. See Cobbing and Meyer, p. 27.

137 Haroldo de Campos, 'La Obra de Arte Aberta,' in Augusto de Campos and others, *Teoria da Poesia Concreta*, pp. 49–50.

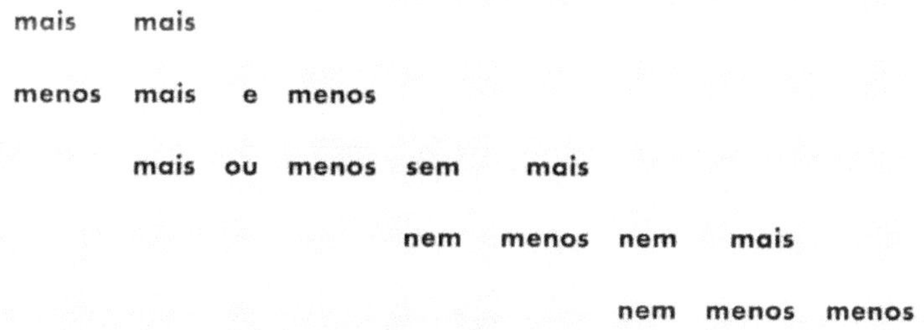

mais mais

menos mais e menos

mais ou menos sem mais

nem menos nem mais

nem menos menos

Fig. 1.3. Haroldo de Campos, 'Mais Mais' (1958). Courtesy of Ivan de Campos.

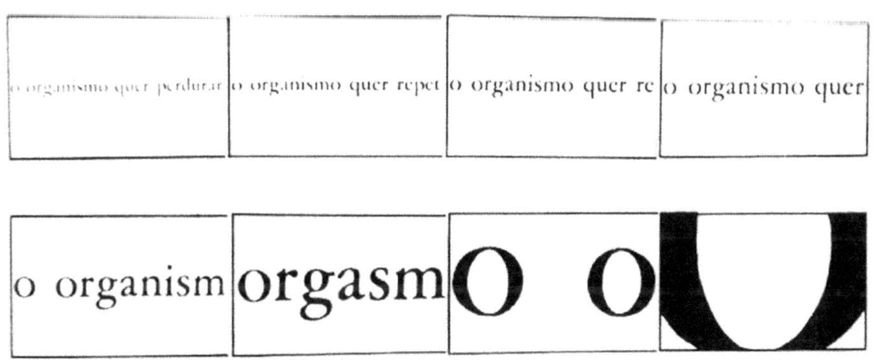

Fig. 1.4. Décio Pignatari, 'Organismo' (1966). Courtesy of Diniz Pignatari.

uma vez
uma fala
uma foz
uma vez uma bala
uma fala uma voz
uma foz uma vala
uma bala uma vez
uma voz
uma vala
uma vez

Fig. 1.5. Augusto de Campos, 'Uma Vez' (1954). Courtesy of Augusto de Campos.

mar azul

mar azul marco azul

mar azul marco azul barco azul

mar azul marco azul barco azul arco azul

mar azul marco azul barco azul arco azul ar azul

Fig. 1.6. Ferreira Gullar, 'Mar Azul' (1957–1958).
Courtesy of María Amélia Mello and Ferreira Gullar's relatives.

choose his/her own path through it. For example, in Augusto de Campos's 'Uma vez' (Figure 1.5), it is unclear in which direction and from where the reader should start. Should one start from the left and move to the right, then top to bottom? Should one begin at the top of the page, reading left to right on each line? Or should one take a different path, such as reading the axis or spine of the poem as a column, or combining the rhyming words in succession? To engage with a concrete poem, one does not read from one beginning or one end, but one can begin from multiple points, read in multiple directions (even off the page, as I will explain in 'A Concrete Example' below) or consume it all at once; the reader's engagement with the text is a function of its being spatial, rather than linear.[138]

Because the subject of a concrete poem is language itself, concrete poems resist the representation of the subject that is so central to lyric poetry; the concrete poets' concern with the material on the page and how it interacts with itself leaves no room for the lyric 'I'.[139] Instead, the focus on this materiality allows the work to become an object, or even a product. There are two outcomes of turning art into an object: first, it contributes to the internationalisation of concrete poetry, something that the concrete poets desired to promote and, second, it raises questions about the relationship between a work of art, traditionally assumed to be 'above' the commercial world, and objects ordinarily associated with that world. Because concrete poetry's sole responsibility is the material used, one's personal, social, or national context rarely fits in directly. Without explicit subjectivity, the poem can escape national borders. Although one might think that a word in a particular language would be inaccessible to a reader who does not speak this language, but because the poem's structure communicates more than through syntax and through a variety of aspects of words, such as their shape and sound, it is accessible to those who do not know the languages in which the poem is composed. Some poems have such an emphasis on the form and spatial arrangement on the page that they become non-linguistic.[140] The poem's focus on the material rather than subjective experience guides the reader to an experience of the poem rather than to an engagement with its author.[141]

138 Other strands of concrete poetry stemmed from the movement of the 1950s and particularly rejected simultaneous readings. For instance, a major movement that occurred in the rival city Rio de Janeiro responded to the São Paulo concrete poetry movement under the name 'neoconcrete poetry'. One of their forerunners was Ferreira Gullar, who recognised many of the principles of the Noigandres group, but rejected the idea that the work should be perceived simultaneously and emphasised the temporal process of reading. This resulted in poems that extended across pages of books, such as *O Formiguero* (1991), or at least, according to Gullar, were supposed to be read word by word, rather than all at once, such as 'Mar Azul' (Figure 1.6). See, for example, 'Teoria do Não-Objeto' (1959). While the poetry and poetics produced by these poets are clearly developments of the initial poems of the Noigandres group, they still adhere to most of the fundamental principles of concrete poetry and therefore can be considered part of the wider movement.

139 All three Chilean poets question and attempt to dismantle the traditional lyric subject and to move the authorial subject from author to reader.

140 See, for example, Augusto de Campos' 'Ôlho por Ôlho' (Figure 1.7) or Dias Pino's 'Solida'.

141 Gonzalez and Treece wrongly characterise the concretist preoccupation with the object as 'an equally uncritical view of the relationship between the poem and the reader, who existed as a passive object to consume or be persuaded by the text.' Gonzalez and Treece, p. 230.

This rejection of the place of the authorial subject does not mean, however, that the poems cannot criticise oppressive features of society; social critique can emerge from the form of the poems. Coming out of a period of industrialisation in Brazil, the Noigandres group wrote many poems that are clearly socially engaged. For instance, Augusto de Campos wrote a variety of poems playing on the words 'lixo' and 'luxo' as what can be considered a critique of capitalistic consumption (Figure 1.8). Moreover, many of their poems were brought to public spaces in order to reach wider audiences and to engage politically, such as Augusto de Campos's 'cidadecitycite', which appeared on multiple media throughout São Paulo in the 1960s.[142] The social critique of the concrete poets is in part achieved by their co-optation of the techniques of commercialised society. Each poem is created not as any object; as Paulo Franchetti claims, 'The concrete poem is produced *as if* it were an industrial product.'[143] The concrete poem is something material and also is like a product for a market, a commodity. Pignatari's 'Beba Coca Cola' (Figure 1.9) criticises commodity culture by mimicking advertising. It was produced not as a product, but as an advertisement (one that does not sell a product). In this poem, Pignatari uses the Coca-Cola brand and emblem in order to deconstruct it.[144] In a world of industrial objects, the concrete poets strive to create poems that, through their objective qualities, both criticise and engage with capitalist society.

These 'committed' poems can be seen as a type of experimentation with reduplication (like the reduplication of mass production), and specifically a type of 'process poetry,' a poetry that highlights the process of a poem's creation.[145] The creation of verbal patterns in the poem on the page (such as in Ronaldo Azeredo's 'Rua', Figure 1.10), invites the reader to continue forming these patterns on their own; the poem has the potential to carry on, and can do so with the help of the reader.[146] The poems give the reader the framework to continue producing the patterns of the poem, just as a factory machine provides the moulds for products so that they can be continually produced. Another example of a 'poema proceso' is Wlademir Dias Pino's poem 'Solida' (without an accent, and therefore either the third person present indicative of 'solidar' or a neologism), in which he offers multiple combinations of the letters of the word 'solida' in various codes, replacing

142 For an in-depth discussion of this poem and its existence as a work of art in public space, see Burghard Baltrusch, 'Traducir lo poético en el espacio público', in *La poesía actual en el espacio público*, ed. by Alba Cid and Isaac Lourido (Binges: Éditions Orbis Tertius, 2015), pp. 23–54.

143 Franchetti, p. 63.

144 As we will see in Chapter 3, Lira similarly uses the forms and language of those whom he is criticising.

145 *Poems for the Millennium*, ed. by Pierre Joris and Jerome Rothenberg (Berkeley: University of California Press, 1998), pp. 302–03. In his essay, 'Commitment', Theodor Adorno reverses the typical definitions of 'autonomous' art (that has been defined as art that is 'free' from reality) and 'committed' art (an art that is politically engaged), arguing that autonomous art, through formal experimentation directed towards the politics of form, in fact is usually more successfully 'committed' than art that explicitly attempts to do so. For a more detailed discussion on Adorno's 'Commitment', see Chapter 4. Adorno, 'Commitment', in *Notes to Literature*, trans. by Shierry Weber Nicholsen, vol 2 (New York: Columbia University Press, 1992), pp. 76–94.

146 Augusto de Campos, *Poesía* (São Paulo: Editora Brasiliense, 1986).

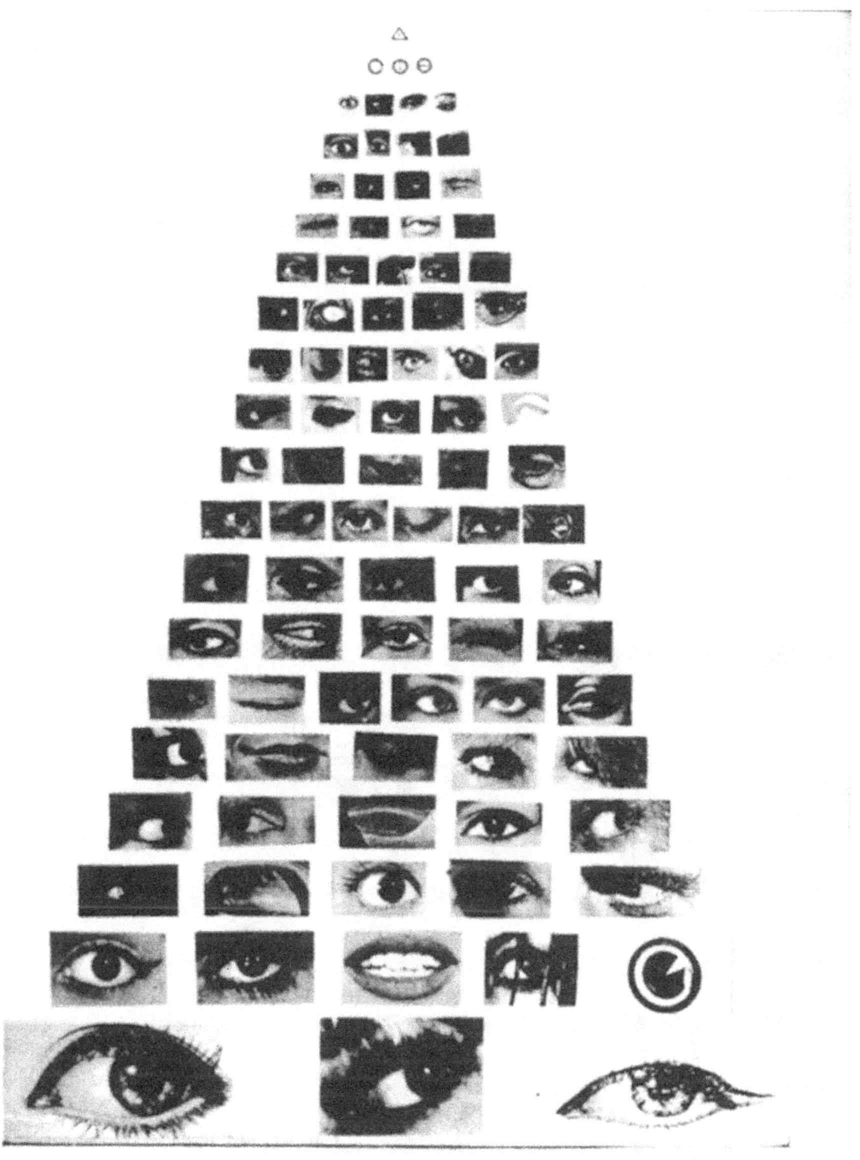

Fig. 1.7. Augusto de Campos, 'Ôlho por Ôlho' (1964).
Courtesy of Augusto de Campos.

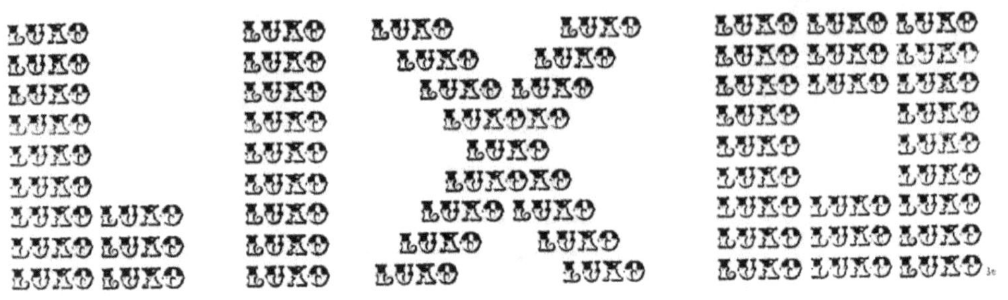

LUXO LUXO LUXO LUXO LUXO LUXO LUXO
LUXO LUXO LUXO LUXO LUXO LUXO LUXO
LUXO LUXO LUXO LUXO LUXO LUXO LUXO
LUXO LUXO LUXOXO LUXO LUXO
LUXO LUXO LUXO LUXO LUXO
LUXO LUXO LUXOXO LUXO LUXO
LUXO LUXO LUXO LUXO LUXO LUXO LUXO LUXO
LUXO LUXO LUXO LUXO LUXO LUXO LUXO LUXO
LUXO LUXO LUXO LUXO LUXO LUXO LUXO LUXO

FIG. 1.8. Augusto de Campos, 'Lixo/Luxo' (1965).
Courtesy of Augusto de Campos.

beba coca cola
babe cola
beba coca
babe cola caco
caco
cola
cloaca

FIG. 1.9. Décio Pignatari, 'Beba Coca Cola' (1957).
Courtesy of Diniz Pignatari.

r u a r u a r u a s o l

r u a r u a s o l r u a

r u a s o l r u a r u a

s o l r u a r u a r u a

r u a r u a r u a s

Fig. 1.10. Ronaldo Azeredo, 'Rua' (1962). Courtesy of Marcelo Azeredo.

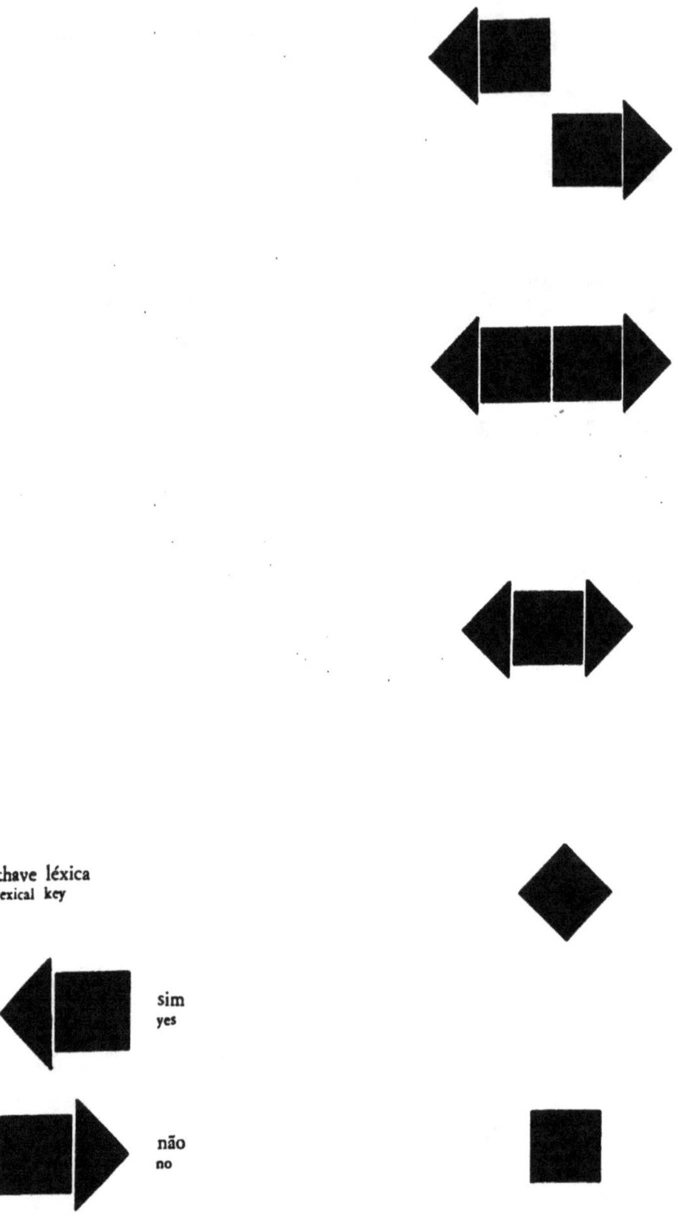

FIG. 1.11. Luiz Angelo Pinto, Untitled (a semiotic poem) (1964).
Courtesy of Luiz Angelo Pinto.

the letters with dots or shapes and repositioning them in a variety of ways.[147] He also gives instances in which the reader can form his/her own patterns with the coded letters.[148] These experiments clearly bring to mind Walter Benjamin's *The Work of Art in the Age of Mechanical Reproduction*. If put in Benjamin's terms, one could argue that the concretists shift the 'aura' in reproducible art from that of an original creator to the reader him/herself.[149]

Because they resist subjectivity, concrete poems come alive through a particularly active interaction between the patterns of the poem and the reader. As the critic Walter Moser describes it, concrete poetry (in particular Haroldo de Campos's work) is a particular kind of experimental poetry embodying a specific definition of 'experimental', that is, the 'experiential'. Using the definition of 'experiment' as 'the action of trying anything', Moser explains that concrete poetry emphasises the 'processive aspect of an act' and forces the reader to engage, or 'experience', language as such: Concrete poetry 'is experimental inasmuch as it makes us experience language, especially its material aspect.'[150] Concrete poetry, as Gomringer explains, calls for a new kind of reader: 'the constellation is a system, it is a playground with definite boundaries. The poet sets it all up. He designs the playground as a field-of-force & suggests its possible workings. The reader, the new reader, accepts it in the spirit of play, then plays with it.'[151] The reader cannot read a concrete poem passively, but must participate in the creation of the poem itself. It is the visual and aural design of a concrete poem that allows for this kind of readerly participation. The creation of space for an active, playful reader promotes a democratic vision in which singular subjectivity or authority is dismantled and multiple subjectivities or authorities are created and recreated. This vision, moreover, is anti-capitalistic: play is the state of mind not controlled by the market economy; therefore, the promotion of play resists an attempt to capitalise the reading process.

Summary: A Concrete Example

Augusto de Campos's 'Linguaviagem' (Figure 1.12), presented at the Brighton Festival in 1967, demonstrates clearly the characteristics of a 'verbivocovisual' concrete poem that encourages the reader to play a part in the creation of the text. The poem consists of four 'pages', each with a word or part of a word on each side. When opened, the pages form a cube, with words printed in blue on the outside and in green on the inside. On one of the pages, de Campos describes the words

147 Another strand of concrete poetry was 'semiotic' poetry, which, similar to process poetry, includes non-verbal patterns paired with a verbal key. See, for example, Luis Angelo Pinto (Figure 1.11).

148 Although Wladamir Dias Pino was not considered a member of the Noigandres group, his work clearly is a direct development of concretist principles.

149 See Walter Benjamin, *The Work of Art in the Age of Mechanical Reproduction*, trans. by J. A. Underwood (London: Penguin Books, 2008).

150 Walter Moser, 'Haroldo de Campos' Literary Experimentation of the Second Kind', in Drucker and others, *Experimental-Visual–Concrete*, pp. 139–54 (pp. 146–47).

151 Gomringer, as quoted by R. P. Draper, 'Concrete Poetry', *New Literary History*, vol. 2 (1971), 329–40 (p. 332).

that can be formed when reading the poem: lingua (tongue), via (via, road or path), linguagem (language), and viagem (voyage).

The form of the poem allows it to be treated as an object. It is a perfectly geometric cube without a top or bottom that creates a hole in the middle, and with writing on every other side. The shape not only subverts the conventional centrality of the line in poetry, but even visual poetry's commitment to two-dimensional space. This shape illustrates the mathematical, geometric approach that de Campos used in the (initial) construction of the poem. This poem looks like a geometric object, rather than like the usual linear, lyrical and subjective poem that appears as a two-dimensional form on the page. One can see that the words have been organised in a specific order so that the words on the inside of the cube correlate with the words written on the outside. The poem is made up solely of nouns, so there are no agents and no actions represented by the words on the page. Not only are there no grammatical subjects, but, apart from one definition of 'via' (as 'by way of' or 'through'), the words themselves don't have any direction, time or movement (unlike conjugated verbs or prepositions). In other words, the object itself does not communicate subjective action.

It is thus up to the reader to assume the role of subject and therefore enter into the creation of the poem. Because there is no true beginning to the poem (although in this version the title suggests a place to begin), the reader can decide where to

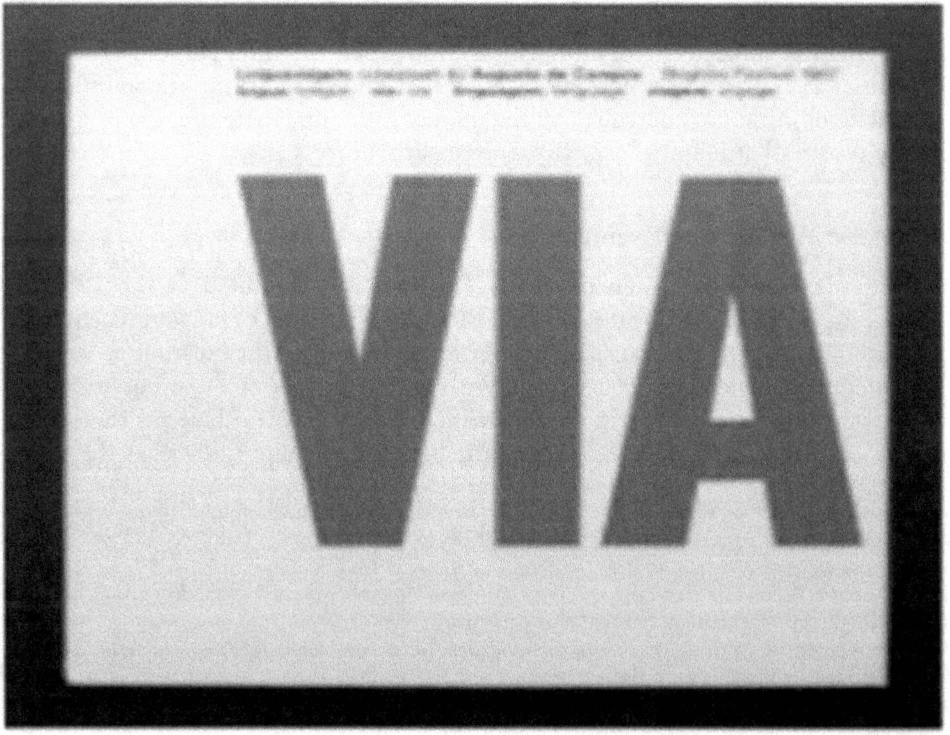

Fig. 1.12 (above, and on next pages). Augusto de Campos, Linguaviagem. Courtesy of Augusto de Campos.

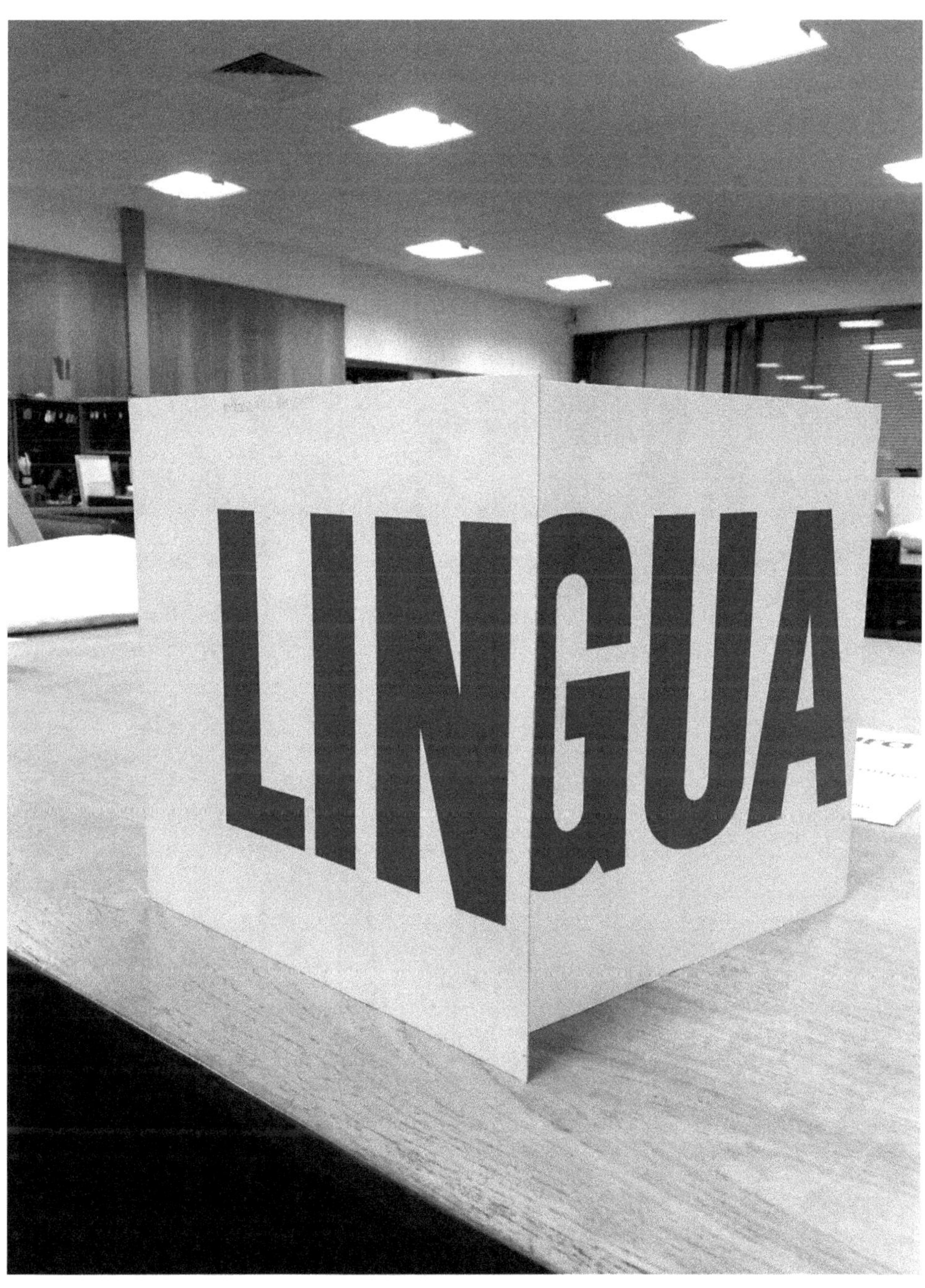
LINGUA

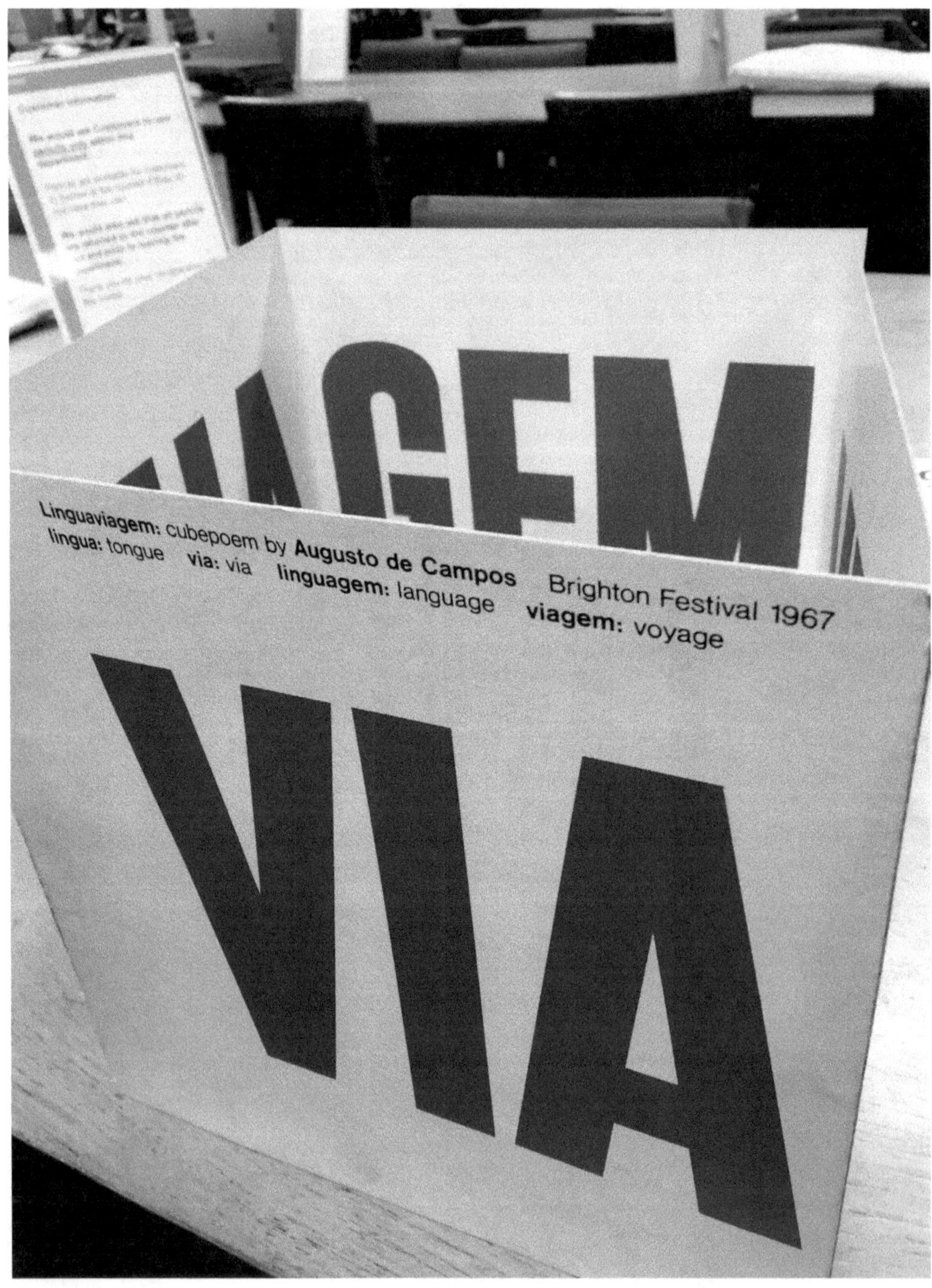
VIAGEM
Linguaviagem: cubepoem by Augusto de Campos Brighton Festival 1967
lingua: tongue via: via linguagem: language viagem: voyage
VIA

start reading and similarly, as there is no end, the reader can decide where to stop. In addition, the poem can be read in multiple directions. One can read it counter-clockwise around the outside and/or inside of the cube, or one can read across from the outside to the back inside or from the back inside to the outside and can do this from most positions around the cube.

'Linguaviagem' encourages the reader to travel, physically and mentally, in order to read (or complete) the text. Firstly, it requires physical movement. Because it is three-dimensional, the poem engages the whole body of the reader; one has to move physically around the poem to be able to read it. (Depending on whether or not it has been already set up in its presentation, one may have to set the poem up from its original folded form, in which case the unfolding also engages the body in an activity that is like turning the page of a book, but an activity that involves a larger degree of movement). Secondly, the poem forces the reader's eyes to 'travel' over the empty space in the middle (for instance, one has to connect the word 'via' to the second part of the word 'gem' on the back inside to create 'viagem'); with his/her eyes, the reader has to act out the word 'viagem'. This exercise thus ties the semantic meaning of the word to *the act of reading*. Moreover, the words 'lingua' and 'linguagem' are semantically connected by the word 'viagem'; the word for 'tongue' physically changes, or 'takes a trip', to its other definition, 'language', or 'linguagem'. Thirdly, this empty space in the middle of the poem (between words, syllables, and pages) brings with it the analogy between the white space and silence that Mallarmé evoked. Just as in Gomringer's 'Silencio' (see above), in which the word 'silencio' is written multiple times to form a box surrounding an empty inner box, this poem questions what empty space is: silence has no meaning except when surrounded by sounds.

In 'Linguaviagem', the three-dimensional 'empty' space exists not only because the pages surround it, but also to allow the reader to perform the words playfully. In other words, like the relationship between sound and silence, the inner space gives meaning to the words that surround it and the words give meaning to the space. Furthermore, the aural and oral aspects of this poem are developed in the words themselves. For instance, the reader can create vocal patterns with the rhymes: the two longer words (linguagem and viagem) and the shorter words (lingua and via) are connected aurally. The semantic meaning of the word 'lingua' also indicates that this 'trip' should be taken with the tongue, that is, one should read the poem aloud. The reading of the poem, then, becomes not only subjective from the position of the reader, but also physical and sensual.

This cubepoem powerfully exemplifies a 'verbivocovisual' object because it allows the reader to engage with it visually, vocally, semantically and even physically. These various qualities that form the object do not exist separately, but blend together to communicate, as the Noigandres group says in their manifesto, as a 'tensão de palavras-coisas no espaço-tempo' (tension of word-things in space-time) that allows the reader to create playfully.[152]

152 Augusto de Campos, 'Poesia Concreta', in Augusto de Campos and others, *Teoria da Poesia Concreta*, p. 42.

CHAPTER 2

Juan Luis Martínez's Concretist Poetics under Dictatorship

Signifier, Author, Nation

Described as both a 'madman' and Chile's 'best-kept secret' by his contemporaries, the poet Juan Luis Martínez (1942–1993) has recently come to be regarded as a key figure in the Chilean neo-avant-garde.[1] Living much of his life as a poet on the margins of a society marked by instability and then by the Augusto Pinochet dictatorship, Martínez subtly, yet sharply, criticises the political corruption under which he wrote. Through his various poetic experiments, Martínez examines the roles that language, author and context play in the reading of poetic works. As the poet and literary critic Jorge Polanco states, 'Juan Luis Martínez lleva al límite el rol precario de las palabras, persistiendo en el cuestionamiento del estatuto del poeta y de la poesía'.[2] In this chapter, I will show how Martínez's 'questioning' of the status of the poet and poetry, especially in his book *La nueva novela*, is a development of the Brazilian concrete poets' attempt to create a purely 'objective' poetry, that is, poems that are at once object-like and not coloured by the point of view of the author or infused with extra-literary concerns. Martínez uses and then problematises the formal, political and ideological principles of concrete poetry to investigate even further than the concrete poets (1) the unstable nature of the signified; (2) the author's status in relationship to his/her work and the reader's active participation that this authorial relationship allows; and (3) the degree to which a poem comments upon the nation in which it is produced. These poetic explorations emerge from Martínez's struggle to understand a world of censorship and oppression (particularly, the nation under Pinochet's military dictatorship) and his quest to find the ideal form of (oppositional) expression under such conditions. Martínez ultimately departs from the poetics of the concretists by proving that a truly objective poetry, at least under censorship and oppression, cannot be made.

Martínez lived (socially and literarily) most of his life as a 'poet on the edge' of Valparaíso and the surrounding metropolitan area.[3] His formal education ended

1 Livon-Grosman and Vicuña, p. 452.

2 Jorge Polanco, *Pajarístico: Aproximaciones a la obra de Juan Luis Martínez* (Valparaíso: Ediciones Universitarias de Valparaíso, 2015), p. 8.

3 See Jesús Sepúlveda, *Poets on the Edge: Vicente Huidobro, César Vallejo, Juan Luis Martínez, and Néstor Perlongher* (Florida: Brown Walker, 2016). He could also be considered a 'poet on the edge of the edge' because Chile is a country on 'the edge' of the world.

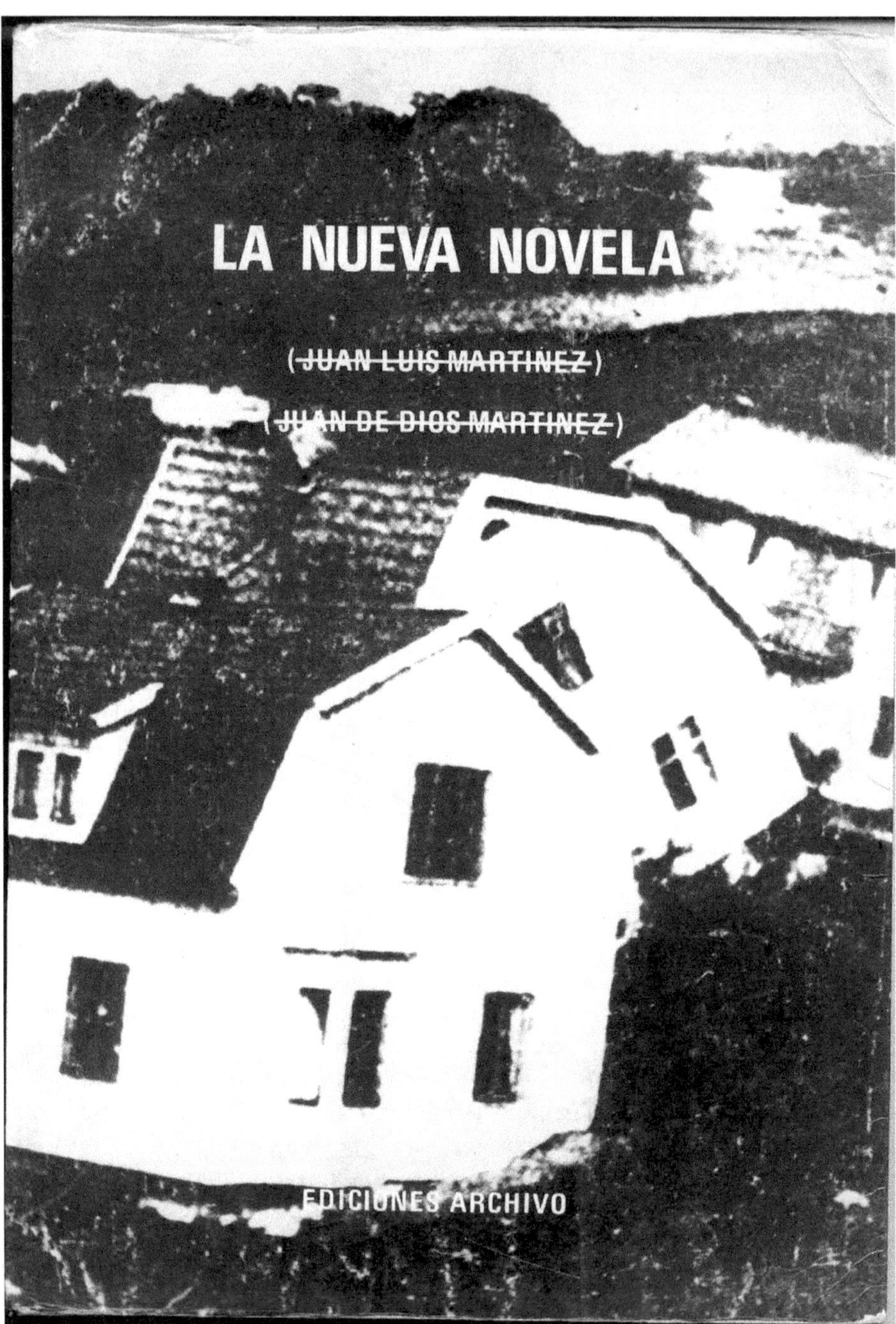

FIG. 2.1. Martínez, cover of *La nueva novela* (Santiago: Ediciones Archivos, 1977). Courtesy of Alita Martínez and Fundación de Juan Luis Martínez.

when he left secondary school and began to experiment artistically at the age of seventeen. As an autodidact, he maintained his position outside of mainstream society from then on, meeting with the members of the literary circles on the margins of Valparaíso. From 1969 to 1973, he conversed with the Chilean neo-avant-garde poets Raúl Zurita (who, in 1971, would become his brother-in-law) and Juan Cameron in the hole-in-the-wall cafés and bars of the port cities of Valparaíso and Viña del Mar.[4] He was adamantly against conforming to societal norms and was a strong opponent of the military dictatorship that began in 1973. Apart from being detained for a few hours, however, Martínez managed to stay under the military regime's radar and continued to carry out his life without much direct interference from the dictatorship.[5] In 1982, he fell sick and lived out the rest of his days with his wife Eliana Rodríguez and his two daughters by his side until he died of a heart attack in 1993. As many have argued, living on the outskirts of society influenced his poetry, a poetry that stretches the boundaries of a variety of conceptual and formal binaries, including those between sense and nonsense, reality and fiction, and literature and visual art.[6]

During his lifetime, Martínez published only two works, both self-published. Although he finished a version of his most renowned work, *La nueva novela*, in 1971, he did not publish it until 1977 when he printed five hundred copies through his own press 'Ediciones Archivos' and later, in 1985, a thousand more copies.[7] The deceptively titled book in fact resembles something far from a novel, new or otherwise (Figure 2.1).

Martínez at first seems to offer a conventional linear novel — he provides a title, a table of contents and seemingly organised sections (Figure 2.2) — but does so only in order to invite the reader to expect that a narrative will follow and then to undermine that expectation.[8] The title directly refers to a literary form called the 'nueva novela'. The Mexican author Carlos Fuentes gave this designation to works associated with the Latin American 'Boom' of the 1960s and 1970s. The 'Boom' included writers who challenged the conventions of preceding Latin American and Western literature (and with it Latin American and Western society) through experimental fiction.[9] Like the 'nueva novela', Martínez's book disrupts traditional,

4 This group has been called the 'School of Valparaíso'. Sepúlveda, *Poets on the Edge*, p. 108.

5 Fondos Cultura: Libro y lectura, *Juan Luis Martínez*, <http://juanluismartinez.cl/jlm/juan-luis-martinez/biografia/> [accessed 10 December 2016].

6 See, for example, Sepúlveda, *Poets on the Edge*.

7 The Editorial Universitaria rejected it in 1971, which led Martínez to leave it untouched until 1977.

8 Gwen Kirkpatrick, 'Desapariciones y ausencias en *La nueva novela* de Juan Luis Martínez', *Revista de Crítica Literaria Latinoamericana*, 25 (1999), 225–34 (p. 225).

9 Carlos Fuentes, *La nueva novela hispanoamericana* (México, D.F.: Editorial Joaquín Mortiz, 1969), p. 30. This title also clearly refers to the *nouveau roman*, the French equivalent of a 'nueva novela', which questions traditional and realist narrative. See, for example, John Sturrock, *The French New Novel* (Oxford: Oxford University Press, 1969), pp. 1–41. As Sepúlveda points out, the abbreviation for the book ('n.n.') was also the abbreviation written on the graves of the detained and disappeared for 'no name'. He also suggests that the abbreviation could refer to Adolf Hitler's 'Nacht und Nebel', thus linking Pinochet's Chile and the Nazi regime. Sepúlveda, *Poets on the Edge*, p. 105. This allusion, along with Martínez's insistence on anonymity (see below), as Peter Leong notes, 'puts [Martínez]

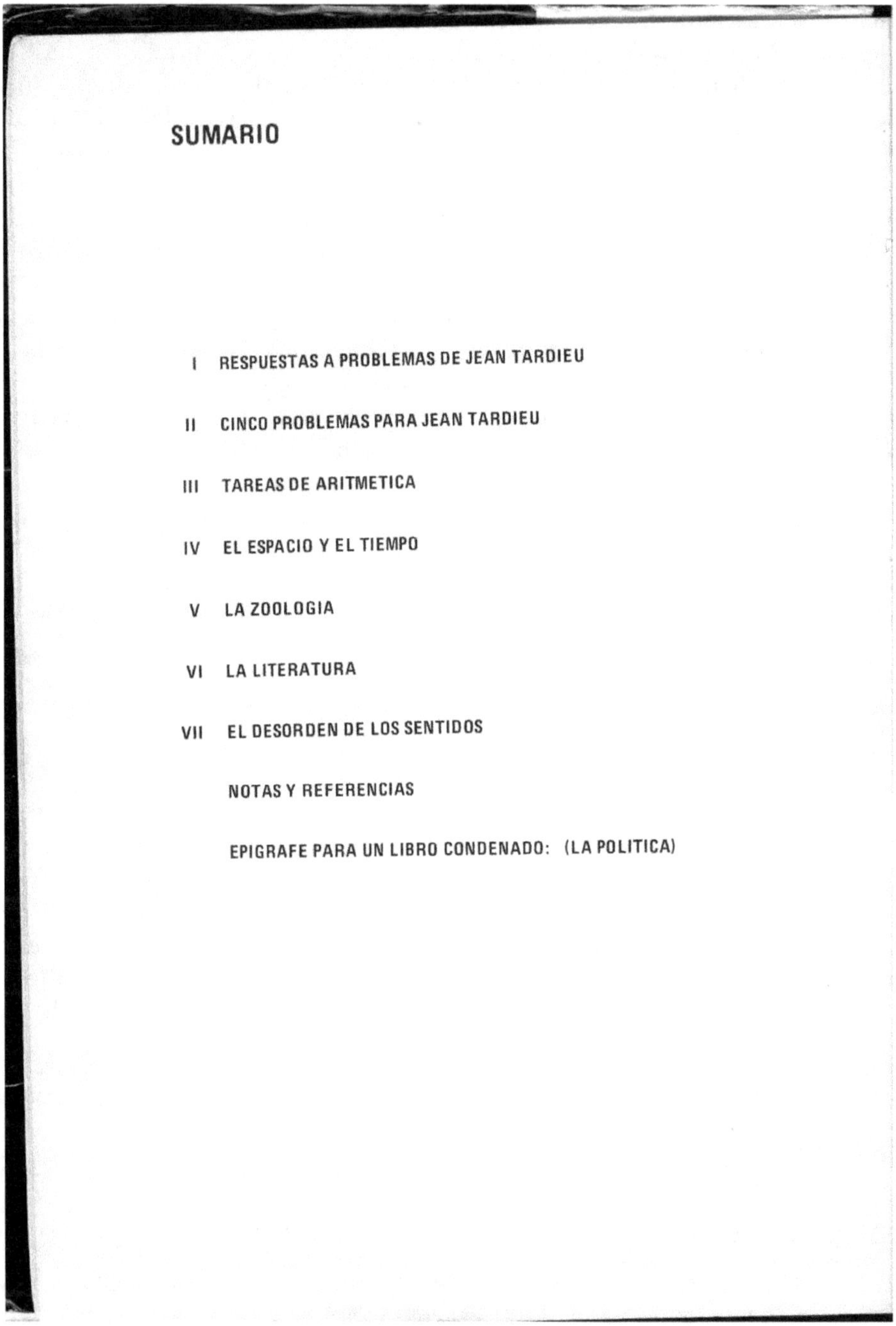

SUMARIO

Fig. 2.2. Martínez, 'Sumario'.
Courtesy of Alita Martínez and Fundación de Juan Luis Martínez.

linear narrative. However, at the same time that he acknowledges his affinities with such authors, he breaks away from his Latin American contemporaries by taking such dismantlings of conventional forms even further. Instead of immersing oneself in a familiar novel form, the reader of *La nueva novela* enters into a 'labyrinth' of photographs, school exercises, prose and verse poems, bibliographies and epigraphs, and 'mathematical' equations in which s/he becomes lost trying to find his or her way through the maze.[10] In Gérard Genette's terms, moreover, this title performs both 'rhematic' and 'thematic' functions: not only does it indicate (albeit falsely) the form of the poem, but it also indicates its theme or subject.[11] The title thus carries the tension between text as subject and text as object that we will see throughout the book.

Through the creation of a collage of miscellaneous poems and items in the book (a Chilean flag, fish hooks, newspaper clippings, reproductions and drawings, to name a few) structured into separate, yet connected, sections, Martínez, like the concrete poets, blurs the line between art and 'non-art'.[12] Just as in both Surrealist art and concrete poetry, objects begin to fill the literary spaces of Martínez's book.[13] As Zenaida Suárez states:

> El objeto literario...está dotado de una concepción artística que lo muestra, no como simple artefacto cotidiano, sino como elemento dotado de la noción de artificiosidad [...] Los objetos [...] operan dentro del libro como textos interpretables en el contexto literario al que han sido adheridos.[14]

Martínez's importation of objects into the 'novel' transforms the quotidian object into a literary or aesthetic object at the same time as it, in line with concretist poetics, changes the book into a quotidian object.

Martínez stretched the limits of what can be considered poetry in other experimental works even further than he did in *La nueva novela*. In 1978, he published the object book entitled *La poesía chilena*. In the shape of a box, this 'book' includes a bag of soil supposedly from Chile's Valle Central, and a booklet that consists of death certificates and library catalogue call cards of the poet's father, Luis Martínez Villablanca and the four 'greats' of twentieth-century Chilean poetry, Gabriela Mistral, Vicente Huidobro, Pablo Neruda and Pablo de Rokha. In this experiment, Martínez blurs the lines between poetry, visual art and quotidian objects. By

in radical solidarity with the detained-disappeared.' Peter Leong, 'Poetry Homework: Pedagogy, Memory, and Politics in the Visual Poetry of Juan Luis Martínez", *A Contracorriente*, 14.2 (2017), 162–88 (p. 178).

10 Oscar Galindo, 'El alfabestiario universal de *La nueva novela* de Juan Luis Martínez', *Revista Chilena de Literatura*, 57 (2000), 21–40 (p. 23).

11 See Genette (1997), pp. 78–79.

12 Zenaida M. Suárez, 'Objetualismo en Juan Luis Martínez: el significante palpable', *Estudios Filológicos*, 51 (2013), 83–98 (p. 84). Rebecca Kosick, along with many other critics, also describes *La nueva novela* as an assemblage of 'mismatched materials that do not communicate a unified message and often do not appear to belong together [...] the book shows itself capable not only of having parts that can detach from it and attach to a different assemblage, but parts that can detach and attach in different places within the same assemblage'. Kosick, pp. 857–71.

13 Suárez, 'Objetualismo en Juan Luis Martínez', p. 87.

14 Ibid., pp. 87–88.

juxtaposing the death certificates of these figures with library call cards of their works, he complicates the role of a (particularly Chilean) canon, the value of the authorial figure and the relationship between author and text.[15] After his death, contrary to his wishes, three more of Martínez's books were published with the help of his widow: *Poemas del otro* (2003), consisting of a handful of translated lyric poems and a series of interviews with the poet; *Aproximación del principio de incertidumbre a un proyecto poético* (2010), a book of visual poems based on the *I Ching* which followed an exhibit of his art objects titled 'Señales de ruta'; and *El poeta anónimo (o el eterno presente de Juan Luis Martínez)* (2012 in Brazil; 2013 in Chile), a collection that was part of another exhibit of Martínez's art objects held at the September 2012 São Paulo Biennial.[16]

Compared to the scant scholarship published on the poetic works of the other poets discussed in this book (Vicuña and Lira), there are many publications on Martinez's works. However, while having a relatively recent 'cult' following in Chile, Martínez has until recently received little attention internationally.[17] During his lifetime, few critics recognised his work (partially because of its limited distribution), and some even questioned his existence. In fact, when the poets Enrique Lihn and Pedro Lastra published one of the first reviews of his work, 'Señales de ruta' in 1987, the critic Luis Vargas Saavedra suspected that Lihn and Lastra had made up the figure of the marginal poet from Valparaíso. Seen as an almost mythical creature, Martínez, like his work, straddled the line between existence and nonexistence.[18]

A number of critics have acknowledged (although have rarely explored fully) Martínez's similarities to concrete poets in general. Suárez, in her recent book on hypertextuality in *La nueva novela*, recognises the influence of concretism in

15 Weintraub discusses the questions Martínez raises about the Chilean canon in terms of mourning. See Scott Weintraub, 'Mourning for the Future: Poetic Inheritance in Juan Luis Martínez's *La poesía chilena*', *Revista Canadiense de Estudios Hispánicos*, 37.2 (2013), 255–78.

16 Only recently (in 2014) did Weintraub discover that seventeen of the lyric poems in *Poemas del otro* were in fact translations of poems by the Catalan poet Juan Luis Martinez (no accent), literally the 'other' Juan Luis. See Weintraub, *La última broma de Juan Luis Martínez: No solo ser otro sino escribir la obra de otro* (Santiago: Cuarto Propio, 2014).

17 In the English-speaking world, there has recently been an explosion of publications in Martínez studies, most of which have appeared in the last few years. One of the reasons few have read Martínez until now might be because of the limited number of copies of his works. In addition, he has been frequently described as a recluse who did not engage in mainstream literary circles (such as C.A.D.A., an organisation in which many of his contemporaries participated), the fact of which might contribute to the limited circulation his works had, at least during his lifetime. The fact that he did not make himself into a public figure, moreover, is in keeping with his distrust of the status of the author (as will be discussed below).

18 Martínez recognised his and his work's place between reality and fiction, claiming that one of his goals was 'de existir y no existir, de ser más literario que real'. Juan Luis Martínez, *Poemas del otro*, p. 64. Despite this lack of early recognition as a poet of import, a variety of critics have subsequently recognised Martínez's experimental works as texts that discuss the tension within literature between existence and nonexistence. See Scott Jackson, 'Juan Luis Martínez: The Novelist of Non-Existence', *Confluencia*, 12.1 (1996), 134–40; Weintraub, 'Juan Luis Martínez y las otredades de la metafísica: apuntes patafísicos y carrollianos', in Polanco, *Pajarístico*, pp. 63–81; Sepúlveda, *Poems on the Edge*; and Suárez, 'Objetualismo en Juan Luis Martínez', pp. 83–98.

Martínez's book.[19] In three articles, Oscar Galindo has noted that Martínez's work follows the same trajectory as concrete poetry. In 'El alfabestiario universal de *La nueva novela* de Juan Luis Martínez', Galindo argues that Martínez forms a bestiary of 'creaciones que merodean "entre otros animales imaginarios y reales"'[20] that emphasises a tension between 'presencia y ausencia, realidad y literatura, transparencia y opacidad'.[21] He argues that this tension is partly due to the fact that 'sus construcciones gráficas y objetuales lo acercan a la poesía concreta y las artes plásticas'.[22] Although he acknowledges Martínez's debt to the concrete poets, Galindo focuses on his creation of imaginary creatures. In 'Palabras e imágenes, objetos y acciones en la postvanguardia chilena', Galindo categorises Martínez as a Chilean neo-avant-garde artist who wrote concrete and object-like poems that foreground expression through the signifier and 'ofrece[n] una pluralidad semiótica'.[23] Lastly, in 'Áreas verdes de la realidad', Galindo compares Martínez to Zurita by close-reading a text by each poet mentioning their similar aims to those of the concrete poets, especially in their rediscovery of the material nature of poetry.[24] Despite recognising that the concrete poets and Martínez share a concern with the materiality of language, Galindo does not develop this comparison in depth.[25]

Many critics have overlooked his development of concretist poetics, focussing instead on how Martínez is particularly interested in stretching the formal boundaries of poetry and that he draws on the experiments of avant-garde poets who influenced the concrete poets. For example, Polanco recognises Martínez's Mallarmean experiments with the visual aspects of poetry: '[Martínez] busca, bajo la herencia de Mallarmé, revolucionar las formas y resquebrajar los interdictos de lo que es posible decir y ver'.[26] The poet Elvira Hernández also notes Martínez's connection to Mallarmé in her discussion of his work as 'juego, obra, [y/o] libro'.[27] Weintraub briefly mentions Martínez's formalist tendencies and explores Martínez's use and development of Lewis Carroll's visual poetics.[28] Although she does not develop the comparison, Valeria de los Ríos mentions the connection between Martínez, Mallarmé and the concrete poets, yet claims that Martínez's work defies

19 Suárez, *Palabras ya escritas: Relecturas de* La nueva novela *de Juan Luis Martínez* (Santiago: RIL editores, 2019), p. 31.

20 Oscar Galindo, 'El alfabestiario universal', p. 24.

21 Ibid., p. 23.

22 Ibid., p. 21.

23 Galindo, 'Palabras e imágenes, objetos y acciones en la postvanguardia chilena', *Estudios Filológicos*, 42 (2007), 109–21.

24 Galindo, 'Áreas verdes de la realidad: Martínez y Zurita en el contexto de la poesía neovanguardista hispanoamericana', *Revista de Crítica Literaria Latinoamericana*, 38.76 (2012), 364–65.

25 I have not included Zurita in my study of the neo-avant-gardes with concretist tendencies because, while some of his work at first glance might look like concrete poetry, he seems to move in a different direction, working with, as Martínez himself explains, the signified, rather than the signifier. Martínez (2003), p. 68.

26 Polanco, p. 16. Suárez also recognises this development. See Suárez, *Palabras ya escritas*.

27 Elvira Hernández, 'Acopio de materiales y algunos andamios para alegrarme de a obra de ~~Juan Luis Martínez~~', in Soledad and Hernández, *Merodeos*, 33–38 (p. 25).

28 Weintraub, in Polanco, p. 72.

categorisation and thus is more ambitious than the avant-garde and concrete poets.[29] In addition, Emma Richter recognises that the concrete poets and Martínez 'están emparentados porque coinciden en recuperar la noción de ideograma que revisa y recrea, en primera instancia, Ezra Pound', but focuses on Martínez's publication of visual art, *Aproximación del Principio de Incertidumbre a un proyecto poético*, and also does not include a comparison of Martínez to the concrete poets in her central argument.[30] Rebecca Kosick also recognises Martínez's emphasis on the materiality of language, defining *La nueva novela* as a 'material poetics of relation'.[31] Although these comparisons to his (and the concrete poets') predecessors are informative, the comparison I will make in this book to concrete poetry particularly brings to the fore the *synthesis* of avant-garde verbal-visual experiments that occurs in both concrete poetry and Martínez's work.

The parallels to concrete poetry in Martínez's work clearly have major implications for the development of Martínez's own poetic project, and it is these implications that have not been examined in depth. By closely reading poems from *La nueva novela*, I will argue that Martínez's particular reworking of the principles of concrete poetry is the means by which he expresses his personal, political and philosophical concerns. In the first section of the chapter, I will discuss how Martínez, like the concrete poets, privileges the visual qualities of signifiers on the page above their signifieds, or conceptual meaning. In his poetics, Martínez focuses not solely on the black marks on a page, but the relationship between the words and white space (and the relationship between sound and silence when read aloud).[32] Part of the way he stretches boundaries, as I have said above, is his inclusion of objects in his

29 In this article, de los Ríos mainly argues that Martínez uses the relationship of photographs and their referents as a model for writing in *La nueva novela*. Valeria de los Rios, 'La fotografía como clave de lectura de *La nueva novela*', *Estudios Filológicos*, 44 (2009), 53–65.

30 Emma Richter, 'Tras los cambios en la poesía: J. L. Martínez', *Estudios Filológicos*, 51, (2013), 115–29. Other explorations of Martínez's works that provide useful interpretations of his radical experiments in stretching the limits of language and literature include the following. In his detailed 2013 book, Rioseco places Martínez in relation to Rodrigo Lira and Diego Maquieira as ludic neo-avant-garde poets, arguing that Martínez questions the structures of logic, language and traditional literature as a *Scriptor Ludens*. Rioseco, *Maquinarias reconstructivas*. Oscar de Sarmiento compares *La nueva novela* to Vicente Huidobro's work, claiming that Martínez continues Huidobro's 'plural, legitimating, creationist Latin American impulse' in 'Intersecting Reflections: Huidobro through Juan Luis Martínez's *La nueva novela*', *Hispanic Issues Online*, 5 (2010), 152–66. Weintraub, the most prolific Martínez critic publishing in English, explores Martínez's moulding of philosophy (particularly of Alfred Jarry's 'pataphysics') and literature. Others have explored the motif of the house (particularly in *La nueva novela*). Andrés Cáceres Milnes compares Martínez to Marcel Duchamp in 'Una lectura de *El gran vidrio* de Marcel Duchamp y *La nueva novela* de Juan Luis Martínez como una articulación meta-poética y autorreflexiva', *Aisthesis*, 55 (2014), 97–115. Juan Herrera argues that *La nueva novela* is 'protohipertextual' (a text that foreshadows new ways of engaging with a text) in '*La nueva novela* de Juan Luis Martínez: Poesía protohipertextual en el contexto de la ideósfera', *Acta Literaria*, 35 (2007), 9–27 (p. 17). Andrés Morales gives a general summary of the role of the reader, the text-as-object, and his 'desacralización del yo poético' in 'Para una lectura interpretativa de *La poesía chilena* de Juan Luis Martínez', *Revista Chilena de Literatura*, 69 (2006), 107–12.

31 Kosick.

32 Jesús Sepúlveda claims that the silence in *La nueva novela* is due to censorship. Sepúlveda (2016), p. 126.

'novel'. Like Martínez, the concrete poets also attempted to separate completely the signifier from the signified, which, in some cases, resulted in 'poems' of non-linguistic patterns. However, these non-linguistic poems usually had a linguistic key, so, in fact, the concrete poets' attempts to rid the sign of the signified could be considered unsuccessful. Martínez explores this 'failure' by experimenting with ways to separate the marks on the page from their conventional meanings even further.

Martínez not only examines the nature of the signifier when detached from its signified, but also, like the concrete poets, challenges the conventional relationship between text and author. Although they were not entirely successful, the concretists, as stated above, nonetheless attempted to make poems that would be completely 'objective', rather than 'subjective', or only 'subjective' in that each reading would be contingent upon whoever engages with the text and in what context it was read. Similarly, Martínez strove to produce texts that would dismantle the conventional role of the author and rid the text of individual ownership, as well as destroy the status of the text as commodity. He concludes, however, that the complete elimination of his role as author is impossible. While he does not want to create a text void of any connection to himself, Martínez rids the text of authorial subjectivity in a variety of ways. It is important to distinguish here between authority and authorial subjectivity: authority designates singular control of what is said and how it is said, whereas the authorial subject may be authoritative in this sense, but could also co-exist with other subjectivities. In the second section of the chapter, I examine how Martínez tries to separate a singular authority of the text from himself as the figure of the author; he aims to create a text that possesses an authority of the many, that is, from its readers and himself as co-creators.

As I will show in the third section of this chapter, Martínez develops the objective aspects of concretist poetics by creating a seemingly universal structure with the use of widely recognised intellectual and academic disciplines for his book and by appealing to an international audience. However, unlike the concrete poets, Martínez ultimately and pointedly exposes his criticism of the national context of Chile within which he wrote. While the concrete poets might claim to create universal texts (i.e. poems that were accessible to any given reader as well as poems structured by universal 'truths', such as mathematics), because of the 'objective' nature of the poems, Martínez, as I will show, realises that such a goal is impossible, and ultimately abandons it, recognising instead the importance of sacrificing the universal for the local as a response to a political crisis. After the military coup, he added to his 1971 version a Chilean flag, thereby bringing the concretist critique into the realm of the Chilean dictatorship.[33]

33 See *Raúl Zurita habla sobre Juan Luis Martínez* (YouTube), <https://www.youtube.com/watch?v=lUFBlbEvLZY> [accessed 24 January 2016].

Signifier and Signified

As discussed in Chapter 1, one of the major aims of the concrete poets, in an attempt to deconstruct conventional and ideologically driven ways of making meaning, was to explore the relationship between the elements of the sign by separating the word's meaning from its aural and visual characteristics. In *La nueva novela,* Martínez tests the viability of this concretist goal. Through myriad examples, Martínez encourages the reader to recognise that visual and sonic patterns are inextricable from meaning. For him (and the concrete poets), space is the visual frame of the signifier of poems. Such consideration of the signifier allows Martínez to challenge conventional understandings of linguistic meaning and accepted ideologies of language, yet also to pose the limits of such a challenge. Drawing on Ferdinand de Saussure's definition of the linguistic sign (*signe*) as containing both a *signifier* (*significant*), or *sound-image*, and a *signified (signifié*), or *concept*, I will illustrate a selection of ways in which Martínez stretches apart the different components of the linguistic sign (making use of nonsense language, translation, the musical nature of poetry and the white space on the page), provoking us to conclude that complete separation is impossible, and how such a result illuminates the limits of concretism.[34]

Just as the concrete poets emphasise the signifier over the signified (see, for example Augusto de Campos, Figure 1.7 or Dias Pino's 'Solida'), Martínez includes nonsense language in *La nueva novela* to illustrate the communicative power of the signifier; he humorously demonstrates how language, especially poetic language, can 'communicate' when the signifier has no semantic meaning attached to it. For example, in 'TAREAS DE POESIA'[35] (NN,[36] p. 95; Figure 2.3), Martínez creates a page that consists of a verse poem with nonsense words followed by six analytical exercises.

This page itself allows for the visual apprehension of iterations of nonsense simultaneously as a means of testing conventional meanings. He begins the page with an eight-line verse poem of nonsense language (ll. 1–8), a poem that, as Weintraub points out, resembles Spanish translations of Lewis Carroll's 'Jabberwocky'.[37] The

34 Saussure argues that, while the relationship between signified and signifier is arbitrary, one cannot separate them because they are 'intimately united, and each recalls the other'. See Ferdinand de Saussure, *Course in General Linguistics*, trans. by Roy Harris (London: Gerald Duckworth and Co., 1983). It is likely that Martínez was influenced by Saussure because of his use of similar terms within *La nueva novela* and *Poemas del otro*. See, for example, Martínez, *Poemas del otro*, p. 68.

35 The capitalised letters in *La nueva novela* do not carry accents.

36 Martínez, *La nueva novela*.

37 Carroll's works are structuring references throughout *La nueva novela*. Weintraub, *Juan Luis Martínez's Philosophical Poetics*, pp. 44–45. For an in-depth investigation of the rhizomatic hypertextuality that Martínez's references to Carroll's work (alongside that of Tardieu, particularly in this poem) creates, see Suárez (2019). Interestingly, Augusto de Campos translated Carroll's Jabberwocky into Brazilian Portuguese. See Lewis Carroll, *Jaguadarte*, trans. by Augusto de Campos (São Paulo: Nhambiquara Editora, 2014). Martínez's poem also could be considered what the Mexican writer Alfonso Reyes defined as a 'jintanjáfora' in 1929, a term he takes from the Cuban poet Mariano Brull's poetry. Martínez could be responding to Reyes's essay and thereby be in conversation with a wider literary tradition of nonsense poetry in Latin America and Europe. See

95

TAREAS DE POESIA

Tristuraban las agras sus temorios
Los lirosos durfían tiestamente
Y ustiales que utilaban afimorios
A las folces turaban distamente.

Hoy que dulgen y ermedan los larorios
Las oveñas patizan el bramente
Y las fólgicas barlan los filorios
Tras la Urla que valiñan ristramente.

EXPLIQUE Y COMENTE:

1. ¿Cuál es el tema o motivo central de este poema?

2. ¿Qué significan los lirosos para el autor?

3. ¿Por qué el autor afirma que las oveñas patizan el bramente?

4. ¿Qué recursos expresivos encuentra en estos versos? :

   "Y las fólgicas barlan los filorios
   Tras la Urla que valiñan ristramente".

5. Ubique todas aquellas palabras que produzcan la sensación de claridad, transparencia.

6. ¿Este poema le produce la sensación de quietud o de agitado movimiento? Fundamente su respuesta.

Fig. 2.3. Martínez, 'Tareas de poesía'.
Courtesy of Alita Martínez and Fundación de Juan Luis Martínez.

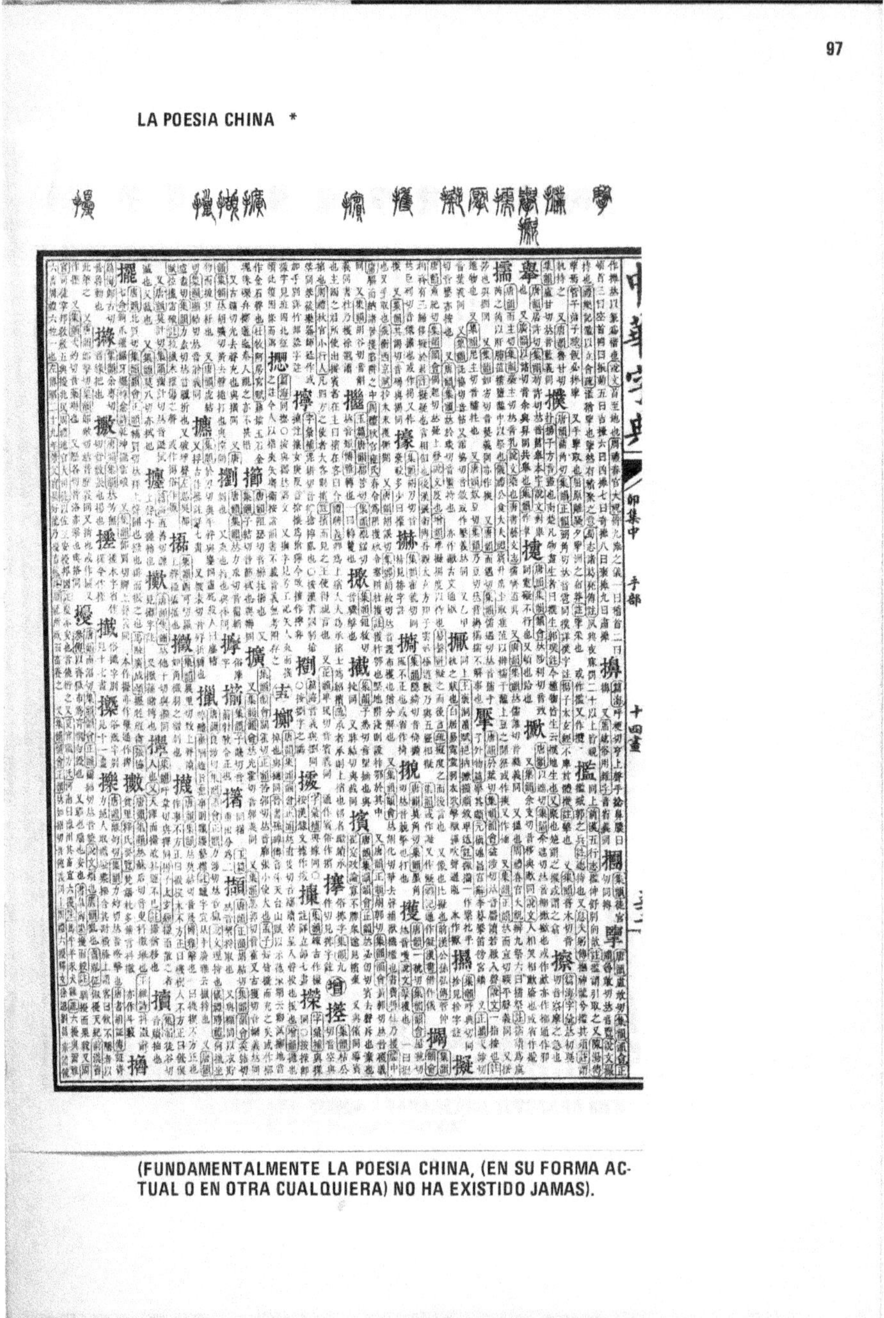

Fig. 2.4. Martínez, 'La poesía china'.
Courtesy of Alita Martínez and Fundación de Juan Luis Martínez.

97

LA POESIA CHINA *

El cuerpo es el árbol Bodhi
La mente el espejo brillante en que él se mira
Cuidar que esté siempre limpio
Y que polvo alguno lo empañe.

Shen-hsiu

Nunca existió el árbol Bodhi
Ni el brillante espejo en que él se mira
Fundamentalmente nada existe
Entonces, ¿qué polvo lo empañaría?

Hui-neng

* (NADIE LEERA NUNCA / OIRA (INTERPRETARA MENTALMENTE) ESTOS DOS POEMAS CHINOS).

(NADIE RECORDARA NUNCA / TARAREARA (EVOCARA MENTALMENTE) ESTOS DOS POEMAS CHINOS).

(FUNDAMENTALMENTE LA POESIA CHINA, (EN SU FORMA ACTUAL O EN OTRA CUALQUIERA) NO HA EXISTIDO JAMAS).

lines of nonsense force the reader to focus on the formal aspects of the words, lines and stanzas:

> Tristuraban las agras sus temorios
> Los lirosos durfían tiestamente
> Y ustiales que utilaban afimorios
> A las folces turaban distamente.
>
> Hoy que dulgen y ermedan los larorios
> Las oveñas patizan el bramente
> Y las fólgicas barlan los filorios
> Tras la Urla que valiñan ristramente. (NN, p. 95, ll. 1–8)

With almost no signifieds in this text, one can only interact with it by looking at the visual and aural patterns created by the words on the page. However, the nonsense language Martínez creates is not *completely* nonsense. Not only does he use phonemes and letters that designate some sort of meaning when combined with others, but also he includes a few recognisable Spanish words, such as conjunctions ('y' and 'que'), a preposition ('a'), articles ('los', 'las', 'el' and 'la'), and the adverb and noun 'hoy'. By glancing at the poem, one can identify seemingly syntactically meaningful lines along with phonemes and morphemes like those found in Spanish. For example, the poet uses words, such as 'Tristuraban' and 'tiestamente', where the suffixes evoke known Spanish meanings; even though the word as a whole has no meaning, its verbal or adverbial suffix (the imperfect tense 'aban' and adverbial 'mente') indicates a degree of morphological function and, furthermore, syntactic coherence. Martínez's foregrounding of syntax illuminates what Roman Jakobson called language's axis of combination, that is, the horizontal, syntactic relationships between signs.[38] While a set relationship between signified and signifier may not exist in Martínez's poem, the horizontal relationship between signs does; he privileges the axis of combination over the axis of selection. By including a syntactically coherent, albeit indiscernible, text, Martínez therefore encourages the reader to see the relationships between words as an essential part of reading a poem.[39]

Just as there are indications of real words in the poem, there are also allusions to meaningful, that is, traditional, abstract poetic forms. One can perceive a metre and a rhyming pattern in this 'nonsense' poem: each line consists of eleven syllables and the lines follow a rhyme scheme of ABAB ABAB. The poem seems as though it were the first eight lines of a sonnet, in particular, a Spanish American *modernista*

Alfonso Reyes, 'La jitanjáfora', in *Revista Libra (1929)*, ed. by Rosa Corral (Mexico City: Colegio de México, 2003), pp. 1–22.

38 Roman Jakobson, *Fundamentals of Language*, trans. by Morris Halle (Gravenhage: Mouton, 1956), pp. 58–62.

39 The roots of many of the words, moreover, are also somewhat recognisable (for example, one can discern 'triste' and 'triturar' from 'tristuraban'). This combination of recognisable phonemes, reminiscent of César Vallejo's blending together of words and parts of speech in *Trilce* or James Joyce's 'montage words', suggests that these 'nonsense' words might actually have multiple meanings. See César Vallejo, *Trilce*, ed. by Julio Ortega (Madrid: Ediciones Cátedra, 1991). This also brings to mind Humpty Dumpty's analysis of 'Jabberwocky'. Lewis Carroll, *Alice's Adventures in Wonderland* (London: Vintage, 2007), p. 256.

sonnet, which is often hendecasyllabic and uses this rhyme scheme. Martínez shows then that the meaning of a poem should be sought less in its semantics than in its visual and aural qualities and its representation of an abstract poetic structure (like a sonnet).[40] As Jean Jacques Lecercle argues in *The Violence of Language*, this kind of nonsensical language, albeit only to a limit, can express meaning at phonological, morphological, and syntactical levels.[41] As he says, 'if no sense is conveyed by the text, a certain quantity of affect is'.[42]

On the same page, by means of a series of questions following the verse poem, Martínez satirises conventional readers of poetry who seek to pin down a poem to its signified meaning alone. Presenting the questions as school exercises for the reader to complete, Martínez humorously criticises the ways in which poetry is typically taught while also illuminating different approaches to reading it. In the first three questions, he ironically[43] asks the 'student' reader to determine the 'meaning' of the poem and its words and to specify the author's intention: '1. ¿Cuál es el tema o motivo central de este poema?/2. ¿Qué significan los lirosos para el autor?/3. ¿Por qué el autor afirma que las oveñas patizan el bramente?' (p. 95, ll. 10–12).[44] On the one hand, Martínez seems to mock typical processes of analysis by giving the reader pointless exercises: how can one find a theme or understand the author's intention without any signifying words? On the other hand, he may be pushing the reader to find meaning by observing the poem's form, that is, its visual and aural structures.

Because the first three questions do not have answers concerning the poem's semantic meaning, Martínez moves the discussion to the 'affect' (in Lecercle's word) of a 'nonsensical' poem.[45] In other words, he questions whether feeling can be conveyed even if the reader cannot find the denotations of individual words.[46] The questions guide the reader to focus on his or her emotional, rather than intellectual, responses. He proposes that certain words within the poem as well as the poem as a whole can produce certain sensational reactions: '4. ¿Qué recursos expresivos encuentra en estos versos? [...] 5. Ubique todas aquellas palabras que produzcan la sensación de claridad, transparencia./6. ¿Este poema le produce la sensación de

40 Moreover, Martínez calls upon common imagery in lyric poetry by providing words with recognisable roots that evoke lyrical and pastoral imagery: 'lirosos' reminds one of 'lírico', 'lira' or 'rosas' and 'oveñas' of 'ovejas', for example.

41 Jean-Jacques Lecercle, *The Violence of Language* (London: Routledge, 1999), pp. 1–6.

42 Ibid., p. 4.

43 It is important to note that the use of irony in Martínez's work is uncharacteristic of concrete poetry. The lack of irony perhaps is due to their attempt to present the thing itself which leaves little room for irony, which involves saying one thing and meaning another.

44 These questions resemble Alice's questions to Humpty Dumpty. Carroll, *Alice's Adventures in Wonderland*, pp. 253–62.

45 The word 'nonsensical' is used here in quotation marks because, as the questions indicate, one can experience some sort of 'sensation'. In addition, one might have to intuit the meaning of the poem. In other words, Martínez plays on the multiple connotations of the word 'sense', or 'sentido', as meaning, bodily perceptive faculties and intuition.

46 He also seems to parody, or at least take to the extreme, Ruben Darío's aesthetics in which the poem's form and musicality are essential for its meaning. See, for example, 'Ama tu ritmo' (1896) or 'Yo persigo una forma' (1896).

quietud o de agitado movimiento? Fundamente su respuesta' (NN, ll. 16–19).[47] While these questions seem to be a humorous criticism of didactic exercises in poetic studies, they nonetheless move the reader to forget about the poem's (and its individual words') definitive signification and to focus on the sensations evoked by and the meaning that can arise from the formal qualities and spatial arrangements of the signifiers on the page. Martínez, moreover, implicitly questions whether this concretist practice of searching for 'meaning' primarily through the formal characteristics of the words on the page is possible and whether it is truly possible to separate the words on the page from semantic meaning. In other words, he asks: has the signified truly disappeared from the poem or not, and can form exist without any semantic import within poetry?

Martínez also demonstrates his resistance to poetry solely of the signifier or solely of the signified through the inclusion of logograms (written characters that represent a word or phrase) in the text. When he includes logograms in the text (recall the concretist preoccupation with the ideogram), he moves the visual aspects of the signifier to the foreground.[48] By looking at the logogram as an object or ideogram in the poem 'La poesía china' (NN, p. 97; Figure 2.4), Martínez questions the possibility (or lack thereof) of translating a word in which its visual characteristics convey meaning more directly than those of Spanish words.

Martínez inserts a page full of Chinese logograms into *La nueva novela* with the title 'La poesía china' and the footnote: '(FUNDAMENTALMENTE LA POESIA CHINA, (EN SU FORMA ACTUAL O EN OTRA CUALQUIERA) NO HA EXISTIDO JAMAS)'.[49] Paradoxically (and humorously), Martínez calls the logograms 'poetry' in the title, while in the footnote he denies that poetry exists in Chinese.

In an implicit questioning of the 'universality' of the concrete principle of ideogrammatic poetry, Martínez seems to claim that, while ideograms are a form of poetry for one who can read the characters as both signifiers and signifieds, they cannot be poetry for the reader who is unfamiliar with reading its characters. As Octavio Paz has noted, the introduction of Chinese ideograms into a poem (for example, in Ezra Pound's *Cantos*) is problematic because the ideograms either demand a translation (into Spanish, or in Pound's case, English) that is not ideographic or that lose semantic meaning.[50] Martínez simultaneously makes explicit the poem's status as a visual object and its lack of literary qualities, and thus questions the circumstances in which a word (or ideogram) is literary, as opposed to a mere image. The logogram's complete meaning can only be understood by those

47 Martínez might also be criticising here the rejection of complicated, 'inaccessible' poetry by poets such as Pablo Neruda. See, for example, Pablo Neruda, 'Oda a la claridad', in *Odas elementales*, 4th edn (Buenos Aires: Editorial Losada, 1977), pp. 43–45.

48 An interesting example of how the concrete poets spin the ideogrammatic method into their poems is one version of Augusto de Campos's 'Lixo/Luxo' (Figure 1.8), in which he forms the word 'lixo' with the patterned repetition of the word 'luxo'.

49 According to Jaime Quezada, these logograms are cut out from Chinese newspapers. Jaime Quezada, 'Juan Luis Martínez: El desórden de los sentidos', *Ercilla*, 23 November 1977, pp. 49–50.

50 Octavio Paz, *Transblanco* (Rio de Janeiro: Editora Guanabara, 1986), pp. 98–99.

who read Chinese characters. Thus, for the reader unfamiliar with the characters, the sign is incomplete because the reader can only interact with the signifier as an image, rather than a sign.[51]

The difficulty of translating both signifier and signified is further illustrated on the next page, also titled 'La poesía china', in which Martínez includes a translation into Spanish of the Bodhi poem by Shen-hsiu and its contradictory response by Hui-neng:[52]

El cuerpo es el árbol Bodhi
La mente del espejo brillante en que él se mira
Cuidar que esté siempre limpio
Y que polvo alguno lo empañe.
Shen-hsiu

Nunca existió el árbol Bodhi
Ni el brillante espejo en que él se mira
Fundamentalmente nada existe
Entonces, ¿qué polvo lo empañaría?
Hui-neng (NN, p. 97)

Martínez then expands the footnote from the previous page: '(NADIE LEERA NUNCA / OIRA (INTERPRETARA MENTALMENTE) ESTOS DOS POEMAS CHINOS). (NADIE RECORDARA NUNCA / TARAREARA (EVOCARA MENTALMENTE) ESTOS DOS POEMAS CHINOS). (FUNDAMENTALMENTE [*sic*])'. Not only does Martínez provide the same title for these last two pages, 'La poesía china', but also he numbers both pages '97'. Martínez contradicts himself: on the one hand, both pages are described as the same poem and are 'Chinese poetry'; on the other hand, in the footnotes, he indicates that both a poem in Chinese (to a reader who cannot read it) and one that is translated from ideograms cannot exist as Chinese poetry. If one treats the signifier as something object-like, then to translate the object to another language would result in the creation of a signifier that no longer signifies in the same way.

Martínez, like the concrete poets, amplifies the presence of the sensuous nature of the signifier by including not only a visual sense, but also an aural one; he equates the language of poetry with the musical patterns of birds in two interconnected poems (Figure 2.5).[53]

51 Suárez, *Objetualismo en Juan Luis Martínez*, p. 89.

52 It is not surprising that Martínez includes these famous contradictory Buddhist poems from the seventh century that question existence as clear examples of the tension between existence and nonexistence throughout the book. Martínez purposefully, perhaps as an exercise in philosophical scepticism, contradicts himself throughout the book. As Suárez cleverly points out, this poem is a multi-layered palimpsest: 'De nuevo se trata de un ejercicio de doble reescritura, en este caso paródica, de una obra de Yoko Ono basada en el absurdo, Pomelo. Un libro de instrucciones de Yoko Ono de 1964, que recuerda mucho a las instrucciones de Cortázar en su Historia de cronopios y de famas (1962) y que nos remite a la importancia del papel del lector en este tipo de obras'. Suárez, *Objetualismo en Juan Luis Martínez*, p. 146). One could consider this act of rewriting as another layer of translation.

53 A good example of the musical element in concrete poetry is the musicians Caetano Veloso and Gilberto Gil's 'Batmacumba' (1968), a song transcribed by Augusto de Campos. Augusto de Campos,

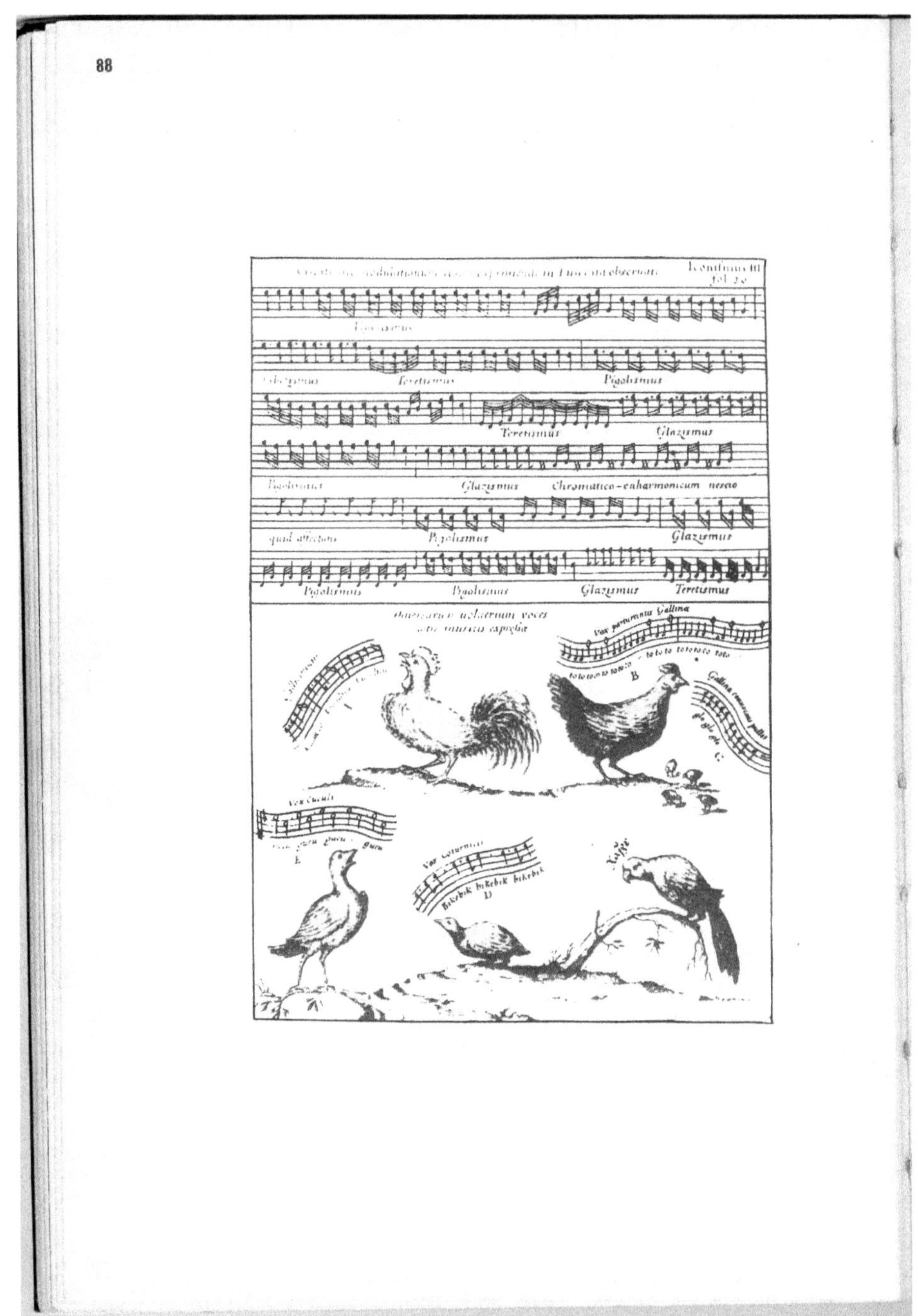

Fig. 2.5. Martínez, 'Observaciones relacionadas...'.
Courtesy of Alita Martínez and Fundación de Juan Luis Martínez.

89

OBSERVACIONES RELACIONADAS CON LA EXUBERANTE ACTIVIDAD DE LA "CONFABULACION FONETICA" O "LENGUAJE DE LOS PAJAROS" EN LAS OBRAS DE J.-P. BRISSET, R. ROUSSEL, M. DUCHAMP Y OTROS

a. A través de su canto los pájaros
comunican una comunicación
en la que dicen que no dicen nada.

b. El lenguaje de los pájaros
es un lenguaje de signos transparentes
en busca de la transparencia dispersa de algún significado.

c. Los pájaros encierran el significado de su propio canto
en la malla de un lenguaje vacío;
malla que es a un tiempo transparente e irrompible.

d. Incluso el silencio que se produce entre cada canto
es también un eslabón de esa malla, un signo, un momento
del mensaje que la naturaleza se dice a sí misma.

e. Para la naturaleza no es el canto de los pájaros
ni su equivalente, la palabra humana, sino el silencio,
el que convertido en mensaje tiene por objeto
establecer, prolongar o interrumpir la comunicación
para verificar si el circuito funciona
y si realmente los pájaros se comunican entre ellos
a través de los oídos de los hombres
y sin que estos se den cuenta.

NOTA:

Los pájaros cantan en pajarístico,
pero los escuchamos en español.
(El español es una lengua opaca,
con un gran número de palabras fantasmas;
el pajarístico es una lengua transparente y sin palabras).

In the first poem, he presents a musical score followed by drawings of birds singing musical stanzas that, when played, sound like various birdsongs. The musical score Martínez includes is that of German Jesuit scholar Athanasius Kircher's categorisation of birdsongs.[54] Because birdsong signifies only through the patterns of signifiers because birds do not have concepts *per se*, it is particularly effective for describing the 'meaning' latent in the signifier. As expressed with recognisable words in the poem on the following page, 'Observaciones relacionadas con la exuberante actividad de la "confabulación fonética" o "lenguaje de los "pájaros" en las obras de J.-P. Brisset, R, Roussel, M Duchamp y otros' (Figure 2.5), the musical notes of the birdsongs act as signs in a language. Just as the photographs in Augusto de Campos's 'popcreto' poem 'Ôlho por Ôlho' (for example; Figure 1.7) act as words, or signifiers, the drawings in Martínez's book act like signifiers. When the musical lines (any musical lines, for that matter) are sung or played, the song is made not only through the production of the notes in themselves, but also by the sonic patterns of noise and silence they create when played together. On the page, their patterns are expressed through the positions and types of the notes and their (linear) relationships to one another. Furthermore, the drawings under the musical score illustrate that the music is coming from the birds' open beaks, as though they were singing. The relationship between the drawings and the musical score urges the reader to consider not solely the notes, but the page in its entirety.

By including this score in which the individual notes are subordinated to the page as a whole and thereby illuminating the power of the visual patterns of birdsong on the page, Martínez shows, as with his nonsense poem, that a poem's strength comes as much, if not more, from its aural and visual patterns as from the meaning of particular words. The musical score on this page, however, includes words (not the lyrics of a song, but rather words linked to the production of sound) that act as a key to understanding what these patterns represent. While many musical scores have words that guide the musician through the music ('*a tempo*', for example), this score contains words that seem to organise the musical stanzas. For instance, almost every musical phrase in the first half of the page is categorised as 'Glazismus', 'Teretismus', or 'Pigolismus'. According to Raymond Monelle, Kircher distinguished between three sound types of birds: 'Glazismus' (close repetition of the same sound), 'Teretismus' (a set of a variety of elements including a noticeable repetition), and 'Pigolismus' (a fast oscillation between two pitches).[55] These terms also draw our attention to the aural rather than the semantic quality of birdsong.[56] Furthermore, the musical lines that accompany the chickens in the second half of the page have

Balanço da Bossa e Outras Bossas, 5th ed. (São Paulo: Editora Perspectiva, 2005), p. 288.

54 Athanasius Kircher, *Musurgia Universalis*, vol. 1 (Rome: Ex Typograpia Haeredum F. Corbellitti, 1650), pp. 30–31. This inclusion of Kirsher's musical score without direct acknowledgement of the artist is an example of how Martínez dismantles the notions of authorship and authority, a discussion that will be developed below in 'Author and Text'.

55 Raymond Monelle, 'Musica Significans: Proceedings of the 3rd International Congress on Musical Signification', *Contemporary Music Review*, 16 (1992), p. 61.

56 Although one could argue that particular birdsongs signal certain meanings (such as if there is food, a predator, etc.), it is the pattern of the song, rather than a concept (or signified), carried with it that signals its meaning.

the sounds they might make written onomatopoeically: 'totototosemtototototo-tototo totototo toto!' or 'glogloglo' (NN, p. 88).[57] The page, at the same time, does not signify purely through musical patterns and drawings, but also provides some form of language so that it can be read.

The score is also supported by the verse poem that follows, which explains (with words) how the 'birdish' language communicates. The musical score is dependent on the poem; it only becomes fully 'readable' when it is physically placed next to a 'conventional' form of literature (a verse poem). In the poem, 'Observaciones relacionadas con la exuberante actividad [...]' (Figure 2.5), Martínez compares the language of the birds, or 'pajarístico' (therefore immediately anthropomorphising the birds) to the language of poets, thus highlighting the importance of the sonic in poetry.[58] The birds' language, like poetic language, communicates through a pattern created by the alteration of silence and sound: 'no es el canto de los pájaros [...] sino el silencio,/el que convertido en mensaje tiene por objeto/establecer, prolongar o interrumpir la comunicación' (NN, p. 89, ll. 13–16).[59] Martínez draws on the well-known association of birdsong and the production of poetry (and of birds and poets): Romantic poets allude to nightingales (such as Samuel Taylor Coleridge and John Keats), modernist and *modernista* poets to swans (such as William Butler Yeats and Ruben Darío), and late *modernista* poets to owls (such as Enrique González Martínez), for example. Juan Luis Martínez explains how poems signify not only through sounds but also through the white space surrounding the words and the silence it produces. If one considers Jakobson's claim that, of the six functions of a speech act (the referential, poetic, emotive, conative, phatic, and metalingual), the poetic function of language is concerned with the message, one can infer that Martínez goes even further to imply that this silence, converted into the message, *is* the poetic function of language (just as it is essential in birdsong); as he states, silence becomes a message ('convertido en mensaje').[60]

The variety of experiments Martínez includes that probe the potential of signs to convey meaning suggests the difficulty that any one way of writing might have in doing so. Martínez explains that the language of birds consists of what he calls 'transparent' signs that seek other meanings only to find that they are also

57 This onomatopoeic representation of birdsong is reminiscent of August Strindberg's 'The Nightingale's Song' and John Clare's metric birdsong from 'The Progress of Rhyme'. *Poems for the Millennium*, ed. by Jeffrey Robinson and Jerome Rothenberg, vol 3 (Berkeley: University of California Press, 2009), pp. 716–17 and 297–98. The equation of birdsong to poetry also reminds us of John Keats's 'Ode to a Nightingale' (1819). Other poems throughout *La nueva novela* allude to birdsong and music, such as with the word 'tararear' in 'La poesía china' (p. 97, see above) and the word 'chirriante' in the poem 'La grafología' (p. 91, see below in 'Author and Text').

58 Felipe Cussen, as an attempt to expand the discussion of Martínez's development of the relationship between birdsong and language, lists other writers and artists who have made similar comparisons in 'Del pajarístico al lenguaje de los pájaros', *Acta Literaria*, 39 (2009), 91–103.

59 There is obviously a difference between birdsong and poetry (birdsong does not have signifieds, or concepts, and only signals particular actions, and therefore could be considered pure communication), but Martínez uses the comparison to foreground the meaning that can emerge from the signifiers in poetry alone.

60 Jakobson, 'Linguistics and Poetics', in *Modern Criticism and Theory: A Reader*, ed. by David Lodge and Nigel Wood, 3rd edn (London: Pearson, 2008), pp. 141–64 (p. 146).

transparent (and perhaps opaque, or solid, clearly defined meanings cannot be found): 'El lenguaje de los pájaros/es un lenguaje de signos transparentes/en busca de la transparencia dispersa de algún significado' (NN, ll. 4–6). He suggests that transparent signs are those empty of 'meaning' (or at least signifieds); birds do not have concepts behind their songs and only communicate through patterns of sounds. The signs of birdsong, just as the words of a poetic language, are in Martínez's vision just as transparent in the sense that they constantly move the reader to search for a meaning attached to the word, but the meaning can never be reached as one can only reach other transparent signifiers.[61] The birds' song, because it does not contain opaque meaning, is therefore empty: 'Los pájaros encierran el significado de su propio canto/en la malla de un lenguaje vacío;/malla que es a un tiempo transparente e irrompible' (NN, ll. 7–9). The transparent signified is trapped in a transparent, yet unbreakable net of signifiers. Even though the signified cannot be reached because it is trapped in this net, meaning is not destroyed but instead opened up to new possibilities. The net of signifiers gains strength (and becomes 'irrompible') as it intertwines with itself to form the page as a whole; it is at the same time transparent, or open to multiple meanings, and unbreakable. Silence is also entangled in this net: 'd. Incluso el silencio que se produce entre cada canto/es también un eslabón de esa malla, un signo, un momento/del mensaje que la naturaleza se dice a sí misma' (NN, ll. 10–12). While the language of the birds contains transparent signs that never reveal one meaning, silence, nonetheless, allows for a degree of communication by existing as an essential component of the patterns within the text (NN, ll. 13–16).

Martínez discusses the ultimate transparency of the words of poetry (and birdsong) as signifiers in opposition to the spoken, quotidian language of human beings that emphasises instead its signifieds. In the 'note' to the poem, he explains that quotidian language is opaque because its meaning overrides its signifiers, even though it contains signifiers that are 'ghosts' (which are many times depicted as transparent) that one can mostly see through: 'El español es una lengua opaca,/con un gran número de palabras fantasmas' (NN, ll. 23–24). The language of birds, in contrast, does not have 'words', in the sense that the words do not signify and are therefore only transparent because there is no sole meaning behind them: 'el pajarístico es una lengua transparente y sin palabras' (NN, l. 25). If poets claim that their words do not signify ('A través de su canto los pájaros/comunican una comunicación/en la que dicen que no dicen nada' (NN, ll. 1–3)), then their language must be 'sin palabras' and only in patterns of silence and sound can they communicate. Martínez thus expands the concrete poets' emphasis on words themselves through his play on birdsong. However, the signified in this poem remains: the musical score requires signs that have semantic meaning in order for it to be read as a literary object (and as a song).

To rid the poem completely of conventional meaning (i.e. the signs' signifieds), Martínez, in 'La página en blanco' (NN, p. 86; Figure 2.6), goes even further than

61 See Jacques Derrida, '...That Dangerous Supplement...', *Of Grammatology* (Baltimore: The Johns Hopkins University Press, 1974), pp. 141–57 (pp. 152–57).

Fig. 2.6. Martínez, 'La página en blanco'.
Courtesy of Alita Martínez and Fundación de Juan Luis Martínez.

the concretists by experimenting with the elimination of signs all together from the poem.[62] He inserts a page into his book that is almost entirely blank, apart from the asterisked title: 'La página en blanco★', located at the top of the page, and a footnote: '(El Cisne de Ana [*sic*] Pavlova sigue siendo la mejor página en blanco)', at the bottom. As the title indicates, the page in its entirety, like the page does for concrete poets, forms the poem — not simply the 'words' or even the 'white' space, but the whole object. The page, despite what the title indicates, is not completely blank. With this poem, Martínez pushes to the limit the relationship between white space and words within a poetic text; in order for the poem to exist and have literary status (and not become solely a sheet of paper), the blank space must stand in relation to words. The title and the footnote structure the blank poem; on the one hand, they border the poem, but, on the other, they *are* the poem because they are a part of the poetic unit, that is, the page.[63] By placing the only sentence on the page not only in a footnote, but also in parentheses, Martínez subordinates the words to the 'blank' space. At the same time, however, the presence of a footnote points to the paradox that words are necessary to convey the meaning of a blank page.[64] By referring to Anna Pavlova's symbolic ballet performance of the dying swan (in which she is dressed in white) in his footnote, Martínez indicates that ultimately only another form of art, ballet, has the potential to succeed in expressing the silence that white space can convey. Yet even dance, which does not use verbal language, cannot completely communicate pure silence because it involves expressive movement and, in many cases, music.

The paradoxical dependence silence has on sound (and vice-versa) brings into question the significance a sign (words) or no sign (white space) can carry. On the one hand, Martínez privileges the page in 'La página en blanco', and thus values the avant-garde idealisation of white space and its evocation of silence (see, for example, the discussion of Mallarmé above). White space carries the possibility for freedom and play within literature and, without words, carries no specific semantic meaning; white space, like words, has the potential to signify, but, unlike words, is not constrained by one authorial signified. At the same time, white space only becomes a sign if there are other signs surrounding it; as soon as one strives for a certain signification, the text becomes imbued with authority. On the other hand, Martínez associates the avant-garde's idealisation of white space with authority itself because, for them, silence seemed to be something for which one could reach, something that has a signified apart from itself that dictates its essence. In this experiment, as with his other experiments in finding meaning in the signifier alone, and in contrast to the concrete poets, Martínez acknowledges the impossibility of a perfect separation of signifier and signified.

62 This poem does not have a page number because of the nature of the poem (see below). However, it has been placed between page 86 and 87 in the section titled 'Literatura'.

63 Martínez uses these paratextual (to use Genette's term) elements as part of many poems in *La nueva novela*. See Genette, *Paratexts*. In addition, Rioseco has a thorough discussion of the paratexts in Martínez's work. See Rioseco, *Maquinarias reconstructivas*, pp. 139–55.

64 This paradox recalls Gomringer's 'Silencio', which suggests that to understand (or even to form) the white space, that is, silence, on the page, one also needs the written word, with both its semantic and spatial meaning.

87

EL CISNE TROQUELADO

I (La búsqueda)

La página replegada sobre la blancura de sí misma.
La apertura del documento cerrado: (EVOLUTIO LIBRIS).
El pliego / el manuscrito: su texto corregido y su lectura.
La escritura de un signo entre otros signos.
La lectura de unas cifras enrolladas.
La página signada / designada: asignada a la blancura.

II (El encuentro)

Nombrar / signar / cifrar: el designio inmaculado:
su blancura impoluta: su blancor secreto: su reverso blanco.
La página signada con el número de nadie:
el número o el nombre de cualquiera: (LA ANONIMIA no nombrada).
El proyecto imposible: la compaginación de la blancura.
La lectura de unos signos diseminados en páginas dispersas.
(La Página en Blanco): La Escritura Anónima y Plural:
El Demonio de la Analogía: su dominio:
La lectura de un signo entre unos cisnes o a la inversa.

III (La locura)

El signo de los signos / el signo de los cisnes.
El troquel con el nombre de cualquiera:
el troquel anómino de alguno que es ninguno:
"El Anónimo Troquel de la Desdicha":

Le $\frac{\text{SIGNE}}{\text{CYGNE}}$ blanc de le $\frac{\text{CYGNE}}{\text{SIGNE}}$ Mallarmé

(Analogía troquelada en anominia):
el no compaginado nombre de la albura:
la presencia troquelada de unos cisnes: el hueco que dejaron:
la ausencia compaginada en nombre de la albura y su designio:
el designio o el diseño vacío de unos signos:
el revés blanco de una página cualquiera:
la inhalación de su blancura venenosa:
la realidad de la página como ficción de sí misma:
el último canto de ese signo en el revés de la página:
el revés de su canto: la exhalación de su último poema.
(¿Y el signo interrogante de su cuello (?) ?:
reflejado en el discurso del agua: (¿) : es una errata).

(¿Swan de Dios?)
(¡Recuerda Jxuan de Dios!): (¡Olvidarás la página!)
y en la suprema identidad de su reverso
no invocarás nombre de hombre o de animal:
en nombre de los otros: ¡tus hermanos!
también el agua borrará tu nombre:
el plumaje anónimo: su nombre tañedor de signos

borroso en su designio
borrándose al borde de la página . . .

Fig. 2.7. Martínez, 'El cisne troquelado'.
Courtesy of Alita Martínez and Fundación de Juan Luis Martínez.

Like the musical score and 'Observaciones relacionadas a la exuberante actividad' discussed above, 'La página en blanco' is followed by a verse poem, 'El cisne troquelado' (NN, p. 87; Figure 2.7), which emerges out of the white space of the page, not moving from infinite possibilities to one, restrictive meaning, but moving from no meaning to the meaning*ful*. As the title indicates, the swan, a symbol of grace, sensuality, and purity (and poetic creation), has been cut, moulded and commodified like a coin ('troquelado') in order to stand as a metaphor for modernism and Spanish American *modernismo*.[65] Martínez plays with the metaphor of the swan and the word 'cisne' itself by connecting it to its homophone 'sign':

> La lectura de un signo entre unos cisnes o a la inversa [...]
> El signo de los signos / el signo de los cisnes. [...]
> Le SIGNE Blanc de le CYGNE Mallarmé
> CYGNE SIGNE (NN, ll. 15–20)

With white space on the page ('El proyecto imposible: la *compaginación* de la blancura', [l. 11, my emphasis]), the poem implies that the goal of the concrete poets (as explained in Chapter 1) is to arrange, or organise, the blank space so that it becomes a language of its own is unrealisable. The word no longer sufficiently expresses, but the blank space ('Le Signe y Cygne blanc') itself conveys meaning. The sign and the swan thus become homophonically the same thing; the swan, something white, is no longer the metaphor that the modernists and Spanish American *modernistas* had used to convey beauty and purity. Instead, the sign itself, a *white* bird, like the *white* space, carries the meaning (the relationship between language and silence). In other words, as the reader moves through the verse poem, words are confused with others ('swan' with 'sign' being the main confusion) and one signifier may no longer carry the same signified. Because both words are signifiers detached from their signifieds, the word 'swan' acts the same as the word 'sign'.

Because these words insufficiently express meaning, the page (or poem), requires something else, that is, blank space, in order to convey something: 'La página signada / designada: asignada a la blancura' (NN, l. 6). Martínez highlights how the Spanish American *modernista* sign for 'swan' can never arrive at its signified, yet the lack of signification can open the reader up to the sign's freedom to reveal multiple meanings. Martínez further undermines the ways in which a fixed signified conveys authority by confounding his name, 'Juan', with 'swan' (and therefore 'sign', see below); just as he again questions the authority of the author, he questions the authority of a signified. When he mentions his name in 'El cisne troquelado', he draws attention to the problem both of the authorial figure and of the sign: '(¿Swan de Dios?)/(¡Recuerda Jxuan de Dios!): (¡Olvidarás la página!)' (NN, ll. 33–34). As soon as he connects the image of the swan to his name through the sign itself ('Swan' and 'Jxuan'), however, Martínez suggests that the poetic unit (the page) will no longer be efficacious once an authority is brought into the poem (the reader will forget the page). The name (Jxuan de Dios), which is repeated throughout *La*

65 See W.B. Yeats's 'Leda and the Swan' (1924), Charles Baudelaire's 'Le Cygne' (1857) and Rubén Darío's 'Los cisnes' (1907), for example. Like the question mark that is the swan's neck in Darío's poem, the 'sign' here becomes the (sign for) the swan and vice-versa.

nueva novela, not only plays on the author's first name, but also on the Spanish saint 'Juan de Dios' and, with a 'cross' placed inside the name (x), the mystic poet San Juan de la Cruz and his search for absolute knowledge. Moreover, the 'x' in 'Jxuan de Dios' recalls that of Julio Cortázar's 'Axolotl'. As Brett Levinson explains, the 'x' in the word 'axolotl' (which is the name for a salamander-esque creature into which the protagonist of Cortázar's story turns) is a 'transliteration' that symbolises the Latin American identity of being at a crossroads between cultures.[66] Similarly, the sign of the swan (and the sign of the author) could be seen as an intersection; it represents poetic freedom from defined meaning, but, at the same time, it negates that freedom by its nature as a symbol.[67]

Martínez equates the swan with the signified to emphasise further the potential tyrannical danger the authorial signified can bring by alluding to the myth of Leda and the Swan ('Swan de Dios'), a myth reused in the works of many of the modernist and Spanish American *modernista* poets. Nonetheless, he argues that a supreme authority ('Swan de Dios', Zeus, the god who rapes Leda) ultimately cannot reveal the meaning of a poem, since the name, or sign, will be forgotten.[68] The change of the sign seems to point here to Martínez's sense of the failure of the modernist and Spanish American *modernista* poets who utilised the swan as a symbol of a freedom free of confined meaning, when, in fact, their use of the symbol confined it to a specific meaning. Martínez understands that authority and meaning, if handled properly (through a poetry of signifiers only loosely connected to signifieds), is crucial for raising a transformative consciousness; danger appears only when authority becomes tyrannical and meaning becomes singular.

Author and Text

Also crucial to Martínez's experimental poetics and his development of concretist poetics is his playful analysis (in its etymological sense, meaning 'loosening', 'breaking up' or 'dissolution') of the status and authority of the author in relationship to the text and reader. The creation of a truly 'verbivocovisual' text, according to the concrete poets, requires the erasure of the author in order to allow the reader to emerge as an equal creator of the text. In an interview by Félix Guattari, Martínez explains that his literary goal is to rid the text of all authority and replace it with anonymity:

66 See Brett Levinson, *The Ends of Literature: The Latin American 'Boom' in the Neoliberal Marketplace* (Stanford: Stanford University Press, 2001), pp. 10–30. It also symbolises the unknown. The Brazilian critic Silviano Santiago also describes Latin American culture as a state of in-betweenness, that is, between 'sacrifice and playfulness, prison and transgression, submission to the code and aggression, obedience and rebellion, assimilation and expression'. Silviano Santiago, *The Space In-Between* (Durham: Duke University Press, 2001), p. 38. I will discuss this state of betweenness further in Chapter 4.

67 Martínez also, as Hugo Rivera Scott points out, was born near the San Juan de Dios hill in Valparaíso. Hugo Rivera Scott, 'Notas para una cautelosa entrada en el oscuro objeto de ceniza que es *El poeta anónimo* de Juan Luis Martínez', in Polanco, p. 60.

68 This poem could also be read from a feminist perspective; the (male) signified authority suppresses the meaning of the (female) signifier.

> mi mayor interés es la disolución absoluta de la autoría, la anonimia, y la ideal, si puede usarse esa palabra, es hacer un trabajo, una obra, en la que no me pertenezca casi ninguna sola línea, articulando en un trabajo largo muchos fragmentos. Son pedacitos incluso que se conectan. Es un trabajo de Penélope.[69]

Just as Penelope wove and un-wove her *text*ile, Martínez presents the author at the same time as he erases the author's (supposed) power. His aim is to create a text in which all the materials, as diverse threads, are separated from a sole speaker. However, he does not want to eliminate the author entirely ('una obra en la que no me pertenezca *casi* ninguna sola línea'). As I shall argue, he wants the text to be attached to and detached from his signature in order for it (and more generally a world) to have no sole authority, but instead for it to be a text in which everyone, including (the figure of) the author, can participate.[70]

With his crossed out and parenthetical signatures as primary examples (see Figure 2.1), Martínez demonstrates his preoccupation with (his conception of) the poet's identity or existence as being fragile or questionable; his signature asserts the presence of the author at the same time as it cancels it.[71] The signature questions the degree to which art can embody this fragility of existence through an orthographic, and therefore visual, act of object-creation. He captures what Jacques Derrida observes of the written signature and its relationship to its creator:

> By definition, a written signature implies the actual or empirical nonpresence of the signer. But, it will be said, it also marks and retains his having-been present in a past now, which will remain a future now, and therefore in a now in general, in the transcendental form of nowness (*maintenance*).[72]

Martínez demonstrates (orthographically and semantically with his signature as well as in particular poems) Derrida's idea that the author exists paradoxically in relation to his or her written text. As Martínez illustrates, the text only comes to

69 Martínez, *Poemas del otro*, p. 82. Throughout his work, Martínez engages in conversation with the works of many French philosophers and critical theorists (such as Derrida, Foucault and Saussure), which, as Rioseco implies, is a way of questioning Western logic. See Rioseco, *Maquinarias reconstructivas*, pp. 115–75. Leong argues that Martinez's 'insistent dialogue with French authors [...] in the context of the early 1970s [...] seems an example of his "virtual exile."' Leong, pp. 168–69.

70 While this attempt to dissolve all authority from a text is apparent in all of Martínez's works, I've included here just one example *La nueva novela*. Other examples include Martínez's translation of the first seventeen poems in *Poemas del otro* (in which the interview with Guattari and his quote about the dissolution of authority appears), written by another Juan Luis Martinez (*sic*), seems to be his attempt to take this destruction of authority to a level beyond that of *La nueva novela*. Without any clear explanation of to whom the poems 'belong', Martínez destroys both his authority as Juan Luis Martínez as well as the role of the signature itself. He also questions the idea of authorship in his 'book' *La poesía chilena*. By placing library calling cards of poetry books and their poets next to the death certificates of said poets, he both satirises the Chilean canon and problematises the role one's name has in relation to one's work.

71 The doubled crossing out of his signature, as Heriberto Yépez notes, also places into question a capitalistic sense of ownership and individual property. Heriberto Yépez, 'The Dialectic of Romantic and Postromantic Ethopoetics (after Certain Hispano-American Visual Poetries)', in *Active Romanticism*, ed. by Julie Carr and Jeffrey C. Robinson (Tuscaloosa: The University of Alabama Press, 2015), 197–211 (p. 206).

72 Derrida, 'Signature Event Context', *Margins of Philosophy* (London: The Harvester Press, 1982), p. 328.

being with a reader, which means it only can exist in the present, the 'now'. With other contemporary theories of authorship, such as Roland Barthes's argument that 'the birth of the reader must be at the cost of the death of the Author'[73] and Michel Foucault's analysis of the author as a 'function'[74] as starting points, I will illustrate how Martínez explores a variety of ways to diminish authorial subjectivity at the same time that he acknowledges the inevitable presence of his authorship. He thus wants to be a subjective presence in his text — recognising that an author as a creator of a poem will always have some degree of connection to the material — but at the same time he does not want to dominate the material.[75]

In this section, I will explore how Martínez, like the concrete poets, in questioning his relationship to his text, attempts to create an egalitarian text in which both reader and author can participate. As I will show, by (1) referring to his life outside of literature with allusions to his family and home, (2) discussing the nature of his signature itself and (3) opening up (to an extent) his text for the reader to participate in its creation, he exemplifies various theoretical positions concerned with the nature of authorship. Through this destruction of the conventional role of author, Martínez demonstrates his own vision of the possibility for a communal art with the collaboration of reader and author rather than the subjection of the ego of the reader to that of a superior author.

Although Martínez attempts to avoid inserting himself (as a person as opposed to an author) into *La nueva novela*, in the poem called 'La casa del aliento,* casi la pequeña casa del (autor)' (NN, p. 90; Figure 2.8), he calls into question the role the biography of the author can play in the reader's experience of a poem by directly referring to part of his life outside the work. The house (and its instability) — a metonym encompassing the biography of the author as a Chilean, of himself as author and his poetry as a constructed thing — is an important motif throughout *La nueva novela*.[76] To begin with, the cover of the book (Figure 2.1) consists of the photographic image of a tumbling house, and its negative reappears in the middle of the book.[77] The house not only refers to one that exists outside the text, that is, to the author's (supposed) house, but also points to an idea of a house as a metaphor for the poetry itself, that is, his poem constructed on the page which 'houses' his ideas; just as the concrete poets are preoccupied with the page as the principal unit of poetry, so Martínez uses the page as a whole to 'house' his description of his

73 Roland Barthes, 'The Death of the Author', *Image, Music, Text* (London: Fontana, 1977), pp. 142–48.

74 Michael Foucault, 'What is an Author?', *Essential Works of Foucault 1954–1984: Aesthetics, Method, and Epistemology*, vol. 2 (New York: The New Press, 1998).

75 The author, for Martínez, like for Foucault, is continuously disappearing. Ibid., p. 206.

76 Sepúlveda specifically argues that the image of the house plays a crucial role in Martínez's politics; for Sepúlveda, the precarious state of the house throughout *La nueva novela* symbolises the insecurities felt under dictatorship. See Sepúlveda (2016), pp. 91–137. Hugo Rivera-Scott also argues that the book, for Martínez, is a house in 'Notas para una cautelosa entrada en el oscuro objeto de ceniza que es *El poeta anónimo* de Juan Luis Martínez', in Polanco, pp. 49–62.

77 Juan Herrera argues that this house in the photograph not only represents Pinochet's Chile (as well as Martínez's Chile at the time he published *La nueva novela*), but also art, writing and the self. Herrera, p. 12.

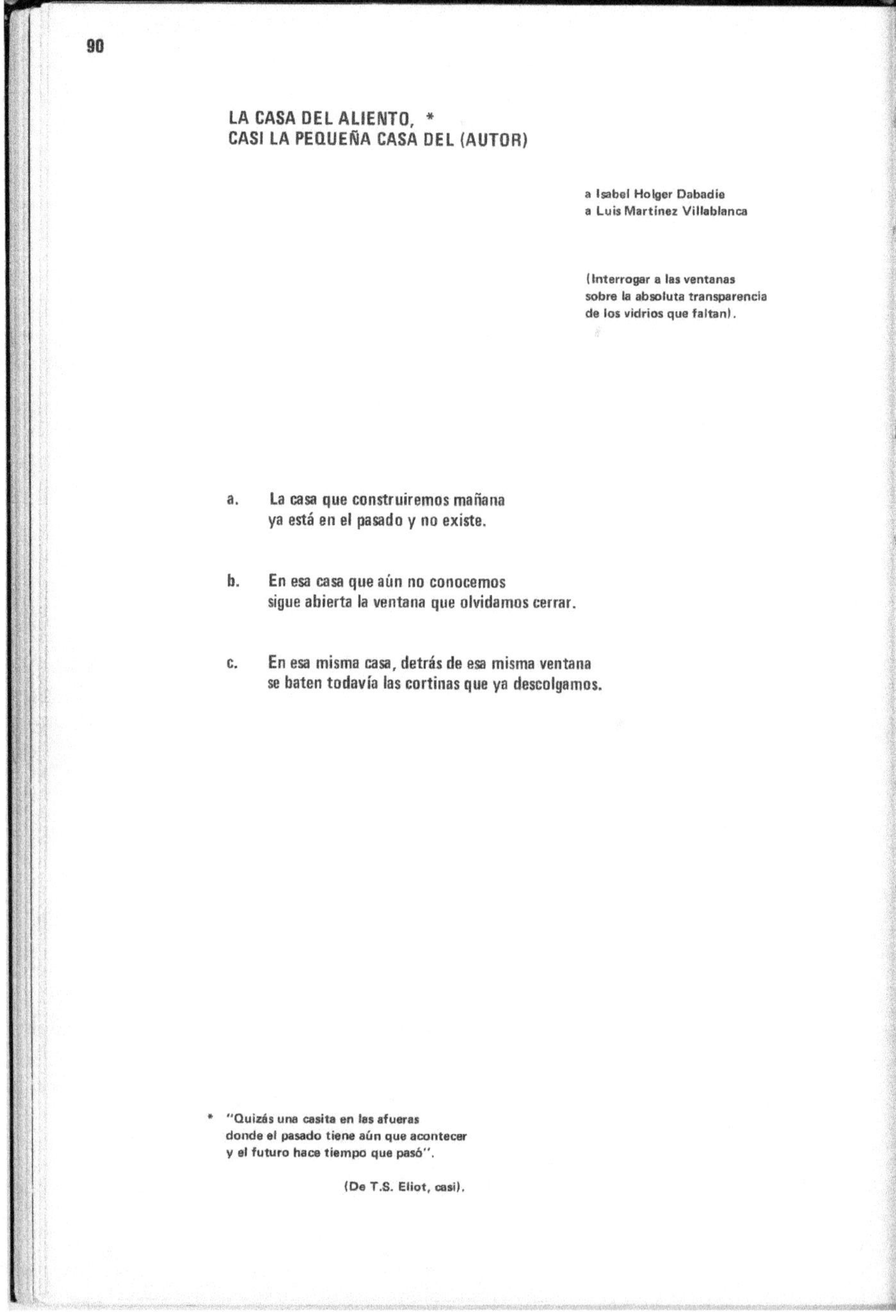
90

LA CASA DEL ALIENTO, *
CASI LA PEQUEÑA CASA DEL (AUTOR)

a Isabel Holger Dabadie
a Luis Martínez Villablanca

(Interrogar a las ventanas
sobre la absoluta transparencia
de los vidrios que faltan).

a. La casa que construiremos mañana
ya está en el pasado y no existe.

b. En esa casa que aún no conocemos
sigue abierta la ventana que olvidamos cerrar.

c. En esa misma casa, detrás de esa misma ventana
se baten todavía las cortinas que ya descolgamos.

* "Quizás una casita en las afueras
donde el pasado tiene aún que acontecer
y el futuro hace tiempo que pasó".

(De T.S. Eliot, casi).

Fig. 2.8. Martínez, 'La casa del aliento'.
Courtesy of Alita Martínez and Fundación de Juan Luis Martínez.

home.[78] This symbol of the falling house, appearing on the cover, signifies the collapse of traditional spaces and therefore signals the breakdown of all traditional coordinates of life, as well as the form of the work that follows in the book. As the title indicates, Martínez (as author) *almost* dwells both in a house outside of the text and in the house on the page; there are indications of his presence within the text, yet he does not fully exist within it.[79]

By naming this house 'la casa del aliento' as 'the house of breath', he describes it as if it were a living, breathing person, or even the biological body that houses the author. The 'breath' could be the material with which the house is built, or it could be a synecdoche for the living, breathing author, and, in turn, for the 'life' of a work of art. However, breath (as well as the other connotations of the word 'aliento' as 'inspiration' or 'encouragement') is intangible and invisible, something that is necessary but ungraspable. This 'house of breath' is something that exists, yet cannot be seen. Similarly, the author of a text, as this poem indirectly suggests, exists only as a figure or character of the text on the page. In the main text of the page, he lists three verse statements about a house:

a. La casa que construiremos mañana
ya está en el pasado y no existe.

b. En esa casa que aún no conocemos
sigue abierta la ventana que olvidamos cerrar.

c. En esa misma casa, detrás de esa misma ventana
se baten todavía las cortinas que ya descolgamos. (NN, p. 90)

At first glance, the 'poem' seems constructed (like a house): the statements are ordered alphabetically and each sentence repeats the word 'casa' in a phrase with one more word (moving from two words to three to four). Furthermore, resembling a pattern poem (see Chapter 1), the lines become progressively longer through the page, almost resembling the shape of a roof. The pattern also could be seen as another 'almost' house as kind of blueprint for a house; just as Mallarmé's 'Un coup de dés' and many concrete poems resemble musical scores and things to be realised (see Chapter 1 for an example), this poem resembles a plan for the construction of a house.

The house that he describes, however, does not belong in a place in time. Martínez obscures the time in which the house exists, deliberately contradicting himself; as he explains, it has yet to be constructed so cannot have existed in the past, but somehow already did exist ('La casa que construiremos mañana/ya está en el pasado y no existe'). It also does not exist in the present, yet has windows and

78 The stanzas, in the etymological meaning of the word, are the 'rooms' for his ideas.

79 The question of where the author dwells, either on or off the page, can be considered within the context of Martin Heidegger's essay 'Poetically man dwells'; Martínez locates that dwelling on the page itself. Moreover, this line, which Heidegger takes from Friedrich Hölderlin, is qualified by 'on Earth', demonstrating, as Heidegger explains, that one dwells poetically not in some universal space, but on this planet. Such thoughts may be behind Martínez's decision, as discussed in the following section, to abandon the goal of the concrete poets to create a universal text. See Martin Heidegger, *Poetry, Language, Thought* (New York: Harper & Row, 1971), pp. 213–29.

curtains that continue to exist in the present ('sigue abierta la ventana [...] se baten todavía las cortinas que ya descolgamos'). Martínez (the author), like the house, does not exist in the present of the text, and the house, like his poem, will only be 'constructed' in the *present* by a collaboration between the reader and whatever traces that remain of a past author.

Martínez creates a house that can only exist in language on the page, and yet this fact does not preclude thinking of the house as 'outside' the work. In the terms of the concrete poets, the poem has become an object.[80] Firstly, in this 'almost' house, the title and its footnote frame the page, just as walls would frame a house. Even the word 'casi' is (homophonically) *almost* the word 'casa'. The diminutive of 'casa' also contains the word itself ('*casi*ta'), a word Martínez includes in the footnote and plays with in the title 'casi la pequeña casa del autor'; the house is *almost* a 'casita'. In addition, one could connect this 'casi' house to his statement 'no me pertenezca casi ninguna sola línea' in the interview quoted above, a link which emphasises his goal to create a text that is almost, but not completely, detached from himself. The word 'casi', moreover, exists both in the title and in the footnote, thereby emphasising the ambiguity of the existence of the author's 'house' and thus of the author's biographical life.

This 'page-house' also includes the author in the title (albeit in parentheses). Furthermore, the 'page-house' contains his lineage in the form of dedications to Martínez's parents: 'a Isabel Holger Debadie/a Luis Martínez Villablanca'.[81] His identity, such as it is, exists beyond the Martínez writing and living in the moment. By including the names of his parents in this poem, he implies, moreover, that the house is not that of just any author, but *his* (Juan Luis Martínez's) house; it occupies the border between 'object' and 'representation', which shows that, paradoxically, Martínez ultimately veers away from the goals of the concrete poets (and of visual poetry in general), particularly the concretist goal of creating a text that does not *re*present, but *presents* itself.

The obscure first-person plural used in the poem mirrors the ambiguity of the house's existence. On the one hand, the 'we' could refer to the author and his parents (because of the dedication), which would add to the image that this house is the author's childhood home. On the other hand, it could refer to the author and the reader to whom he gives the directions that follow the dedications to his parents: '(Interrogar a las ventanas/sobre la absoluta transparencia/de los vidrios que faltan)'. In this case, the house is that of the text itself (i.e. the page), where the author only exists insofar as he is a character in the poem and therefore a 'function'

80 Moreover, it has become an object that does not completely belong to the author; Martínez questions his ownership of the poem-as-house and thus more generally private property.

81 While dedications usually do not pertain to the body of a text, we can assume that this dedication is part of the poem itself if we consider the page as a whole to be the poem. There are many poems throughout *La nueva novela* with dedications, footnotes and epigraphs in which this consideration is helpful. In addition, Martínez designates an entire section of poems as 'notes', even though they should be considered poems in and of themselves (as well as in relation to the other poems of the book).

of the text, rather than an actual person.[82] In other words, the book passes by the *filiative* (that is, vertical, linear and familial) community that traditional homes (or poems) would house for the *affilliative* community (that is, non-hierarchial and horizontally-formed relationships including the reader) with the precarious house that is being made in the active participation in reading and/or making the book.

The image of the window of this house emphasises the position the author's life has in relation to the text, one that exists *almost* on the page itself; Martínez uses the image of the window as a means to explore the presence and absence of the guiding author in the text. According to the note provided at the beginning, the windows in this house exist as part of the house's border (the walls), yet, at the same time, disrupt the border by allowing one to look through them. Their ability to serve as boundaries is further diminished by the fact that they do not have glass windowpanes: 'la absoluta transparencia/de los vidrios que faltan'.[83] However, how can something be transparent if it does not exist? Martínez claims that the only way one can achieve absolute transparency (in language) is by not existing at all (although one's nonexistence, at the same time, has to be represented to some extent), like the lack of meaning in birdsong (see previous section). The author's position resembles that of these windows. On the one hand, the author has to exist in reality in order to create the text; like a window's frame, the author frames the images on the page. On the other, he, like the windowpanes, does not exist on the page itself and at the time of the reading of the text.[84]

The questions of authorship raised throughout the book are reinforced by the allusion in the footnote. Set up as a quote, it both expands upon the title of the poem and alludes to T. S. Eliot's 'Burnt Norton' in *Four Quartets:*[85]

> 'Quizás una casita en las afueras
> donde el pasado tiene aún que acontecer
> y el futuro hace tiempo que pasó'.
> (De T. S. Eliot, casi). (NN, p. 90)

Martínez rewrites Eliot's poem; he pretends to take words from someone else, implying that they might not be his own. With the word 'casi' (and alluding to his previous use of 'casi'), however, he negates this false appropriation; as much as he wants to move his own authority from the text, he fails to do so completely.

82 See Foucault, 'What is an Author?'.

83 These windows are reminiscent of Carroll's looking glass, a symbol that allows the reader to move between the world of sense and nonsense.

84 The window without glass could also be interpreted as the page/poem itself or even the words as transparent signs (see above).

85 Martínez places his house in the 'present' and 'past' that Eliot describes: 'Time present and time past/Are both perhaps present in time future,/And time future contained in time past./If all time is eternally present/All time is unredeemable./What might/have been is an abstraction/Remaining a perpetual possibility/Only in a world of speculation./What might have been and what has been/ Point to one end, which is always present'. T.S. Eliot, 'Burnt Norton', in *Collected Poems of T. S. Eliot: 1909–1935* (New York: Harcourt, Brace and Company, 1936), pp. 213–20. This allusion to an overtly religious poem also emphasises Martínez's satirical view of religious authority.

91

LA GRAFOLOGIA

~~a R. Barthes~~

a F. Le Lionnais

"El nombre que puede nombrarse
no es el verdadero nombre".
Tao Teh King

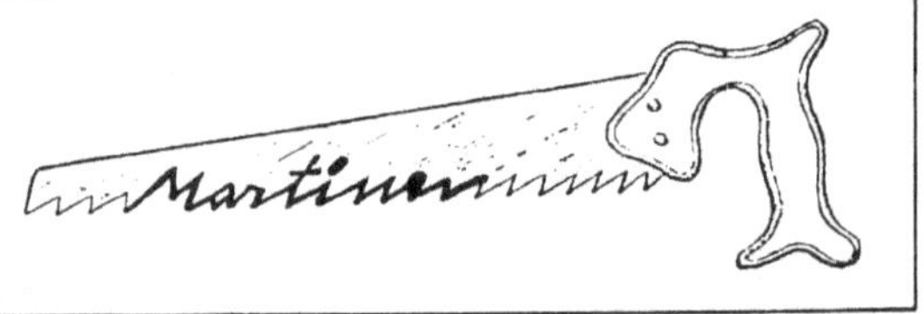

*

A sílabas entrecortadas quiso repetir un nombre: (Jxuan de Dios), ¡Ah, ese si que hubiera sido un verdadero nombre! , mas como un serrucho trabado en el clavo oculto (que maldice el carpintero), sólo pudo pronunciar, a duras penas, tartamudeando - atragantado por el aserrín de sus palabras - las chirriantes sílabas de su apellido: (Mar - mar - ttí - nnez).

* (En numerosos poemas modernos y en varios cuadros de Picasso aparece también, sin que exista ninguna necesidad objetiva de ello, una sierra o por lo menos los dientes de un serrucho, colocados oblicuamente sobre superficies geométricas. No es necesario pensar en ninguna posible influencia: la aparición de ese símbolo de la sierra o del serrucho es de categoría negativa y sólo puede explicarse como uno de los signos que mejor traduce la coacción ejercida por la estructura sobre la poesía y el arte modernos a partir de la segunda mitad del siglo pasado).

FIG. 2.9. Martínez, 'La grafología'.
Courtesy of Alita Martínez and Fundación de Juan Luis Martínez.

Similarly, Martínez tries to deny himself authority in the first stanza of the main text: 'a. La casa que construiremos mañana/ya está en el pasado y no existe'. While on this page, Martínez does not deny that these words are his own, in the poem 'Nota 1. LA DESAPARICION DE UNA FAMILIA' on page 121 he quotes the same line, only changing one word from the first person plural to second person ('construiremos' to 'construirás'): '"La casa que construirás mañana, ya está en el pasado y no existe"'. He denies ownership of this line, however, and instead attributes it to 'Anónimo'.[86]

The following page demonstrates the nature of the tool with which reader and author can construct it. 'La grafología' (p. 91; Figure 2.9) begins with a crossed out dedication to 'R. Barthes' followed by a dedication to 'F. Le Lionnais'. By crossing out Roland Barthes's name (and thereby his works, including 'The Death of the Author' and *Roland Barthes* — by Barthes), Martínez clearly sets up the question of the name of the author and its role in the text.[87] Moreover, in contrast to the previous page, Martínez uses only 'family names' and 'replaces' the dedications to his parents' with literary theorists, implying that his parents are not only biographical, but also literary (or at least that he has an emotional attachment to theorists). Identity, whether familial or intellectual, belongs to the past. Martínez, however, does not want his art to belong to the (filiative) past, but to be a poetic intervention of the present world. By replacing the dedication with one to the mathematician and Dadaist François Le Lionnais, one of the founders of the Ouvroir de Littérature Potentielle (OuLiPo), Martínez implies that the following poetry will in some way be constructed with certain limiting 'inspirations' or with a design in which the poem can flourish.[88] In other words, Martínez replaces the authorial symbol (his name or signature) for the idea of the death of the author with a shocking, surreal metonym of material function, a hand-saw used in building a house, one that represents the idea of an author who crafts and controls that which is written.[89]

In the main part of the page, the identity of the creator of the text is unknown because the subject (who is doing the 'sawing') is ambiguous. It begins with a drawing of a handsaw with the letters 'Martínez' outlined into its sharp teeth, which is clearly an example of a concretist tendency to blend the visual with the semantic

86 To add to the obscurity of the poem on page 121, Martínez does not include this second quote in a note for 'La casa de aliento', but instead refers to three other poems of the book.

87 See Barthes. Kosick argues that these dedications demonstrate that although '*La nueva novela* works to dissolve the authorial subject, its reading subjects are already dispersed'. Kosick, p. 860.

88 See Warren Motte, 'First and Second Manifesto', in *Oulipo: A Primer of Potential Literature*, ed. by Warren Motte (Lincoln: University of Nebraska Press, 1986), pp. 26–29. This reference to a movement based on defined, constraining structures adds to the allusion to structure and control throughout the book. However, the control is not in the hands of the author; a poet of OuLiPo would leave the poem to its 'potential' once he or she has chosen a structure.

89 Martínez seems to use satirically the title of this poem, the study of handwriting that (supposedly) investigates connections between individuals and their handwriting, as a way to question his own relationship with the words he writes and types. The title also recalls Jorge Luis Borges's 'Pierre Menard, autor del Quijote' as well as Pierre Menard himself, who studied graphology. See Borges, 'Pierre Menard, autor del Quijote', in *Ficciones* (Buenos Aires: Emecé, 1956), pp. 47–60.

in a poem. In this image, the name of the author is part of the tool that is to be used (to build a house, for instance, or a page). It is followed by a descriptive paragraph:

> A sílabas entrecortadas quiso repetir un nombre: (Jxuan de Dios), ¡Ah, ese si que hubiera sido un verdadero nombre!, mas como un serrucho trabado en el clavo oculto (que maldice el carpintero), solo pudo pronunciar, a duras penas, tartamudeando –atragantado por el aserrín de sus palabras — las chirriantes sílabas de su apellido: (Mar — mar — ttí — nnez).

Martínez compares the process of repeating his name to a saw stuck on a hidden nail. It is unclear, however, who is attempting to repeat the name: is it Martínez himself as author? Is it the carpenter who curses the nail? Or is it the handsaw, and thus the name, itself? This ambiguity of the identity of the subject trying to say a name highlights the uncertain status of the author as the sole authority of the text. The unknown subject, moreover, does not create a new name, but repeats one. The subject does not create something *ex nihilo*, but appropriates language that supposedly has already been spoken. Martínez not only denies the author agency in this naming process, but also ownership of his own name. In this way, he implies that this page is an example of his ideal text, one in which the author remains anonymous and in which every word has been taken from somewhere else; even though his name still exists on the page, the poem is a *heteroglossic* text in which even the author's name is an appropriated word.[90]

On this page, Martínez suggests what it might mean to create an anonymous text. He demonstrates that naming is a fraught enterprise by showing how difficult ('a duras penas') the process of repeating a name is. Firstly, like the edge of a saw, the syllables are intermittent ('entrecortadas'); the subject cannot say the name clearly.[91] Secondly, the unknown subject is not successful in repeating the name it wants to, that is 'Jxuan de Dios', and instead can only write the last name of the author, 'Martínez'. However, in the paragraph, the name that exists on the page is clearly written (although in parentheses): '(Jxuan de Dios'), and the word that is claimed to be pronounced is written phonetically as stuttered (also in parentheses): '(Mar — mar — ttí — nnez)'. Martínez claims that the name that the subject cannot repeat (Jxuan de Dios) would have been a 'true name', referring back to the epigraph in which he refers to the Tao Teh King: ('"El nombre que puede nombrarse no es el *verdadero nombre*"', emphasis added); because it cannot be named, it could be a true name.[92] The name, however, cannot be true because it has in fact been written in the paragraph.

90 See Mikhail Bakhtin, 'Discourse in the Novel', in *The Dialogic Imagination: Four Essays* (Austin: University of Texas Press, 1981), pp. 259–422.

91 It is worth noting that these intermittent syllables form other words, such as the French word 'nez' and 'Martí (suggestive of the poet José Martí). This process of taking apart words in order to find new ones is reminiscent of Vicuña's PALABRAR*mas* (see Chapter 3) and many concrete poems (see Introduction). Moreover, the syllables are cut up by the saw's 'teeth', indicating that the sound is occurring in the mouth. In other words, the name is being spoken.

92 For an English translation of the Tao, see Lao-Tzu, *Tao Te Ching*, trans. by Stephen Addiss and Stanley Lombardo (Indianapolis: Hackett Publishing Company, 1993). See previous section for a discussion of the name 'Jxuan de Dios'.

The image of the saw, moreover, illustrates how the process of writing the name of the author is one of cutting, engraving into a material, or branding (like the swan that is cut in 'El cisne *troquelado*'). The name appears on the tool itself, but when it begins to cut, it becomes worn down. The jagged edges of the saw are analogous to the lines made by the pen when it writes his name (or anything) and performs the same double action of creating (making, building) and destroying (cutting, breaking apart).[93] In order to build something, both saw and pen make permanent changes to the material with which they engage. Martínez implies that the act of writing something (e.g. a name) to a certain extent is a painful and (relatively) permanent act; however much the author may distance him or herself from the text s/he has written, as soon as his or her name is written on the page, complete separation of author from text is impossible.

Martínez complicates the relationship between signature and person by claiming that his name was uttered in the past, as opposed to solely written or drawn. Here, Martínez demonstrates an idea that Derrida explores in 'Sign Event Context', that neither the author nor the speaker in any given speech or written act is ever fully present; he implies that as soon as a word is written or uttered (even if this word is the name of the author him or herself), the intentions of the author are, a least to a certain extent, separated from the signs written or spoken.[94] The connection the author has to his text, like the stammered name, is not direct, but also not nonexistent. Instead, the author's role in his text appears as a distorted name. Representing the condition of the poet who (subjectively) produces anonymous art, the stuttered name captures the tension between his desire to erase his authority and his knowledge that this is impossible. The stuttering sound, like the image of the name does visually, creates an aural connection to the image of the handsaw. Like the concrete poets, Martínez here plays with visual, aural and semantic meaning of the word. By putting his name on the teeth of the saw, he absorbs the role of author into the present-tense act of making (*poiesis*). The name as an image (as opposed to text) brings the author into the image while at the same time distancing the author even further from the poem. The multiple signs for the author on the page also call into question the nature of the sign and the relationship between signifier and signified; as I discuss in the previous section, Martínez attempts to separate the signifier from the signified, but ultimately does not succeed in doing so. Similarly, the relationship between text and author, as Martínez discusses and demonstrates, can neither be unified nor completely separated.

This poem also questions the role of the signature in relation to an author's *oeuvre*. In the footnote, he explains that (supposedly) the image of the saw has appeared numerous times in modern poetry and art. However, he claims that it appears so without the participation of a particular influence:

> (En numerosos poemas modernos y en varios cuadros de Picasso aparece también [...] una sierra o por lo menos los dientes de un serrucho, colocados oblicuamente sobre superficies geométricas. No es necesario pensar en ninguna

93 This is similar to what we will see in Lira's work and reminiscent of Blake's engravings.

94 See Derrida, *Margins of Philosophy*, p. 328.

> posible influencia: la aparición de ese símbolo [...] solo puede explicarse como uno de los signos que mejor traduce la coacción ejercida por la estructura sobre la poesía y el arte modernos a partir de la segunda mitad del siglo pasado). (NN, p. 91)

Martínez (perhaps satirically) argues that the image of the saw or handsaw has appeared throughout modern art not because of any particular tradition or person, but rather from a structure imposed upon modern art from the previous century.[95] Nonetheless, by alluding specifically to the works of Picasso, he cannot escape the use of particular names and thus referring to authorial figures and their *oeuvre*.[96] In other words, a reader might try to steer away from looking at the author as the influential creator of a sign, but cannot escape him or her completely.

Just as concrete poetry encourages the active participation of the reader (who is invited to respond to the visual and aural features of a poem), Martínez's movement away from the text gives the reader the space to interact sensually (and intellectually) with the production of the text, a co-maker of the 'house-poem'. From 'housing' one authority, the poet has allowed for multiple authorities (alongside his own subjectivity).[97] In a variety of poems in *La nueva novela*, he provides questions and school exercises for the reader to complete. For instance, the poem 'La psicología' (NN, pp. 16–18; Figure 2.10) consists of a series of questions and tasks, as well as space on the page to which the reader can respond.[98]

Martínez not only asks the reader to respond generally to his questions ('¿Cómo se representa usted la falta de pescado?'), but also asks him or her to enumerate answers ('¿Cómo hace usted para sorprender a los personajes indeseables que se deslizan entre sus pensamientos? Enumere diversos procedimientos'), draw answers ('¿Cómo se representa usted la falta de pescado? DIBUJELO'), physically carry out his instructions ('A fin de remontarse en sus recuerdos, aplique una escalera contra la pared, pero no empiece a subir sin haberse provisto de una cuerda, uno de cuyos extremos será sólidamente fijado al piso y el otro enrollado alrededor de su puño izquierdo') and take precautions for inherent dangers ('Por no haber tomado esta precaución, muchas personas nunca han vuelto').[99] The provision of these questions followed by white space in a way acts as Martínez's own answers to the initial question of how to represent the lack of a fish. One possible answer

95 It is possible that Martínez is also referring to the definition of the word 'sierra' from which the name for the tool emerged, 'mountain range', which has a similar shape to a saw. Here, he also seems to be satirising and criticising the violent and destructive nature of modernist art and literature.

96 He only refers to Pablo Picasso by his first surname. Picasso is also particularly famous for his signature. As Foucault describes, one of the operations of the author function is to categorise multiple works written by the same person. See Foucault, 'What is an Author?', pp. 207–16.

97 Ibid.

98 The question of how to represent the lack of a fish also relates to the question of how to represent silence; the lack of something can only be recognised with something framing it, just as words frame the white space on the page.

99 It is interesting to note that Martínez asks for the representation of 'pescado', not 'pez', perhaps in order to emphasise the referent's particular relationship to the person attempting to represent it: a 'pez' only becomes 'pescado' when it is conceived of as a consumable object (that is, as potential food) for humans, whereas a 'pez' is assumed to have its own subjectivity.

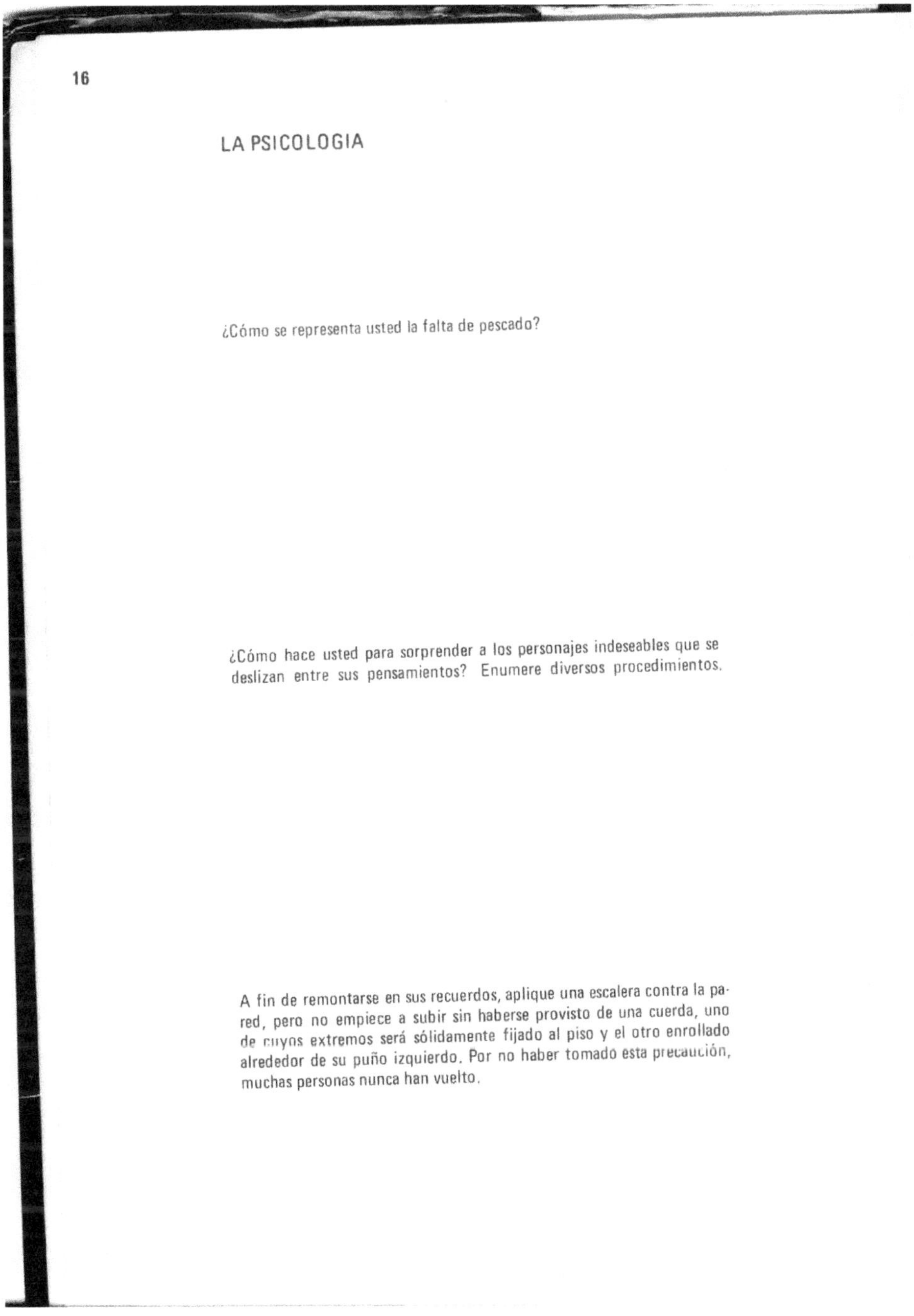

16

LA PSICOLOGIA

¿Cómo se representa usted la falta de pescado?

¿Cómo hace usted para sorprender a los personajes indeseables que se deslizan entre sus pensamientos? Enumere diversos procedimientos.

A fin de remontarse en sus recuerdos, aplique una escalera contra la pared, pero no empiece a subir sin haberse provisto de una cuerda, uno de cuyos extremos será sólidamente fijado al piso y el otro enrollado alrededor de su puño izquierdo. Por no haber tomado esta precaución, muchas personas nunca han vuelto.

FIG. 2.10. Martínez, 'La psicología'.
Courtesy of Alita Martínez and Fundación de Juan Luis Martínez.

17

¿Cómo se representa usted la falta de pescado?

DIBUJELO:

(Vea tres ejemplos en la página siguiente).

18

A.

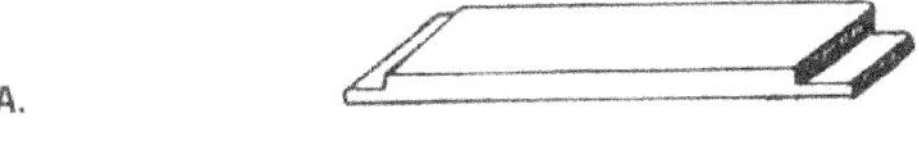

B.

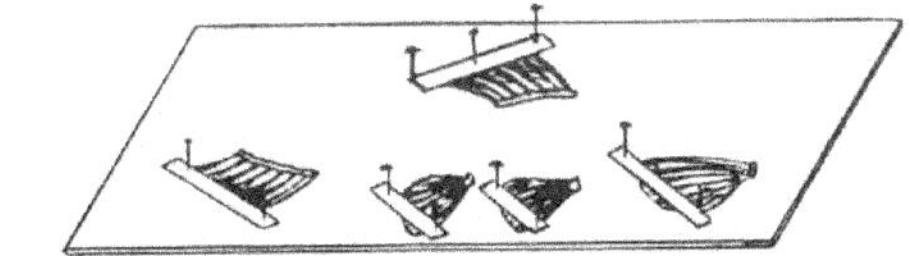

C.

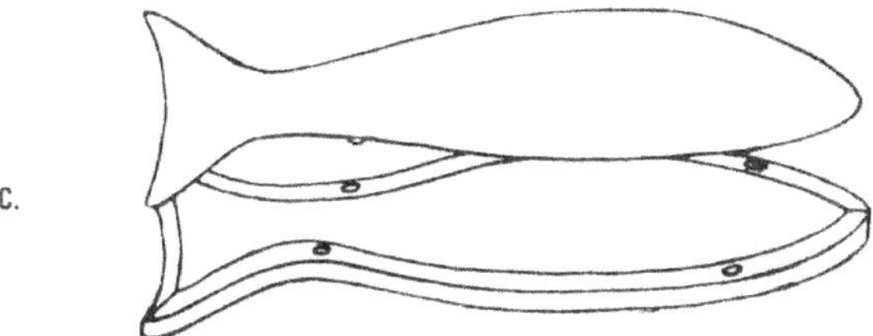

(Estos son sólo ejemplos).

he provides is on the page itself; the white space following the question itself could be a representation of the lack of a fish (there are no fish on the page), and the words on the page act as the defining borders of this lack. Another possible answer could be seen in the question itself: the fact that the line is a question illustrates the uncertainty Martínez has about the possibility of the representation of lack. Or, perhaps, as the invitation to the reader to respond allows, the *re*presentation of lack has infinite manifestations.[100]

This poem includes suggestions that resemble the concrete poets' provision of patterns or jumping-off points for the reader to continue on his/her own off the page.[101] Martínez playfully suggests examples of responses to the question that asks the reader to draw the representation of a fish: he provides three drawings, one of a cutting board, one of fins pinned down, and one of an open box shaped like a fish, but with nothing (or, more accurately, with white space) inside. These examples guide the reader in a particular direction more so than the questions do, but the final answers, within the limits of the choices given, are left open to each reader; he says, '(Estos son sólo ejemplos)'. With examples as well as a repeated question with only a minor change (an additional instruction to draw the answer), this poem resembles the 'poema proceso' that developed from the concretist movement, as in Dias Pino's poem 'Solida' (see Chapter 1).[102]

Martínez not only allows, but *forces* the reader to replace (or at least stand in for) the author, whose identity has become ephemeral, as agent. While Martínez's clever games might seem to be tricks that force the reader into confusion, as though the key to the game is a 'secret' of the author, they also can be read as 'playful'. As play, they can (and do in *La nueva novela*) create, as Rioseco argues, a space for the reader of freedom between reality and fiction.[103] For example, he instructs the reader to flip back and forth between pages in order to find the author. In the poems 'La página sesenta y uno' (NN, p. 61; Figure 2.11) and 'La página noventa y nueve' (NN, p. 99; Figure 2.12), the reader has to find the author who is moving around the book.[104] The poem on page 61 follows a logical sequence organised in an outlined structure of five sections, each of which corresponds to a photograph or space for a photograph. In each note of the outline, Martínez explains where 'people' (pictures

100 'La falta de pescado' is also a telling economic comment; Martínez may be criticising how Chile could allow people to grow hungry, especially considering Chile's long coast. In other words, while there was access to food in Chile, many starved.

101 A different realisation of this encouragement of readerly participation off the page is, for example, the Uruguayan writer Felisberto Hernández's *Libro sin tapas* (1929), in which he indicates the work can be written before or after its beginning and end: 'Este libro es sin tapas/porque es abierto y libre:/se puede escribir antes/y después de él'. Felisberto Hernández, *Los libros sin tapas* (Buenos Aires: El Cuenco de Plata, 2010), p. 45.

102 Kosick explains that this poem illustrates the book's movement: 'A lack of a fish [...]is not an emptiness that threatens the wholeness of *La nueva novela*. For one, [the fish's] lack contributes materially to the book. But also their movement in and out of the book is precisely what makes *La nueva novela*'. Kosick, p. 869.

103 See Rioseco, *Maquinarias reconstructivas*, pp. 1–31.

104 Suárez links these poems to chapters 61 and 99 of Julio Cortázar's *Rayuela*, illustrating Martínez's expansive network of references (Suárez, *Palabras ya escritas*, pp. 147–51).

LA PAGINA SESENTA Y UNO

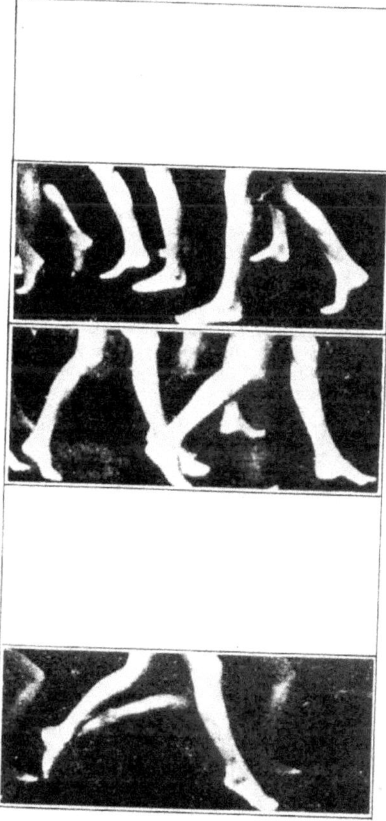

A.
En este cuadro hubo personas que ya no es posible encontrar en esta página, pues ellas se dirigen a presenciar los acontecimientos de la página 99.

B.
Las personas que pueden observarse en este cuadro, regresaron sólo minutos antes que usted tomara este libro. Ellas venían de leer las notas del final y luego de haber estado detenidas durante varios días en la página 99.

C.
Suponga ahora que las personas de este tercer cuadro vienen directamente del prólogo y se dirigen ya al cuadro B de la página 99 donde usted las encontrará viniendo de releer las notas del final del libro.

D.
Suponga también que las personas que deberían encontrarse en este cuadro se encuentran en alguna página intermedia entre las notas del libro y el cuadro C de la página 99.

E.
La persona que en este cuadro se ve en primer plano es (el autor) del libro y no deseando atrasar a su lector se dirige rápidamente a esperarlo en la página 99.

Fig. 2.11. Martínez, 'La página sesenta y uno'.
Courtesy of Alita Martínez and Fundación de Juan Luis Martínez.

LA PAGINA NOVENTA Y NUEVE

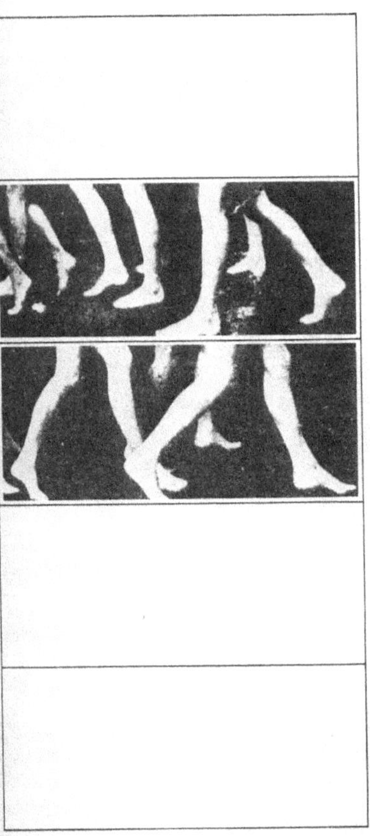

A.
En la página 61 usted debió suponer que las personas del cuadro A llegarían a presenciar los acontecimientos de esta página. Esas personas se encuentran ahora en el cuadro B de de la página 61 después de haber estado algunos días en esta página.

B.
Las personas de este cuadro son las mismas que usted encontró en el cuadro C de la página 61. En ese instante venían de leer el prólogo. Ahora usted las encuentra de regreso a esta página, viniendo de releer las notas del final del libro.

C.
Suponga que las personas de este tercer cuadro son las mismas que usted debió encontrar en el cuadro D de la página 61 y que en ese instante se encontraban en alguna página intermedia entre el cuadro D de la página 61 y este cuadro.

D.
Las personas que usted ya no encuentra en este cuadro, se han alejado rápidamente de esta página en dirección a la página 61. (Si usted ha leído ordenadamente este libro debería haberlas encontrado en alguna página intermedia).

E.
Las intenciones del (autor) eran esperar al lector en este cuadro, pero habiéndose el lector atrasado demasiado en su lectura, (el autor) ya se encuentra nuevamente en la página 61, esperando a un siguiente lector, que más rápido en su lectura, alcance a encontrarlo en esta página.

FIG. 2.12. Martínez, 'La página noventa y nueve'.
Courtesy of Alita Martínez and Fundación de Juan Luis Martínez.

of legs) have gone or have been within the book. For example, in the last section he explains, 'E. La persona que en este cuadro se ve en primer plano es (el autor) del libro y no deseando atrasar a su lector se dirige rápidamente a esperarlo en la página 99' (61). The speaker claims that, while supposedly seeing the author's legs 'leaving' and with his title of 'author' in parentheses, the reader can actually find him waiting on page 99. On page 99, however, within a similarly structured page, there is no picture at all next to point 'E', and the note indicates that the author will be back on page 61: 'E. Las intenciones del (autor) eran esperar al lector en este cuadro, pero habiéndose el lector atrasado demasiado en su lectura, (el autor) ya se encuentra nuevamente en la página 61, esperando a un siguiente lector, que más rápido en su lectura, alcance a encontrarlo en esta página' (99). Martínez forces the reader to act as a detective, investigating the author's whereabouts; the reader is now acting as subject and producer of meaning. However, the reader is led on a wild goose chase; s/he will never find the author and thus will never 'solve' the mystery of the authority of the book. Martínez thus humorously makes apparent the impossibility (and perhaps the undesirability) of the concretist attempt to remove all subjectivity from a poem. At the same time, Martínez widens the focus beyond the poet and the audience as an individual by making readers essential to *poiesis*.

National and International

Martínez extends his playful unravelling of the status of the author in *La nueva novela* to the apparently contradictory scope and extent of the work: an international, and even 'universal' reach on the one hand, and a national and local focus (the contemporary literary and political context) on the other. Martínez seeks to express the universal first by broadening his frame to move beyond the local and to include the international (especially by including many international references and appealing to an international audience) and then the universal by articulating universal truths (particularly through the 'universal' science of mathematics, a tool the concrete poets claimed to use in their poetic constructions) to organise and frame the texts. While the concrete poets aimed to write poems that had international appeal (i.e. poems that were accessible to any given reader from any nationality), Martínez attempts to create a universal text while at the same time commenting on a national context. To summarise my major point above, his play on the simultaneous presence and absence of signified and author suggests that the concretist goal of a completely objective poem is unrealisable. In part because of those partially unerasable presences, the poems will inevitably or necessarily express, at least partially, a politically localised subjectivity however much they may at the same time reach for the universal.

Although he strives to construct an anonymous and heteroglossic text in *La nueva novela*, one that escapes the specificity of an author's engagement with a particular political moment, Martínez ultimately cannot avoid including a specific political critique of his local context, that is, Augusto Pinochet's dictatorship. Weintraub, amongst other critics, recognises that the text is: 'intensely political in its critical self-reflexivity as a *Chilean* book that very clearly attempts to situate itself outside of Chilean intellectual-poetic space, through the erasure of the author as well as its radical use of *bricolage*, citationality, translation, and interdisciplinarity'.[105] Even though the pictorial dimension of concrete poetry helps dislodge poetry's rootedness in a particular place and time that language often carries, thus allowing it to be more accessible across nationalities and languages, the concrete poets, one might argue, do not succeed in creating completely universal texts. Indeed, as many theorists and linguists have argued, because language itself ultimately cannot be separated from its context no writer can.[106] Many concrete poems, for instance, are in Brazilian Portuguese, a factor that automatically connects the texts to a specific country (and era) and simultaneously limits access to Portuguese speakers only (although this has been partially reconciled by an additional mediation with the use of keys with translations in anthologies or at exhibitions).[107]

The national in *La nueva novela* is partly hidden because Martínez creates the impression of an international and even a universal text. For example, he includes a plethora of international allusions and languages, which suggests he is addressing an international audience. He further extends the international text into a universal one by 'disappearing' its foundations in present-day certainties; the technique is to blend together the real and the imaginary, and sense and nonsense, so that any stable perspective is lost. In particular, he uses non-Euclidean geometry and Lewis Carroll's 'Looking Glass' as metaphors for the reality behind the conventional logic and appearance of stability and order that a fascistic regime might upon its people; through these transnational points of reference he exposes the lies that a totalitarian regime might impose.

Martínez creates an international focus in *La nueva novela* through direct and indirect references and dedications not only to literary figures (Mallarmé, Carroll, William Shakespeare, and Pablo Neruda, just to name a few), but also to visual artists (such as Jean Tardieu and Francis Picabia), psychiatrists (Karl Jaspers, for example), political figures (such as Adolf Hitler), philosophers (including Karl Marx, Gilles Deleuze and Plato), mathematicians (such as Euclid, Lobatchewsky and Gauss), and 'muses' (for instance, Alice Liddell, the real-life source for Carroll's Alice).[108] The majority of these references are to Europeans (such as Barthes and André Breton), but some are to North Americans (such as Denis Oppenheim, T.S. Eliot and Pound), South Americans (such as Alejandra Pizarnik and Miguel Serrano) and Asians (such as Shen-hsiu and Hui-neng). In addition, while *La nueva novela* is composed mostly of text (in multiple forms, from verse and prose to school exercises

105 However, although Weintraub recognises that the book is in fact Chilean, he fails to recognise the tension that exists between the local and international. Weintraub, *Juan Luis Martínez's Philosophical Poetics*, p. 94.

106 Jakobson, for example, argues that context is one of the six key elements necessary for communication. Jakobson, 'Linguistics and Poetics', pp. 43–47.

107 In addition, some poems created after the initial concretist poetic movement directly comment on Brazilian society. For example, Pignatari's poem 'Agora' alludes to the famous Brazilian football star Pelé. Pignatari, *Poesia Pois é Poesia: 1950–2000* (São Paulo: Ateliê Editorial, 2004), p. 157.

108 For an extensive account of expansive hypertextuality of *La nueva novela*, see Suárez, *Palabras ya escritas*.

and bibliographies), it also consists of photographs of people and places (of William Butler Yeats and the Parthenon, for example), drawings of things and animals (such as of a handsaw and a fox terrier), maps (in particular, a map of the globe[109]), collages of newspaper clippings (of advertisements and photographs of Rimbaud and Marx), letters (for example, a letter written by Ezra Pound) and even objects (such as the Chilean flag and fish hooks). Martínez even diversifies the 'material' of the text, that is, he writes in multiple languages; while he writes the majority of the text in Spanish, he includes (his own or others') texts in English, French, German, and Chinese.[110] In constructing a text that refers to many international figures, Martínez therefore aims to fulfil the concrete poets' intentions of creating an objective poetry that does not dwell in the Chilean literary context.

While its myriad allusions, languages and materials form an international text, the book moves even further in the concrete direction to become a *universal* one in two principle ways. Firstly, the book appeals to universal truths, such as mathematics, that do not pertain to clearly defined places in the world that we can perceive with our senses. Secondly, in *La nueva novela*, 'the universal' (or even 'utopic', as we will see) appears through the obliteration of the outlines of apparent certainties; dichotomies and categories are intentionally confused: genres, sense and nonsense, and place and non-place.[111]

With many references to Lewis Carroll throughout the book (as we have seen above), for example, the constructed text does not exist in Wonderland or in reality, but instead acts like the looking glass itself, moving between sense and nonsense and thus offering a way to restructure reality.[112] A copy of Carroll's photographed portrait of Alice Liddell appears on several pages throughout the book titled 'Portrait study of a lady' (for example, NN, p. 86; Figure 2.13).[113] Here, the image of the character of Alice moves between reality and Wonderland. Moreover, the character of Alice is removed from the photograph of Liddell at a variety of levels. Firstly,

109 The poem 'Un problema hemisférico' (p. 57), in which Martínez includes the map of the globe, highlights the text's international vision.

110 Although the use of multiple languages seems to allow the text to appeal to an international audience, it is obvious that this use also restricts the readership; only one who speaks these languages has complete access to the text. The plethora of allusions also can be seen as rather elitist. Nevertheless, by making the semantic not always accessible to readers who are not multilingual, he brings to the fore the elements of language which are not semantic, but universal.

111 The poem in 'nonsense' language, as discussed in the first section of this chapter on Martínez, in fact demonstrates some meaning, thus existing as both sense and true nonsense. While Martínez confuses place and non-place to illuminate the tension between the two, Vicuña, as we will see in Chapter 3, writes from and forms 'non-places' as the space for creation.

112 There are many other recurring references that bind the book together, such as those to Edward Lear, Jean Tardieu, Julio Cortázar, among many others. See Suárez, *Palabras ya escritas*.

113 Martínez most likely takes this title from T. S. Eliot's poem because Martínez follows it with another allusion to Eliot ('Eyes that I saw in tears') on a couple of the pages titled 'Portrait of a Lady'. The title could also refer to Henry James's novel (1881). Moreover, Martínez, with this title, seems to satirise Charles Dodgson's relationship with Alice; the speculated assumption was that Dodgson's falling out with the Liddell family was because of his questionable relationship with Alice, a girl, not a lady. See Stephanie Lovett Stoffel, *Lewis Carroll and Alice* (London: Thames and Hudson, 1997), pp. 81–82, or Robert Douglas-Fairhurst, *The Story of Alice* (London: Harvill Secker, 2015), pp. 95–138.

86

PORTRAIT STUDY OF A LADY

"¿Qué es una niña?".

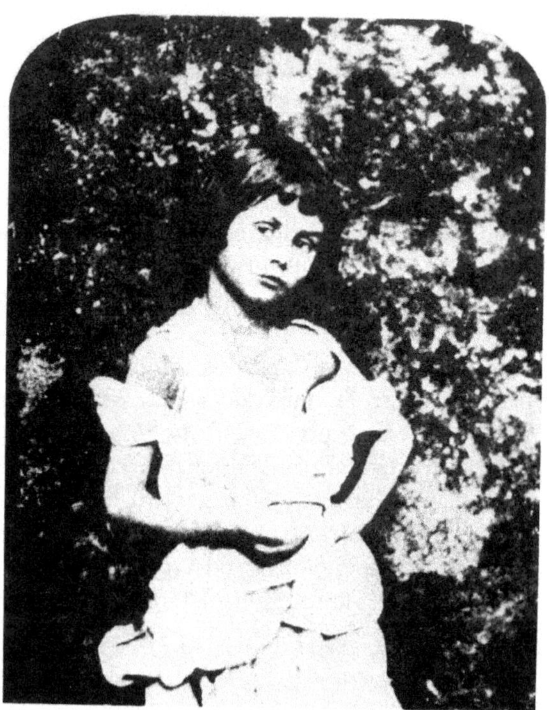

La máquina fotográfica no agregó mayores detalles de ilusión a la realidad, pues fue el fotógrafo, quien en su necesidad de hacer aún más tangible la belleza sensual de esta niñita, descifró en ella una mirada interrogante y atrevida, cuyo alcance podría perfectamente no ser sólo un simple fraude óptico.

Fig. 2.13. Martínez, 'Portrait Study of a Lady'.
Courtesy of Alita Martínez and Fundación de Juan Luis Martínez.

the photograph is not a representation of Alice (the character) in Carroll's novel, but rather a photograph of Carroll's 'muse', Alice Liddell. In addition, on multiple pages of the book, there is an image of a rabbit, another principal character in *Alice's Adventures in Wonderland* who moves (fast) between reality and Wonderland.[114] The image itself is a reproduction of Albrecht Dürer's 'Young Hare' (1502), but clearly refers to Carroll's rabbit or hare because of the plethora of references to it throughout the book. The rabbit, as a repeated image in *La nueva novela*, also signals to the reader that s/he should act like Carroll's rabbit by moving in and out of sense and nonsense. Martínez makes explicit these references to *Through the Looking Glass* on page 142 by titling the page 'Throught [*sic*] the Looking-Glass, and what the poet found there' with a reproduction of Dürer's 'Young Hare' followed by an instruction for the reader to look up *Alice's Adventures in Wonderland.*[115]

Just as Martínez runs Carroll's looking glass as a thread throughout the book, he creates a figure of a fox terrier called 'Sogol' to frame the text and to 'string together' its pages.[116] As the name suggests (the reverse of 'logos'), the dog represents Martínez's attempt to confuse both logic and language. In the section titled 'La zoología', Martínez provides poems that discuss both real and imaginary animals (such as elephants, fish, and the Cheshire Cat).[117] At the end of the section, he includes four pages that describe his 'character' Sogol (NN, pp. 80–83; Figure 2.14). The first page contains a large picture of a fox terrier crossed by the intersection of two lines, one labelled 'Avenida Lobatchewsky [*sic*]' and the other 'Avenida Gauss' (which is written twice). By referring to two non-Euclidean mathematicians, Martínez already implies that the following scenarios are going to deal with ideas that are not logically linear; just as it is difficult to understand the curved mathematics of non-Euclidian geometry, it will be difficult to understand (at least linearly) the 'scientific' problem that Martínez provides in order to deconstruct linear logic.[118] The (non-Euclidean) reality is 'truer' than the apparent (and ideologically determined) 'linear' logic and order asserted by dictatorship (and, in particular, the neoliberal agenda of Pinochet's regime).

The page and poem that follow at first seem scientifically/mathematically (and therefore logically and universally) structured.[119] Firstly, there are a variety of

114 This image could also refer to the March Hare in *Alice's Adventures in Wonderland.* See Carroll (2007), or to an animal commonly hunted for sport or food.

115 Scott Jackson argues that Martínez uses Carroll's looking glass as a metaphor for the reader entering in and out of the world of nonexistence. Jackson (1996), pp. 134–40.

116 Martínez's use and personification of Sogol breaks down the human/animal hierarchical distinction and therefore furthers the image of the disruption of logical categories and hierarchies. As Suárez argues, the fox terrier 'Sogol' leads us down a rabbit hole of literary references, such as to Carroll's character, Fury (who has been argued to be a fox terrier in Dodgson's life), which brings us to the Furies in Greco-Roman mythology. Suárez, *Palabras ya escritas*, pp. 77–79.

117 Galindo develops the idea that *La nueva novela* exists between the real and the imaginary in his argument that this section presents a universal bestiary of animals. See Galindo, 'El alfabestiario universal', 21–40.

118 The fact that Dodgson was a mathematician (particularly a scholar of Euclidian geometry) adds to the allusions to and uses of mathematical structures throughout the book, see Stoffel (1997), p. 111.

119 Many of the concrete poems are (supposedly) patterned mathematically. For example, Haroldo de Campos creates a mathematical equation (albeit an illogical one) in 'Mais Mais' (see 'Mais Mais',

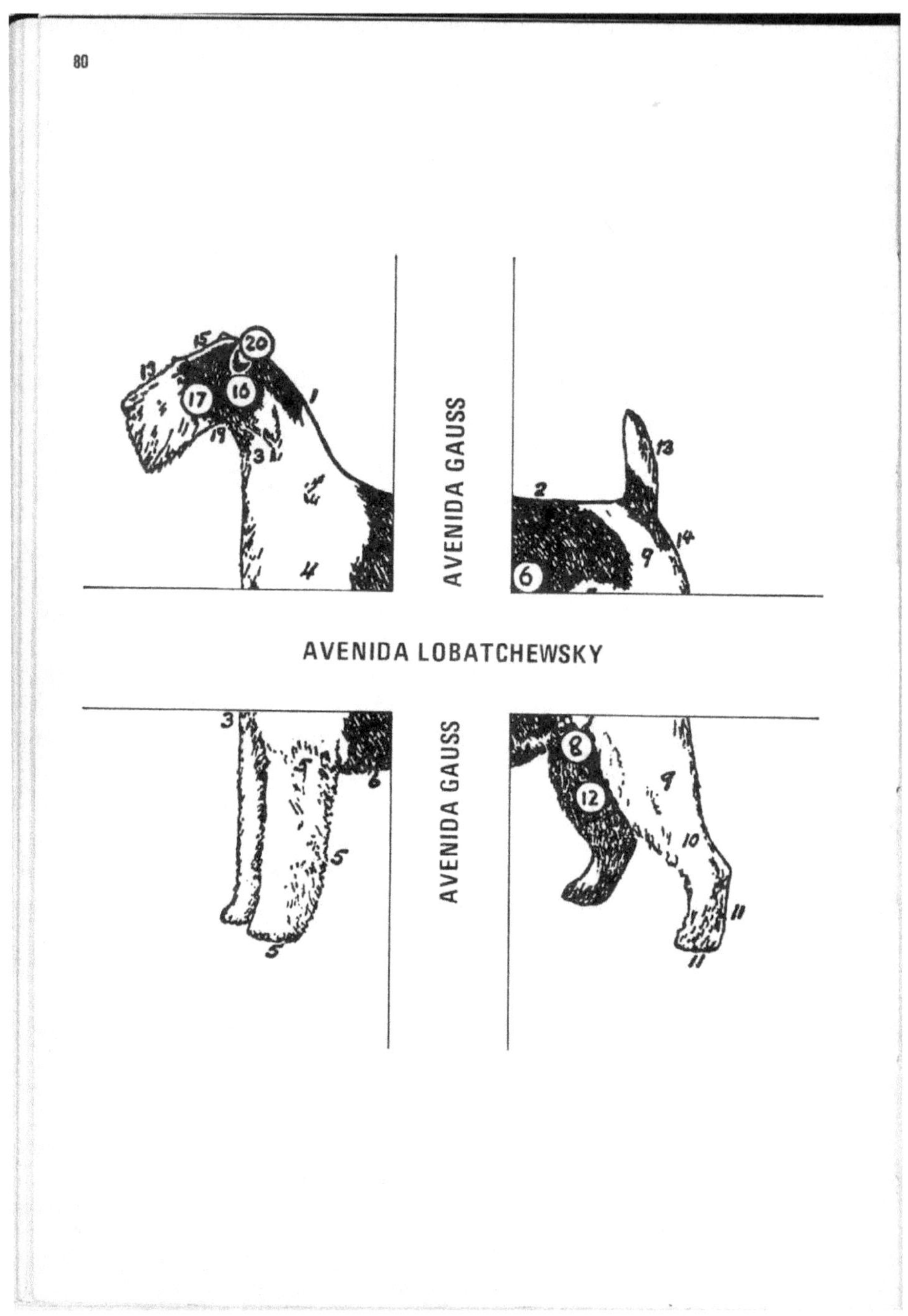

Fig. 2.14. Martínez, 'Fox Terrier'.
Courtesy of Alita Martínez and Fundación de Juan Luis Martínez.

81

FOX TERRIER DESAPARECE EN LA INTERSECCION
DE LAS AVENIDAS GAUSS Y LOBATCHEWSKY *

Suponga que su perrito de raza Fox Terrier, de pelaje a manchas negras sobre fondo blanco y que obedece al nombre de "SOGOL", se dirige por una avenida y al llegar a la esquina de otra, desaparece súbitamente. AVERIGÜE DONDE Y COMO PUEDE VOLVER A ENCONTRARLO.

1.

a. La avenida Gauss sólo es invisible
en su punto de intersección con la avenida Lobatchewsky.

b. La avenida Lobatchewsky sólo es visible
en su punto de intersección con la avenida Gauss.

2.

a. Que las avenidas Gauss y Lobatchewsky
sean invisibles en uno u otro punto de sí mismas,
no significa que el Fox Terrier no sea visible
en cualquier punto de ambas avenidas.

b. Que el Fox Terrier sea visible
en cualquier punto de ambas avenidas,
no significa que en la intersección de las 2 avenidas
no pueda haber un punto donde el Fox Terrier sea invisible.

c. Si el Fox Terrier se encontrara detenido
en la intersección de ambas avenidas,
sería visible desde cualquier punto de la avenida Gauss.

d. Si el Fox Terrier se encontrara detenido
en la intersección de ambas avenidas, en forma invisible,
sería visible desde cualquier punto de la avenida Lobatchewsky.

3.

a. Sólo es posible suponer que el Fox Terrier
haya desaparecido en esa fisura precisa e infinitesimal
en que se intersectan ambas avenidas.

b. Dado que esa fisura precisa e infinitesimal
pertenece a las geometrías no euclidianas
la única solución es que el Fox Terrier
regrese por sus propios medios desde esa otra dimensión,
cuya entrada y salida se encuentra en la intersección
de las avenidas Gauss y Lobatchewsky.

* "Todas las calles son invisibles. Las visibles son falsas, aunque algunas visibles son la parte final de las invisibles".

Yoko Ono

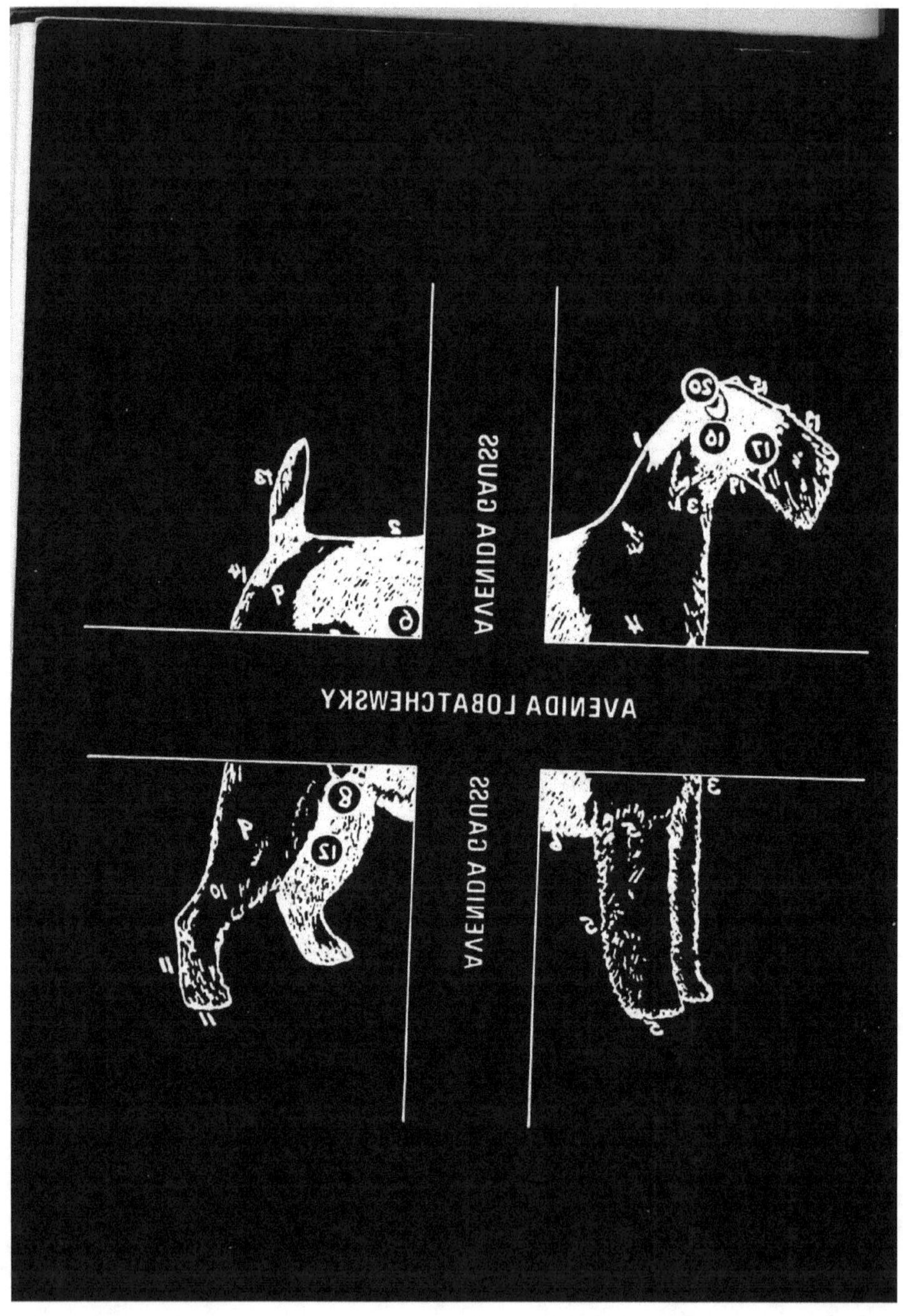
AVENIDA GAUSS
AVENIDA LOBATCHEWSKY
AVENIDA GAUSS

**FOX TERRIER NO DESAPARECIDO NO REAPARECE
EN LA NO-INTERSECCION DE LAS NO-AVENIDAS (~~GAUSS Y LOBATCHEWSKY~~)**

Suponga que su perrito Fox Terrier es visto por última vez cuando a razón de un trotecito constante de 10 Kms.,/Hr. se dirige desde su no-casa hacia la no-intersección de las no-avenidas donde debe desaparecer. Usted sale tras él a igual velocidad, realizando la misma trayectoria, pero sin lograr alcanzarlo. Usted regresa entonces a su no-casa donde advierte que ya han transcurrido 30 minutos desde que el Fox Terrier iniciara su recorrido. CALCULE EXACTAMENTE LA DISTANCIA QUE HAY ENTRE SU NO-CASA Y LA NO-INTERSECCION DE LAS NO-AVENIDAS GAUSS Y LOBATCHEWSKY.

1.

a. Las no-avenidas Gauss y Lobatchwsky
son a tramos igualmente falsas o verdaderas, visibles o invisibles.

b. Los tramos visibles e invisibles de cualquiera de las 2 no-avenidas
son también los tramos falsos y verdaderos de la otra no-avenida.
(Y viceversa).

2.

a. En su trayectoria desde la no-casa
hasta la no-intersección de las 2 no-avenidas
el Fox Terrier atraviesa tramos falsos y verdaderos,
tramos visibles y tramos invisibles.

b. A tramos falsos y verdaderos,
a tramos visibles e invisibles
el Fox Terrier logra cubrir la distancia
que mediaba entre la no-casa y la no-intersección de las 2 no-avenidas.

c. La trayectoria del Fox Terrier
a través de tramos falsos y tramos verdaderos,
de tramos visibles y tramos invisibles
puede ser también falsa o verdadera, visible o invisible.

d. Según atravesó en su trayectoria tramos falsos o verdaderos
el Fox Terrier fue un perrito falso o verdadero,
así mismo cuando atravesó tramos visibles o invisibles
el perrito sólo fue un Fox Terrier visible o invisible.

3.

a. Es posible suponer que el Fox Terrier no haya desaparecido jamás
en esa no-fisura no-precisa ni infinitesimal
en que se intersectan las 2 no-avenidas
(como en ese ningún otro punto donde no se intersectan las 2 no-avenidas).

b. Dado que esa no-fisura no-precisa ni infinitesimal
no pertenece a las geometrías euclidianas
la única no-solución es que el Fox Terrier no regrese jamás
desde esa otra no-dimensión donde jamás desapareció,
pero cuya entrada y salida seguimos encontrando
en la intersección de las avenidas Gauss y Lobatchewsky.

numbers written on various spots on the dog, making the drawing look like a scientific diagram. Secondly, this page is followed by a poem 'FOX TERRIER DESAPARECE EN LA INTERSECCION DE LAS AVENIDAS GAUSS Y LOBATCHEWSKY' that begins with an assignment for the reader: 'Suponga que su perrito de raza Fox Terrier....se dirige por una avenida y al llegar a la esquina de otra, desaparece súbitamente. AVERIGÜE DONDE Y COMO PUEDE VOLVER A ENCONTRARLO', followed by an outlined list of 'conditions', or, as Weintraub describes them, 'labyrinthine logical-poetic postulates'.[120] The conditions at first glance seem logical given the scientific structure of the poem and its mathematical allusions.[121]

Through a seemingly structured form, Martínez ironically presents an illogical scenario by proposing that the avenues and the dog can be visible and/or invisible at certain points.[122] The first postulate, as Weintraub points out, is followed by fourteen lines that resemble a sonnet.[123] This form gives the poem at once a mathematical and a poetic structure. In the final 'condition', however, the dog has to pass not just to another street, but through another dimension:

> Dado que esa fisura precisa e infinitesimal
> pertenece a las geometrías no euclidianas
> la única solución es que el Fox Terrier
> regrese por sus propios medios desde esa otra dimensión,
> cuya entrada y salida se encuentra en la intersección
> de la avenidas Gauss y Lobatchewsky. (NN, ll. 22–27).

The exercise of how to find the dog seems impossible, at least in logical and linear terms. In other words, as the poem states, the scenario exists in non-Euclidian terms (in which lines follow curved, rather than straight trajectories) and in a space that one cannot represent two-dimensionally.

Martínez flips again this already destabilising scenario: on the following page he includes the inverse of the drawing of the fox terrier on the first page — the dog and words are reversed and the colours are inverted so that the background is black and the lines and words are in white. On the following page, Martínez again provides the reader with an apparent mathematical exercise, but in this case he negates both the actions and places he describes in the first poem. Titled 'FOX TERRIER NO DESAPARECIDO NO REAPARECE/EN LA NO-INTERSECION DE LAS NO-AVENIDAS (~~GAUSS Y LOBATCHEWSKY~~)'[124], the poem begins with an

in *Plano-Piloto para Poesia Concreta*, Figure 1.3); see Chapter 1.

120 Weintraub, *Juan Luis Martínez's Philosophical Poetics*, p. 80.

121 Rioseco argues that this poem, as a purely geometric problem 'se transforma en una reflexión en torno a la representación matemática de la realidad y a la composición real del universo'. Rioseco, *Maquinarias reconstructivas*, pp.166–267.

122 The (in)visibility of Sogol and the question of his existence are reminiscent of Schrödinger's cat that is simultaneously alive and dead when given radioactive poison in the box until the box is opened and the cat is observed.

123 Weintraub, *Juan Luis Martínez's Philosophical Poetics*, p. 81.

124 Note the triple negation of the names of these 'avenues'; just as he crosses out and puts in parentheses his name, Martínez attempts to negate the authority of these names. As Weintraub mentions (although he does not expand upon the idea), this poem is yet another example of 'the ethos

instruction that structurally looks like a logical mathematical problem (and looks like the problem given in the previous poem):

> Suponga que su perrito Fox terrier es visto por última vez cuando a razón de un trotecito constante de 10 Kms./Hr. se dirige desde su no-casa hacia la no-intersección de las no-avenidas donde debe desaparecer. Usted sale tras él a igual velocidad, realizando la misma trayectoria, pero sin lograr alcanzarlo. Usted regresa entonces a su no-casa donde advierte que ya han transcurrido 30 minutos desde que el Fox Terrier iniciara su recorrido. CALCULE EXACTAMENTE LA DISTANCIA QUE HAY ENTRE SU NO-CASA Y LA NO-INTERSECCION DE LAS NO-AVENIDAS GAUSS Y LOBATCHEWSKY. (NN, p. 83)

In the list of 'conditions' that follow, Martínez explains that the variables are at once true and false and visible and invisible: 'Las no-avenidas Gauss y Lobatchwsky [*sic*]/ son a tramos igualmente falsos o verdaderas, visibles o invisibles...En su trayectoria desde la no-casa...el Fox Terrier atraviesa tramos falsos y verdaderos,/ tramos visibles y tramos invisibles' (NN, ll. 1–9). If, just as the second picture of the fox terrier is the inverse of the first picture, this poem is supposed to be the inverse of the previous one, the result is that dichotomies are confused so much so that the 'variables' have become 'non-variables'. The places of the poem have become 'non-places', to use Marc Augé's term, that is, a space between in which one 'checks in' one's identity.[125] Martínez thus proposes a world that exists in a 'non-place' (in this case between reality and fiction).[126]

Unattached and unrooted existing in a non-place, *La nueva novela* gestures, like concrete poems, towards transcending the national (even though it fails) and towards the universal; if the text exists as a 'non-place', it, like an ideal concrete poem, can be accessed by any given reader and can continuously be moulded, can always be *becoming* every time it is read.[127] While Martínez writes with reference to the universal principles of the concrete poetry movement, at the same time he seeks to address their apparent contrary: the social conditions of Chile during the 1960s and 1970s. In the context of this 'universal' poem, the turn to social and political immediacy may feel like a disruption. (Yet one must remember that Martínez intends to bring the principles and techniques of political critique found in concrete poetics to bear on the Chilean situation.) Unlike concrete poetry, '*La nueva novela*' contains poems in which the poet's national identity comes to the

of "writing under erasure" as described with respect to Martínez's own proper name, the concept of authorship, the multifarious enigmas of the Cheshire Cat, and so on'. Weintraub, *Juan Luis Martínez's Philosophical Poetics*, p. 82.

125 Marc Augé, *Non-Places: An Introduction to Supermodernity*, trans. by John Howe, 2nd edn (London: Verso, 2008), pp. 74–76. As I discuss in Chapter 4, in this non-place, while one may not have any solid 'roots' in one place or another, one has the potential to create continuously, never becoming stuck in one place or another.

126 Sepúlveda argues that Martínez himself is a 'poet on the edge' and that *La nueva novela is* a liminal text. See Sepúlveda, *Poets on the Edge*, pp. 91–137.

127 As I argue in Chapter 4, a 'nomadic' text that does not pertain to any specific place or culture allows the text to be moulded continuously by international readers and thus continuously to come into being.

fore, mostly as political critique. The book has a total of three direct allusions to Chile itself (as well as two references to Chilean writers — Miguel Serrano and Pablo Neruda). The first allusion is in the epigraph on the first page (Figure 2.15), in which Martínez provides both the original and translated verses of Edward Lear:

> 'Había una Vieja Persona de Chile,
> su conducta era odiosa e idiota.
> Sentada en una escalera comía manzanas y peras
> esa Imprudente y Vieja Persona de Chile.'
>
> 'There was an Old Person of Chili
> Whose conduct was painful and silly
> He sat on the stairs eating apples and pears
> That imprudent Old Person of Chili.'
>
> Edward Lear (NN)

Martínez opens the book with an explicit allusion to nonsense poetry (particularly a limerick), setting the stage for the (humorous) tension that he creates between sense and nonsense throughout the rest of the book.[128] However, unlike the instances before in which he foregrounds the form of the poem, in this case his translation into Spanish is mostly a semantic one; rather than focus on a key element of a limerick, the rhyme (apart from a most likely incidental rhyme 'escalera' and 'peras'), he mostly translates the English literally. This reversal of emphasis when referring to Chile both adds to the tension he creates throughout the book and distinguishes it from the more objective poems. In this epigraph, Martínez, in spite of the Chilean reference, gives it an international dimension by referring to and quoting the poem in English and translating it into Spanish. This expression of two directions at once — one towards the international and the other to the local — therefore illuminates the tension he will create between the national and the universal. On the one hand, the epigraph is from an English text that to some extent exoticises Chile. The country is also spelled incorrectly, so ultimately the country of the 'Old Person' does not literally exist, making him not from this world. On the other hand, from the first page, Martínez brings his nation into the text.

Citing Chile for a second time in the introduction before the table of contents, Martínez clearly frames his entire book with national meaning. In this page, Martínez transcribes dedications written by the Chilean diplomat, journalist and author Miguel Serrano on the page titled 'DOS DEDICATORIAS ENCONTRADAS POR (EL AUTOR) EN UN EJEMPLAR DEL LIBRO DE MIGUEL SERRANO: "ANTOLOGIA DEL VERDADERO CUENTO EN CHILE"' (NN, Figure 2.16). This allusion to Serrano and his dedicatees acts as a bridge between Europe and Chile; because Serrano was interested in the Third Reich and proposed a new philosophy and religion for the Aryan race, Martínez evokes the particulars of the Chilean dictatorship at the same time he points us

128 Suárez suggests that, stemming from Jean Tardieu's work, *La nueva novela* presents us with not just the tension between sense and nonsense, but also an 'antisentido [...] necesario para llenar el vacío semántico en que queda el sinsentido'. Suárez, 'Objetualismo en Juan Luis Martínez', p. 86. Limericks, like concrete poetry, emphasise the oral and aural aspects of language in a playful manner.

a Roger Caillois

"Había una Vieja Persona de Chile,/ su conducta era odiosa e idiota./ Sentada en una escalera comía manzanas y peras/ esa imprudente y Vieja Persona de Chile".

"There was an Old Person of Chili/ Whose conduct was painful and silly/ He sate on the stairs eating apples and pears/ That imprudent Old Person of Chili".

Edward Lear

Fig. 2.15. Martínez, 'Edward Lear'.
Courtesy of Alita Martínez and Fundación de Juan Luis Martínez.

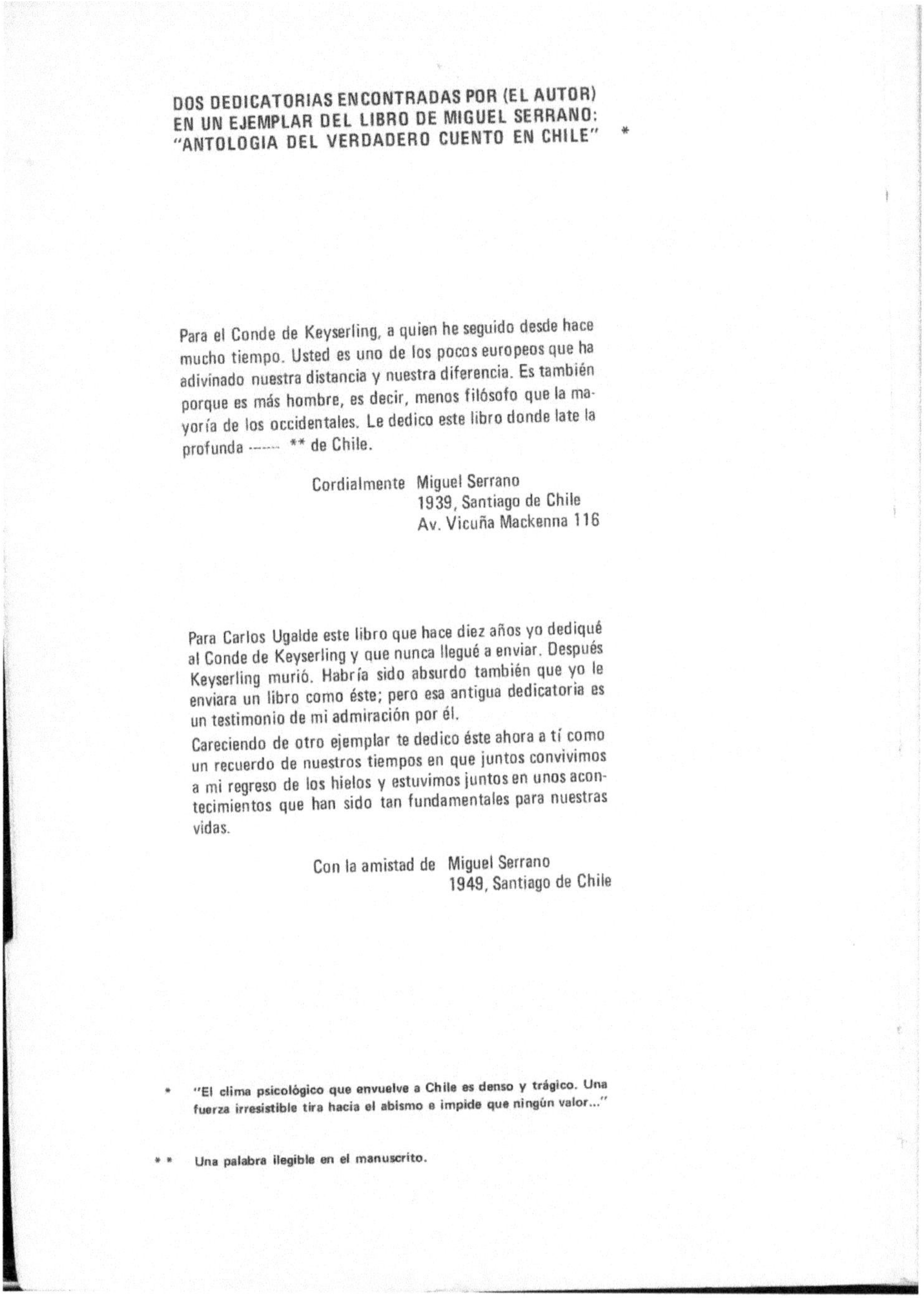

DOS DEDICATORIAS ENCONTRADAS POR (EL AUTOR)
EN UN EJEMPLAR DEL LIBRO DE MIGUEL SERRANO:
"ANTOLOGIA DEL VERDADERO CUENTO EN CHILE" *

Para el Conde de Keyserling, a quien he seguido desde hace mucho tiempo. Usted es uno de los pocos europeos que ha adivinado nuestra distancia y nuestra diferencia. Es también porque es más hombre, es decir, menos filósofo que la mayoría de los occidentales. Le dedico este libro donde late la profunda ------ ** de Chile.

Cordialmente Miguel Serrano
1939, Santiago de Chile
Av. Vicuña Mackenna 116

Para Carlos Ugalde este libro que hace diez años yo dediqué al Conde de Keyserling y que nunca llegué a enviar. Después Keyserling murió. Habría sido absurdo también que yo le enviara un libro como éste; pero esa antigua dedicatoria es un testimonio de mi admiración por él.
Careciendo de otro ejemplar te dedico éste ahora a tí como un recuerdo de nuestros tiempos en que juntos convivimos a mi regreso de los hielos y estuvimos juntos en unos acontecimientos que han sido tan fundamentales para nuestras vidas.

Con la amistad de Miguel Serrano
1949, Santiago de Chile

* "El clima psicológico que envuelve a Chile es denso y trágico. Una fuerza irresistible tira hacia el abismo e impide que ningún valor..."

** Una palabra ilegible en el manuscrito.

FIG. 2.16. Martínez, 'Dos dedicatorias...'.
Courtesy of Alita Martínez and Fundación de Juan Luis Martínez.

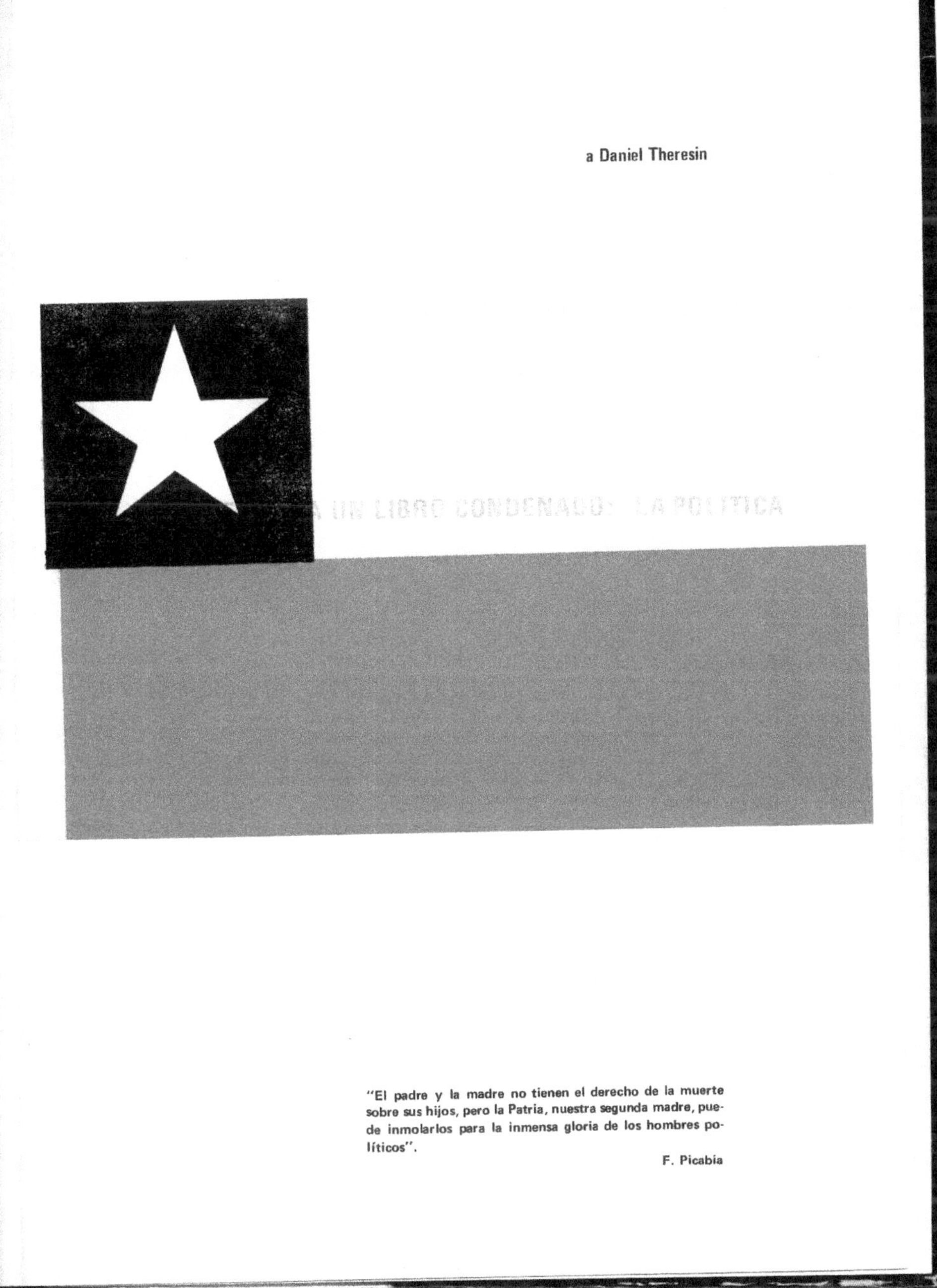

Fig. 2.17. Martínez, Chilean Flag.
Courtesy of Alita Martínez and Fundación de Juan Luis Martínez.

137

LA DESAPARICION DE UNA FAMILIA

1. Antes que su hija de 5 años
se extraviara entre el comedor y la cocina,
él le había advertido: "-Esta casa no es grande ni pequeña,
pero al menor descuido se borrarán las señales de ruta
y de esta vida al fin, habrás perdido toda esperanza".

2. Antes que su hijo de 10 años se extraviara
entre la sala de baño y el cuarto de los juguetes,
él le había advertido: "-Esta, la casa en que vives,
no es ancha ni delgada: sólo delgada como un cabello
y ancha tal vez como la aurora,
pero al menor descuido olvidarás las señales de ruta
y de esta vida al fin, habrás perdido toda esperanza".

3. Antes que "Musch" y "Gurba", los gatos de la casa,
desaparecieran en el living
entre unos almohadones y un Buddha de porcelana,
él les había advertido:
"-Esta casa que hemos compartido durante tantos años
es bajita como el suelo y tan alta o más que el cielo,
pero, estad vigilantes
porque al menor descuido confundiréis las señales de ruta
y de esta vida al fin, habréis perdido toda esperanza".

4. Antes que "Sogol", su pequeño fox-terrier, desapareciera
en el séptimo peldaño de la escalera hacia el 2º piso,
él le había dicho: "-Cuidado viejo camarada mío,
por las ventanas de esta casa entra el tiempo,
por las puertas sale el espacio;
al menor descuido ya no escucharás las señales de ruta
y de esta vida al fin, habrás perdido toda esperanza".

5. Ese último día, antes que él mismo se extraviara
entre el desayuno y la hora del té,
advirtió para sus adentros:
"-Ahora que el tiempo se ha muerto
y el espacio agoniza en la cama de mi mujer,
desearía decir a los próximos que vienen,
que en esta casa miserable
nunca hubo ruta ni señal alguna
y deesta vida al fin, he perdido toda esperanza".

FIG. 2.18. Martínez, 'La desaparición de una familia'.
Courtesy of Alita Martínez and Fundación de Juan Luis Martínez.

towards an international context of European fascism.[129] Moreover, by referring to Serrano, Martínez emphasises the easy deception that seemingly ordered and reasonable thought can produce. The dedications are followed by two footnotes, one explaining that a word was illegible in the manuscript and the other describing the Chilean context: '*"El clima psicológico que envuelve a Chile es denso y trágico. Una fuerza irresistible tira hacia el abismo e impide que ningún valor..."' (ellipsis in original). The quote immediately illustrates Martínez's criticism of Serrano's ideals and the psychological and political atmosphere in Chile as tragic.

The third direct reference to Chile is Martínez's inclusion of a miniature Chilean flag made out of blotting paper preceding the section titled 'La política' (NN, Figure 2.17). Although Martínez wrote the majority of *La nueva novela* before 1973, according to an interview with Raúl Zurita, he added for the 1977 publication (i.e. during Pinochet's dictatorship) a crucial page: the Chilean flag.[130] Therefore, although he had written the majority of the book before the dictatorship began, once under dictatorship Martínez apparently found it necessary to specify the relationship his poems had to Chile's political and social context. Moreover, the only allusion to Chile within the principal part of the book is not text but an object. It is as though the name itself would be too provocative, so another, more 'objective' symbol is necessary to represent the context in which he writes. However, the placement of the flag before the section 'La política' emphasises that Martínez finds it impossible not to comment on politics, at least within the particular political context in which he writes. As a synecdoche, the flag brings the people and nation of Chile, in its current political and social context, into immediate view.[131]

Although *La nueva novela* contains only a few explicit references to Chile, some of the poems within it are indirect, yet highly critical, allusions to the national context in which the book was written; that context and Martínez's response to it loom larger in the work than is immediately apparent. For instance, the poem 'La desaparición de una familia' (NN, p. 137; Figure 2.18) implicitly alludes to the *desaparecidos* of the military rule under Pinochet.

In this poem, Martínez juxtaposes a formal mask of order and logic with the chaos and devastating illogical real-life occurrences caused by the dictatorship. This is one of only a few pages that contain a structured verse poem. Each stanza is numbered, all in logical order from one to five. Moreover, the use of anaphora at the beginning of every stanza, 'Antes que...', and a refrain at the end of each stanza that only changes slightly each time, gives the poem a sense of stability and readerly security. Just as a room within a house would provide shelter and security for a

129 Miguel Serrano proposed the philosophy of 'Esoteric Hitlerism', a philosophy that looks at mythological evidence that the Aryan race is superior to all other races. Curiously, however, he found Pinochet's regime unsympathetic to his beliefs.

130 YouTube, *Raúl Zurita* (2016).

131 Suárez argues that the flag is an 'invulnerable' object because Martínez does not change its form or material to integrate it into the text (unlike some other objects within the text that have been changed in one way or another), and thus it is impossible to consider it without its political meaning in mind. Suárez, 'Objetualismo en Juan Luis Martínez', pp. 88–94. Martínez also includes a Chilean flag in *La poesía chilena*.

family, the poem, like the poem of the 'almost house' (NN, p. 90) of the previous chapter, encloses its images in its notable form.

On the surface, the poem thus seems to present a stable, predictable narrative. When looking more closely, however, one sees that it is not logical and the space it shelters is not secure; as the title suggests, the family members are disappearing.[132] Martínez emphasises the absurdity of this situation of the disappearances by explaining exactly where each member disappeared, becoming more exact as the poem progresses: 'Antes que su hijo de 5 años/se extraviara entre el comedor y la cocina [...] Antes que "Sogol", su pequeño fox-terrier, desapareciera/en el séptimo peldaño de la escalera hacia el 2° piso' (NN, ll. 1–23).[133] In the final stanza, the last family member (probably the father), who warns the rest of the family of the pending erasure of order that will lead to the loss of hope, disappears not from a specific spatial place, but from a place in time: 'Ese último día, antes que él mismo se extraviara/entre el desayuno y la hora del té' (NN, ll. 29–30). Both time and space can no longer be used to give rational order to the house. In the last refrain, the speaker explains that there was in fact no order in the house, and thus all hope had already been lost (NN, ll. 32–37). Just as the house presents a façade of order and security masking a place where hope is lost, conventional poetic form also masks what can occur in the space of poetry. The poem mirrors Pinochet's dictatorship that gave the appearance of and promoted order and stability (especially as a response to the supposed 'chaos' under Salvador Allende), when in fact thousands of its citizens were tortured and killed without reason. More specifically, this poem alludes to the *desaparecidos*, a technique of the Southern Cone dictatorships that denied their citizens legal due process as well as the opportunity to mourn.[134] Like Sogol, who both exists and does not exist in his disappeared form, the *desaparecidos* were both alive and dead for those who loved them.

Although the commitment of the concrete poets to universality in all its various meanings might have carried an implicit social critique of their local society, in Martínez's *La nueva novela* that critique is explicit. As Kirkpatrick explains, 'a pesar de que extrae sus fuentes de una esfera universal, [Martínez] termina por darle una angustiada y muy personal expresión al estado de su mundo'.[135] Martínez seems unable to escape writing about the harsh social reality of Chile under a dictatorship (a social structure under which the Brazilian concrete poets did not begin their movement), and thus finds himself in a paradox: the book illustrates a need to express his dissent against the regime, even though, by doing so, he hinders his goal of creating a fully objective work. In this regard, Martínez manifests what Adorno

132 The disappearance of the family registers with the work's dynamic movement between filiative to affiliative communities.

133 The dog 'Sogol' that appears throughout the book, including as the 'guardián del libro' on the front and back cover, disappears along with the family. Martínez seems to poke fun at the idea of a 'logocentric' poem.

134 Without the addition of the Chilean flag, however, this allusion to the *desaparecidos* would carry less weight, as the poem was written before the military coup. As Suárez points out, the poem could be contextually linked to World War II and literarily to Carroll, Dante, Guiseppe Ungaretti and T. S. Eliot. See Suárez, *Palabras ya escritas*, pp. 137–41.

135 Kirkpatrick, p. 226.

has said is true of lyric poetry, that a poem 'is always the subjective expression of a social antagonism'.[136] For Martínez, it is as though the concretist agenda on its own cannot be realised under a dictatorship, and thus it is inevitable that his authorial voice will infuse the book in order to criticise the regime.

Conclusion

Just as the concrete poets considered the page as the poetic base for their object-poems, Martínez in *La nueva novela* uses all aspects of the page (writing, images, and white space) to challenge the limits of conventional and even experimental literature. His transformations of the traditional novel ('the new novel') speak to Martínez's connection with the concrete poets in his search to discover a form for challenging the kind of language and authorial literature produced under capitalism, but also to his need to go further to intervene in the authoritarianism of the dictatorship where he lives, in a 'casa de aliento', that is, the page.

He stretches apart (although not entirely separates) the (supposed) binaries of signifier and signified, author and text, and national and universal in *La nueva novela*. He uses his poetic experiments, resembling in part concretism, to demonstrate the coexistence of contrary ideas, suggesting that the interpretation of the notion of universal truths and logical order as authoritarian structures is a necessary (and often humorous) way to understand how the contemporary world really is.

La nueva novela can be seen as a text that seeks to intervene poetically in the Chilean dictatorial regime by resorting to a modification of concretist principles and techniques. In particular, the concrete poets challenge the primacy of the signified, emphasise the objective — which includes both the idea of poem as object and poem as authorless —, formally relies on the page and strives for universality. Martínez combines these principles and techniques into a formal critique of the traditional narrative-based novel.

This combination firstly results in an interrogation of the sign itself and the question of 'meaning'. Both the concrete poets and Martínez attempt to take meaning away from social and ideological authorities in order to bring it back to the people, which requires moving the emphasis from the signified to the signifier and is expressed through the spatial relationships on the page. This poetry of the signifier and the page particularly draws on comprehension through the senses and brings the experience of the reader to the present. Whereas the concrete poets wanted the complete destruction of the signified, Martínez recognises that complete separation of signified and signifier is impossible in a meaningful text. The emphasis on the signified immediately activates the role of the reader in establishing meaning or significance, which leads to the partial (allegorical and physical) deletion of the author, further allowing space for the reader to become a major agent in the production of 'meaning'. Like the concrete poets, Martínez wants a text that is not hindered by the direction of one controlling authorial voice and thus strives to create 'objective' poems. However, whereas the concrete poets

136 Theodor W. Adorno, 'On Lyric Poetry and Society', *Notes to Literature*, ed. by Rolf Tiedemann, vol 1 (New York: Columbia University Press, 1991), p. 45.

(at least theoretically) wanted the author to disappear altogether, Martínez desires a text in which both author and reader can participate equally; his goal is to present a book of anonymous words alongside some of his own.[137]

He recognises that complete objectivity cannot address the particular situation on which he is commenting. By framing the book with Chilean references, he locates the book in a Chilean context, modifying the concretist emphasis on the universal in the direction of the local. The concretist texts were attempts to deny one person's authorial opinion or perspective. Martínez also appreciates the force of such objectivity, but wants to locate the readers (or other authors) in the local in order to bring them to experience his direct comment on the Chilean political context of both the past and the present. As with the advertisement-like poems of the concrete poets, which were both produced and consumed internationally as 'objective' and therefore 'universal' texts, *La nueva novela* in many ways acts like a text that both crosses borders and uses objective 'truths' as its structure. However, unlike the concrete poets (at least regarding the texts produced in the 1950s), Martínez purposefully criticises his own nation, showing that this search for objectivity can sometimes cover the chaos that exists beneath.

Martínez's developments of concretist poetics allow for active reading that disrupts traditional expectations and principles and that remakes self and community. By rethinking a poem as an unstable house, requiring first its destruction and then its recreation according to affiliative remakings of a society on democratic, not autocratic and traditional, principles, the reader of *La nueva novela* is forced to realise the poem through a radical destabilisation of his/her perspective and vision of both poetry and society. As we will see in the following chapters, this process of destruction and recreation through active readerly participation is essential to both Rodrigo Lira's antipoetry and Cecilia Vicuña's plastic poetry. All three poets significantly transform the universalist concretist position towards the reader as proposals for a reconfiguration of society.

137 Martínez, *Poemas del otro*, p. 82.

CHAPTER 3

Nothing New under the Sun: Literary and Non-literary *Détournement* in the Poetry of Rodrigo Lira

As one who shapes, appropriates and exploits poetic and colloquial languages and forms as the material basis of his works, the Chilean poet Rodrigo Lira (1949–1981) was considered a 'manipulator of language' (by himself and others).[1] In particular, he 'manipulated', often with sharply humorous criticism, both the poetry of his Chilean predecessors and of his contemporaries. Following Nicanor Parra's antipoetics (to be discussed below), Lira, to use his own choice of word, 'robs' antecedent poetic form and content and turns them into his own. Both Lira and Parra, often in colloquial language, satirise conventional notions of poetry. However, Lira creatively stretches the limits of the accepted poetic field further than Parra by criticising and dismantling even the specifically innovative elements in the twentieth-century poetic experiments he engages, including those of Parra himself, as though he has discovered the conventional within the purportedly innovative. Lira, in a sense, becomes the anti-poet to Parra's antipoetry. In order to achieve this status, Lira reworks poems that were well known (at least within Chile) into intertextual collages that stress the local and the quotidian; he sees such characteristic reformulations as a radical, often aggressive, intervention in the cultural field. His reworkings are reactions to the conventional, the customary and the ideologically charged in society and poetry, to the biblical phrase that I have chosen for this chapter's title; nothing comes from nothing, but something comes from 'nothing new'.

Lira's poems are generally known for their sharp humour, but it is his innovative collages (of literary and non-literary materials) and his emphasis on the space of the page that make his work stand out.[2] Lira creates *verbivocovisual* texts that are diverse in both form and content. Ranging from pattern poems to prose poems, satirising both political and literary figures, and making use of found material, from

1 'Rodrigo Lira', *Memoria Chilena* (Santiago: Biblioteca Nacional de Chile) <http://www.memoriachilena.cl/602/w3-article-3693.html> [accessed 15 June 2017].

2 It is important to note the difference between the kind of humour found in concrete poetry and Lira's work. As we will see, Lira's humour tends to be sardonic and satirical, while that of the concretists is at best whimsical.

advertisements to well-recognised photographs and paintings, his poems stretch the limits of the practices even of his avant-garde forebears. He not only stands in critical relationship to conventional and even experimental texts, but also is often self-critical, questioning his function in relation to the text as poet and the function of poets in general.[3]

Formally, Lira combines a preoccupation with the space on the page and a concern for the aural qualities of spoken Chilean Spanish. Challenging the notion of a single, nationalised linguistic system, he represents his colloquial dialect on the page with misspellings and phonetically transcribed words. He juxtaposes this colloquial local language and quotidian materials (such as advertisements and popular song lyrics) with hyper-literary references. He 'robs' and 'destroys' texts (by direct quotation, reference and rewriting) from his Chilean (and sometimes global) predecessors and contemporaries.[4] These 'crimes' result in a *détournement* (that is, the reworking of previous texts, especially with humorous, yet political intent) of the traditional lyric and of antipoetic texts; he utilises myriad allusions from other poets in order to satirise them. In addition, through his lively combination of colloquial, quotidian and literary materials, Lira creates objects that, as multiple critics have emphasised, straddle the line between reality and language, life and text. His aggressive refiguring of what has been said before and what has traditionally been accepted as 'given' demonstrates his often playful critique of that which is supported by the hegemonic commercial powers of Chilean society.

His endeavours at first glance may not resemble concrete poems, but looking closely, one can see how his texts employ and renovate concretist principles. Lira, like the concrete poets, utilises the space of the page (the relationship between the white space and the words on it) as a means of emphasising language's materiality. While Martínez strives to delineate it as a universal space (even though he ultimately fails to do so) and Vicuña's page designates a space of between-ness (as we will see in the following chapter), for Lira, the space of the page is used to highlight the renewability of particularly Chilean literary and non-literary language and structures as a means of social critique. In this chapter, I will explore the ways in which his texts, as reworkings of Chilean literary and non-literary materials and forms, exemplify and develop concrete poetics, especially its emphasis on

3 See 'Autocríticas, uno', for example. Rodrigo Lira, *Rodrigo Lira: Proyecto de obras completas,* edited by Milagros Abalo (Santiago: Ediciones Diego Portales, 2013), p. 47. The criticism of the role of the poet results in a portrayal of a self that is fractured. As Rioseco discusses, Lira's work reflects the fractured psyche of the poet himself, a young man with schizophrenia living under an oppressive dictatorship. See Rioseco, 'La escritura exasperada', *Hispamérica*, 108 (2007), 101–08.

4 See Lira, 'Ars poétique', *Rodrigo Lira*, p. 26. I also have used the term 'robs' here to emphasise the reputation Lira has as a 'maldito'. See, for instance, Alejandro Aliaga Rovira, 'Rodrigo Lira, poeta chileno: Muerto en Navidad... vivo en el papel', *El Mercurio de Antofagasta*, 21 April 2001, p. 5. In addition, in his poem 'Ars poétique', he changes the opening lines of Vicente Huidobro's 'Arte poética' (1916): 'Que el verso sea como una llave/Que abra mil puertas' to 'Que el verso sea como una ganzúa/Para entrar a robar de noche', implying that poetry should be a process of theft. See Vicente Huidobro, *El espejo de agua* y *Ecuatorial* (Buenos Aires: Pequeño Dios Editores, 2011), p. 13. In addition, this word, 'robs', supports Lihn's description of Lira's work as picaresque and Bravo's categorisation of Lira's poems as *barroco* or *neobarroco*. Enrique Lihn, 'Prólogo a la primera edición', in Lira, *Rodrigo Lira*, pp. 155–71 and Eduardo Bravo, 'El caos tras la poesía', *El Centro*, 9 April 2000, p. 11.

language's physical qualities, its destruction of the authorial position, and its use of advertising techniques and other non-literary forms. In his works, Lira reconfigures the universality of the concretist 'object-poem' into an exploration of the material properties of a localised, colloquial language and history.

Like Martínez and Vicuña (as we will see in Chapter 4), Lira was involved in the experimental poetry and art scene in Santiago during the 1970s and was in contact with other neo-avant-garde poets, but he and his works remained out of the spotlight.[5] Yet despite the fact that only a small number of critics have investigated his poetry, contemporary poets and critics have recognised Lira as an important neo-avant-garde figure of his time. While his poetry was only published in journals or distributed by hand during his lifetime, after Lira's death in 1981, the majority of his works were gathered into *Rodrigo Lira: Proyecto de obras completas* (1984).[6]

Lira entered the literary scene in Santiago at an early age. After studying at La Pontificia Universidad Católica in Santiago from 1966 and during Salvador Allende's administration, Lira worked sporadically for the Editora Nacional Quimantú writing children's stories.[7] In 1971, he was diagnosed with schizophrenia, a disease that would in many ways define him and his work from then on.[8] During the dictatorship, he went back to studying, where he wrote the majority of the poems that Lihn would publish posthumously. After his suicide in 1981, Lira was transformed into a cult figure within the literary scene, particularly because of his biting, humorous criticism of his predecessors, of his contemporaries and of the nascent neoliberal society as a whole, and because of his outsider position exacerbated by his disease.[9]

5 'Rodrigo Lira', *Memoria Chilena.*

6 Lira's poems that were published during his lifetime appeared in a variety of Chilean journals. The one that received the most attention was '4 tres cientos sesenta y cincos y un 366 de once' published in *La bicicleta*, after winning the journal's 'Concurso de poesía'. Perhaps due to or a contributing factor of the lack of publication, Lira was known as a performer. He performed his work at various events, held interventions, and, notably, soon before his suicide, used his performance skills as a means to make some money by presenting his work on the television competition "¿Cenúto vale el show?" See Roberto Careaga, *La poesía terminó conmigo* (Santiago: Ediciones Universidad Diego Portales, 2017), pp. 240–47. Many of the individually published poems differ visually from those published in the compilation. While the (word) layout is generally similar, many of the journal publications and those passed among friends and scholars informally include collaged photographs and newspaper clippings. Throughout my chapter, I will consider all versions to which I have access. Another collection (which includes six more texts than *Proyecto de obras completas*) was published in 2006: Lira, *Declaración jurada* (Santiago: Ediciones UDP, 2006). His poems and drawings were recently compiled in *Buelos barrios: Boladas boludas*, ed. by Marcelo Gatica (Santiago: Piélago, 2016).

7 Although it is known that Lira worked for Editora Nacional Quimantú, it is uncertain whether these stories survive (the online archive does not include them). This might be because many of the publications were burned when this publishing house was shut down by the dictatorship in 1973.

8 While an obvious reading of his poetry as a whole would be in relation to the poet's schizophrenia, I will refrain from doing so in fear that the focus on his illness would diminish or distort the value and proper characterisation of his works. Nonetheless, convincing arguments have been made, especially in Deleuzean readings of Lira's poetry as rhizomatically schizophrenic. See, for example, Julio César Aguilar, 'Rodrigo Lira: Una aproximación neobarroca a su poética de genial esquizofrénica', *Crítica.cl* (2016), 1–14.

9 'Rodrigo Lira', *Memoria Chilena.*

Apart from a variety of short newspaper articles and brief mentions in academic articles, there are currently only a handful of critical discussions that contribute to our understanding of Lira (including the prologues to both editions of *Rodrigo Lira: Proyecto de obras completas*). These studies productively recognise Lira's 'antipoetic' style and applaud his postmodernist parodies and satires of conventional and contemporary poetry (including his own works). Jaime Blume Sánchez argues, through two close readings of poems, that Lira is a postmodern poet because he valorises, like Parra, the destruction of the traditional lyric 'I'.[10] Eduardo Bravo also describes Lira's work as postmodern, categorising it not as a nihilistic poetry, but as a *neobarroco* or postmodern *barroco*, one that fills in the gaps of, or makes more complete, Parra's antipoetry.[11] Andrés Morales discusses Huidobro in relation to Lira and other Chilean poets, briefly mentioning Lira's 'Ars poétique' in comparison with Huidobro's 'Arte poética'.[12]

There are a few critics who recognise, although only cursorily, the qualities I bring to light in this chapter: Lira's subtle political criticism, his distrust of the authorial subject and his preoccupation with the dismantlement of poetic language. One of his principal critics, Marcelo Rioseco characterises Lira's texts as critiques of Chilean poetry and as manifestations of Lira's literary subject as 'un maldito'.[13] Along with many other critics, Rioseco argues that Lira's poetry is the testimony of those whose words have been censored. In his view, Lira's work is political poetry in which the fractured (anti-) traditional poetic lineage and his disintegrated self stem from and represent the fractured Chile of his time.[14] Rioseco explains that Lira creates his political poetry by representing a colloquial oral language on the page: 'No quiere escribir poemas, sino largos textos orales que pueden ser representados'.[15] In his recent and thorough book *Maquinarias deconstructivas*, Rioseco argues that Lira expresses through parody and satire the oppression under which he wrote.[16]

Other critics who also address these elements in Lira's work include Nicolás Folch Maass, who compares Lira to Juan Luis Martínez and analyses their use of nonsense and their deconstruction of conventional Chilean poetics.[17] Andrés Cáceres Milnes, Alexis Candia Cáceres and Patricio Landaeta Mardones also acknowledge Lira's deconstruction of the Chilean poetic tradition, and recognise his destabilisation of Christian ideals and even his own biography through his distrust of reason, his lament for a loss of collective values and his psychological harshness.[18] Cristóbal

10 Jaime Blume Sánchez, 'Rodrigo Lira, poeta posmoderno', *El Instituto*, 7 (1994), 145–59.

11 Bravo, 'El caos tras la poesía', p. 11.

12 Andrés Morales, 'Vicente Huidobro y la poesía chilena actual', *Anales de Literatura Chilena*, 9 (2008), 235–40 (pp. 237–38).

13 Rioseco, 'La escritura exasperada', pp. 101–08.

14 Ibid.

15 Ibid., p. 103.

16 In this book, Rioseco places Lira amongst poets (including Martínez) of the 'ludic neovanguardia'. While he recognises Lira's political force, Rioseco focuses on Lira's use of humour rather than on Lira's concretist characteristics. Rioseco, *Maquinarias reconstructivas*, pp. 60–108.

17 Nicolás Folch Maass, 'Rodrigo Lira revisitado', *Cyber Humanitatis*, 44 (2007), 1–8.

18 Mariela Fuentes Leal and Juan Zapata Gacitúa, 'La escritura del lenguaje en Enrique Lihn y Germán Marín', *Universum*, 31 (2016), 45–66. They also make a brief parallel between Juan Luis Martínez and Lira's destabilisation of their poetic Chilean lineage in a footnote. Ibid., p. 53.

Joannon focuses attention on Lira's creation of hyper-literary objects, in describing Lira as 'un poeta tomado por el lenguaje', influenced by Parra, Lihn, Claudio Bertoni, Erick Pohlhamner, and Roberto Merino. The poet Roberto Merino recognises that Lira's poetry can be difficult, claiming that it contains 'cierto registro de ilegibilidad', but at a closer glance he finds that the texts represent 'el grito sordo de una intelligencia escondida'.[19]

In the supplementary material of *Rodrigo Lira: Proyecto de obras completas*, Lihn and Milagros Abalo bring to light the primary elements of Lira's antipoetics. In the prologue to the first edition of the volume, Lihn, after a detailed discussion of his frustrating personal relationship with Lira, describes Lira's work as one that exists between reality and text; he claims that Lira, as an 'anarcofrancotirador', intervenes in reality through parody and hyperliterary antipoetics.[20] However, he argues that Lira does not create 'acciones de arte' (as the members of the Colectivo Acciones de Arte [C.A.D.A.] did, for example), poetic or artistic events performed outside of traditional artistic spaces (such as the museum), but brings spoken language to the page.[21] In addition, he concludes that Lira's social and literary context influences him to produce, as we will see in the following readings, an absurd or exaggerated version of antipoetry.[22] The complexity of Lira's poetry is clear, but Milagros Abalo, in his brief description of Lira's complicated relationship with the texts, concludes that, as difficult reading Lira's antipoetic poetry may be, it is worthwhile.[23] However, none of these critics have drawn the connection between Lira and the Brazilian concrete poets, a comparison that will illuminate key features of his poetry.

Antipoetry

Given the centrality of the idea of 'antipoetry' for Lira, I will briefly explain the term, which he inherits from his two predecessors: Nicanor Parra (1914–2018) and Enrique Lihn (1929–1988). While the term antipoetry could be applied to a variety of poets and poetry, it is associated primarily with Parra, who has been seen as its father, and his 1954 volume *Poemas y antipoemas*.[24] From this book onwards, Parra attempted to disrupt and redirect the path poetry had taken and was projected to take. Aiming to create a poetry that questioned the accepted definitions of Poetry (with a capital 'P'), Parra felt that previous literature had lost contact with the rest of society and therefore sought a new poetic form suitable to express reality as it is.[25] Furthermore, he strove to undermine the assumptions made by the literary

19 Roberto Merino, 'La llamada elíptica', *Talleres Gráficos*, 268 (1988), iv–v.
20 Lihn, in Lira, *Rodrigo Lira*, pp. 155–71.
21 Ibid.
22 Ibid.
23 Milagros Abalo, in Lira, *Rodrigo Lira*, pp. 9–13.
24 While the word and idea of 'antipoetry' has been used by many poets, Parra is known as the first principal promoter of such poetry.
25 'Nicanor Parra', *Memoria Chilena*, (Santiago: Biblioteca Nacional de Chile) <http://www.memoriachilena.cl/602/w3-article-3629.html> [accessed 16 June 2017].

establishment concerning those who should be able and allowed to read and understand poetry, especially the assumption that to read poetry one must be an erudite, elite reader. As he stated in his famous 'Manifiesto', 'Los poetas bajaron del Olimpo' (l. 4), Parra wanted to pull poets down from their pedestals and create a poetry for the masses.[26]

Even though his predecessors also restructured the lyric by rearranging language, rethinking the page and the concept of literature itself, Parra attacked previous poetic practices by 'rewriting' previous texts.[27] This critical rewriting occurs particularly at the formal level, where he uses a variety of verse lengths and metres, with flexible rhythms and colloquial vocabulary, as opposed to the conventional line lengths, metres and diction of previous poetry. His poetic language, as William Rowe explains, was not just ordinary spoken language, but instead an assemblage of different forms of the spoken and the written word.[28] Moreover, as Felipe Cussen argues, antipoetry attempts not only to show that 'una banalidad puede convertirse en gran literatura, sino también que la gran literatura puede convertirse en una banalidad'.[29] Parra aimed to dismantle conventional poetic language by continually evaluating what had been left outside the poetic sphere and bringing these traditionally 'unpoetic' aspects into the work.[30]

While Parra's poems are not overtly political, his reworking of literary forms can be read as a political statement in and of itself. The critic Ivan Carrasco, explaining the political implications of Parra's work, states that Parra's poetry is anarchic in its attempt to destroy all previous hierarchies that have defined literature in the past.[31] Parra took apart the hierarchies of the poet and reader and even questioned his own role as anti-poet (see, for example, 'Autoretrato'). Moreover, Carrasco further outlines two principal factors with particular elements that define an antipoem:

26 Nicanor Parra, 'Manifiesto', *Obra gruesa* (Santiago: Editorial Universitaria, 1969), pp. 211–14. This particular line is in part a clear reaction to Vicente Huidobro's claim in his 'Arte poética' that 'El poeta es un pequeño Dios' that creates his own world apart from reality on the page. Huidobro, 'Arte poética', *El espejo de agua* y *Ecuatorial*, p. 13, l. 18. Parra refers to Huidobro's statement later on in the same poem: 'Nada más, compañeros [...] La poesía de pequeño dios'. Parra, 'Manifiesto', pp. 211–14, ll. 101–05).

27 For example, he parodied Gabriela Mistral, Vicente Huidobro and (especially) Pablo Neruda.

28 William Rowe, *Poets of Contemporary Latin America: History and the Inner Life* (Oxford: Oxford University Press, 2000), p. 31. Importantly, according to the critic Eduardo Milán, this attention to orality as the language of poetry is what Parra's antipoetry shares in common with concrete poetry. See Eduardo Milán, 'Parra en dos tiempos', *Revista de Teoría y Crítica de Poesía Latinoamericana*, 6 (2018), pp. 108–19.

29 Felipe Cussen, 'Versos sueltos, lugares comunes, poemas encontrados', *Acta Literaria*, 46 (2013), p. 18.

30 Rowe, *Poets of Contemporary Latin America*, pp. 29–77.

31 Parra, although he has sometimes contradicted himself, has identified as an anarchist. Ivan Carrasco, 'La antipoesía: Manifestación política heterogénea', *Atenea (Concepción)*, 510 (2014), 95–109 (p. 97).

> [El antipoema] opera a partir de dos factores textuales: *una instancia antipoetizante* o *texto trans y extratextual*, que actúa sobre *la instancia antipoetizada* por medio de *tres operaciones de reescritura*, que a su vez incluyen procedimientos particulares: la *homologación falsa o aparente*, la *inversión* y *la deformación satírica del modelo* elegido. La ironía, la parodia, los diversos *genus dicendi*, la paradoja, la cotidianidad, la carnavalización, el humor negro, el chiste, y los demás procedimientos textuales que ha señalado la crítica, constituyen elementos o constituyentes parciales de las figuras anteriores. La instancia antipoetizada es un texto particular, un género literario o referencial (histórico, filosófico, mítico, religioso), un discurso oral, o un modelo no verbal, como ser lugares, personas, entidades de diversa índole, es decir, referentes parciales o totales existentes en el extratexto.[32]

These factors work together to create a committed poetry, in the positive sense in which Theodor Adorno defines commitment: for Adorno, successful art is not ideologically driven and politically explicit, but rather is political through its form.[33] The commitment of antipoetry comes not from an overt discussion through content, but through formal disruptions and decisions. While Parra's antipoetry at times explicitly expresses ideologically governed stances (which in some cases contradict one another[34]), his work overall is committed in its formal stance against and opposite to an inaccessible, reified and authoritarian poetry. In other words, one could argue that antipoetry is inherently, albeit implicitly, politically committed through the formal ways in which it combats authoritarianism and the status quo (as outlined in the quotation above).

Parra's *Artefactos* (1972), in particular, illustrates his antipoetics.[35] In this project, he not only challenged the traditional form of a lyrical poem (such as one created solely of words on a page within a book) by creating poems that included images or drawings accompanied by short written phrases, but also rearranged the expected physical form of the book of poetry by writing each poem on a postcard so that they could be sent to multiple readers as well as read in any order. These satirical postcard 'poems' that humorously criticised society and literature in general could thus be read as separate from the book *Artefactos* as a whole, as well as in distinct places and at various times. Because of the poem's existence as a mailed communication assumed to be read in multiple geographical locations, each part of the same book simultaneously adds an individual part to the event of the text. He completely takes apart the conventional form of the verse poem and creates instead 'artefactos',

32 Carrasco, 'Antipoesía y neovanguardia', *Estudios Filológicos*, 23 (1988), pp. 38–39.

33 Adorno, 'Commitment', in *Notes to Literature II*, trans. by Shierry Weber Nicholsen (New York: Columbia University Press, 1992), pp. 76–94. See below for a detailed explanation of Adorno's definition of 'commitment'.

34 See Carrasco, 'La antipoesía: Manifestación política heterogénea', 95–109.

35 Although Parra did not call the Artefactos 'antipoems' and they are not considered to be 'classical' antipoems, I argue that the poems carry the traits of antipoetry as described above. In addition, various critics have claimed that the Artefactos are in fact antipoems. For example, as William Rowe explains, the Artefactos can be taken as the explosion of the world of the antipoem (Rowe, *Poets of Contemporary Latin America*, p. 73), and Carrasco categorizes the Artefactos as avant-garde antipoems: 'La antipoesía de Parra, tanto a través de los antipoemas clásicos (los que asumen la apariencia de un poema convencional) como de los artefactos (que asumen el aspecto de un texto vanguardista)'. Carrasco, 'Antipoesía y neovanguardia', p. 41.

in both senses of the Spanish term as an object made by a person as well as in its figurative military definition as an explosive device. In other words, like concrete poems, the poems are no longer solely things to be read, but are material objects to be handled as such. Moreover, unlike the *creative* force Vicente Huidobro, for example, expects of poetry (or, in other words, the poet's ability to create *ex nihilo*), poetry for Parra (and especially for Lira, as we will see) has the *destructive* force of an 'artefacto'.

Through his engagement with Parra's antipoetics, the Chilean poet and cultural figure Enrique Lihn also significantly influenced Lira's projects. A prolific poet, novelist, artist and critic, he was present in Santiago's literary scene in the mid-twentieth century. Just as Parra did, Lihn used colloquial language and drew on the life of the city to express his scepticism about the Chilean poetic heritage as well as to criticise the society and politics of his time, especially the neoliberal reforms and privatisation of space under the dictatorship. He particularly tried to avoid, to use critic Christopher Travis's term, the 'fetishisation' of his own works, responding to the fetishisation that affected the great Chilean poets (for example, Neruda, Mistral, Huidobro and even Parra).[36] His work has also been described as 'literatura de contrabando' (a phrase he himself used), breaking down literature's traditional forms and limits in much the same way as Parra's does.[37] Irony and parody, as well as formal experimentation, shaped his critique of literature and society. In visual projects and installations, both Parra and Lihn moved poems off the conventional poetic page and physically into the city. For example, along with Parra and the poet, film director and artist Alejandro Jodorowsky, Lihn created a series of poetic interventions titled *Quebrantahuesos* (1952). In these interventions, they used public space and language to form collages of cut outs from journals and newspapers, pasting them on walls throughout Santiago. Just as the concrete poets used advertising spaces, these artists took poetic language out of the book and into the public spaces of the city.[38]

Although they had much in common, Lihn's poetics expanded upon and differed from Parra's, especially through his focus on written language.[39] In an interview with Marlene Gottlieb, he explains that, apart from 'los aspectos que incluyen el "reduccionismo" y excluyen el trascendentalismo profético', his work diverges from Parra's antipoetry in part because, instead of wanting to destroy all poetic language completely, he wishes to create new poetic language.[40] The feature of Lihn's work that most distinguishes it from that of Parra is his preoccupation with written language, as opposed to speech 'acts' (for example Parra's distribution of

36 Travis provides an excellent account of Lihn's adversion to felishisation as Adornian and reads his poetics through an Adornian lens. See Christopher Travis, 'Beyond the Vanguardia: The Dialectical Voice of Enrique Lihn', *Romance Quarterly*, 49.1 (2002), 61–74 (p. 64).

37 Mariela Fuentes Leal and Juan Zapata Gacitúa, 'La escritura del lenguaje en Enrique Lihn y Germán Marín', p. 154.

38 See Introduction.

39 Some describe Lihn's poetry as 'contrapoesía', that is, self-sceptical poetry that does not trust the poetic word. Andrés Cáceres Milnes and others, 'Una Lira desolada: Parodia y frustración en Proyecto de obras completas y declaración jurada', *Universum*, 31 (2016), 45–66 (p. 49).

40 Marlene Gottlieb and Enrique Lihn, 'Enrique Lihn', *Hispamérica*, 36 (1983), 35–44 (p. 36).

the *Artefactos* as an action); as Lihn himself explains, '[Parra] cree en una poesía o antipoesía de hechos y no de palabras [...] se declaró enemigo de la retórica [...] En cuanto a mí [Lihn], soy un retórico confeso. Practico una poesía hecha de palabras y de palabras escritas.'[41] In other words, Lihn privileges the physical permanence of the poem on the page. Moreover, as Travis explains, Lihn never called himself an antipoet because he believed that that designation promoted a counterproductive canonisation of antipoetry; he saw that the celebration and promotion of Parra undid many of the fundamental aspects of antipoetry.[42]

Although he had a difficult personal relationship with Lira, Lihn was a principal promoter of the latter's work and encouraged him to write.[43] As readers of Parra and antipoetry, both Lira and Lihn at the same time appreciated and criticised the work of the father of antipoetry from a removed position. What distinguishes Lira from other antipoets is his particularly destructive tone and his exaggerated characterisation of his predecessors. As Carrasco argues:

> El procedimiento usado por Lira para desmitificar el carácter transgresor de los antipoemas y negarlo del todo, es la interpretación literal de los textos de Parra y su comparación con los hechos del extratexto, para demostrar su inutilidad y su falsedad, por supuesto que de modo caricaturesco, por lo tanto, también de modo ambiguo y, por ello, antipoético.[44]

Throughout his work, Lira caricatures his predecesors (such as Neruda, Huidobro, and Mistral), his contemporaries (Parra, Lihn, Martínez and Zurita, for example) and indeed himself.

Antipoetics shares with concretist poetics an attempt to go beyond the limits of what has been conceived previously as poetry by transforming previous ideas, techniques and even poems into new ones; they do not critique *ex nihilo* but rather work from other texts. Although the Chilean neo-avant-garde did not seem to have a direct relationship with the Brazilian concrete poets at the time, Lira's adaptation of the antipoetics of Parra and Lihn does echo certain aims of the concrete poets. While the majority of Lira's critics recognise his poetry as antipoetic, none has developed the links between his antipoetic works and concrete poetry.

In the first section of this chapter, I will argue that Lira creates poetry that engages the politics of the time through this *détournement*.[45] Just as concrete poems bring together the practices of the European historical avant-garde and sometimes directly engage with earlier texts, Lira's poetry could also be seen as a synthesis, but specifically of Chilean and Latin American avant-garde and neo-avant-garde practices. Through collage and phonetic spellings and misspellings of previous poetic experiments, Lira emphasises the materiality of a particularly Chilean language.

41 Ibid., p. 37.

42 Travis, 'Beyond the Vanguardia', pp. 66–77.

43 Lihn and Lira often disagreed and would frustrate each other. As Lihn says, 'El recuerdo que tengo de Rodrigo Lira me disgusta conmigo mismo. Era alguien que ponía a prueba la capacidad para desestabilizar los códigos de comportamiento en la relación interpersonal'. Lihn, *Rodrigo Lira*, p. 155.

44 Carrasco, 'Antipoemas de la antipoesía', *Anales de Literatura Chilena*, 3 (2002), 53–62 (p. 60).

45 See the conclusion of this chapter for further explanation of Adorno's definition of commitment.

The primary materials with which he works are thus the poetic experiments of his predecessors. Because his work engages the local, Lira, like Martínez, ultimately rejects the concretist goal of completely erasing societal specificity through the elimination of subjectivity.[46] Like the concrete poets, Lira illustrates a disdain for the poet who claims authority over the writing and reading of the poem. However, while the concrete poets tried to eliminate the authorial subject altogether, Lira retains enough of the subject in order to attack both his predecessors and the general concept of an omniscient, elite poet.

Not only does Lira appropriate and distort the language of his predecessors, he also integrates materials and structures from sources typically not related to poetry. Just as the concrete poets did, Lira makes politically committed poems out of the variety of material he collages together.[47] The intertextual range of the material of his poems, from weather reports and academic articles to collaged photographs and magazine clippings, reinforces the anti-poetic nature of his texts and furthers the concern he shares with the concretists to highlight the materiality of language. In the second section, I will discuss how he criticises both local and international societal structures not directly, but indirectly through 'non-literary' *détournement*. While the concrete poets commented generally on consumerism and capitalism, Lira develops these techniques in order to criticise his society under dictatorship in Chile.

Lira expands upon concrete poetry in three main ways. Firstly, by reworking the texts of his predecessors, he, like the concrete poets, criticises the literary status quo; both by re-contextualising and re*forming* these texts, he launches a general attack on Pinochet's oppressive regime. Secondly, he maintains a direct relationship to his reality by creating objects and materials that exist within reality (that is, daily life). They are not thematic representations of that reality, but become part of that reality formally (such as the form of a weather report) and through quotation (such as direct quotes and references to certain figures and an informal Chilean Spanish). In the terms of concrete poetry, he makes his poems into objects with which one could engage in real life. Thirdly, he criticises the authoritarian nature of the poet, that is, a subject that assumes his/her point of view to be authoritative.

Détournement

Through reworking previous texts, Lira creates an attitude for change; he does not directly state his criticisms of his predecessor's works, but manipulates their texts and transforms them into his own arguments. Through the application of certain concretist principles, he takes on questions of authorship and authority in his own poetry, and his act of reworking these texts is a political statement in and of itself.

46 In Chapter 2, I also discuss the question of subjectivity, authority and context in relation to the text. Both Martínez and Lira write about their social context implicitly, most likely because they both were writing under an oppressive dictatorship. While Martínez, however, mostly refers to Chile through inference, Lira directly addresses his local society.

47 Although both Parra and Lihn did the same, Lira's satire is sharper and darker than their criticisms.

While it is somewhat difficult to categorise his reworkings of previous texts, and a variety of categories could apply, I will focus on his technique of *détournement* because it brings 'back into play' previous poems.[48]

What is *détournement*? According to the Situationist International (SI), the term is: 'Short for "détournement of preexisting aesthetic elements." The integration of present or past artistic productions into a superior construction of a milieu. In this sense there can be no situationist painting or music, but only a situationist use of those means.'[49] Guy Debord, a leader of the SI, provides a more general definition: 'the reuse of preexisting artistic elements in a new ensemble'. Or he defines it even more generally without the qualifier 'artistic': 'any elements, no matter where they are taken from, can be used to make new combinations'.[50] In another text, Debord characterises poetry with *détournement* as the antithesis of consumerism:

> It brings back into play all the unsettled debts of history[...] Poetry is becoming more and more clearly the empty space, the *anti*matter [emphasis added], of consumer society, since it is not consumable (in terms of the modern criteria for a consumable object: an object that is of equivalent value for each of a mass of isolated passive consumers). Poetry is nothing when it is quoted, it can only be *detourned*, brought back into play. Otherwise the study of the poetry of the past is nothing but an academic exercise.[51]

48 For example, Lira's poems can be seen as a parody, a particular type of what Genette calls hypertext. Genette defines parody as a type of transformation (as opposed to a pastiche, which is that of imitation) of the hypotext that can be satirical (which he calls 'travesty') or playful (which he calls 'parody proper'). See Gérard Genette, *Palimpsests: Literature in the Second Degree*, trans. by Channa Newman and Claude Doubinsky (Lincoln: University of Nebraska Press, 1997), pp. 1–24. Lira does not attempt to assume the voices of others, but critically reforms them into parodic travesties. While the terms 'contrafactum' and 'parody' have been conflated (especially in music), Lira's poems, if we take the basic definition of 'contrafactum' as the rewriting of lyrics while maintaining the same music, do not fit the definition. Instead, Lira rewrites not only sections of the lyrics, but also the musicality of the poems (that is, he tends not to stick to the same metres or rhymes of the hypotexts). In these regards, Lira's poems could be seen as not quite as contrafacta, but as parodic travesties. For more on the distinction of contrafactum and parody (especially in music), see Robert Falck, 'Parody and Contrafactum: A Terminological Clarification', *The Musical Quarterly*, 65.1 (1979), 1–21. Oliver Noble Wood also provides a detailed account of a contrafactum in '"Ensíllenme el asno rucio": Parody and Burlesque in a Contrafactum', in *A Poet for all Seasons: Eight Commentaries on Góngora*, ed. by Nigel Griffin and Oliver Noble Wood (New York: Hispanic Seminary of Medieval Studies, 2013), pp. 1–23.

49 *Internationale Situationniste #1: Definitions*, trans. by Ken Knabb (June 1958), <http://www.cddc.vt.edu/sionline/si/definitions.html> [accessed 5 July 2016]. Because it is a technique, one could argue that many avant-garde experiments use the technique of *détournement*. However, unlike other modernist works, I will argue that Lira's use of *détournement* helps him create particularly Chilean object-like poems.

50 'Detournement as negation and prelude', in *Situationist International Anthology*, ed. and trans. by Guy Debord and Ken Knabb (Berkeley: Bureau of Public Secrets, 2006), pp. 67– 68. And Debord and Wolman, 'A User's Guide to Détournement', in ibid., pp. 9–21. For more information on Détournement, see *Detournement as Pedagogical Praxis*, ed. by James Trier (Boston: Sense Publishers, 2014).

51 Debord, 'All the Kings Men', quoted in *Poems for the Millennium: From Post War to Millennium*, ed. by Pierre Joris and Jerome Rothenberg, vol 2 (Berkeley: University of California Press, 1998), pp. 417–19.

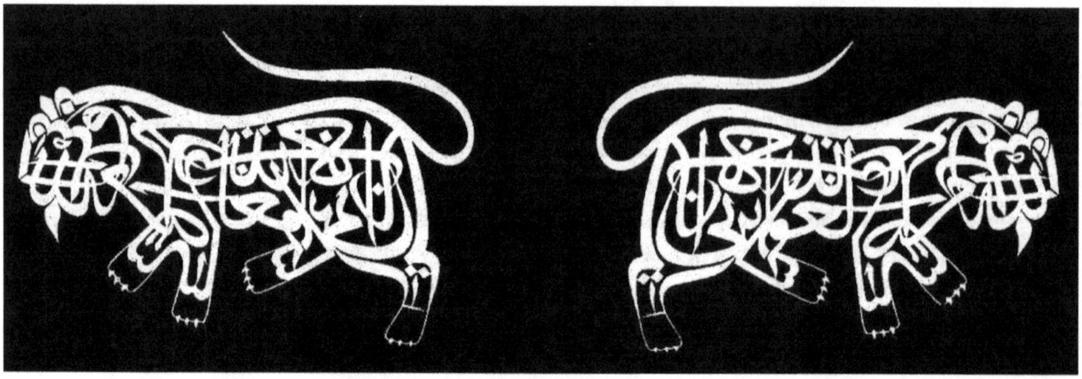

FIG. 3.1. Augusto de Campos, 'O Tigre' (1977). Courtesy of Augusto de Campos.

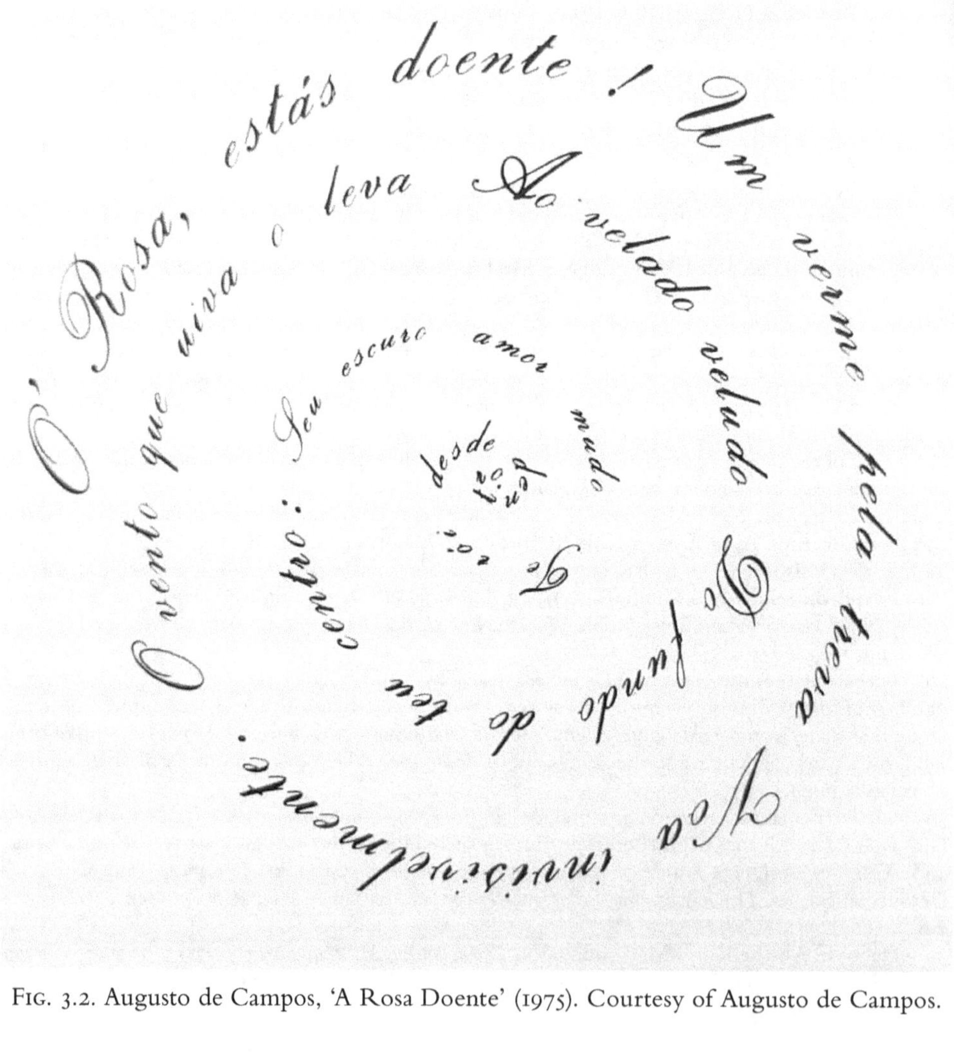
Ó Rosa, estás doente!
Um verme pela treva
Voa invisivelmente.
O vento que uiva e leva
Ao velado veludo
Do fundo do teu centro:
Seu escuro amor mudo

FIG. 3.2. Augusto de Campos, 'A Rosa Doente' (1975). Courtesy of Augusto de Campos.

In this regard, one can connect both Lira's poetry and concrete poetry to *détournement* in that both emphasise that poetry is antithetical and antipathetic to consumerism. I will examine Lira's work as *détournement* in order to highlight its antipoetic nature.

While the concrete poets tended to synthesise avant-garde practices into one poetics in general, they also rewrote (or used *détournement* for) a variety of famous poems. For example, Augusto de Campos restructured and translated lines from William Blake's 'The Tyger' and 'The Sick Rose' into calligrammatic poems (Figures 3.1 and 3.2). Similarly, Lira combines and rewrites specific poems by his Chilean predecessors in order to criticise and question the literary history of his nation. In particular, he reworks their language into (particularly Chilean) object-like poems. Through *détournement*, Lira emphasises the materiality of language, particularly used language, and therefore creates poems that, like concrete poems (although they should not be considered such), present, rather than represent, themselves. Many of his poems are 'artes poeticae', of which I will look at the two that he designates as such: 'Ars poétique' (Figure 3.3) and 'Ars poétique, deux' (Figure 3.2). In 'Arts poétique', Lira discusses what poetry should do and how it should do it, and in 'Ars poétique, deux', focusing more on the poet than on poetry, he postulates why and when one should write.

As a critique of canonical Chilean poetry, 'Ars poétique' can best be described as an antipoem that deconstructs and reconstructs previous texts. In particular, Lira reconstructs Vicente Huidobro's 'Arte poética', now considered by most readers a poem of the Chilean establishment. The monumentalised poems of his predecessors, for Lira, end up assuming and controlling the subjectivity of others by not making space for other subjectivities other than a singular authority. Lira thus attempts to take apart these 'monuments'. For Lira, an antipoem requires what he dramatically calls the destruction of other texts (particularly of 'monumental' texts), and from the 'rubble' left over, one can create a new text;[52] poetry is a process of both the destruction of previous poetry and the reformation of its remaining parts into a heteroglossal work.[53] Through the destruction and reworking of Huidobro's poem, he expands concretist *object*ivity by both criticising and engaging with material that already exists within society and then creates a new object within that society. He does not make explicit his critique, but rather illuminates it through its *re*formation.

Lira insists, from the first line of the poem, that the creation of poetic texts comes from the destruction of a previously existing one. Huidobro begins his 'Arte poética' with the line 'Que el verso sea como una llave/Que abra mil puertas', implying that he hopes that the poetic line can open up many new worlds. Lira's poem begins with the same phrase 'Que el verso sea como una' but then changes from the word 'llave' to 'ganzúa'. This substitution of words drastically changes the

52 Vicuña discusses this creation out of something in PALABRAR*mas* (see Chapter 4). Martínez's image of the falling-down house also evokes this image of rubble, or at least, an image of the destruction right before the rubble is created (see Chapter 2).

53 This calls to mind Alfred Jarry's call for the destruction of everything, including the rubble: 'Pa Ubu.-Hornstrumpot! We shall not have succeeded in demolishing everything unless we demolish the ruins as well'. Alfred Jarry, 'Ubu Enchained', in *The Ubu Plays*, trans. by Cyril Connolly and Simon Watson Taylor (London: Methuen, 1968), p. 91. Whereas Jarry wants to destroy even the ruins, Lira uses the ruins from the destruction for creation.

ARS POÉTIQUE

para la galería imaginaria

Que el verso sea como una ganzúa
Para entrar a robar de noche
Al diccionario a la luz
De una linterna
sorda como
Tapia
Muro de los Lamentos
Lamidos
Paredes de Oído!
cae un Rocket pasa un Mirage
los ventanales quedaron temblando
Estamos en el siglo de las neuras y las siglas
y las siglas
son los nervios, son los nervios
El vigor verdadero reside en el bolsillo
es la chequera
El músculo se vende en paquetes por Correos
la ambición
no descansa la poesía
está c
ol
g
an
do
en la dirección de Bibliotecas Archivos y Museos en Artí
culos de lujo, de primera necesidad,
oh, poetas! No cantéis
a las rosas, oh, dejadlas madurar y hacedlas
mermelada de mosqueta en el poema

El Autor pide al Lector diScurpas por la molestia (Su Propinaes Misuerdo)

33

FIG. 3.3. Lira, 'Ars poétique' (Lira, *Rodrigo Lira*, p. 33). Courtesy of Elisa Lira.

meaning of the line; both 'key' and 'crowbar' are tools with which to open doors, but the latter opens destructively and prevents the lock from ever being used again. Lira thus immediately proposes that poetry is a destructive, criminal force, unlike Huidobro, who implies that poetry is creative (or at least not destructive). Both the line as key and as crowbar, moreover, allow for the reader to enter into the creation of poems, as concrete poems often do, but Lira's crowbar denies the chance to close that entrance; in other words, once it is open, for Lira, poetry should be accessible to all, not opened for a few and then closed off again.

Lira stresses that the crowbar is a tool often used for illegal activity. The altered phrase is followed by the line 'Para entrar a robar de noche'. As opposed to the key that 'abra mil puertas', Lira's crowbar is used to break through an entry. In particular, the line is used to steal 'Al diccionario a la luz/De una linterna' (ll. 3–4). Instead of following Huidobro's advice to 'cuida[r] tu palabra' (Huidobro, l. 6), Lira suggests that poetry should rob with the help of the dictionary and by the light of a lantern. Lira does exactly that: he steals from and destroys Huidobro's poem by replacing some of Huidobro's words with his own. Because it is night when this robbery is taking place, Lira specifies one would be using a 'linterna' for light; as opposed to the Romantic view of composition as 'natural', this light is artificial.[54] Unlike for Huidobro, for Lira the poetic line does not create something out of nothing, but instead violently appropriates words that have already been written and destroys things that have been made.[55] Importantly for his poetics, he 'illegally' rejects the biblical-Romantic tradition of creation *ex nihilo* that Huidobro celebrates.

In this poem, *détournement* has a particular relation to sight and sound, that is, the 'vocovisual' aspects of poetry that both Lira and the concrete poets emphasise. Moving away from direct allusion to Huidobro's poem, Lira anthropomorphises the lantern by claiming that the object used for sight cannot hear: 'De una linterna/sorda como' (ll. 4–5). He further compares the lantern to an object through which God is supposed to hear, the Wailing Wall: 'sorda como/Tapia/Muro de los Lamentos /Lamidos/Paredes de Oído!' (ll. 5–9). For Lira, the Wailing Wall, the remaining ruins of a temple that had been destroyed by the Romans in 70CE (which today has become the holiest place of prayer in Judaism) does not listen. Lira makes his *détournement* through linking sounds.[56] The cries, in the process of attempting to be listened to, morph into things that are tasted, or licked ('lamidos'). Ironically, they are tasted through an aural connection of the words 'lamentos' and 'oídos' to produce 'lamidos'. Just as the concrete poets connect words through their aural

54 Huidobro, *El espejo de agua y Ecuatorial*, p. 13. The setting at night is reminiscent of José Martí, who finds that the night is when he can be most creative, out of the 'light' of the Spanish colonisers. See José Martí, 'Dos patrias', *Obras completas*, vol 16 (Habana: Centro de Estudios Martinianos, 2001), p. 252.

55 Kenneth Goldsmith claims that all poetic language is appropriated language and exemplifies this appropriated nature in his poetic experiments by 'stealing' entire texts and placing them in new contexts. See Goldsmith, *Uncreative Writing: Managing Language in the Digital Age* (New York: Columbia University Press, 2011).

56 This technique is apparent in almost all concrete poems, but, to give just one example, see 'Linguaviagem', in which Augusto de Campos brings together the words 'linguagem' and 'viagem' aurally (as well as spatially).

qualities in order to evoke the sensuous engagement of the reader, Lira explicitly plays on the semantic and vocal expressions of the text.

This violent act of destruction leaves unstable rubble from which the poet can create. The 'muro' might refer to Parra's poet that 'construye su muro' (Parra, ll. 12). In other words, Lira's poet has destroyed the wall that Parra's poet has constructed in order to pick up the pieces and construct again. What remains of this wall is unstable: 'cae un Rocket pasa un Mirage/los ventanales quedaron temblando' (ll. 10–11).[57] In particular, the shaking remains are the windows, which allow one to see in and out of a fixed structure. In other words, what is leftover are frames; it is not the image that the windows frame that remains, but only its frame.[58] Lira literalises José Ortega y Gasset's distinction between modern art and traditional art, in which he asserts that modern art focuses on the frame. Like modern art, here all that remains from this destruction is the focus on art as an *object* of art, rather than a representation of some object.[59] Moreover, the window frames were left shaking as a rocket and a French fighter jet ('Mirage') pass by.[60] Lira scrambles the time of the Wailing Wall by placing the rocket and mirage in the present tense and then the wall's shaking in the past. He includes the imagery of the Wailing Wall and of war not as a direct political statement, but to contrast war as destruction with poetry as a force of both destruction (particularly of a 'monumental' poetry) and creation.

Like the concrete poets' dismantlement and reformation of individual words, Lira's destruction and manipulation does not solely occur metaphorically and at the level of the image, but also at the level of the word. He 'robs' from another line of Huidobro's poem, changing 'Estamos en el ciclo de los nervios' to 'Estamos en el siglo de las neuras y las siglas/y las siglas' (ll. 12–13). Instead of being in a 'cycle of nerves', we are in a 'century of mania and maniacs', or, alternatively, a 'century of abbreviations'. Although he changes the meaning of the word 'ciclo', he retains the connection to the word phonetically ('ciclo' to 'siglo'). He also changes the word 'nervios' to 'neuras', retaining both some phonetic and semantic similarity. Here, just as the material of a word in a concrete poem informs its meaning, it is the phonetic connection of the words 'siglo,' 'sigla' and 'neuras' to those in Huidobro's poem that inform the meaning of the line. The addition of the word 'siglas' emphasises that the time that we are in is one of reduction; just as the Wailing Wall is the only sign that remains of the Holy Temple, what remains of a name is just the first letter. In other words, names have been stripped down of their full signifiers

57 Here, Lira's images of the Middle East bring to mind the Six-Day War in 1967 and the October War of 1973 (which, although its fighting mostly took place outside of Jerusalem, was just a month before Pinochet's coup).

58 A comparison could be made between Lira's windows and those of Martínez, as discussed in Chapter 2.

59 See José Ortega y Gasset, *La deshumanización del arte y otros ensayos estéticos*, 4th edn (Madrid: Revista de occidente, 1956), pp. 7–13. Moreover, whereas Parra's poet (as he describes in his 'Manifesto'), is a builder: 'El poeta es un hombre como todos/Un albañil que construye su muro/Un constructor de puertas y ventanas' (Parra, ll. 11–13), Lira's poet destroys everything that surrounds the frames that Parra's poet has built.

60 'Mirage' applies to a variety of types of fighter jets designed by the French company Dassault Aviation and have been used both by the Chilean and Israeli armed forces.

into signs of signs. Instead of being a simulacrum, this substitution allows one to see the destruction on the page itself; Lira allows the words to become materials that can face destruction.

Lira shares with the concrete poets a preoccupation with consumerism. What remains in this poem is not a memory or the remnants of a memory, as it is for Huidobro, and does not remain in our heads, but instead has monetary value and can easily be exchanged; what remains changes from a mental phenomenon to a commodity.[61] Huidobro claims: 'Estamos en el ciclo de los nervios./El músculo cuelga,/Como recuerdo, en los museos;/Mas no por eso tenemos menos fuerza:/El vigor verdadero/Reside en la cabeza' (Huidobro, ll. 8–13). Lira's poem, however, insinuates that this imagination today can be sold: 'El vigor verdadero reside en el bolsillo/es la chequera/El músculo se vende en paquetes por Correos' (Lira, ll. 15–17).[62] He criticises both poetry and societies that he believes value (or come to value) money, rather than the body and the mind.[63]

This monetarily valued poetry, for Lira, is in fact weak, like hanging muscle ('El músculo cuelga'). In Lira's poem, it is not the muscle that hangs, as it does in Huidobro's poem, but poetry itself: 'la ambición/no descansa la poesía /está/c/ol/g/an/do'. He mocks the calligramme or pattern poem (from which the concrete poets draw) by having the word 'colgando' 'hang' down the page from the previous line like a thread and therefore indicating that even experimental forms of poetry are unstable.[64] The ambition does not rest physically on the page as the word 'descansa' runs right into the following phrase without a break or punctuation mark. Like the unstable Wailing Wall, poetry is unstable on the page. However, it is a particular poetry that Lira discusses, the poetry of the institution: 'la poesía/está/c/ol/g/an/do/en la Dirección de Bibliotecas Archivos y Museos en Artí/culos de lujo, de primera necesidad' (ll. 19–26). Lira satirises poetry that is written to be placed in archives, in the institution of art that is accessible only to an elite few. In particular, by cutting the word 'Artículo' with a line break, he humorously compares these archives to 'arses of luxury'.[65] In other words, Lira suggests that, if poetry is to be hidden and kept safe (as a commodity) from destruction and is intended to be read only by a select few, its instability (hanging as if by a thread) will not form a space for potential creation.

Lira explains that poetry that allows itself to be unstable and yet accessible to the masses, far away from the 'culos de lujo', has the potential to stimulate the creation

61 Lira also seems to dissolve the romantic tradition's privileging of memory.

62 The capitalisation of 'Correos' implies that Lira is referring specifically to Correos Chile, thereby tying the poem directly to Lira's local context.

63 The concrete poets make similar criticisms by constructing poems as selling tools themselves, as advertisements (see Introduction).

64 This spacing is similar to that of pattern poems (see Introduction). It is also reminiscent of the spacing in Vicuña's quipu-like poems, and particularly her poem in *cloud-net* that begins 'Hanging by a thread' (see Chapter 4). Lira especially could be mocking Neruda's opening to *Estravagario*, which begins with a line that moves up and across the page: 'Para/subir/al/cielo/se/ne/ce/si/tan'. Neruda, *Estravagario* (Buenos Aires: Losada, 1958).

65 'Artículo de lujo' might also be a reworking of Parra's line in 'Manifiesto' that 'la poesía fue un objeto de lujo' (Parra, l. 6).

of something new. In the final three lines, he changes Huidobro's famous lines 'Por qué cantáis la rosa, ¡oh Poetas!/Hacedla florecer en el poema;' (Huidobro, ll. 14–15) to: 'oh, poetas! No cantéis/a las rosas, oh, dejadlas madurar y hacedlas/mermelada de mosqueta en el poema' (Lira, ll. 27–29). Using a similar register to that of Huidobro, Lira urges the poets to press the roses into rosehip marmalade instead of letting the roses grow in the poem.[66] Again, Lira implies that the writing of a poem should destroy overused tropes or clichés, but nonetheless has the potential to create something sweet, that is, something new and pleasant, out of a traditional, overused symbol of love. He also juxtaposes the Spanish register of *vosotros* that Huidobro also uses with a particularly local, Chilean food (mermelada de mosqueta), therefore bringing the text into his local reality.

By stealing and reforming Huidobro's poem, Lira contradicts exactly what Huidobro's poetry calls for; he does not create his own world out of nothing, but forms his poem through materials used before. Lira seeks a direct (albeit destructive) engagement with the material of (literary and social) reality. In Lira's implicit view, Huidobro's *creacionismo* removes itself completely from a given reality in order to become an object in and of itself, but, in doing so, loses its creative force within the reality of which it is no longer a part. Lira's demonstration, in contrast, uses materials from that reality. Indeed, to 'destroy' these materials — or at least their poetic manipulation — may be Lira's way of acknowledging a materiality in poetry that a poet like Huidobro does not wish to recognise. Similarly, the concrete poets, through their use of a variety of media and material from quotidian life (including from earlier texts), allow their objects to participate as objects of reality (rather than as separate things outside this world, as Huidobro attempts to create).

If 'Ars poétique' is an antipoem in that it *destroys* poetry that has been considered part of the canon (or the Spanish language canon, at least) and thus 'beyond' material reality, 'Ars poétique, deux' (Figure 3.4) is another anti-poem that dismantles even the works of the anti-poets themselves. In this poem, Lira expands upon the concretist concern for the destruction of a singular authority of the poet through the manipulation of the material of language. Through his collage of reworkings of texts by Lihn and Parra (and others), he articulates or emphasises the contradictions in his predecessors' particularly antipoetic works that have, surprisingly, fallen into the category of institutionalised or elitist art.[67] In other words, Lira suggests that the antipoets ultimately fall into the same traps of authority and capitalism that they claim they have attempted to dismantle in their antipoetry.

Through the poetic 'ejercisio' of *détournement* as a destabilising act (or even one of destruction), Lira in this poem emphasises the instability of the poet's existence in relation to writing, in particular the poet's control over poetry and over him/herself in order to advocate a political, yet non-authoritative, poetry. While the concrete poets attempt to rid the text of authorship completely, Lira, like Martínez, prefers

66 Here he addresses 'poets' and earlier uses first person plural, perhaps thereby including himself in the group of 'poets'. However, he dedicates the poem to 'la galería imaginaria', thus implying that these poets are imagined, or at least, that the readership of his poetry does not exist at the time of writing.

67 See Bürger, Theory of the Avant-Garde, above.

ARS POÉTIQUE, DEUX

Porque escribo estoy así Por
Qué escribí porque escribí 'es
Toy vivo', la poesía
Terminóo con-
        migo.
            huero V a c u o
        gastado e in-*nútil* ejer
Cisio: "el adjetivo mata, Matta...!"
Fri-*volidad* ociosa, tediosa y
Esporádica
        –hasta un cierto punto:

  sobrevivo a una muerte
  que podría vivirse. Ademáas,
la poesía
Me abandona a medio día;
                    cuando escriba,
no conduzca no
Corra: poesía hay en todas partes
Sólo para n o s o t r o s mueren
todas las cosas   el Sol:
            bajo   nada
Nuevo: decadentismo de tercera
Mano a mano hemos quedado
a o a a o   o   a o
              los poetas
                    e
son unos pequeñísimos reptiles:
ni alquimistas ni
            albañiles ni
andinistas: bajaron del monte
Olimpo, cayeron de la montaña
Rusa se sa-
caron la cresta paaalabaraa
en la noche ya nada.
  en la noche ya nada
        está en calma Poetry

34

Fig. 3.4. Lira, 'Ars poétique, deux' (Ibid., p. 34)
Courtesy of Elisa Lira.

May be Hazardous[1] to Your
Health
¡Oh, Poesfiah!
Il nostro
Ayuntamiento
k
a c a b a /
a a

[1] Can Seriously Damage (it
was determined *so* later than
the statement quoted *supra*)

35

to use the poem as an investigation into the role of poet as a singular authority. He begins 'Ars poétique, deux' by unravelling a line from a poem by Enrique Lihn titled 'Porque escribí'. He takes Lihn's final lines: 'Pero escribí y me muero por mi cuenta,/ porque escribí porque escribí estoy/vivo' (Lihn, ll. 85–87) and rewrites them. He both cuts Lihn's stanza up and moves it from the past to the present: 'Porque escribo estoy así Por/Qué escribí porque escribí "es/Toy vivo", la poesía/ Terminóo con-/migo' (Lira, ll. 1–3). He cuts the word 'estoy' with a line break, suggesting that this lyric 'I' has multiple selves in the present of the page (because he — and Lihn — choose 'estar' instead of 'ser'), one of the present (escribo) and one of the past (escribí). In addition, after it has moved from the present to the past, the present (in this sentence) has moved to direct speech: '"es/Toy vivo"' (ll. 2–3). The inclusion of the extra 'o' at the end of 'Terminóo' perhaps indicates the Chilean pronunciation (of enlongating words), which therefore brings Lira's poem to a particular Chilean present.

While the concrete poets describe their poems as 'alive' through their complete objectivity (see Chapter 1), Lira suggests that a poem can be 'alive' by objectively presenting subjectivity; for Lira, a subject can exist within a poem-as-object. Because the poet is alive ('es/Toy vivo'), in the present of the written words, he lives only as long as the poem (or poetry) continues: 'la poesía/Terminóo con-/migo' (ll. 3–5). While Lihn says he would die on his own account, Lira loses control of his death because he is only alive in the written language (which is desirable because the writing process gives him life). In other words, for Lihn, writing is a (perhaps *the*) cause of being alive. For Lira, writing itself is what is alive; it is inextricably part of himself and vice-versa. The authoritative poet creates a monumental *re*presentation of a subject, but a poet who keeps in check his authority, or questions as opposed to answers it, can create a poem that *presents* a subjectivity. In other words, such a poem is one that is 'vivo'. While the concrete poets attempt to create objects in and of themselves by attempting to remove the lyric subject entirely, Lira's (ideal) poet *presents* subjective objects; the subject *becomes* within the object. The enjambment that splits the word 'conmigo' on the one hand emphasises this inextricability of the author and the poem by highlighting the word 'with' at the end of the line and separating it from the first person subject, but, on the other hand, places more emphasis on 'migo' by putting it on its own line. Lira's relationship to the poem is therefore ambiguous. The misspelling with the extra 'o' on 'terminó' might imply that the poem or poetry has been dragged out, or has not quite finished; the word itself has been dragged out on the page. Moreover, the direct and then indirect quotations from Lihn make the subject ambiguous. Is the subject Lihn? Lira? Lira-as-poem? Through this ambiguity, Lira both takes away credibility away from Lihn, himself and the figure of the poet as authority in general.[68]

Lira adds to this ambiguity his own critique (through both his lexical and formal manipulation) of the value of poetic exercise as a practice in general. He begins the

68 In his satirical meta-poem, 'Sermón de los hombrecitos magentas', Lira criticises the poet who places himself and is placed on a pedestal, particularly his contemporary Raúl Zurita: 'el superpoeta zurita se pasea/con un cristo bizantino por las calles de santiago/con el habla...el superpoeta es objeto' (Lira, *Rodrigo Lira*, p. 140).

sentence with two synonyms for vacuous: 'huero V a c u o" (l. 6), materialising the meaning of the words with the repetition of the concept in different forms and the spaces he places between the letters of 'vacuo'; repetition can both emphasise and make automatic meaning (in this case Lira seems to attempt the latter), and the white space, as in many avant-garde and concrete poems, represents emptiness, or at least an absence.[69] Returning to and reworking Huidobro's words in his 'Arte poética', Lira then explains that this 'emptiness' is wasted in (what is implied as) the exercise of poetry, or at least of the use of descriptive words: 'gastado e in-nútil ejer/Cisio: "el adjetivo mata, Matta...!"' (ll. 7–8).[70] He omits a crucial phrase from Huidobro's line 'El adjetivo, cuando no da vida, mata' (Huidobro, l. 7). Adjectives, for Lira, are empty and useless, and do not give life, but rather only kill. This statement is ironically followed by three adjectives describing a noun: 'Fri-volidad ociosa, tediosa y/Esporádica' (ll. 9–10). However, he then modifies his statement, responding to the previous statements with the line: 'hasta un cierto punto:' (l. 11), which, again ironically, ends with two points (the colon) instead of one and is followed by a blank line or stanza break. The poetic exercise might be useless or dangerous, but for Lira, poetry that is useless and dangerous might in fact be valuable.

In 'Ars poétique, deux', the poetic exercise is unsafe (as the verb 'matar' suggests) for the poet himself. Through the personification of poetry and death, he oscillates between describing poetry as life and poetry as death. He begins by claiming that he has survived a death (perhaps through living in or as poetry) that could have lived: 'sobrevivo a una muerte/que podría vivirse' (ll. 12–13).[71] This nonsensical combination of subject and verb emphasises the ambiguity of where and how the poet is alive. He also anthropomorphises the poem by claiming that it abandons the subject: 'Ademáas,/la poesía/Me abandona a medio día;/cuando escriba,/ no conduzca no/Corra: poesía hay en todas partes' (ll. 13–18).[72] The subject explains that poetry has abandoned him and yet, by claiming that poetry exists in everything, he cannot escape it.

Lira emphasises this inescapability through his rearrangement of a phrase he manipulates throughout his work. He spatially organises the biblical phrase 'nothing new under the sun':

69 In concrete poetry, while white space may represent 'emptiness', it nonetheless gives essential meaning to the poem. The most explicit of these poems is Gomringer's 'Silencio'.

70 Similarly, Gertrude Stein finds adjectives useless, as she explains how adjectives and nouns are the least interesting words because they are stable, unlike verbs, adverbs or prepositions that allow for movement and mistakes. See Stein, 'Poetry and Grammar', *Lectures in America* (New York: Random House, 1935), pp. 211–12. The various misspellings also suggest the spoken word, which presents an interesting relationship between the writing exercise and poetry he is discussing and the colloquial, spoken language of his life. The misspelling of 'Matta' might also refer to the Chilean artist Roberto Matta, or to the nineteenth-century Chilean politician who founded the Partido Radical, Manuel Antonio Matta (or even the street named after him).

71 This seems to be a reference to Parra's 'Manifiesto', in Obra gruesa, pp. 211–14: 'No podemos vivir sin poesía' (l. 9).

72 The use of the word 'además', especially because of the emphasis through the misspelling (with the extra 'a' to exaggerate the word's meaning), could be taken from Parra's 'Manifiesto' in the line 'Además una cosa' (l. 20). The extra 'a' might also represent a Chilean pronunciation of the word (see above).

Sólo para n o s o t r o s mueren
todas las cosas   el Sol:
bajo nada
Nuevo: (ll. 19–22).

The 'we' is ambiguous, but could refer to poets. Even if there is poetry everywhere, everything new under the sun has died for them; in other words, it has all been done before. However, the way he spaces the phrase on the page indeed creates new paths of reading the well-known biblical line; because of the spatial arrangement of the words on the page, one can read it in many different ways, as one does with concrete poetry.[73]

Lira *verbivocovisually* reworks the following reference to Nicanor Parra's 'Manifiesto' to emphasise his criticism of Poetry (with a capital 'P'). He directly quotes from Parra's manifiesto: 'decadentismo de tercera Mano' (Lira, ll. 22–23, Parra l. 73), which he quickly *détourns* into a foreign form of the tango, that is, a line from the famous Argentinean tango 'Silencio' by Carlos Gardel: 'Mano a mano hemos quedado/a o a a o o a o' (Lira, ll. 23–24).[74] He distils the line even further into only the vowel sounds of the lyrics, perhaps as a way of distancing the song from himself aurally to emphasise its foreignness. He then takes Parra's criticism of poets and poetry even further by claiming that they are 'unos pequeñísimos reptiles:/ ni alquimistas ni/albañiles ni/andinistas: bajaron del monte/Olimpo, cayeron de la montaña/Rusa se sa-/caron la cresta paaaaalabraaa' (ll. 27–33). Implicitly, he formally and semantically disrupts the first three stanzas of Parra's 'Manifiesto':

Señoras y señores
Ésta es nuestra última palabra.
— Nuestra primera y última palabra —
Los poetas bajaron del Olimpo.

Para nuestros mayores
La poesía fue un objeto de lujo
Pero para nosotros
Es un artículo de primera necesidad:
No podemos vivir sin poesía.

A diferencia de nuestros mayores
Y esto lo digo con todo respeto
Nosotros sostenemos
Que el poeta no es un alquimista
El poeta es un hombre como todos
Un albañil que construye su muro:
Un constructor de puertas y ventanas. (Parra, ll. 1–13)

Lira rewrites Parra's 'Manifiesto' (and refers to Parra's poem 'La montaña rusa') into its extreme version with vulgar Chilean idioms and spatial liberties. In addition, with the use of 'pequeñísimo', as well as critiquing religious authority, Lira *détourns*

73 Lira, like Parra, was particularly critical of the authority of religious language.

74 Carlos Gardel, *Silencio*, <https://www.youtube.com/watch?v=rO3ytWP9i78> [accessed 10 July 2017].

Huidobro's 'pequeño Dios' as the ultimate authoritative poet through Parra's allusion to Huidobro; the poet, for Lira, is no longer Huidobro's little god, and he is even less significant than Parra's attributions — the poet is but a mere tiny reptile. Because the poet does not practice any of the professions Lira (and Parra) list (and the list implies all other professional identities), s/he cannot successfully assume their voices. Moreover, Lira degrades the written word itself, elongating the word 'palabra' as though it were spoken slowly (or sung in a tango or screamed from a roller coaster), as the concrete poets might do to create a *verbivocovisual* poem. Through this allusion to Huidobro through Parra's reworking of the 'pequeño dios', Lira further separates the 'authority' of the poet's words from the poet himself.

The biblical phrase 'nothing new' seems to include not only what there is 'under the sun', but also what is 'under the moon', with the repetition of Gardel's line 'en la noche ya nada' from the song 'Silencio' (1932). Unlike the Cuban poet José Martí's famous night, in which there is space for creativity and poetry, for Lira neither the sun nor the moon allows for such poetry.[75] There is no longer a place for the traditional poet of inspiration. Moreover, the poetry of the night is no longer provocative but calm: 'está en calma Poetry' (l. 36).[76] Calm poetry, however, seems to contradict what Lira calls for, which is to say, a poetry that destroys and moves.

This Poetry with a capital 'P' that the authoritative author controls may be 'calm', as Lira says, but, as he implies in his *détournement*, like the tools of advertising, it is manipulative. In other words, the authoritative poetry he criticises is masked as part of the market economy. He juxtaposes the calm he refers to with what resembles a familiar health warning of the dangers of tobacco products: 'May be Hazardous to your/Health' (ll. 41–42). Just as the concrete poets use advertising techniques in order to criticise advertising itself (the most obvious example being Pignatari's 'Beba Coca Cola', Figure 1.9), Lira steals an advertisement in order to criticise it as well as to criticise a poetry of 'calm' as being manipulative and 'calming' like an advertisement. Although poetry may calm one down in the present (just as a cigarette might), in the long run, it will likely be harmful. Lira's allusion to this warning emphasises how the tobacco companies skew words in their (publicly-mandated) warnings (i.e. 'may' instead of 'will'), or at least used the warnings, in order to sell more.[77] The use of the phrase (as well as the word 'Poetry' in the line above) in English suggests not only the dominance of English-language poetry and literature, but also its identification with the market economy.[78] It is the capitalist, consumerist society (which the English-speaking world and English word dominate and control) in which noxious products are sold solely for a profit that is truly

75 See José Martí, 'Dos patrias', *Obras completas*.

76 Lira switches to English, perhaps emphasising the imperialistic prominence English poetry has within the institution, forming the majority of the world canon.

77 See, for example, the 1973 memorandum about the advertising for the youth market: *Research Planning Memorandum on Some Thoughts about New Brands of Cigarettes for the Youth Market* (Minnesota Documents, 1973), <https://www.industrydocumentslibrary.ucsf.edu/tobacco/docs/#id=gmnx0096> [accessed 1 February 2018].

78 For example, the 'Chicago Boys' (an English term used in Chile) from the United States of America with their neo-liberal ideology provided the theory on which Chile's economic and social structure, beginning under the dictatorship, was tested.

harmful and seemingly unredeemable, as Lira suggests in the final lines of the poem. He includes an apostrophe to poetry and equates it to the municipality before he claims it ends (as the poem ends, including the dissolving of the word 'acabar' itself: '¡Oh, Poesíah!/Il nostro/Ayuntamiento/k/ acaba /a a' (ll. 43–48). 'Poetry' that does not itself take issue or in fact may be complicit with the market economy will end up eliminating all poetry. Because the market economy is so pervasive, moreover, in order to transcend it, one has to *destroy* it. If it is controlled by neoliberal values, however, poetry, according to Lira, will end in only destruction without creation.

Just as a forest burns in order to regenerate itself from the ashes, he transforms the ashes of previous texts into new poetry. He does not completely detach himself from the works of his predecessors, but repurposes their materials both to criticise their faults and to work them into new objects of the world. However, both 'Ars poétique' and 'Ars poétique, deux' warn that, in an Adornian sense, if poetry turns into products to be sold and consumed, one will no longer be able to create from its destruction.[79] He implies that the works of his predecessors ultimately lend themselves to this commodification.[80] Instead, Lira's work suggests that one has to treat the poem not as an object of consumption that will lose its value once it has been consumed or used, but as one that has the potential to be reformed into something of lasting value. In the following section, I will consider ways in which the principles expressed in the *artes poeticae* of destruction and (re)creation reveal themselves and are developed in other poems by Lira.

Détournement with Non-Literary Materials

Not only does Lira 'steal' materials from other poetic texts in his *détournement*, he also uses materials from, allusions to and structures found in quotidian life in Chile. Just as the concrete poets did, and as I illustrated in the discussion of 'Ars poétique, deux', Lira brings consumerism's advertising techniques and forms into his work. However, instead of commenting on society in general as the concretists do, he criticises his own society under Pinochet's dictatorship. Unlike Martínez's book that addresses his local context subtly through general allusions to the nation and Vicuña's utopian poems (which we will see in the following chapter), Lira's work directly engages with Chilean society through the quotidian material and forms he both includes and reworks. By creating objects drawn from daily life, not as an attempt to imitate but to become part of reality (that is, to become objects in and of themselves), he articulates a general criticism of consumerism and society under Pinochet. In the following two examples, he manipulates the structure of weather broadcasting and the techniques of advertising to form poetic objects.

79 See, for example, 'On the Fetish-Character in Music and the Regression of Listening', in which Adorno argues that music (and other art forms) cannot escape its superficiality because of the way it has been advertised and designed for mass consumption. Adorno, 'On the Fetish-Character in Music and the Regression of Listening', in *Essays on Music*, ed. by Richard Leppert (Berkeley: University of California Press, 2002), pp. 288–318.

80 One could argue that concrete poems also have been commodified.

POEMAS ECOLÓGICOS

WEATHER REPORT[1]

–ecológicos I–

ad memoriam
Willy Duarte

"(...) sanísima, de mucho contento, tiene quatro meses de Invierno no más, que en ellos, si no es quando hace quarto la Luna, que llueve un día o dos, todos los demás hacen tan lindos Soles (...)"

Pedro de Valdivia al Rey don Carlos I

En el transcurso deste mes de junio
con la excepción de un nublado y una lluviecita
para la luna nueva, el primer día del invierno,
el tan mentado *smog* ha resultado ser casi puro
smoke
humo casi puro en tanto que sin *fog*
(neblina).

Pero al ir la luna entrando en creciente
apareció una gasa blanquecina de humedad
la tal gasa se puso gris
desde un comienzo
de modo que la Muy Noble Ciudad de Santiago
tuvo al fin
un *smog* propiamente tal ensartado en sus edificios.

[1] "informe del tiempo", en español. Nombre de un conjunto de *jazz-rock* (Wayne Shorter, saxo; Joe Zawinul, teclados; Miroslav Vitous, contrabajo; Alphonse Musson, batería; Airto Moreira, percusión).

36

FIG. 3.5. Lira, 'Weather Report'. Courtesy of Elisa Lira.

Mi vecino el Sr. Rojas, Administrador de los colectivos estos donde vivo
–quema lo del incinerador[2] todas las mañanas a las cinco a eme–:
"*chimeneas más altas...*"
la mayoría de la gente entrevistada por *El Mercurio*
(pequeños burócratas comerciantes, dueñas de casa, jubilados, un "ren
tista"): "*que actúe la Municipalidad*".
El doctor Grau, ecólogo (y piedras semipreciosas y boquillas *tar-gard*)
"*...crear Ministerio del Ambiente*".
Rolf Behncke Concha, de Odeplan:
Multas. "*El que contamine, que pague*".
El Arzobispo de Santiago: "*Oración...*"
NEM-D: "¡Acción Directa!"

El Fablante Lírico (un servidor):
–alcohol de azúcar de remolacha en todos los servicentros[3]
–chimeneas industriales con mangueras conectadas a cámaras de vacío
(para invertir el tiraje)[4]
–aviones cisternas lavando avenidas de 6 a 7 y de 10 a 11 todas las ma-
ñanas
(el ruido que meterían los tales aviones
me parece preferible al que mete
el pito del lechero a las 7, a las 9, a las once y media
los solos de batería de los vendedores de gas licuado
y los pregones de los compro ropa-zapato que contaminan,
con su infernal barullo,
el espacio
de mi pieza.

---

[2] la *basura*. Los incineradores –que no debieran usarse como tales, según explícitas órdenes del Ministerio de Salud– están en unos sótanos en los que podrían funcionar, sin grandes inversiones, miniplantas de recuperación –o simple clasificación– de *basuras* (metal, papel, restos orgánicos biodegradables y plásticos) que actualmente –lo que sobrevive a esas quemazones matutinas, se entiende– se traslada, a bordo de unos camiones amarillos que echan humo como contratados, a unos botaderos amarillos do se cubre –según entiendo– de tierra.

[3] IANSA –Industria Azucarera Nacional– ha acumulado, desde 1976, deudas a razón de 20 a 30 millones de dólares al año, teniendo a comienzos de este año una deuda de arrastre de 80 millones de dólares. Para este año, se esperan cifras de sólo veinte mil hás. –algo más de 500 mil tons.– de remolacha, lo que significa 120 mil tons. de azúcar, dentro de un consumo nacional total de 380 mil tons.

Agréguese a esto la escasa calidad nutritiva del azúcar industrial, que aporta cals. sin los desechos necesarios para el funcionamiento intestinal, ni nutrientes, y que posiblemente provoca hábito por sus efectos sobre el S. N. C., además del bien estudiado asuntillo de las caries.

Por otra parte, el Sr. Presidente de los EE.UU. del Brasil demostró-comprobó personalmente la factibilidad de la propulsión de un automóvil con alcohol como reemplazante total de la bencina. Esta sustancia, que se puede elaborar en forma asaz sencilla a partir del azúcar industrial, no es contaminante ni siquiera en motores de dos tiempos.

[4] el hollín resultante puede ser utilizado en materiales de construcción.

37

Extending the concretist exploitation of the structures of consumerism to present new, yet critical, texts, in 'Poemas ecológicos' (Figure 3.5), Lira frames his work within the structure of Chilean broadcasting. With the insertion of quotidian and historical Chilean references that highlight the relationships between people, and between people and the environment, he subtly reveals his criticism of the Chilean dictatorship. While in his *artes poeticae* he reworks other poetic or literary material, in 'Poemas ecológicos' he combines historical, literary and quotidian material and forms for his *détournement*. In particular, he appropriates the language, structure and themes used in daily weather reports. As we will see, however, his report describes a capitalism-induced 'weather', that is, a natural atmosphere infused with pollution caused by capitalism.

A weather report, a form of news broadcasting, claims to distribute neutral information to mass audiences. However, a footnote explains that it will not be an ordinary weather report; that it will not be unbiased.[81] He begins with a subtitle 'WEATHER REPORT/-ecológicos I' followed by a dedication and an epigraph, all on the right-hand margin. Just as a television broadcast might have credits or sponsor acknowledgements at the beginning of the show, he uses the entire page to frame and organise his weather report. He also provides a footnote that explains why he has chosen to title the poem in English: '"informe del tiempo", en español. Nombre de un conjunto de jazz-rock (Wayne Shorter, saxo; Joe Zawinul, teclados; Miroslav Vitous, contrabajo; Alphonse Musson, batería; Airto Moreira, percusión)'. By referencing an American jazz-fusion band of the 1970s and 1980s, he points out that this 'weather report' might actually be musical, poetic, or perhaps a fusion of different genres, as well as a fusion and/or juxtaposition of languages and cultures. This explanatory footnote allows the poem to engage with a familiar form of reality without falling into mimesis; by implying that his weather report is not typical, Lira evokes the familiar without claiming the authoritative stance of a conventional report. These paratexts he uses add to the dismantlement of the conventional poetic form into something more prosaic. In addition, they break down the sole authorial voice of the speaker of the poem by layering reflective voices.

Lira narrows down this familiarity to ensure Chilean-audience recognition of his references. He dedicates the poem to 'Willie Duarte [*sic*]',[82] referring to the famous Chilean weather reporter who presented on the Chilean broadcasting network TVTiempo from 1970 to 1979, followed by an epigraph from a letter written by Pedro de Valdivia to the emperor Carlos V from the colonisation of Chile in the sixteenth century: 'sanísima, de mucho contento, tiene quatro meses de Invierno no más, que en ellos, si no es quando hace quarto la Luna, que llueve un día o dos, todos los demás hacen tan lindos Soles'.[83] Because what Valdivia claims about

81 Lira's use of footnotes plays this role throughout his poetry.

82 There are a lot of instances in which Lira misspells (here he misspells Willy Duarte's name). It is difficult to tell if many of these are intentional misspellings or if they indicate a lack of precise editing (which is possible considering the history of his publication).

83 Valdivia wrote this letter on 4 September 1545 describing the newly conquered land that is now Santiago. See Pedro de Valdivia, *Carta al Emperador Carlos V. 4 de septiembre de 1545* (Universidad de Chile) <http://www.historia.uchile.cl/CDA/fh_article/0,1389,SCID%253D11303%2526ISID%253D

the weather in Santiago is clearly false, it can be seen as a form of propaganda to promote Chilean exploration/exploitation. The inclusion of both a contemporary figure and this quote, supposedly one of the first 'weather reports' of Chile's colonial existence brings together Chile's past and present into the present of the poem. By comparing the past colonisation and present nation through descriptions of weather, a temporarily changeable yet overarching constant throughout most of human history, Lira subtly points to a repeating pattern of exploitation and propaganda from the start of the region's nationhood. The use of the form and content of a weather report also allows him to set the stage for this comparison without explicitly criticising Chilean politics.

The verse poem begins with a description of the weather of the first month of winter in Santiago that is in the form of a deconstructed sonnet: there are fourteen lines on the first page, many lines of which contain eleven syllables. Lira organises his description by the phases of the moon, connecting his poem to the epigraph: 'con la excepción de un nublado y una lluviecita/para la luna nueva...Pero al ir la luna entrando en creciente' (ll. 2–8). In the first stanza, he describes the smoke and smog that covers the city: 'con la excepción de un nublado y una lluviecita/ para la luna nueva, el primer día del invierno,/el tan mentado *smog* ha resultado ser casi puro/*smoke*/humo casi puro en tanto que sin *fog*/(neblina)' (ll. 2–7). In this description, the material, or language, is particularly a Chilean one. For example, he uses the diminutive ('lluviecita'), a typical characteristic of Chilean Spanish. Peppering the largely Chilean Spanish text with three English words, he describes the weather at the beginning of winter: 'smog', 'smoke', and 'fog'. Through partial translation, he suggests that this 'smog' is not exactly smog, but closer to smoke: 'el tan mentado *smog* ha resultado ser casi puro/*smoke*/humos casi puro en tanto que sin *fog*/(neblina)' (ll. 4–7). The clouds over Santiago are not naturally created and do not result from the water cycle, but are produced by man, probably from burning fuel or waste; the weather of his Santiago is not an environmental phenomenon unaffected by man; it is in fact created by him. Lira also plays on the word 'puro', claiming that this man made, unnatural smog on top of the city is somehow 'pure' (a word typically used with 'natural' and 'clean' when referring to the weather) or is like a 'cigar', a product that burns and contaminates.

Lira connects this 'pure' smog to nobility, emphasising that the ecology of Santiago is created and controlled only by a select few. In the following stanza, Lira's sarcastic mention of the 'Muy Noble Ciudad de Santiago' in its formal register hints at a criticism of the political and cultural situation of the time, while also referring back to colonial Chile. Again, he blends together the past and present: 'desde un comienzo/de modo que la Muy Noble Ciudad de Santiago/tuvo al fin/ un smog propiamente tal ensartado en sus edificios' (ll. 11–13). In the course of its development, beginning with the time when the Spanish first made contact with Chile, the city created its own (literal and metaphorical) smog.

When Lira zooms in from an aerial view of Santiago to a specific neighbourhood in his illustration of the city, he, like the people he describes who subvert authority

405%2526PRT%253D11300%2526JNID%253D12,00.html> [accessed 30 June 2017].

under the radar, masks his form of resistance within his weather report.[84] Moving from the poetically 'authoritative' and disinterested viewpoint to a participatory one, this poem dramatises the very critique of authority that Lira practices. The subject of the poem enters in the following stanza with an introduction to his neighbour: 'Mi vecino el Sr. Rojas, Administrador de los colectivos estos donde vivo' (l. 14).[85] The inclusion of the lyric 'I' places Lira within the social context on which he comments. In the following line, he indicates that in his neighbourhood, and in these collectives, subversive activity is occurring: 'quema lo del incinerador todas las mañanas a las cinco a eme' (l. 15).[86] Moreover, one cannot ignore the connotations of the Holocaust (and other massacres) carried by the word 'incinerador'.[87] However, the occupants of the building do not use the incinerator as one might expect: as the footnote attached to the word 'incinerador' explains, the ministry of health has explicitly prohibited the use of the incinerator as they are using it: '*La basura*. Los incineradores — que no debieran usarse como tales, según explícitas órdenes del Ministerio de Salud — están en unos sótanos en los que podrían funcionar' (Footnote 2). The combination of the line and the footnote imply that the collectives of artists are engaging politically through the subversion of quotidian rules placed on them by the government. The fact that further explanation is hidden in a descriptive footnote, about trash, moreover, physically emphasises the need to carry out acts of civil disobedience *incognito* under the dictatorship; just as the trash is being burned in the basement, Lira's description of the act is in a footnote.

A plethora of references both masks and supports his resistance to the regime. He lists quotes from scientists concerned with ecology and the environment interviewed in the conservative newspaper *El Mercurio*, referring to the archbishop of Chile, Dr. Juan Grau (1917–2009, known as the father of ecology in Chile), and Rolf Behcke,[88] one of Pinochet's advisors on population and family protection issues: 'La mayoría de la gente entrevistada por El Mercurio [...] El doctor Grau, ecólogo (y piedras semipreciosas y boquillas *tar-gard*)/ "...crear Ministerio del Ambiente"/ Rolf Behncke Concha, de Odeplan:/Multas. "El que contamine, que pague"/El Arzobispo de Santiago: "Oración..."/NEM-D. "¡Acción Directa!"' (ll.17–25, ellipsis

84 It does not seem likely that his motivation for this 'masking' of his resistance was out of worry for the consequences because of his explicit, biting criticisms of his contemporaries throughout his work; however, it might be an implicit criticism of overt political engagement in poetry.

85 He perhaps refers to the prominent Chilean poet Gonzalo Rojas, who brought together avant-garde poets and artists in Santiago. Lira directly refers to him in other poems, such as 'doQ.mentos del/antayer Q.atro/gatos.s.'

86 By writing out 'a.'m' phonetically, he emphasises the spoken word over the written. He uses this technique throughout his works, such as in 'Epiglama oliengtaleh', in which he writes out a specific accent. In contrast, in other poems, such as 'doQ.mentos del/antayer Q.atro/gatos./s.', he replaces certain phonemes with a sole letter that contains the same sound (as seen in the title). In all cases, it is the sound of the words that he privileges.

87 The word 'incinerador' also brings to mind the burning of books that occurred on 23 September 1973 in Chile. As in the Holocaust, while there were public book burnings, many books were burned in the privacy of the home, apparently out of fear.

88 See Carmen G. Sepúlveda Zelaya, *The Legal and Political Battles over the Distribution of Emergency Contraception in Chile Under the Presidencies of Ricardo Lagos (2000–2005) and Michelle Bachelet (2006–2010)* (unpublished PhD thesis, University College London, 2014), p. 121.

in original). Alluding to these figures of authority under the dictatorship, Lira at first glance creates an atmosphere of control through the quotation of commands given to the people. However, because the quotes are material taken from other resources and inserted into the poem, Lira in a sense reappropriates these commands, again mocking their initial force.

Lira questions the authority of the one who brings together these commands, the poet. He equates the speaker of these commands to the lyric subject and then to one who supposedly serves the state and the corporations that support the state:

> El Fablante Lírico (un servidor)
> -alcohol de azúcar de remolacha en todos los servicentros(3)
> -chimeneas industrials con mangueras conectadas a cámaras de vacío (para invertir el tiraje)(4)
> -aviones cisternas lavando avenidas de 6 a 7 y de 10 a 11 todas las mañanas (ll.26–30).[89]

He connects the lyric speaker to the following list with the prefix 'servi-'. While in the previous stanza the quotes from the newspapers indicate that the state is preoccupied with the environment, in this stanza he lists industrial projects that are in fact corrupt or derelict financially, environmentally and nutritionally. For example, the footnote explains that IANSA, the national sugar industry, has produced and promoted a food that has no nutritional value and that is potentially harmful:

> Agréguese a esto la escasa calidad nutritiva del azúcar industrial, que aporta cals. sin los desechos necesarios para el funcionamiento intestinal, ni nutrientes, y que posiblemente provoca hábito por sus efectos sobre el S.N.C., además del bien estudiado asuntillo de las caries.

He therefore implies that the lyric, disinterested 'I' is a servant of this capitalist corruption.

This poem reveals vividly how Lira's discussion and inclusion of the lyric subject helps explain the distinctive kind of (non)authority he advocates in contrast to the concretist goal of complete authorial eradication. Although he includes a lyric subject in this poem, Lira refuses to place himself in a position of supposedly disinterested authority, but rather places himself in one of proximate observation. While the lyric 'I' previously appears in the poem, it is only in a parenthetical aside at the end in which he comments on his personal experience of his surroundings. His personal experience is expressed as a preference towards different sounds, that is, the fusion of music that he mentions in the footnote at the beginning of the poem (ll. 31–38). His description of these daily noises as musical performances, such as 'el pito' and 'los solos de batería', is followed by his explanation of them as contaminating the space of his room. For Lira, it is not only the smog that contaminates but also the noise that commerce creates on a daily basis. In other words, the 'music' of poetry can become unbearable, incoherent noise that contaminates both aurally and

89 He often misspells words beginning with 'h', changing it to the medieval spelling with 'f' instead of 'h', perhaps as a way to emphasise that the literature he *détourns* can be traced back through the history of the Spanish language.

visually on the page, or more specifically, within the subjective 'stanza' (or room): 'el espacio/de mi pieza' (ll. 37–38).

The language used to describe this space is not only musical, but is also particularly Southern Cone Spanish: by using the word 'pieza' for 'room', he indicates that both his personal space as well as the space of his society is from the southern part of the continent. While he draws parallels between his room and all of Santiago, because his 'lyrical' discussion is within parentheses, he manages to connect his experience with that of the Santiago collective while at the same time acknowledging his individual experience. In other words, he does not distinguish between his private, idiosyncratic experience and that of his fellow Chileans. In this poem, Lira, through the 'used' form of a weather report, dismantles the singular lyric 'I' at the same time that he expresses his own experiences.

Lira highlights the heteroglossal and dialogic nature of poetry through his *détournement* of used advertisements and trademarks in the poem 'Nil Novi' (Figure 3.6).[90] In this poem, Lira demonstrates what can be considered one of his principles of poetry by reworking the phrase 'Nothing new under the sun'; that is, creating something from already used materials. Just as in concrete poetry where the reader has to make his/her own path out of the words, Lira (and his reader) make new connections with used words.

The poem, which is a page long (in the online version) and forms a pattern poem that is vaguely in the shape of a bottle of the oil treatment 'STP', concerns both the use of material within poetry as well as the nature of the material of advertising. Instead of attempting to give voice to the oppressed, Lira, following a primary strategy of concrete poetry, writes with the language and structures of the oppressors to dismantle it from within. While in the previous poem he frames his critique with the structure of a weather report, in this poem, Lira takes material and techniques of advertising to structure his criticism, just as, for example, Pignatari does in 'Life' or 'Beba Coca Cola' (Figure 1.9). In order to express his distrust of capitalism and consumerism, he structures the poem with the form of and references to the product STP, its uses and its representation as material from his reality. Moreover, it is through his illustration of poetry as something that consists of 'recycled' material that Lira expresses that distrust.

Lira begins the poem by demonstrating the general principle upon which his poetry works, that is, by *détournement*. In the first lines, he manipulates a common phrase, specifically a phrase from a text of authority, into something original. In the version that appears in the Ediciones Universidad Diego Portales publication, Lira begins by repeating the phrase 'Nada Nuevo' (ll. 1–4) twice, with one word on each line.[91] He completes the common biblical phrase on the next line with 'Bajo el Sol' (l. 3).[92] In other words, he takes the common phrase (which he refers to in

90 See Mikhail Bakhtin, *The Dialogic Imagination: Four Essays* (Austin: University of Texas Press, 1981).

91 In the *Memoria Chilena* version he only states the phrase once. The repetition of the line, just like the repetition in any concrete poems, reminds one of the repetitive process and creation of the product in a factory line.

92 The phrase comes from the Book of Ecclesiastes, in which Solomon expresses the limitations of human beings within the vast order of the world that we cannot fully know: 'What has been will

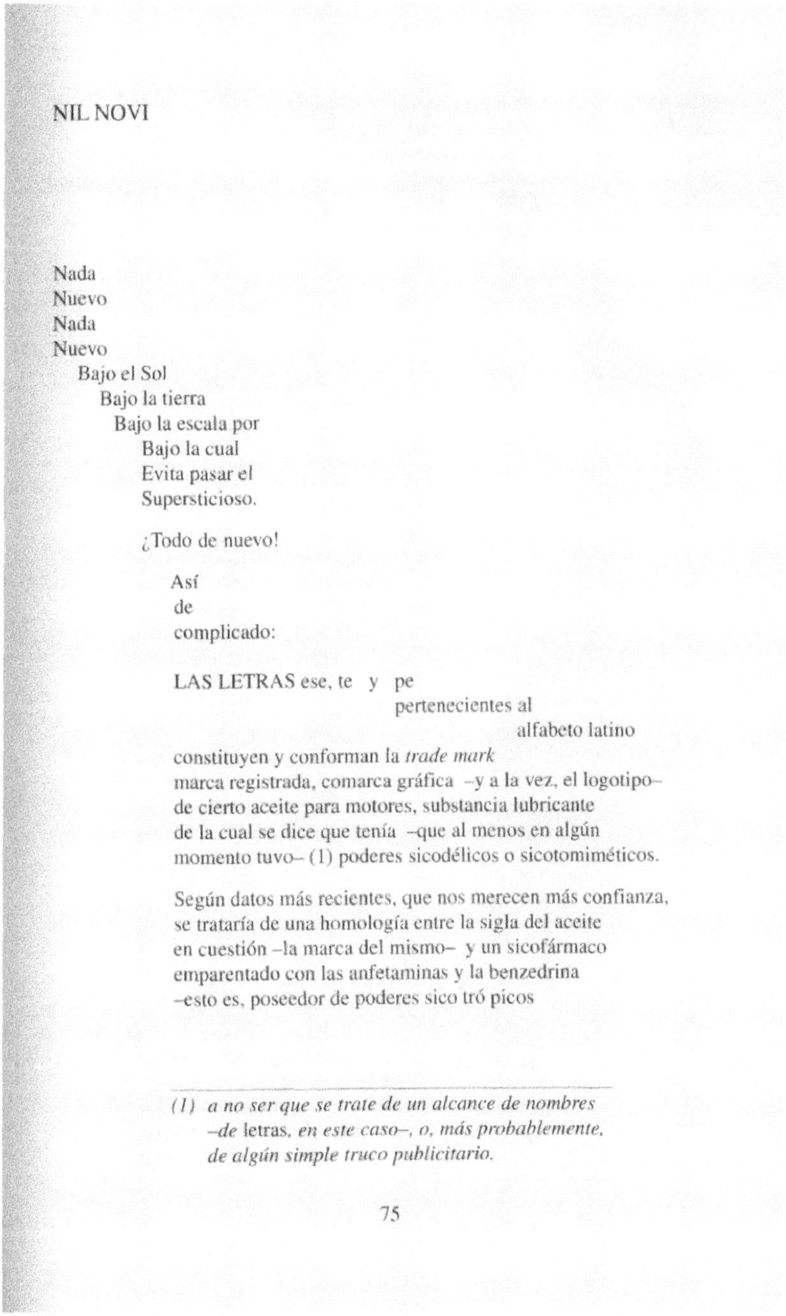

NIL NOVI

Nada
Nuevo
Nada
Nuevo
  Bajo el Sol
    Bajo la tierra
      Bajo la escala por
        Bajo la cual
        Evita pasar el
        Supersticioso.

¿Todo de nuevo!

Así
de
complicado:

LAS LETRAS ese, te y pe
pertenecientes al
alfabeto latino
constituyen y conforman la *trade mark*
marca registrada, comarca gráfica –y a la vez, el logotipo–
de cierto aceite para motores, substancia lubricante
de la cual se dice que tenía –que al menos en algún
momento tuvo– (1) poderes sicodélicos o sicotomiméticos.

Según datos más recientes, que nos merecen más confianza,
se trataría de una homología entre la sigla del aceite
en cuestión –la marca del mismo– y un sicofármaco
emparentado con las anfetaminas y la benzedrina
–esto es, poseedor de poderes sico tró picos

(1) a no ser que se trate de un alcance de nombres
–de letras*, en este caso–, o, más probablemente,*
de algún simple truco publicitario.

75

Fig. 3.6. Lira, 'Nil Novi' (ibid., p. 75).
Courtesy of Elisa Lira.

(El establecer la relación entre lo anterior y el ejercicio
escrito, especulación, experimento técnico, juego,
simiento texto plegaria súplica, temblor pánico.
soledad tétrica, poema y/o payasada
que se copia a continuación
queda a cargo de la sagacidad del lector.)

'Ars Poétique, deux') about the absence of newness to emphasise that his source also is not new.[93] He even recycles words that are his own through his repetition (in this case, from the words in the first two lines).[94] Nonetheless, Lira manages to create something new out of the common phrase. The phrase spins out physically on the page, its noun changing on each line from 'el Sol' to 'la tierra' to 'la escala' to 'la cual': 'Bajo el Sol/Bajo la tierra/Bajo la escala por/Bajo la cual' (ll. 3–6). The left margin of each line is indented as though the lines were spiralling into new words and, eventually, into a new clause: 'Evita pasar el/ Supersticioso' (ll. 7–8). The change of words and meaning not only occurs semantically, but also spatially; the lines act as steps of a ladder ('escala') for the reader to walk down to arrive at the new clause. In the new clause, Lira claims that the 'superstitious one' avoids passing beneath the ladder in order to avoid (the supposed) bad luck. At the same time that he emphasises that nothing can be created out of nothing, he insinuates that something might be created outside of the space under the sun, or at least under the stairs.

The dismantling of the phrase also occurs physically on the page (and, in this case, what is physically under the word 'escala', or ladder) and through a focus of the material of the signifier, rather than through the signified. Just as the concrete poets use the spatial arrangement on the page to convey meaning, Lira allows the material of the signifiers on the page to defamiliarise the biblical phrase to make it new. In the following line, for example, Lira repeats the word 'new' yet again, but in the phrase for 'again' ('de nuevo'), he plays on the multiple connotations of the phrase (or at least the phrase's individual words), while repeating a word that is not new to this page; everything is at the same time new but repeated again (thus not new, but *re*newed).[95] In this situation, repetition itself makes new. Although he argues throughout his work that 'newness' comes from the rearrangement of previously used material, he still allows for the possible thought of potential creation *ex nihilo* outside of our current framework. While strongly implying that one can only

be again, what has been done will be done again; there is nothing new under the sun' (Ecclesiastes 1:9).

93 By reworking this phrase in two different poems (that is, rewriting his own work), he adds another layer to his *détournement*. However, it is unclear which poem was written first.

94 In the draft version published by *Memoria Chilena*, Lira directly refers to Juan Luis Martínez and *La nueva novela*, on a page of what seem to be footnotes, by copying and pasting Martínez's cover page and collaging his poem 'Tareas de poesía' (see Chapter 2). In the published version, this page (without the collage) is included as 'Nil novi sub sole (4)', on which, in a list of epigraphs and footnotes, he references Martínez directly: '(3) à propos de La Nueva Novela, libro de Juan Luis o/y/ Juan de Dios Martínez, Ediciones Archivo, Santiago, 1977, en el artículo Dichas y Desdichas de la Poesía. El Mercu-/rio de Santiago, domingo 4 de junio de 1978/(S. del C.)' (p. 79). ('S. del C.' stands for 'subrayado del compilador', which Lira slowly abbreviates as he moves through the page from: 'subrayado del compilador' to 'subrayado del C.' to 'S. del C.'). By cutting out Martínez's work and pasting it onto a page about 'nothing new under the sun', Lira shows his allegiance to Martínez by playing with Martínez's title of the 'new novel' and appropriates the title page and a poem within the book by making a collage with his words and Martínez's pages. It is this new combination of works that makes this list of epigraphs and images into something 'original'.

95 The reworking of used material is reminiscent Vicuña's 'precarios' and 'palabrarmas' (see Chapter 4).

rearrange the already given, he maintains that there is always a slight possibility that he is wrong.

Lira emphasises the contradiction of reformation as something original with his use of punctuation in the phrase: '¿Todo de nuevo!' (l. 9). The phrase opens as a question, but instead of finishing the question, it concludes as an exclamation. In addition, while it is still a form of a line and a period, it has now straightened into something different and has been rotated 180 degrees; even the punctuation can be 'reworked' in the process of a line. For Lira, the biblical phrase over time has become conventional and its authoritative promoters use it in support of the status quo; to disrupt its form implies the possibility of authorial change.[96]

For Lira, the process of (re)creation is 'complicated': 'Así/de/complicado:' (ll. 10–12). In the etymological sense of the word 'complicado', writing anew, for Lira, is a process of 'folding together', a physical process of intertwining different materials. The materials used in this instance are distinctly combined letters. In the *Memoria Chilena* version of the poem, this statement is followed by four 's's, four 't's, and six 'p's, with one of each letter capitalised. Lira places the letters somewhat randomly (it does not form any immediately obvious image, although each letter forms more or less a diagonal line. In a way, it looks as though the capital letters are growing out of the repetition of the lower case letters. The letters are followed by the statement: 'LAS LETRAS ese, te y pe/pertenecientes al/alfabeto latino' (ll. 13–15). Here, Lira writes out the pronunciation of the three letters, claiming that they are those letters and that they are part of the Latin alphabet. However, while the letters about the statement are letters and are letters of the Latin alphabet, the phonetically written 'letters' are words, and thus consist of actual letters; the graphemes are realised differently as phonemes.[97] He therefore emphasises the physical signs of the letters on the page in order to illustrate their power as signs rather than referents (that is, the thing itself).

These letters, STP, are not any letters, but have powerful resonance in contemporary capitalist society and their association with the power of advertising. STP is the trademark for an oil lubricant that was a product from the United States first introduced in the 1950s. Lira explains what these letters of the Latin alphabet, when placed together, create: 'LAS LETRAS [...] constituyen y conforman la *trade mark* ––a la vez/el logotipo — marca registrada, comarca gráfica/de cierto aceite para motores' (ll. 16–18). Through his explanation, the letters move from just neutral letters to signifying a product (a particular brand 'STP' that stands for 'Scientifically Treated Petroleum'). He then describes its properties: 'substancia lubricante/de la cual se dice que tenía ––que al menos en algún/momento tuvo–– poderes sicodélicos o sicotomiméticos' (ll. 18–20).

Lira also depicts the referent, the oil, as something that in the past had been said to possess psychotomimetic actions to emphasise its mimetic abilities. Lira puns on the

96 However, if one is not careful, the change might solely be a transfer of authority to the author, rather than a change in the singular form of the authority itself. Lira, as we saw in the previous section, implies that the antipoets have fallen into this trap.

97 The repetition of the syllables 'pe' and 'al' sound as though this phrase is being stuttered, which stresses the oral aspects of the phrase.

acronym for the synthetic drug STP (Serenity, Tranquility and Peace, often referred to as DOM), the street name for '2, 5-Dimethoxy-4-methylamphetamine', a drug that has psychedelic and psychotomimetic powers.[98] This product copies in order to present it in a new light. If consumed, and with Lira's schizophrenia in mind, it imitates the symptoms of a psychosis, a distorted version of subjectivity. This equation brings into question the nature of poetry as an imitation or *re*presentation of subjectivity. But here, the 'subject' is not a person, but seems to be the product and its sign, or acronym, STP. The repetition and appropriation of the first lines are reflected in the nature of the product (for example, '*s*ico*t*ro*p*icos'). Like a typical pattern poem, even the shape of the poem mimics the shape of the STP can.

However, Lira mimics in order to criticise mimicry. In other words, he uses a technique that can take over the voice of the other in order to criticise that technique; instead of attempting to represent the voice of the oppressed, he takes the voice of the oppressor to criticise it from within. In the following stanza, or, more accurately, block of text, he continues to question the nature of the letters as signs or symbols and their relationship with the product and its abilities. For example, he equates the letters to initials 'la sigla del aceite/en cuestión' (ll. 22–23). He therefore connects the sign of oil to an abbreviation. Moreover, initials are signs of a sign, one step further removed from the thing itself. However, Lira states that they are 'la marca del mismo' (l. 23); initials are the sign of a sign, but the initials STP become the sign itself. In particular, he discusses the relationship between this sign itself and not the product as it is intended to be used, but its psychedelic powers: 'se trataría de una homología entre la sigla del aceite/en cuestión [...] y un sicofármaco emparentado con las anfetaminas y la benzedrina/ — esto es, poseedor de poderes sico tró picos' (ll. 22–25). It is the relationship between the signifier and the signified, or, at least, a signified that contains these powers. STP does not gain its power because of its representative qualities, but because of the (advertising and, he suggests, psychedelic) power of the letters themselves (or the coincidence between the acronyms) on the page.

Lira's explanation following the presentation of these letters is yet another clear criticism of capitalism and consumerism. As the concrete poets play on words, Lira here plays on the multiple connotations and the materiality of the letters STP. The letters STP are an abbreviated version for quick consumption. In the footnote, he states: 'a no ser que se trate de un alcance de nombres/––de letras, en este––, o, más probablemente,/de un simple truco publicitario.' Lira satirically relates advertising to magic.[99] In addition, he separates the word 'sicotrópicos' into three words, the last meaning peaks, beaks, and, in Chilean slang 'dicks'. In other words, Lira satirises the 'powers' of the product.[100]

These psychedelic 'powers' of the product exist in writing; the energetic transformation of the given into the 'new' occurs through writing. In a parenthetical

98 STP (Global Information Network About Drugs) <http://www.ginad.org/en/drugs/drugs/407/stp> [accessed 20 July 2017].

99 'Simple truco publicitario' also repeats the letters STP.

100 In the version on *Memoria Chilena*, Lira includes what looks like a doodle of mountains, or 'picos' under the line that contains the word 'picos'.

note at the end of the poem, he connects the relationship between the logotype and the product with the exercise of writing to 'lo anterior' (supposedly the principle part of the poem): 'El establecer la relación entre lo anterior y el ejercicio escrito, especulación, experimento técnico, juego,/ simiente texto plegaria súplica, temblor pánico./soledad tétrica, poema y/o payasada/que se copia a continuación/ queda a cargo del lector.)' (ll. 25–31). In a paratactic list, Lira further relates writing to a variety of things including a technical experiment, a game, a poem and a 'payasada' ('nonsense', 'buffoonery' or even 'mimicry'). This writing exercise/ game/poem/etc., is one continuously copied and requires the responsibility of the reader. This phrase ties us back to the beginning of the poem: the writing exercise is a (playful) process of copying (and defamiliarising). In order for the poem to become an object of reality, it needs to come from previous material, but has to allow for active readings — responses to a presentation — so that it does not slip solely into *re*presentation.

Conclusion

As an anti-poet (of conventional poetry and anti-poetry), Lira employs poetic and quotidian materials to dismantle existing authorities in both literary and daily scenes, with the intention of revealing more about the cultural and social consequences of an authoritarian regime, particularly that of Chile. Lira expands on the concrete poets' emphasis on the materiality of language as a means of generally criticising the consumerist society in which they wrote, by using 'destructive' *détournement* of both literary texts and quotidian forms to create objects that are both part of and critical of his society. Breaking with the authoritarian nature of the conventional subject, his reworking of literary and non-literary materials, the 'nothing new', becomes an immersion in which the subject is diffused in the new work, from which s/he can comment on his/her society. This political as well as poetic 'commitment' that we see in all the poets, concrete and Chilean, but particularly in Lira's work, can be understood in the Adornian sense.[101] Adorno insists that poetry has to stay with the

101 Adorno, *Notes to Literature*, pp. 76–94. In this essay, Adorno addresses the limits of what are usually categorised as 'autonomous' and 'committed' art. Typically, 'autonomous' art has been defined as art that is 'free' from reality, that is, 'art for art's sake', whereas 'committed' art is (supposedly) actively politically engaged. He characterises the two types of art as 'attitudes to objectivity' that artists and critics have pitted against each other, but argues that this distinction between autonomy and commitment in the end fails to produce successful art. He criticises (supposedly) committed artists for attempting to capture reality in its own terms; by attempting to recreate reality (especially of the oppressed), the work, instead of actually engaging with reality, ends up with the same discourse that is used to oppress those whom the work is supposedly attempting to free (p. 76). In other words, if one tries to represent the oppressed, one gets caught into the web of the discourses of the oppressors. On the other hand, (supposedly) autonomous art, in its 'freedom', Adorno concludes, through the mere act of not directly engaging the political, is in contrast a form in which commitment can be expressed. Although he initially criticises so-called autonomous art for in effect claiming a domain beyond the political altogether, he eventually concludes that: 'the emphasis on the autonomous work [...] is itself socio-political in nature' (p. 91). In other words, claiming that poetry is autonomous is deceptive because all poetry (and language itself) is social by nature. Formal decisions have the potential for reworking propaganda into poetry because propaganda emerges in a

truth of its subjective position, that is, both with the fundamental nature of lyric poetry as a subjective view of the world beyond the subject and (therefore) with the implied subjectivity (and otherness) of the other. To assume and ventriloquise the language of the other undermines the attempt to reveal such subjectivity. For Adorno, true commitment does not come from a direct thematic political agenda, but instead from an appeal through form:

> It need only be added that this appeal [from art] does not stand in any direct relationship to the thematic commitment of the literary work. The unqualified autonomy of works that refrain from adaptation to the market involuntarily becomes an attack. That attack, however, is not an abstract one [...] There is no content, no formal category of the literary work that does not, however transformed and however unawarely, derive from the empirical reality from which it has escaped. It is through this relationship, and through the process of regrouping its moments in terms of it formal law that literature relates to reality.[102]

He suggests — in what applies accurately to Lira — that truly 'committed' political art should exist not exactly between the autonomy and what seems to be committed art, but rather should have a particular (formal) relationship with reality.

The work of art becomes an object, or artefact, within reality, but avoids reducing itself to propaganda.[103] According to Adorno, commitment expressed through the disruption of propaganda's form means the imagining of a better world. Lira does precisely what Adorno calls for at the local level: by emphasising the materiality of language through the appropriation of previous poetic works and by utilising materials and forms of reality (that is, literary and non-literary *détournement*), he manages to disrupt the authoritarian forms he criticises without assuming the voices of the oppressed nor becoming the ideological voice of authority. Until the poet 'robs' it and *détourns* it, propaganda's discourse is always already 'nothing new'.

form that is ideologically driven. Because of the nature of the relationship between art and reality, commitment, then, can only be expressed through form: 'The moment of intention is mediated solely through the form of the work, which crystallizes into a likeness of an Other that ought to exist' (p. 91).

102 Ibid., p. 89.

103 Ibid., pp. 77–89.

CHAPTER 4

Cecilia Vicuña's Plastic Poetry at the Level of the Word, the Page and the Book

As painter, sculptor, singer, performer, literary commentator and poet, Martínez and Lira's contemporary Cecilia Vicuña asks that the reader be an active participant in making meaning. She displaces authority away from the author and towards the reader or readers, and creates a form of art that acts as a medium for a renewed democratic society. Like Martínez and Lira, Vicuña develops and expands upon concretist poetics. However, unlike Martínez and Lira, who stay in Chile under Pinochet, Vicuña leaves the country. Her exile results in her incorporation of (often feminist) weavings and performances on and off the page; she creates these performative *text*iles in order to produce an egalitarian and visionary poetics that both expresses and reconciles her condition as an exile. In this chapter, by considering a representative selection of her written works, I will show how her distinctive poetics shares with concretist poetics the encouragement of continuous active reading that engages both the mind and the body, but also moves beyond it to express a democratic and feminist vision. She does so through her creation of plastic poetry (that is, poetry that is easily mouldable by the reader). Although her critics have commented on her democratic and feminist poetics, no one has yet fully explored how plasticity, as a development of concrete poetry, serves her vision.[1]

In the following chapter, after a brief synthesis of Vicuña's biography and review of the terms I will use throughout, I will present three examples of Vicuña's many projects, PALABRAR*mas* (1984), *Instan* (2002) and *cloud-net* (1999), in order to demonstrate the plasticity she creates in her works at three different levels: the

1 Jessica Becker, in her doctoral thesis, has categorised Vicuña's work with the Brazilian concrete poets, but as part of a wide tradition of Latin American poetry that emphasises the materiality of language rather than in direct relation with each other. Jessica Becker, *Poetics of Materiality: Medium, Embodiment, Sense, and Sensation in 20th– and 21st-Century Latin America* (doctoral thesis, University of California Berkeley, 2014). Vicuña has also been categorised as 'hypervistalist', neo-avant-garde, counter-canonical and counter-cultural. See Oscar Galindo, 'Neovanguardias hipervitalistas en la poesía hispanoamamericana (1958–1976): nihilistas, revolucionarios, solidarios y amorosos', *Taller de Letras*, 52 (2013), 11–37; and Magda Sepúlveda, 'Cecilia Vicuña: La subjetividad poética como una operación contracanónica', *Revista Chilena de Literatura*, 57 (2000), 111–26.

word, the page and the book.[2] I will show first how Vicuña emphasises language's materiality, which indicates that language itself is something to be moulded or 'woven'; and second, how Vicuña illustrates that the space and time of the poem is contingent upon the reader/viewer/listener's (and potentially the author's) participation with not only the final product, but also with the process of creating the work itself. Through the idea of the participatory reader/viewer, Vicuña, I will further show, in her use of plasticity, enacts in miniature a more democratic and less totalitarian society.

Vicuña was born in Santiago in 1948. From a family of artists, she began her artistic projects at a young age. At sixteen, she completed her 'Esculturas precarias' in Concón, which consisted of sculptures made of pieces of rubbish found by the sea. In this project, she founded her concept of 'lo precario' ('the precarious') as a spatial poetics realised in undeveloped settings, on the streets and in museums.[3] Her preoccupation with the precariousness of the world pervades the rest of her work.

Vicuña's commitment not only to individual expression but also to collaborative efforts led her to join with others to found the group 'Tribu No' in 1967. The group included artists and poets including Claudio Bertoni, Marcelo Charlín and Coca Roccatagliata, who associated themselves with the 'hippie' phenomenon, a countercultural social and artistic movement, as well as with socialism and the Chilean Unidad Popular.[4] Specifically, as the group name indicates, they were brought together by a concern for the indigenous ('Tribu'), and negation of and opposition ('No') to the conservative and materialistic society within Chile and much of the Western world.[5] In particular they, like many of their contemporaries, negated and opposed singular and elitist authorship.[6] In Tribu No's manifesto, curiously published in the conservative newspaper *El Mercurio*, they declared their adherence to their rejection of the notion of the sacrosanct and elitist author: 'Nada menos revolucionario, ni menos humano, ni menos vivo que esta burocracia de la literatura, que esta supuesta cara del escritor. Ustedes son a la poesía lo que a la Iglesia sus tergiversadores.'[7]

Vicuña's first experiment with plasticity came when she brought a provocative use of space to the fore in 1969, creating 'La pieza del hilo azul', crossing a thread around a bedroom in her beach house, connecting different points of the room and impeding the normal circulation of interior space. In this piece, she reconfigured

2 Because *cloud-net* chronologically precedes *Instan* –– that is, because Vicuña did not expand her poetry of the page to poetry of the book over time –– my discussion's movement between word, page and book should not be seen as a temporal progression. Rather, each work should be taken as a distinct manifestation of plasticity.

3 Cecilia Vicuña, 'Sobre Cecilia Vicuña', Cecilia Vicuña. <http://www.ceciliavicuna.org/esp_sobre.htm> [accessed 4 December 2014].

4 Soledad Bianchi, *La memoria: Modelo para armar* (Santiago: Dirección de Bibliotecas, Archivos y Museos, 1995), pp. 145–88.

5 Ibid., p. 150.

6 See, for example, Nicanor Parra, *Artefactos visuales* (Concepción: Universidad de Concepción, 2002).

7 'Cecilia Vicuña', *Memoria Chilena* (Santiago: La Biblioteca Nacional de Chile, 2014) <http://www.memoriachilena.cl/602/w3-article-3330.html> [accessed 15 May 2015].

the domestic space by foregrounding within it a perceived and traditionally female activity of weaving. Vicuña's interest in such experiments in plasticity continued in her next major work of 1971–72, 'Otoño', when she filled a room of the Museo Nacional de Bellas Artes in Santiago with thousands of leaves picked from the grounds of the capital's various parks and gardens.[8] Here, she brought nature's 'throwaways' (also called 'precarios') into the space of art, as sort of 'ready-mades' of nature.

After obtaining her degree in art from the Universidad de Chile in 1971, Vicuña travelled to London in 1972, where, in the following year, she would begin her years of exile.[9] There, she founded the group 'Artists for Democracy' and published her first book of poems in 1973, *Saborami*, which was written before and after Pinochet's military coup. Comprising a mixture of poems, photographs and statements against totalitarianism and in favour of socialism and democracy, the book becomes, as Magda Sepúlveda writes, 'una escritura visual y verbal de un recuerdo', that is, a memory of a Chile that no longer exists under the dictatorship.[10]

Given her socialist-leaning work and her visible connections to the Unidad Popular, Vicuña remained in exile during that period.[11] The frustrations of being in exile, of being in a constant state of in between-ness (between cultures, languages, etc.), of existing in a 'non-place' (a term that Vicuña uses herself and that calls to mind a concept described by Marc Augé, which I will explain below in the section 'The Page'), helped to shape her notion of the precarious. Vicuña's plastic poetry, I will show, manifests betweenness nomadically.[12]

Now even more invested in the culture and art of indigenous peoples of the Americas, she returned to Latin America in 1975 (though she was still exiled from Chile).[13] She articulated her commitment to the collaborative aspect of the plasticity of her work when, in Bogotá, she founded the group 'Taller de nueva plástica'. In

8 Vicuña's work has been discussed as ecocritical. For example, Yenny Karen Ariz Castillo explores, from an ecocritical perspective, the relationship between the poetic-visual works of Vicuña and Soleda Fariña in 'Ecología y literatura en la poesía chilena contemporánea: *Semi ya*, de Cecilia Vicuña, y "Cardosanto", de Soledad Fariña', *Mitologías Hoy*, 12 (2015), 294–311.

9 Claudio Bertoni joined Vicuña in London and Paris in 1972 but returned to Chile in 1976. 'Claudio Bertoni', *Memoria Chilena* (Santiago: Biblioteca Nacional de Chile, 2014) <http://www.memoriachilena.cl/602/w3-article-3338.html> [accessed 15 January 2015].

10 Sepúlveda, 'Cecilia Vicuña: La subjetividad poética como una operación contracanónica', p. 114.

11 Vicuña, 'Re: cloud-net and other questions'. I argue that, while politically Vicuña has now been able to return, culturally she remains in a place between.

12 De Zegher claims that Vicuña's art exists as a 'nomad space' that, because it occupies a space of the between, promotes a continuous process of defining. I will expand her discussion of Vicuña's 'spatialised' art to the written text. See Catherine de Zegher, '*Ouvrage*: Know a Not, Notes as Knots', in *The Precarious: The Art and Poetry of Cecilia Vicuña*, ed. by Catherine de Zegher (Middleton: Wesleyan University Press, 1997), pp. 17–47.

13 Vicuña often draws on traditions and forms of indigenous cultures of the Americas. See, for example, Kenneth Sherwood, who exposes the tension between her written work and her performances of those works and claims that her poems, influenced by indigenous oral forms, are re-oralised in her performances, which in turn implies that her 'readings' are not mere recitations, but are also acts of *poiesis*; Sherwood, 'Sounds Written and Sound Breathing: Versions of Palpable Poetics', in de Zegher, *The Precarious*, pp. 73–93.

conjunction with the Chilean artistic group Colectivo Acciones de Arte (C.A.D.A), she exhibited *Vaso de leche* (1979) for the first time. The mixed media installation presented a bottle of milk tied by a red thread set and then spilled on a road in Bogotá. It was then made permanent in three photos illustrating the moment in which it spilled. In 1984, she published PALABRAR*mas*, a collection including concrete poems that emphasise the materiality of words themselves.

In 1987, she moved to New York, where she has been living ever since, making frequent trips to Chile. There, she has worked with many contemporary poets, such as the L=A=N=G=U=A=G=E poet and promoter of experimental poetics, Charles Bernstein, and avant-garde poet and anthologist of 'ethnopoetics', Jerome Rothenberg. She has had many exhibitions and installations in various venues in the United States, the most well-known being *cloud-net* (1999). While living in New York, she also published *Instan* (2002), which includes drawings, a string-like poem, and poetical statements about poetry.

Plasticity

The term 'plastic,' originally used in the eighteenth century to describe how objects are formed in architecture and sculpture, is applicable in many instances to concrete poetry, but comes to take a central place in Vicuña's work. As objects in the plastic arts are 'easily shaped or moulded' (a common definition of 'plastic'), Vicuña creates poems that are 'mouldable' by the reader. By emphasising the process of moulding through performance and visual art techniques, she also includes a meta-discourse in her poems on their plasticity. Her plastic poetry accords with Charles Bernstein and Jay Sanders's definition of 'Poetry Plastique' as poetry that is 'off the page or outside of normal typographic constraints [...] Pushing the boundaries of textuality', in which 'literary and visual artists move poetry into a new dimension that emphasizes the concreteness and materiality of the written word'.[14]

An important feature of plasticity, like that of concretism, is that it requires a certain spatial and verbal agreement that allows a reader/viewer to engage actively in the creation, or moulding, of the poem. Such readerly participation in plastic art is preceded by a disruption of the reader's expectations of the space that s/he ordinarily occupies. The critic Jessica Smith defines 'plasticity' as 'those aesthetic features that reinforce the concomitance of space and time, simultaneity and succession' to explore the 'virtual reading spaces' of poetry.[15] Drawing on and developing Smith's definition, I will show how Vicuña's work invites the reader to interact with the text as though it were three-dimensional and to engage in the continuous production of this mouldable 'virtual space', that is, space in essence. While the concrete poets attempt to create object poems that are disconnected from particular contexts, Vicuña moves beyond them by connecting the objects to past and present actions of the moment that create space for both author and reader to

14 Charles Bernstein and Jay Sanders, *Poetry Plastique* (New York: Granary Books, 2000), pp. 7–8.
15 Smith uses this term briefly in relation to Vicuña's *precarios*, or found-objects, but not in relation to her written work. Jessica Smith, 'The Plasticity of Poetry', *Literature Compass*, 3 (2006), 613–24 (pp. 614–16).

participate. Vicuña emphasises both the physicality and sensuality of the poem-as-object, and the process of art and making as an engaged interaction between people and object. In this development of plasticity, Vicuña models a more democratic and less totalitarian society; the failure of social relationships in a totalitarian society is challenged by a poetic act that, by creating bonds outside of the existing social structure, turns that failure into a social success.

Vicuña's development of the concretist emphasis on readerly participation is consonant with emerging trends in the visual art world where, especially in the 1990s onward, there was a push towards a new, overt way to encourage participation in the 'making' of the artwork. While her visual artwork has been associated with the plastic and kinetic arts, and could be compared to the Situationist and Fluxus movements, her visual and written work, I suggest, is best associated with what Nicolas Bourriaud designates as 'relational art', that is, 'an art taking as its theoretical horizon the realm of human interactions and its social context, rather than the assertion of an independent and private symbolic space' and one that 'points to a radical upheaval of the aesthetic, cultural and political goals introduced by modern art.'[16] Many artists, Vicuña among them, were moving towards installations and other forms of performance art with which the viewer could interact and participate in the making of the work. For example, Félix González-Torres initiated a variety of works that, while not necessarily performance-based, were determined by the viewers' involvement with the piece. In 1991, he placed colourfully wrapped candies in the corner of a gallery which viewers were welcome to take as they pleased. Not only did the work itself change as people came in and out of the gallery as the pile of candies diminished, but part of it also included people's reactions to it, as they considered such questions as whether to take candies from the work, how many candies they took when they became aware that the work would eventually disappear if everyone were to take some, and so on.[17] These producers of relational art were attempting to destabilise the authority of a single artist in a given work. Both the concrete poets and Vicuña translate to the realm of literature this artistic promotion that the viewer is no longer a spectator, but a participant in the work's creation.

Because the relationship between viewer and object becomes the focal point of this type of art, the realisation of the artwork relies on the agency of the viewer, and therefore could be said to have an ephemeral or precarious existence. The opposite of 'precarious' art would be 'monumental' art that, in theory at least, stands permanently and alone, needing no active participation from the reader/viewer. For Vicuña, monumental art would presumably be associated with state-sponsored or corporate establishment art whose effects can be predicted, whereas a precarious poem would represent a variety of possibilities with unpredictable outcomes. Vicuña's work, then, parallels the ways in which the concrete poets inserted a similar precariousness into otherwise 'monumental' object-poems through their engagement of the active reader.

16 Nicolas Bourriaud, *Relational Aesthetics*, trans. by Simon Pleasance and Fronza Woods (Dijon: Les Presses du Réel, 2002), p. 14.
17 Ibid., p. 39.

In her poetry and art, Vicuña plays, as we will see in throughout the chapter, on the ambiguity of the word 'precarious'. She firstly evokes that which is 'not securely held or in position; likely to fall; dependent on chance; uncertain'.[18] Secondly, she brings to the fore the word's secondary etymological meaning, coming from the Latin root, prex or prec-, which means 'prayer'.[19] The critic Juliet Lynd describes Vicuña's precarious aesthetic as 'the vehicle for attaining an open-ended mode of representation that denies fixed meanings and privileges creative connections, positioning the ephemeral as a gesture of hope against hegemonic discourses of power'.[20] In order to demonstrate a state of precariousness as well as a means to fight against it, Vicuña blends together different media, their juxtaposition often allowing (and requiring) the reader/viewer to participate actively.[21]

Vicuña's distinctive means of expressing openness and non-hierarchical precariousness works through the particularly feminine and indigenous images of the web and acts of weaving that produce webs.[22] Vicuña makes especially effective use of the traditional Inca form of 'writing' called the quipu, which, although not formed by traditional weaving, was formed by knots tied in particular places along strings. The exact purpose of the quipu is debated amongst historians and archaeologists (although it is generally agreed that it was used as an accounting system).[23] However, Vicuña claims that the Inca thought memories would be lost in written language, and would only persist through quipu writing.[24] Weaving

18 *The Concise Oxford Dictionary*, ed. by Judy Pearsall, 10th edn (Oxford: Oxford University Press, 1999).

19 A noun for prayer in Spanish, 'plegaria', also has the same root. Ibid., and Joan Corominas, *Breve diccionario etimológico de la lengua castellana* (Madrid: Editorial Gredos, 1987), p. 464.

20 Juliet Lynd, 'Precarious Resistance: Weaving Opposition in the Poetry of Cecilia Vicuña', *PMLA*, 120 (2005), 1588–1607 (p. 1592).

21 Kelly Gordon emphasises this juxtaposition, focusing on the precarious relationship between the photographs and the word in *QUIPOem* and *Precario/Precarious*. See Gordon (2010), pp. 93–102.

22 Vicuña's weaving has been a major focus within her criticism. See Lucy R. Lippard, 'Spinning the Common Thread', in *The Precarious* (1997), pp. 7–15; Lynd (2005), pp. 1588–1607; de Zegher, *The Precarious*, pp. 17–45; Meredith G. Clark, 'Warping the Word: The Technology of Weaving in the Poetry of Jorge Eduardo Eielson and Cecilia Vicuña', *Textile*, 10.3 (2012), 312–27; Hugo Méndez-Ramírez, 'Cryptic Weaving,' in de Zegher, *The Precarious*, pp 59–71; Julie Phillips Brown, '"Touch in Transit": Manifestation/*Manifestación* in Cecilia Vicuña's *cloud-net*', *Contemporary Women's Writing*, 5 (2011), 208–31; Ariz Castillo 'La red espiritual de Ollantaytambo en *La Wik'uña*, de Cecilia Vicuña: Agua, piedra y luz', *Revista Humanidades*, 5.2 (2015), 1–28; and 'Los animales en la *Wik'uña* de Cecilia Vicuña: Figuras opuestas y complementarias', *La Palabra*, 23 (2013), 51–62.

23 See, for example, Gary Urton, 'Writing the History of an Ancient Civilization Without Writing: Reading the Inka Khipus as Primary Sounds', *Journal of Anthropological Research*, 73.1 (2017), 1–21.

24 Vicuña, *cloud-net*, p. 20. De Zegher explains that Vicuña has always understood weaving not only as an alternative discourse, but also as a form of female participation in political activities. She draws from the example of the Panamanian Kuna. In this indigenous group's communal meetings, the most eloquent men engage in verbal discourse in the centre of a circle, surrounded by rows of women who work on textiles while the chiefs chant. De Zegher, *The Precarious*, p. 27. Another important example of textile-making as a form of political discourse or resistance is the *arpilleras* that were initially stitched by women as a means of expressing experiences and hardships under Pinochet. See, for example, Jacqueline Adams, *Art Against Dictatorship: Making and Exporting Arpilleras Under Pinochet* (Austin: University of Texas Press, 2013).

has been understood as a particularly female form of writing or expression (that is, *text*ual production) in literature. To name a few paradigmatic examples, Ovid's Philomela, after her rape and having her tongue cut out, communicates her story through weaving, and Homer's Penelope weaves and unweaves her textile every day until Odysseus comes home. Drawing upon both indigenous and literary traditions, Vicuña strives to create her own discourse alternative to the partriarchal one that dominates the Western world today.[25] Through her weaving of 'precarious' threads that are manifested as words, poems, pages, and even in the form of actual threads, she aims to strengthen relationships in the world that have become precarious and will continue to be so unless they are repeatedly woven together. Weaving exemplifies (metaphorically and literally) the plasticity of her poetry in a variety of ways. Firstly, in order to weave, one must use one's hands. Secondly, weaving is an act that produces connections between the various threads themselves, as well as between the thread and the hands that guide them. Plastic poetry, like *verbivocovisual* concrete poetry, requires one to focus on the materials being used to create the work, as well as on one's physical position, manifested semantically, visually, aurally, and even tactilely in relation to that material.

While Vicuña had no direct personal relationships with the concrete poets, she was deeply influenced by them and their poetics.[26] Like the concrete poets, Vicuña allows the reader to engage with an object-like text not solely semantically, but explicitly through its visual characteristics. As we shall see in PALABRAR*mas*, she allows the reader to do so at the level of the word. The spatial arrangement of the words on the page in *Instan* at times requires the reader to read, or engage, the text both visually and kinetically. Her non-hierarchical, democratic and feminist vision of artistic creation does not exist as a message to be received by her audience, but comes into being in the experience of reading her work. Vicuña encourages the reader, in one way or another, to join with the other readers in a performance; her work becomes communally 'performative in its own right'.[27] Particularly like the concrete poems that were performed and put to music or filmed, the project *cloud-net* allows the participant to connect to others literally in the performances and installations, and forces the reader of the book to be aware of the bonds made in those events and to continue weaving the connections virtually. Vicuña and the concrete poets all invite active readerly participation in order to give freedom to the reader. For Vicuña, this freedom for the reader has to be fought for with words as weapons, with 'palabr*armas*'.

25 Lynd argues that, in *QUIPOem*, Vicuña's weavings are a new way of representing the memory of the female and indigenous voice. See Lynd, *Precarious Resistance*.

26 Vicuña, 'Re: cloud-net' and other questions.'

27 Gordon, 'Weaving Sight-Weaving Life', p. 94.

The Word

Vicuña's plasticity is manifest at the level of the word. In 1984, Vicuña published the first edition of PALABRAR*mas* in Buenos Aires because she could not publish in Chile under the dictatorship.[28] In 1994 in Scotland, she published a different version in a small, accordion style booklet, which, on the facing pages, includes translations into Scots by the concrete poet Edwin Morgan. She finally published a third edition in Chile in 2005 (Figure 4.1).

As we will see, this collection's poems are clearly similar to those of concrete poetry: like these poets, Vicuña brings the materiality of language to the fore, claiming that one can find hidden words and meanings among other words.[29] Of the works studied here, the poems in this collection are the closest to resembling actual concrete poems. As mentioned above, Vicuña herself considers PALABRAR*mas* to contain concrete poems.[30] Vicuña, just as the concrete poets do, designs some of the poems plastically to be read non-linearly and in multiple ways, which allows the reader to create his/her own path with(in) words themselves and thereby to help mould the poem (see, for example, Figure 1.12). For instance, she can take apart a word and form new words and phrases, where some words or parts of words will be foregrounded. Each path that a reader takes contributes to an invisible 'web' that holds together the words of the poem. This web of words, I will show, is rhizomatic (to use Gilles Deleuze and Félix Guattari's term), that is, it is internally reformed every time it is read, and while its individual readings fall away or break, new readings form or reform to maintain it.[31]

PALABRAR*mas* exists in multiple forms. Published in 1984, the first edition of the book consists of seventy pages divided into four sections, preceded by an introductory verse poem. In the introductory poem, Vicuña explains how she 'encountered' (to use her term) the poems of the first two sections to follow and what she attempted to achieve with them. The first main section, 'Adivinanzas', consists of short poems that contain a question and an answer (see Figure 4.2 for an example).

28 Jazmín Lolas, 'Mi trabajo ha sido censurado durante cuarenta años' (Las Últimas Noticias, 2006), <http://www.letras.s5.com/cv200106.htm> [accessed 20 January 2015].

29 Vicuña, PALABRAR*mas* (Santiago de Chile: RIL editores, 2005), p. 40.

30 Vicuña, 'Re: cloud-net and other questions'.

31 See Gilles Deleuze and Félix Guattari, *A Thousand Plateaus*, trans. by Brian Massumi (Minneapolis: University of Minnesota Press, 1987), pp. 3–25. It would be interesting to investigate and compare Vicuña's rhizomatic poetry with other Latin American poets and artists whose have similarly been described as rhizomatic, such as those of Néstor Perlongher, Coral Bracho, and the group Ala Plástica. See, for example, Benjamin Bollig *Néstor Perlongher: The Poetic Search for an Argentine Marginal Voice* (Cardiff: University of Wales Press, 2008) and Vera Coleman, 'Emergent Rhizomes: Posthumanist Environmental Ethics in the Participatory Art of Ala Plástica', *Confluencia*, 31.2 (2016), 85–98. Within this framework, one could productively argue that Vicuña could be considered a poet of the *neobarroco*, a category that Perlonger defines as folding, which exists in a state of in-betweenness, and as rhizomatic weaving, which manifests as nomadic, annihilates the subject and materialises language; it is 'una verdadera desterritorialización fabulosa'. See Gilles Deleuze, *The Fold: Leibniz and the Baroque*, trans. by Tom Conley (London: The Athlone Press, 1993) and Néstor Perlongher, *Medusario: Muestra de poesía latinoamericana*, ed. by Roberto Echavarren, José Kozer and Jacabo Sefamí (México, D.F.: Fondo de Cultura Económica, 1996), pp. 19–20. However, in this chapter, I will restrict my comparision to concretist poetics.

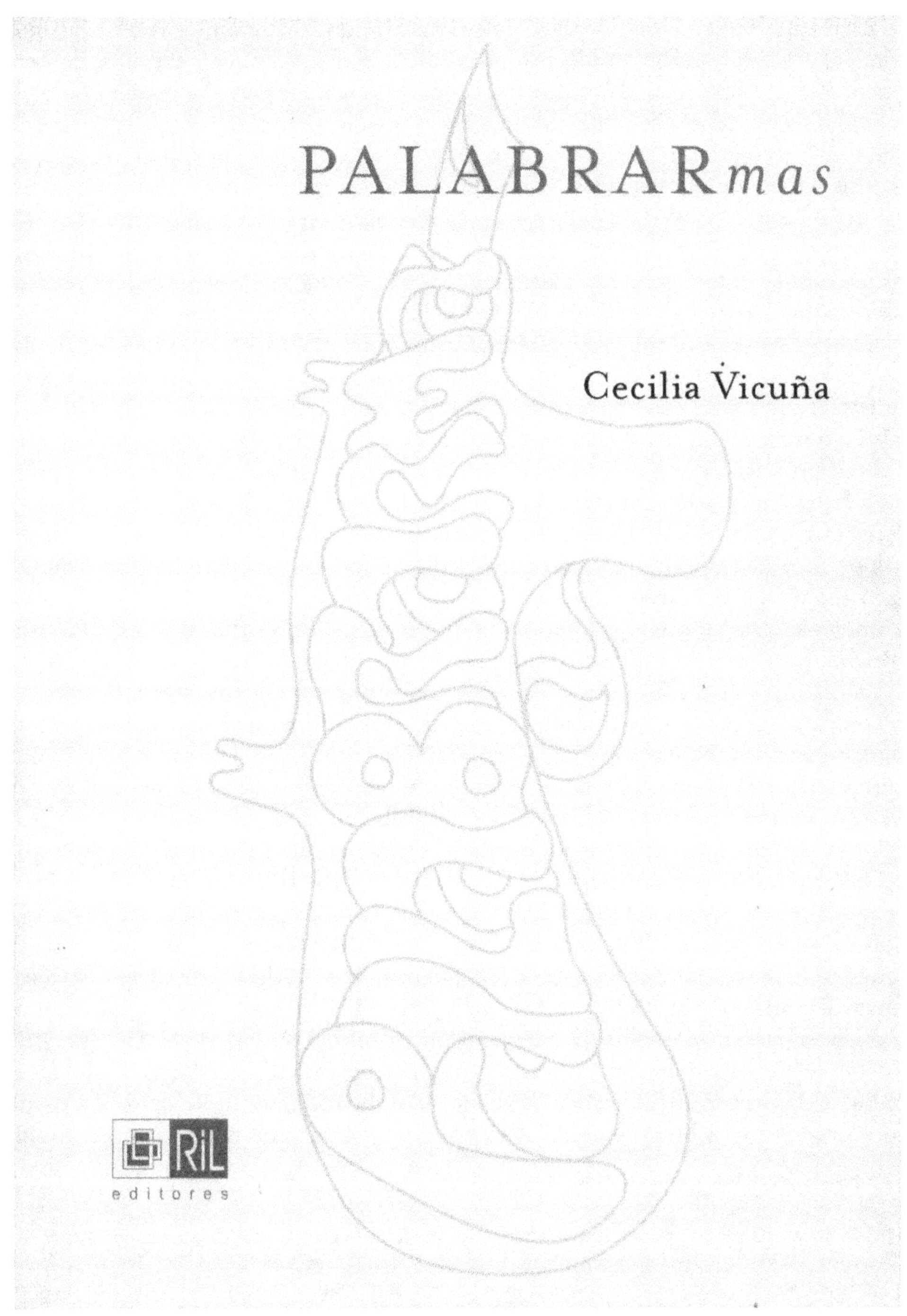

Fig. 4.1. Vicuña, Cover of PALABRAR*mas* (2005).
Courtesy of Cecilia Vicuña.

Each page presents one of these questions and one answer in a relatively small font, which allows most of the page to remain blank. Although the introductory poem and the first section inform the reader rather than give the reader complete freedom to create his/her path through these poems, they can be seen as guides for the reader to understand how they can form new readings in the following section. In this sense, Vicuña provides these sections not as authoritative instructions, but as useful tools.[32] In 'PALABRAR*mas*', Vicuña plays with the typography of words or short phrases to reveal new combinations and meanings within the words. Each page consists of one of these 'palabrarmas' (each containing one word or phrase), leaving the majority of the page blank (see Figure 4.3 for an example).

These poems recall the typography of many concrete poems, in which particular words are enlarged or bolded and therefore stand out to form new combinations of letters and words (see, for example, Augusto de Campos's 'Caracol', Figure 4.4). In the third section, 'Palabrir', Vicuña dissects the word 'palabra' in verse and with reference to the etymology of 'palabra,' 'metáfora,' and 'poesía'. Written in prose and verse, the fourth and final section, 'Incidir juntos en la unión', is a form of reflection on the previous two sections and includes quotes of and references to the importance and divinity of words in myths, religions, and philosophies from all over the world and throughout time.

In 1994, she published a shortened edition of the book that only includes the 'Palabrarmas' section of the first edition. In this book, each poem is mirrored by a translation into Scots by the Scottish concrete poet Edwin Morgan, with an accompanying poetic explanation. Here, the three-dimensionality Vicuña evokes in her poetry (particularly through virtual and literal weaving) is realised physically: certain pages fold out of the book, calling the reader's attention to the spatiality of her conception. In a more recent edition published in 2005 (to which I will mostly refer in my discussion), she adds a poetic introduction that further explains and reflects upon the poems of the first two sections of the first edition.[33]

In all of the editions divided into parts, the sections, apart from the principal, concrete-like ones of 'Adivinanzas' and 'PALABRAR*mas*', present what I call 'poetical poetics' in that, in verse or poetical prose, they provide an explicit meta-discourse about 'Adivinanzas' and 'PALABRAR*mas*'. They explain how the reader can engage with the poems of the principal two sections. Her 'poetical poetics' sections to some extent restrict readerly freedom if read alongside the other sections. However, if the reader choses to read them, they can be used as a useful tool or guide in a broad sense.[34] While she does not quite provide an *ars poetica*,

32 Nonetheless, the sections ultimately restrict the reader's complete freedom in interacting with the text on the page.

33 In 2006, she made a four-minute movie with Ignacio Poblete, in which they experiment with the typography of a variety of poems from both the 'Adivinanzas' and 'PALABRAR*mas*' sections. The words on the screen fade in and out, grow bigger and smaller, overlap each other, etc. Cecilia Vicuña and Ignacio Poblete, *Palabrarmas* (2006), <https://vimeo.com/67557355> [accessed 25 January 2015]. She also has performed and exhibited her 'Palabrarmas' in different forms in a variety of international exhibitions, one of the latest being at the Neubauer Collegium for Culture and Society in Chicago, from March 29 to June 3, 2018.

34 In this sense, they can be compared to Martínez's example answers or the 'guides' the concrete

¿dulces enajenados de color morado?

los enamorados

42

Fig. 4.2. Vicuña, PALABRAR*mas* (2005): An example from 'Adivinanzas'. Courtesy of Cecilia Vicuña.

vi

la i da

55

FIG. 4.3. Vicuña, PALABRAR*mas* (2005): An example from 'Palabrarmas'. Courtesy of Cecilia Vicuña.

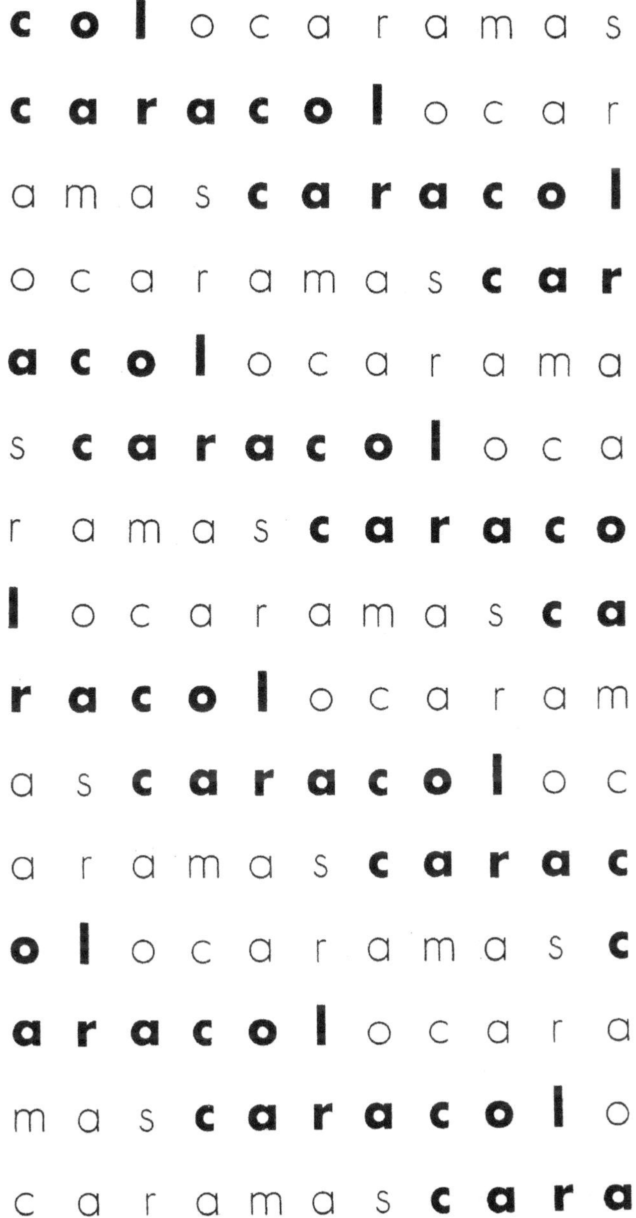

Fig. 4.4. Augusto de Campos, 'Caracol' (1960).
Courtesy of Augusto de Campos.

Vicuña invites the reader to engage with the particular poems of 'Adivinanzas' and 'Palabrarmas' at the same time that s/he thinks about the poetics of her work. In that spirit, I will use the poetics of these sections as explanatory support for my interpretation of the poems.

I will now demonstrate how, in her book PALABRAR*mas*, Vicuña manifests the fundamental plasticity of words. The poems in this book grant (virtual) three dimensions to words themselves and thereby bring to the fore their mouldability. Vicuña provides examples of words that, when read, form strong woven textures of multiple possible interpretations. The character of these weavings can best be explained with reference to Deleuze and Guattari's concept of the rhizome.[35] The rhizome, as they explain, exists as a structure of multiple and equal parts (as opposed to as a binary and hierarchical structure), that form three-dimensional, every-changing pathways.[36] The reader constructs nonlinear, rhizomatic weavings as s/he interacts with the word on the page. In her focus on the genesis of words, Vicuña creates three-dimensional, precarious virtual 'objects' — precarious because, as Vicuña explains, they are thrown out by chance waiting for a reader to engage them. Looking into words by bringing together ('armar') and dismantling ('desarmar') their parts, Vicuña emphasises that multiple meanings exist within the words themselves, which represent, for Vicuña, the 'mestizo' nature of the Latin American experience. Like Oswald de Andrade's notion of 'anthropophagous' writing (see Chapter 1), these crafted words reflect the multiplicity of cultures that emerged in Latin America from the (ongoing) clash between Europe, Africa, Asia and American indigenous groups (or the clash between culturally and/or economically different settlers).

Vicuña asks that words be defamiliarised in order that they may regain their original freshness. Words, for Vicuña (as for the concrete poets), have become static material objects in modern capitalist societies, but, when the reader engages with them, they become something living and even 'divine', as we will see shortly. Vicuña suggests that language itself exists not solely as a tool for basic communication, but as something that can help create strong relationships through which people can fight against the inequalities that exist in the current structures of the world. As the title indicates, these poems are not only mechanisms for bringing together and dismantling, but are also word-weapons ('armas'): to 'palabrir' (to engage in the process of making 'palabrarmas') implies 'to fight' against something, which can be done by opening ('abrir') words ('palabras').[37] Through the 'weapons' made by the weaving of 'palabrarmas', Vicuña calls for a fight against the status quo, that is, against patriarchy, authoritarian structures and linear logic.

These rhizomatic word-weapons are precarious. The word, for Vicuña and the concrete poets, does not exist solely on the two-dimensional page as a sign for a referent, but instead suggests, as Morgan's reworking of the book indicates, as

poets provide in their poems. See Chapter 2.

35 Deleuze and Guattari, *A Thousand Plateaus*, pp. 3–25.

36 Ibid. While de Zegher recognises some rhizomatic features of Vicuña's art, she does not develop her argument about those features in Vicuña's poetry. See de Zegher, *The Precarious*, pp. 29–35.

37 'Palabrarmas' also contains the word 'pala' ('shovel'), signifying that the 'palabrarmas' are tools.

a virtual three-dimensional object, yet an object that remains unstable without a reader. A connection can be made between the poems of 'Adivinanzas' and 'Palabrarmas' and Vicuña's 'precarios', or 'throwaways,' that she had found in nature or on the sides of roads and from which she produced pieces of art. Drawing on both the denotation of the word 'precarious' as unstable or uncertain, and its etymological meaning, prayer, Vicuña calls these objects 'precarios' both to convey the instability of the object's creation and being and to imply that they are prayers. Here, prayers are precarious in the sense that they are addressed to a divine being who might not answer, and yet they declare the person's conviction that a problem can only be solved or an object celebrated by means of a divine response. Vicuña similarly introduces the 'Adivinanzas' and 'Palabrarmas' as precarious things of language that she has found by chance.[38]

Vicuña finds what she deems to be the divinity of words in their plastic qualities.[39] In the opening verse poem, Vicuña describes how she came to see the divine in words. She opens the book with the lines:

> Primero vi una palabra en el aire
> sólida y suspendida
> mostrándome
> su cuerpo de semilla (p. 33, ll. 1–4)

Vicuña immediately describes the word she finds as something material ('sólida'). Instead of allowing the reader to look through a transparent word to find its signified or to reduce it to a single definition, this word is some*thing* in and of itself. She moves the image of language into the domain of plastic arts; as soon as the signifier is pulled away from its usual signified, it becomes precariously open to new readings. Not only is the word tangible, but, as Vicuña explains, it also exists in a three-dimensional space as it is 'suspendida' in the air. In many of Vicuña's works, words are virtually and visually strung together precariously by threads. Here, the suspension of the word implies that the word is hanging from something just as the knots on a quipu 'hang' on threads. In addition, the word 'suspendida' implies instability, which is itself precariously 'suspended' at the end of a short line. Vicuña does not say what the word is suspended from, so the word is hanging from something unknown.[40] Perhaps, then, 'divinity' lies in the risky quality of something at once solid yet 'precariously' suspended.

38 One could consider the 'Adivinanzas' and 'Palabrarmas' as 'precarios' found in language.

39 While I do not develop it for the purposes of this book, an important difference to note between Vicuña and the Brazilian concretists is her vision of poetry (and its process) as divine, or even spiritual.

40 Even though she does not tend to use invisible wire or string in her visual work, she does suspend large lines of yarn in many of her visual works from a variety of places, including from participants (who can move around, creating an unstable suspension). See, for example, photographs of her 'Menstrual Quipu', which was installed in the *Documenta 14* exhibit in Athens, 8 April–17 September 2017. This and her quipu-like poems are reminiscent of Peruvian artist and writer Jorge Eduardo Eielson, who makes beautiful 'quipus' that remain contained within the borders of the canvas as well as poems that evoke quipus and weaving. See Clark, 'Warping the Word', 312–27.

This precarious word appears first to the speaker as a seed out of nowhere: 'Primero vi una palabra/mostrándome/su cuerpo de semilla' (p. 33, ll. 1–4), suggesting the first event of creation. The reader (and seemingly the speaker) does not know of the word's existence before the encounter, and the word thus seems to come out of nowhere and nothing, or at least not from anywhere or anything known; yet it still exists and is immanent to the poem. Clearly drawing on the theological notion of *creatio ex nihilo*, Vicuña (unlike Lira, as we saw in the previous chapter) explains that it is from nothing that words emerge. One of the poems from 'Palabrarmas' illustrates how nothing creates:

nadada (p. 62)

One can read this poem in a variety of ways: as 'nothing gives', 'nothing gives nothing', 'nothing', the word 'nada' itself gives, nothing gives the word 'nada', 'swimming (another form of suspension, in water) gives', 'nothing Dada' (surely referencing how Dadaists create art out of everyday objects), and so on. In the introduction to PALABRAR*mas*, Vicuña explains that creating from nothing is fundamental to poetry:

¿El hacer de la nada haciéndose?
poiesis (p. 22)

Poetry, for Vicuña, means creating something out of nothing through words themselves. This process of making from nothing is also precarious: it is 'suspended' (as we saw above), and there is no guarantee that the process will work.

Instead of coming from something known, the encounter with the word seems to occur by chance or by fate, which brings us to the title of the first section, 'Adivinanzas'; it is in our interactions with poetry, or stanzas (adivin*anza*) that the divine (a*divin*anza) occurs fortuitously. On the first pages of this section, Vicuña explains in verse that she had, by chance, found words that contained a question and an answer at the same time:

Las primeras preguntas se presentaron
como visión:
veía palabras que contenían una pregunta
y una respuesta
a la vez.

Las llamé adivinanzas [...]

La adivinanza
Juega a ser en chanza
La diva de la lanza (pp. 39–40, ll. 1–15)

Vicuña states that this chance occurs in words that emphasise, in the Derridean sense, their inherent deconstructive nature: 'Quizás toda adivinanza sucede al interior de una palabra que la contiene como un espacio y desarmarlo en chanza' (p. 11).[41] The word 'Adivinanza' itself carries with it the meaning of 'chance': 'Adivinanza' (riddle, guess) relates to the verb 'adivinar' (to guess), which has its

41 See Derrida, *Of Grammatology*.

Latin root 'divinus', meaning 'of god'. Vicuña explains that the words are guesses:

> Ellas decían:
>
> la palabra es la adivinanza
> y adivinar
> es averiguar lo divino (p. 39, ll. 7–10)

Rather than coming to be by following a stable, planned path, these words come to Vicuña as the result of guesses. The openness to the unknown that guessing requires is what Vicuña describes as poetry: 'La adivinanza es la palabra "poesía"' (p. 22). The word 'poetry,' as Vicuña quotes in the third section, comes from the Greek word 'poiesis', creation, and 'poiein', to make (p. 92). Thus, for Vicuña, the divinity of poetic creation is tied to the speaker's heroic willingness to risk dwelling in and pursuing uncertain knowledge.

This pursuit of uncertain knowledge can occur in the poem because language, for Vicuña, exists for the divine. In the Mayan creation myth *Popul Vuh*, as Vicuña herself points out in both the last section of PALABRAR*mas* and in her essay 'An Introduction to Mestizo Poetics', the gods created language so that humans could pray to them in a poetic way.[42] In the final section of PALABRAR*mas*, Vicuña explains that many other creation myths contain similar stories about the genesis of words. In Guaraní myths, for example, love, language and hymns were created simultaneously so that humans could be conscious of the gods:

> En el pensamiento guaran [*sic*] la palabra *es* el alma
> otorgada a los hombres
> para que tengan conciencia de la divinidad. (p. 100)

She also quotes from the Gospel of John in the New Testament: 'En el principio era el verbo y el verbo era con Dios, y el verbo era Dios' (p. 102). In Christianity, the Word made flesh is God. In other words, the ability to create exists in language. She further underscores the divinity she sees in words by referring to poets and philosophers, such as Ernest Fenollosa, Friedrich Hölderlin and Martin Heidegger, who all comment on the word's divinity and/or its meaning as the tool of language to address the gods (p. 103–07).[43]

In many of the creation myths to which Vicuña alludes, the sound of words is as important as their meaning because, according to these myths, it is through sound in prayer that one can communicate with the divine. For many South American indigenous religions, creation, and the subsequent reproduction of created forms, involves sound.[44] For example the Baniwa of the Brazilian rainforest, as Vicuña

42 Livon-Grosman and Vicuña, *The Oxford Book of Latin American Poetry*, p. xxi.

43 Vicuña not only includes these references and quotations to illustrate the similarities between the myriad creation myths revolving around the word as divine and as creation itself, but she also uses them to underline the multiplicity of cultures of which Latin America consists and the divinity of Latin American languages. This assemblage of quotations is reminiscent of Martínez's collage of international references (see Chapter 2). However, whereas Martínez uses the collage as a means to achieve universality, Vicuña attempts to express a specifically Latin American and exilic experience with her blend of allusions.

44 Vicuña, *V*, p. xxi.

herself explains, 'see all forms of reproduction as a "communication of sounds"'.[45] According to Vicuña, 'Language, poetry, and song are forms of reproduction', and therefore are forms of sound.[46] This reproduction seems to be used in the biological connotation in which reproduction is linked to 'creation'. Reproduction, however, implies that what is being created, words or life, is not created *ex nihilo*, but from pre-existing forms. The 'nothingness' from which the word comes (as sound), as described in PALABRAR*mas*, must in fact be a pre-existing form.[47] In PALABRAR*mas*, Vicuña explains that the word is a combination of silence and sound: 'La palabra es silencio y sonido articulado' (p. 88). If we look at the poem 'nada' above, potential readings are created out of the physical word 'nada' as written on the page. In other words, the signifieds that are or can be produced do not come from other signifieds, but from signifiers. Just as the pauses or breaths in a song are equally important to the notes, the word requires both sound and silence. As articulated in concrete poems (such as Gomringer's 'Silencio') and in Juan Luis Martínez's poems about music and poetry (see Chapter 2), silence (the 'nothing' of sound) is, in fact, something that can be articulated, or reproduced. So what about the written word? For Vicuña, even that, like a musical score, assumes sound when it is being read. In the opening poem, the words are singers, but simultaneously noiseless: 'Esperan silentes y cantarinas' (p. 35, ll. 54–55). They also have musical bodies:

Música corporal
sus formas transforman' (p. 36, ll. 68–69)

The creation of words and the creation of the relationships between word and reader involve musical sound that consists of patterns of noise and silence.

Divinity, for Vicuña, comes not only from the creation of words, but also from the relational activity of conversation. In 'Adivinanzas', Vicuña claims that the words presented themselves as both question and answer in one (p. 39, ll. 1–5). The words appeared *as* a conversation, the result being, for example: '¿la pasión del compañero?/la compasión' (p. 46). The question and answer reveal and exist as the 'advinanza', the 'divine' riddle.[48] These poems create a Socratic form of dialogue: the use of questions sparks critical thinking and helps ideas develop.[49] Vicuña, through a 'PALABRAR*mas*' exercise, specifically states that knowledge comes from conversation:

La palabra pone al lado lo conocido y por conocer
CON o SER
ser con
El ser palabra para ser con,

45 Ibid.
46 Ibid.
47 As we saw in Chapter 3, Lira also concludes that creation *ex nihilo* is impossible.
48 They also reveal the word 'compás' ('rhythm', 'beat'), suggesting that this conversation is musical.
49 Vicuña most likely had Plato in mind when writing these poems because, in the final section of the book, she refers directly to Socrates (p. 107).

dialoga
o qué dice la palabra del ser
es lo que vamos a conocer. (p. 87)

Through a dialogue with the word, the reader can understand what 'to be' means, which also means 'to know'.[50]

Just as Plato's Socrates converses with real and fictional characters to try to understand the world, in 'Adivinanzas,' conversation mainly occurs between the speaker and Vicuña (or between parts of an individual's mind). If the 'adivinanzas' are taken alone, Vicuña falls short in her creation of rhizomatic webs. Instead of creating an open-ended, rhizomatic dialogue in which the question does not ask for a sole answer and in which ephemeral connections can be made from the conversation, she provides both a limiting question and answer. Nonetheless, Vicuña recognises that the main conversations in these poems do not emphasise the reader's role because they are circular (that is, they fold in on themselves because each 'advinanza' contains a question and an answer),[51] and claims that the 'adivinanzas' (and 'palabrarmas') in this book serve as invitations to the reader to continue the conversation outside of the text: 'este texto no es más que una meditación que avanza por fragmentos y sugerencias, desde y para la imaginación' (p. 83). Like concrete poems, in which the reader is encouraged to continue the pattern that the poet has created on the page (see, for example Figures 1.5 and 1.10), the poems instruct the reader how to follow so that they too can participate in the creation of 'palabrarmas'.[52]

In 'Palabrarmas' the reader can participate more directly in the making of a particular poem than in 'Adivinanzas' because the poem involves the reader's repeated active destruction and construction of words and phrases. In the opening to the section, Vicuña states that these exercises require one to bring together and take apart certain words:

Palabrar más o palabrir
es armar y desarmar palabras
para ver qué tienen
que decir. (p. 54, ll. 1–2)

She implies that the constructing and disassembling of words requires both an agent to do so and a recipient to listen to (or 'see') what is said. The words thus require a reader to become a 'palabrarmador'.

The process of constructing and dismantling words recurs every time one reads them. Just as in most concrete poems, the reader can read the poem in a variety of ways. For example:

50 Vicuña uses 'conocer' instead of 'saber', probably to emphasise the act of knowing, rather than the possession of knowledge.

51 This circularity is dissimilar to, for example, the unanswered questions in Pablo Neruda's *Libro de preguntas*, which remain open-ended. Pablo Neruda, *Libro de preguntas* (Buenos Aires: Losada, 1974).

52 As discussed in Chapter 2, Martínez does this explicitly in *La nueva novela* where he states that some of his poems are mere examples.

organicamente
izar (p. 65)

One could read these typographical elements by reading the letters in order: 'organicamente izar'; one could begin with the letters in the larger font: 'organizar organicamente'; one could then continue the process by using the various words produced as jumping off points to continue this deconstructing-constructing process: 'órgano (in the biological and/or musical sense) izar', 'organismo orgánicamente organiza', and so on. In some of these readings, the words act out their meanings: they are organising themselves on the page and enact their organic nature when read (that is, the reading makes the words an extension of the organic being, the reader).[53]

In PALABRAR*mas*, the invisible connections the reader creates form a non-linear and non-binary rhizomatic network.[54] Instead of a poem inviting a single, precarious 'string' from a linear reading, these poems allow for the creation of a strong weaving of crossing readings: 'Cruza y combina formas de energía' (p. 88). Despite the precariousness of its individual parts, the weaving is strong because it is a lot more difficult to break a woven fabric than a single string. The reader weaves ephemeral strings that connect the words together each time it is read. The more it is read, the more weavings are produced. This weaving, like the rhizome, is not dominated by one subject (or weaver) or one object (or thread), but instead gains its strength from the many possible weavings that can be produced by multiple readers.[55] Even the poet does not become an authoritative subject of the text, but instead considers herself as one among many participants in a collective production of meanings. Foregrounding the intensely involved readerly process of moulding or shaping, the poem exists as a continuous breaking down and rebuilding of the word: 'Construye y destruye a la vez' (p. 88). This process also occurs in the rhizome, in which, according to Deleuze and Guattari, there occur ruptures that reform creating new unpredictable connections. A characteristic of a rhizome is the:

> principle of a signifying rupture: against the oversignifying breaks separating structures or cutting across a single structure. A rhizome may be broken, shattered at a given spot, but it will start up again in one of its old lines, or on new lines.[56]

The ruptures strengthen rather than weaken the rhizomatic structure. Because it is ceaselessly changing and renewing itself, the shoots of the rhizome cannot grow old or become fixed in a vulnerable, linear path. Similarly, the ruptures in

53 This is clearly also reminiscent of Mallarmé's *Un coup de dés* and recalls Pignatari's 'Organismo' (Figure 1.4).

54 The rhizome, for Deleuze and Guattari, is structured in multiple ways, unlike the root-tree that is structured only by binaries. Deleuze and Guattari, *A Thousand Plateaus*, p. 4.

55 Deleuze and Guattari in fact use the metaphor of weaving when discussing how a puppet, as a rhizome or multiplicity, works: 'Puppet strings, as a rhizome or multiplicity, are tied not to the supposed will or an artist or puppeteer but to a multiplicity of nerve fibres, which form another puppet in other dimensions connected to the first: "Call the strings or rods that move the puppet the weave."' Here, the weave is a multiplicity that acts rather than a subject manipulating the weave; the weave moves itself. Deleuze and Guattari, *A Thousand Plateaus*, p. 8.

56 Ibid., p. 9.

the poems are made so that new lines can be formed or old lines can grow in new ways. In other words, Vicuña's weavings, like rhizomes, never have solidified, but instead are continuously, in Deleuze and Guattari's terms, *becoming*.[57]

Because the rhizome exists as a network of many shoots instead of one single vulnerable root, the whole will remain strong even if individual shoots break. Similarly, the mouldable, plastic webs in PALABAR*mas* are always in the process of forming in all directions (or dimensions), and thus will, even if one thread breaks, maintain their strength, or even gain transcendental strength; the process of breaking allows for subsequent experiences. In fact, it is through breaks and divisions that new threads come to exist. In the introduction, Vicuña, by taking apart and reconnecting the words 'vida' and 'divina', explains that the divinity of life comes from dividing and multiplying: 'La vida es divina porque se divide y multiplica a sí misma/Ser vivo es ser parte de la divinidad' (p. 22). Vicuña sees divinity within the possibilities and multiplicities of life itself — life is part of divinity.[58] Just as cells divide and multiply themselves, the divine as Vicuña sees it does not consist of one, separate entity, but has multiple lives within it; the cell differentiates itself, it 'divides' in order to create. Therefore, by calling for multiple readers to create the poems, Vicuña, like the concrete poets as well as Martínez and Lira, abandons the idea of a single, authoritative, divine creator. Her vision is not only one of the relationship between the human and the divine, but also, in its implicit critique of totalitarian regimes, one of a more egalitarian political structure.[59]

Vicuña goes further to suggest that the 'palabrarmas' are not only material, plastic entities, but are living beings.[60] Vicuña equates the 'palabrarma' with a flower, something three-dimensional and a living thing. The word first appears as a seed (p. 33, ll. 1–4). The word is not a transparent signifier leading to a signified, but is a solid, opaque body that forces the reader to confront the signifier itself. Moreover, it exists as a body of a seed, something that has the potential, with the right nutrients, to divide itself and create a plant. By describing the word as a body made up of organic material, Vicuña indicates that the word itself has the ability to come alive when it is seen. Similarly, the concrete poets describe their poems as objects that are alive.[61] Vicuña emphasises the animate nature of the word though the word's

57 Ibid., pp. 1–28.

58 The emphasis on divinity is not something one tends to find in concrete poetry. However, they do recognise the 'life' of the poem (see below).

59 States (such as the United States or Israel, for example) and some terrorist organisations have applied rhizomatic and other Deleuzean structures as a tactic to carry out oppressive or devasting acts. See, for example, Eyal Weizman, 'Walking through Walls: Soldiers as Architects in the Israeli-Palestinian Conflict', *Radical Philosophy*, 136 (2006), 8–22. However, these tactics tend to be used as tools for ultimately authoritarian or hierarchical goals. Vicuña, on the other hand, uses the rhizomatic organisation for the sake of creating non-hierarchical communities. Even though there will always be, to some extent, the authority of the author, she attempts to create, on clearly a small scale, rhizomatic connections between author, reader(s) and text.

60 While Deleuze does not make the link between life and divinity per se, he does equate life with immanence, and immanence defines the transcendental field. Immanence is also like a rhizome — it exists as 'becoming' and as 'possibility'. See Deleuze, *Pure Immanence: Essays on a Life*, trans. by Anne Boyan (Zone Books: New York, 2001), pp. 25–33.

61 Augusto de Campos states: 'como um objeto dinâmico, uma célula via, um organismo

actions (it shows her something, for example); the word is a grammatical subject throughout the poem, and thus carries out actions. The word begins as a seed that appears in the air, not sprouting from a root stuck in the ground, but instead is suspended; the word, even in its initial stages, is not 'rooted' in a single meaning or reading. Like a flower, the word grows as it opens:

Se abría y deshacía
y de sus partes brotaban
asociaciones dormidas' (p. 33, ll. 5–7)

It opens itself up to the speaker, but also undoes or dissolves itself. Just as a flower's bulb becomes undone as it opens, the word undoes itself. A bulb, moreover, opens itself into multiple parts. Similarly, the word multiplies into parts, which allows for new associations to form from it; it is in its multiplicity that it is understood.

This multiplicity, however, only emerges from the process of dissolution and rupture.[62] Dissolution can imply harm, but from harm new things can sprout. On the page, the line after 'asociaciones dormidas' is indented to the middle of the page, and the following two are indented even further to the right, breaking away from the left margin:

Enamorados
        en amor, morado
        enajenados (p. 33, ll. 8–10)

With the left-hand margin as the conventional placement of ordinary consciousness in a poem, the word 'enamorados' requires a break from the previous line and from the left margin in order to be understood in a new way. In the word for 'in love', Vicuña finds the word love, but also the word for purple (maybe to indicate royalty, with its association to the divine) or bruised (implying pain). If one looks at the parts of a (broken) word, one can find new insights into its meaning. Here, Vicuña suggests that love involves both pleasure and pain, a combination that can make one somewhat demented or alienated ('enajenado'), or other ('ajeno'). However, the pain is what makes the word 'enamorado', and thus allows one to be in love. Vicuña pluralises 'enamorado', illustrating that to be in love is not a singular state, but a multiple and yet still unified one.[63]

This dissolution also creates poetry. In the break between 'canto' ('song' or 'edge') and 'dome' (this could be the subjunctive conjugation of 'domar', 'domesticate' or 'tame' in Spanish; or could be the English word for 'round-shaped roof' or colloquially 'head') song can emerge:

en el quiebre
entre canto y dome
canto (p. 33, ll. 16–18)

When they are read together, they are temporally brought together in the present continuous temporality of song: 'cantándome'.

completo, com propiedades psico-físicoquímicas, tacto antenas circulação coração: viva'. Augusto de Campos, 'Poesia Concreta', in *Teoria da Poesia Concreta*, p. 42. See Figure 1.4 for an example.

62 This process is reminiscent of what is essential to Lira's poetry (see Chapter 3).

63 However, it might not be very radical because it is still only dual, as the words rhyme with 'dos'.

When and where does this break between 'canto' and 'dome' occur? One could argue that breaks happen constantly within the web created by the readings, but the poem also breaks from logocentric structures of thought. In other words, Vicuña argues that breaking away from, or dissolving the logical social structure is needed to create the web she desires. Being in love also requires a bit of insanity or alienation ('enajenados'). In one of her 'palabrarmas', she emphasises that letting go of logic can result in something productive:

cada
error (p. 69)

One could read this poem as: 'cada error caer', 'cada error da', 'caer da error', etc. Just as the words formed in Augusto de Campos' 'Linguaviagem' 'travel' with the reader across the box of pages (see Chapter 1 and Figure 1.12), the words in Vicuña's poem fall down a line on the page, yet, in doing so, they do not die, but exist as different, ephemeral combinations. Vicuña illustrates that falling ('caer') comes from every mistake, but, by falling from a logical, supposedly mistake-free structure (like a root-tree), one can give ('dar'). In the opening poem, when the speaker falls, she sings:

Encantándome se sucedían
domos y cúpulas de encanto
cantaban en mi

Ascendía en el vertigo
Desbarrancándome

en el quiebre[...]
canto (p. 33, ll. 11–18)

Instead of attempting to avoid mistakes and avoid falling down from the peak of a linear structure, the poem implies that the mistakes and the fall (which also can be associated with risk and chance) are important elements in the creation of poetry; creation requires risk, destruction and (re)construction.

Vicuña's acceptance and promotion of error indicates a rejection of logical, neat order, one which the patriarchy promotes, just as in Gertrude Stein's in 'Patriarchal Poetry', in which Stein urges people to 'make it a mistake', instead of adhering to the orderly, 'neat' logic of patriarchy.[64] Vicuña similarly encourages a criticism of the phallogocentric system. The creation of words, as she claims in the first poem of the book, occurs by means of the figure of a woman:

La imagen tiene muslos
en su fractal
caderas y llagas
por donde entrar

Es madre y ventolera
su cuerpo fino
acomete y espera (p. 34, ll. 24–30)

64 Gertrude Stein, 'Patriarchal Poetry', in Gertrude Stein, *The Yale Gertrude Stein* (New Haven: Yale University Press, 1980), pp. 106–46 (p. 124).

For Vicuña, woman and mother are the body of creation, and man is no longer the protagonist of this creation story. The 'weapon' of her poetry as she fights against logocentrism results in a critique of patriarchy. However, the imagery of opening up and entering the 'image', as well as the act of opening up and entering words (even the term 'palabrir' contains the word 'abrir', 'to open') throughout the book, could be seen as images and acts of penetration. Vicuña seems to evoke here Luce Irigaray's notion of the speculum as a male tool for further penetration of a woman that, paradoxically, imitates the same shape of that which it seeks to illuminate and in which he may see nothing except himself reflected.[65]

Unlike patriarchies and other hierarchies that thrive on a teleological 'story' of their success structured by a beginning and ending, her poems, with no beginnings or endings, do not lend themselves to linear readings; rather, her structure recalls the plateaus of the rhizome that exist in a middle space, with no orientation toward a summit.[66] Similarly, Vicuña attempts to create poems that exist in the middle, that is, poems that are not defined by their beginning and end. Although the text invites beginnings, there is never one starting place or origin. To refer to Deleuze and Guattari's terms again, the text is always *becoming*; the poem is a process of movement and change.[67]

Vicuña explains that she had to become part of the words in order to 'palabrir': 'El cuerpo de las palabras se abría para dejarme entrar y yo sentía su interior como ellas me sentían a mí. Cambiábamos de lugar con la fluidez de un gozo corporal' (p. 14). Because there is a 'change of place', the relationship between the speaker and the words is not only mutual, but also is bodily, sexually or maternally, so. One has to enter physically into the body of the word to truly see the divinity of the word, and thus to live. Vicuña explains that the exercise of making 'palabrarmas' is to live in words: 'Palabrir es vivir en las palabras, experimentarlas como si fueran recién nacidas, y ellas y nosotros llegáramos al encuentro por primera vez' (p. 24). 'Palabrir' is to engage from inside of the words in order to see, and thus understand, them in a new light. Such becoming one with the body of the word is an instance of Vicuña's modification of concrete poetics.

To see words anew is not just an individual act, but a universal and collective one. As Vicuña states, 'La insistencia en *ver* las palabras, en su doble sentido interior y exterior, es uni*ver*sal' (p. 82). The universal act of 'seeing' these words therefore is a shared experience that, through rhizomatic readings, becomes collective. This collective act is communication:

común
unica
acción (p. 67).

65 Vicuña could be attempting to reappropriate the tool, or, perhaps, on the other hand, she has fallen into a phallocentric endeavour. For a discussion of Irigaray, see Toril Moi, *Sexual/Textual Politics* (Methuen: London, 1985), p. 131.

66 Deleuze and Guattari, *A Thousand Plateaus*, pp. 21–22.

67 Ibid., pp. 1–28.

From within the words and from the words in relation to one another, the reader can *see* new words and meanings. The words themselves communicate 'communication', but that act is both common and unique. Vicuña shows that the word 'comunicación' requires 'unique' individuals to act *with* one another. In other words, communication requires both individuality ('única') and sharing ('común'). Whereas the concrete poets' aim is to separate the text from the individual in favour of the universal, the tension between universal and individual in Vicuña's poem, like in Martínez's work (see Chapter 2), is productive. Vicuña uses the form of a concrete poem in order to explain that making and maintenance of a community requires individual action.

In sum, the word as a 'palabrarma' is at the same time something other, divine, and something formed with the reader. Vicuña particularly creates object-poems to allow for strong, divine bonds. To be divine, for her, does not mean to be an authoritative other, but requires conversations with and within words — with the reader and also her own absorption in them. Words are 'plastic' because they are material and separate, but also because they are *mouldable*, not yet fully moulded; that is, with the reader's engagement, they can continuously form. A sense of urgency, but also danger and a sense that something powerful is at stake are conveyed by Vicuña's creation of a word suspended from an unknown source, a prayer made with uncertain results, and a structure in which everything is hanging by a thread. Seeming to pray for a reader who can connect the threads into a strong, powerful weaving, Vicuña at once exploits the principles of concretism but radically moves beyond its secularism.

The Page

Turning now to her book, *Instan* (2002), I aim to show how Vicuña's use of the page creatively furthers the project in plasticity that she achieves at the level of the word in PALABRAR*mas*.[68] All of the features of her plastic poetry are grounded in the use of the page, or two-dimensional space, as the poetic unit. Expanding on the concrete poets' 'poema-constelação mallarmeano', Vicuña draws 'word-constellations' ('palabras estrellas' [77], as she has said), that is, words or parts of words that are strewn across the page, sometimes connected by lines.[69] With these

68 This subsection has been developed from my previously published article: Rachel Robinson, 'Plastic Poetry of the Page: Cecilia Vicuña's Instan', *Latin American Literary Review*, 40.90 (2018), 33–43. Vicuña's book *I-tu* (2004), is a development of *Instan*, but this analysis will focus solely on *Instan*.

69 Haroldo de Campos, 'La Obra de Arte Aberta,' in Augusto de Campos, *Teoria da Poesia Concreta*, p. 28. A few critics have investigated Vicuña's vision of the universe. For example, Coleman insightfully explores the materiality and relationality of Vicuña's work from a subatomic lens looking at subatomic parts to a macroscopic level of the body and towards the universe. Vera Coleman, 'El huso en el centro del universo: el entrelazamiento cuántico en la poesía visual de Cecilia Vicuña', *Letras femininas*, 42.1 (2016), 179–93. Candice Amich proposes that Vicuña, in her poetic film *Kon Kon*, refigures precarity under neoliberal globalisation into planetarity by looking at precapitalist cultures that do not distinguish or aim to eliminate the distinction between nature and culture. Candice Amich, 'From Precarity to Planetarity: Cecilia Vicuña's Kon Kon', *The Global South*, 7.2

constellations, she, like the concrete poets, makes the page (as opposed to the word or even the line) fundamental to this collection and encourages the reader through the contemplation and physical engagement of the page to reconstruct his/her perceptions of space. In this regard, the two-dimensionality of the page promotes virtual three-dimensionality. Fundamental uncertainties of space are characteristic of the condition of the exile, the primary human type that appears in *Instan*. The reader, like Vicuña, becomes an 'exile' whose space can either be one of isolation or of new connections. The spatiality of the poems occasions and results in the image of a created web. The poetic unit in *Instan* is not so much the word as the images the words create on the page, images of webs that evoke webs of human connections and of 'translations' across boundaries of an exilic isolation.

The structure of *Instan* informs its plasticity of the page. *Instan* is a single book of poems eighty-two pages long, consisting of five interrelated sections. The first section, titled 'gramma kellcani (the drawings)', contains pencil-drawn 'poems' (that can either be read separately or as parts of one continuous poem) that consist of words, parts of words, or letters connected by lines (see Figure 4.5 for examples). In the majority of the 'drawings', the words and/or letters float above or beside the lines; some break the lines up, and some flow into the lines or become part of them. The first and last pages of this section, however, contain no lines, and the last drawing consists only of dots. While Vicuña offers a largely visual poem in the first section, in the second section, titled 'el poema cognado/the poem', she provides a legible version of the same poem. This poem, which is eight pages long, consists of two or three line stanzas, with each line containing only one or two words. Like many other poems throughout her *oeuvre*, this poem looks like a quipu string, with each stanza 'acting' as a knot. The words and stanzas of this poem, more importantly, correspond almost directly to the drawings of the first section (that is, the words of the drawings are the same as those in the poem, although there are a few words in the drawings that do not exist in the poem).[70] As Vicuña defines it in the title ('el poema cognado'), the poem in this section is the legible cognate of the visual poem of the first section. These first two sections are calligrammatic: the pages of the first section contain visual webs formed by the words and lines, and the pages of the second section seem to portray precarious threads that have yet to be connected into a web.

The next section, titled 'fábulas del comienzo y restos del origen//fables of the beginning and the remains of the origin', contains a short 'poetical poetics' that includes quotations, notes and stanzas in verse. In the fourth section, Vicuña includes what she titles 'carta or end note' which, written in prose, explains how she 'encountered' the idea of the book.[71] The final section, called 'dixio nary a diction', is a dictionary that provides Vicuña's own definitions of most of the Spanish and Quechua words she uses in the drawings and the poem.

(2013), 134–52.

70 Although this poem acts as a guide, it might, as I will discuss later, restrict the interpretations of the drawings.

71 This is similar to the first and final sections of PALABRAR*mas* (see 'The Word').

Fig. 4.5. Vicuña, *Instan* (drawings).
Courtesy of Cecilia Vicuña.

com
prehend
pel
plement
miserate

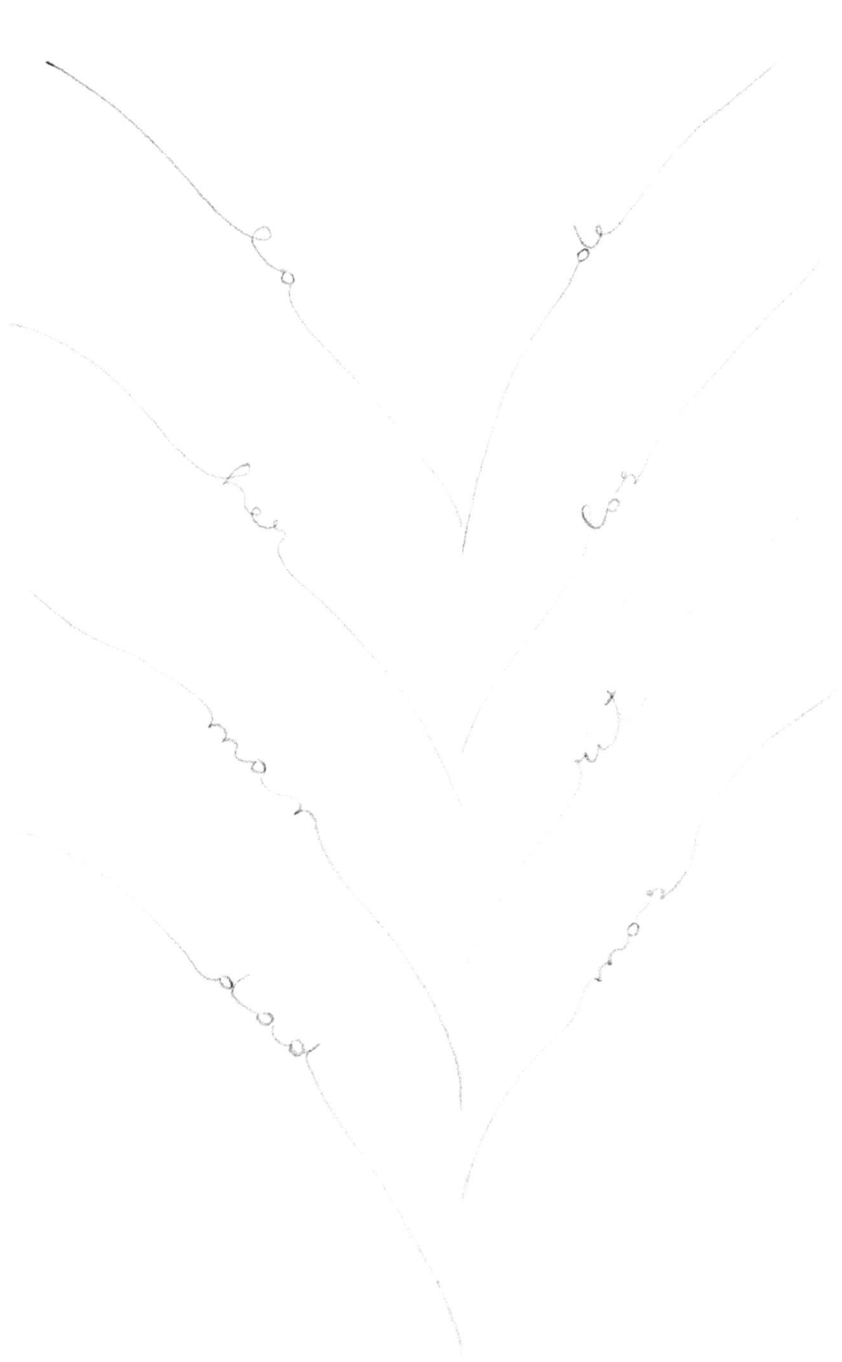

For Vicuña, the page allows for a poetry that recreates the experience of exile. At the same time, it responds to and transforms that condition. She conveys her understanding of the context from which she writes, a position of exile in a contemporary world where people tend to be unaware of, or give no weight to, the connections they have with one another. She supplies a poetic response that attempts to 'heal', or strengthen, the links between people. Like the space of exile she inhabits, Vicuña's poems, and the words within them, are, in her own terms, 'non-places': 'A word is a non-place for the encounter to take "place"' (*Instan*, p. 71). Vicuña's 'non-place' recalls one defined by the contemporary French anthropologist Marc Augé: 'If a place can be defined as relational, historical and concerned with identity, then a space which cannot be defined [as such] will be a non-place.'[72] In contrast to what he calls an 'anthropological place', a 'non-place' refers to a location in which 'inscriptions of the social bond [...] or collective history' cannot be seen.[73] A 'non-place' in Vicuña's work seems to be a space of perpetual betweenness.[74] She, however, does not create these 'non-place' poems in order to wallow in the state of the deterioration of connections she perceives; instead, she uses the condition of exile to transform displacement into strength. In *Instan*, Vicuña allows for the possibility of encounters 'taking place' and for identities to exist, albeit in a fluid form.

The individual poems of this book, as well as their relationship between the sections, can clearly be seen as a development of concretism in their words' spatial arrangements. With the final sections as guides, the reader follows the paths of the lines in the first section with his/her eyes and with his/her body, in a kind of visual and kinetic consciousness, to connect the letters and form words and phrases. Many of the drawings do not have a beginning or an end, so, as it is in concrete poetry, it is up to the reader to decide how to read them (see, for example, Figure 1.12). The 'guides', while more communicative and defining than concretist codes, resemble the keys and poems that 'guide' the reader in many concrete poems (especially in process poems). However, unlike the concrete poets, Vicuña particularly emphasises that the connections between the words are manifestations of bond-creation. The drawn lines and lack of a clear linear reading suggests an emphasis on a place *between* narrative, time, and space. Vicuña illustrates the movement of a nomad: just as a nomad moves (albeit patiently) from place to place, never settling completely in one place or another, the text moves (and invites the reader to move) from language to language, from drawing to poem and vice-versa, always remaining between. In other words, the text exemplifies a place of 'crossing over', that is, 'translation' in its etymological sense; as Bourriaud argues, 'translation is in essence an act of displacement.'[75] The between place of the lines and the movement between languages, I will argue, represents the place in which one in exile exists, that is,

72 Examples of Auge's non-places include airports, supermarkets, hotels, motorways, etc. Augé, *Non-Places*, p. 63.

73 Ibid., viii.

74 Following Augé, I will use the term 'space' in this way throughout to further the definition of 'non-place', that is, a space that cannot yet be defined as a place. Augé, *Non-Places*, p. 63.

75 Bourriaud, *The Radicant*, p. 54.

between cultures, but a place between that allows for strong, albeit precarious, connections.[76]

Vicuña defines the poems and drawings in *Instan* as urgent responses, expressed visually on the page and aurally when read aloud, to the alienation contemporary society produces.[77] In the 'end note', Vicuña defines the word *Instan*: '*Instan* is the third person plural of the infinitive "instar," meaning, "to urge, to press, to reply." It first appears in Spanish in 1490 and is associated with political demands. In English it means 'to stud with stars', and Vicuña tells the reader what it means for her: 'For me it suggests a movement inward, towards the sta, the inner star "standing" in the verb "to be": estar [...] Instan, el libro de la palabra estrella, is the journey inside the word *Instan*' (p. 77). Because 'instan' refers to stars, being, and response, the word brings together a sense of someone responding to the world in a 'non-place,' which may not be of this world, but instead is located elsewhere in the cosmos. The page in *Instan* thus represents the cosmos, and is 'studded with stars', or words.

Vicuña's title and her definition of it evoke, and most likely allude to, Mallarmé and the concrete poets' 'poetic constellations' that constitute the page.[78] To these poets, a poem is like a constellation, a drawn map created by the spatial relationships between the stars, that is, the words on the page. It is not just the words that form the poem, but the white space between them that connects them. In the drawings section, Vicuña creates her own visual poetry, that is, her versions of constellations, but, as we have seen, she takes the divinity of them more seriously than do most concretists. For Vicuña, the constellation is a cosmic response to the world. In *Instan*, each page in its entirety is a constellation (many with the lines between the 'word-stars', or 'palabras estrellas', already visibly drawn for the viewer), and the pages together create a series of constellations that form a night sky (Figure 4.5, for example). Just as concrete poems do, Vicuña's 'drawings' encourage the reader to focus on the spatial relationships between the letters and words. In fact, Vicuña emphasises the spatial relationships so much so that they become just as, if not more, 'meaningful' than the words themselves (see, for example, Figure 4.5, in which the words literally translate, or 'cross over' one another). The words, as in concrete poetry, become separated from the signifieds behind them, and thus become material. Ceasing to be merely signs, they become material insofar as they can communicate through means other than those ascribed to conventional language. In Vicuña's 'drawings', not only do the words become material, but the connecting space between them becomes visible and solid in the form of drawn lines.

76 Many have argued that the Latin American condition itself is one of betweenness (see, for example, the discussion in Chapter 2 of Cortázar's 'Axolotl'). Santiago also describes Latin America as the space in-between, within which 'to speak, to write, means to speak against, to write against'. Santiago, *The Space In-Between*, p. 31. Vicuña's position is even more precarious as an exile between the 'space in-between' and the 'West' and perhaps therefore more urgent, leading her to write 'Palabrarmas', or word-weapons, to 'write against' that precariousness.

77 Vicuña's explanatory 'poetical poetics' that she includes throughout her work could be seen as 'instructions for use', like those one finds in non-places. See Augé, *Non-Places*, p. 77.

78 Mallarmé, *Un Coup de dés*, pp. 121–22, and Haroldo de Campos, 'A obra de arte aberta', in *Teoria da Poesia Concreta*, pp. 30–33. In addition, the word 'constellation' appears in Mallarmé's poem. Mallarmé, *Un Coup de dés* , pp. 144–45. See Chapter 1.

Coupled with translations into multiple languages, the 'crossing over' of the lines and readings of these poems literally enacts on the page translation in its etymological sense.[79] The poems create a 'non-place' of translation; the poems on the page then are nomadic, in that they are constantly changing, crossing over, that is, translating, from language to language, and never staying still in one side or another.[80] Translation, moreover, furthers the mirroring effects of the page, for each translation reflects and responds to the preceding language. By translating between languages and never privileging one language over another, Vicuña illustrates the poems' ability to be constantly remoulded and renewed. In the poem(s) of section one and two, Vicuña writes in Spanish, English, Greek, and Quechua.[81] Joris explains that nomadic poems do not simply offer translations or words to be translated, but rather keep many languages in play at the same time.[82] Similarly, Vicuña does not merely translate literally, but combines the different languages by playing with cognates, both visually and aurally, and with definitions of certain words in various languages.[83] For instance, she places Spanish words next to (or close to) their translations into English, creating stanzas in which the sequence of words mirror each other (although with a slight difference):

madre
del habla [...]

mother
of time (p. 59, ll. 9–16, Figure 4.5)

In this case, she mirrors the first stanza in the last, but switches languages from Spanish to English. In addition, she changes the last word of the mirrored phrase from 'habla' to 'time'. It thus seems as though the mother of speech is also the mother of time (I will discuss the connection between origin and word further below). The translation also evokes a sense of conversation, and thus connection, between the two languages.

While there is a connection between both languages, they are still expressed (visually and aurally) distinctly. The 'drawing' of the first stanza of this passage is an inward-moving spiral with the letters detached from the lines, whereas the last stanza's 'drawing' (Figure 4.5) looks like a large asterisk made of four lines, each line

79 Drawing on Deleuze and Guattari's concept of 'a line of flight', de Zegher proposes that Vicuña's sculptures, as weavings, also exist as a space between. De Zegher, *The Precarious*, pp. 30–31.
80 Pierre Joris, *A Nomad Poetics* (Middletown: Wesleyan University Press, 2003), pp. 5–6.
81 It is worth noting that the titles of the sections are all in some way translated, but each translation is connected to its cognate in a different way: with parentheses, a slash, a line break, the word 'or', or a play on the multiple translations within one word: 'contents//1. gramma kellcani (the drawings)//2. el poema cognado/the poem//3. fábulas del comienzo y restos del origen//fables of the beginning and remains of the origin//4. cartas or end note//5. dixio nary a diction'. The entire book is thus based on translation — beginning with visual poems that are translated into a 'verse' poem, which is translated to poetics, and then into a dictionary.
82 Although nomads might not be multilingual, their movements between places are similar to those movements that one in exile might take between languages.
83 Even the poem section is a cognate for the drawings, as Vicuña calls the section 'el poema cognado'. Moreover, the sections are maternally linked: they are 'born together' (cognado).

beginning and ending with a syllable or letter. While there is a connection between both languages, they are still expressed (visually and aurally) differently. Thus the conversation occurs not only through the translation of language, but also through a visual translation of the form of the language; the reader, like a nomad, passes through both meanings and forms of language.

Vicuña mirrors languages through her use of the spelling and sound of cognates and false cognates. For example, she 'crosses' between languages within the words:

el sign
o
no es
si no
insi
nua t
ción (p. 59, ll. 17–23)

She takes apart the word 'signo' to find 'sign', a word with the same meaning in English, and then 'translates' aurally: 'signo' has the aural 'cognate' of 'si no'. With the cognates 'insinuation' and insinuación', the 't' visually demonstrates the crossing point between the two languages.[84]

Vicuña also 'translates' within the same language by taking words apart into their roots and prefix parts. For instance, she takes apart the word 'respond':

a pond
res ponds

libar
the way
you
re spond (p. 61, ll. 59–64)[85]

The body of water (a pond) answers (responds) by re-sponding.[86] In other words, it creates itself anew.[87] Renewal occurs when one looks at words in a new way, either by taking apart the word and finding new ones inside it or by translating it into other languages. Mirroring is a vital principle in *Instan*. It can be understood as a form of renewal: a pond reflects, or mirrors, its surroundings, creating a new, yet similar, image. The mirrored image comes after the original one, and in this

84 When discussing Vicuña's 'precarios,' Lippard similarly proposes that 'the cross form that recurs in the sculptures [...] might also be a symbol of bicultural experience, paths that both meet and depart'. Lippard, 'Spinning the Common Thread', in *The Precarious*, p. 11. Again, this cross is also reminiscent of the 'x' of Cortázar's Axolotl and its connotations (see Chapter 2).

85 These stanzas do not have corresponding 'drawings'. The deconstruction of the word 'respond' is reminiscent of what Vicuña does in PALABRAR*mas*. In addition, 'pond' can be translated into Spanish as 'estanque' or 'estanco', each containing the stem of 'in*stan*', which further connects the English word to the rest of the book.

86 Vicuña emphasises the relational nature of understanding art with the image of the pond. As a reflective surface, the pond responds to the person looking at it, that is, the reader/viewer.

87 Another way one could read the line is in a Heideggerian or Steinian sense that 'a pond ponds'; or, like Borges's language of Tlön, the 'pond' does not have an essence, only its action. See Borges, 'Tlön, Uqbar, Orbis Tertius', *Ficciones*, pp. 13–37.

way is a response; unlike the reflection of Narcissus, this reflection responds. This process of mirroring, for Vicuña, is the act of offering (libar, spond), and it requires one to do it not once, but continuously: 're', going back and doing it again.[88] Mirroring, as an act of translation, thus requires constant refiguring and continuous 'crossing over.'[89] Translation also occurs as poetic form: 'spond' makes one think of 'spondee,' and the line 're spond' is a spondaic foot. Translation therefore occurs in poetic form used as a libation to the divine (from 'libar').

The special character of the drawings in *Instan* is also formed by 'translation', or 'carrying/crossing over'. In many of the 'drawings,' Vicuña solidifies the 'crossing over' from one letter or word to another by drawing a line between them (Figure 4.5). In these 'drawings', the lines not only cross over to different words, but also cross over themselves. Each line, on its own, could be seen as vulnerable, or in a *precarious* position (although less so than the 'invisible' lines in PALALBRAR*mas* or in most concrete poems because in *Instan* they are actually drawn), but, the more lines are drawn, the stronger the network becomes. The instances of translation in nomadic poetry, as Joris explains, inform its rhizomatic qualities.[90] Each line is like an 'offshoot' of a rhizome, which, when alone, is vulnerable and may easily break, but when joined with other offshoots, becomes stronger and less precarious. Vicuña's translations create a network of crossing threads that do not remain stagnant in one language because the signs and various meanings of the signs move between multiple languages.

Vicuña not only translates words and lines from language to language, but 'crosses over' different modes of artistic expression. Like Martínez, Lira and many concrete poets, Vicuña weaves together drawing, poem, poetics, letters and didactic texts into one book. She not only blends together or makes a collage of the genres, however, but also allows for a constant movement between them, creating what Joris describes as a 'material flux of language matter'.[91] In the third section, she states: 'A continuous displacement, a field of "con," togetherness.//A word disappears, the connection remains' (p. 71). As difficult as this might be, Vicuña seems to call for an acceptance of her position within a 'non-place' and advocates for a continuous movement between cultures.[92]

Vicuña maintains this continuous movement in part by forcing the reader/viewer to focus on the changing movements *between* the words and languages. In the poem, Vicuña emphasises the space between words:

luz y del qué
the space
between words
imantando

88 The act of offering adds to the precarious nature of the poems; they are pleas.

89 This kind of mirroring is distinct from mimesis or imitation, in which one tries to create a perfect copy of the original, whereas this mirroring emphasises the continual process of renewal.

90 Joris, *A Nomad Poetics*, pp. 5–6.

91 Ibid., p. 5.

92 Ibid., p. 6. This is not to say that one cannot linger in one place or another, only that one should not remain static. Joris explains that a poem is 'a stop in the moving along the nomad line-of-flight'; Vicuña's poems, as 'instants', act in a similar fashion (pp. 46–47).

el cruzar

crossing
magnet (p. 60, ll. 32–38, Figure 4.5)

Like the concrete poets who foregrounded spatial relationships between words, Vicuña here explains that the space between words is not empty, but rather is full of light ('luz') and energy ('imantando', 'magnet').

The space between words that manifests on the page, for Vicuña, can be compared to a threshold through which people can pass, but one that continuously changes its location:

luz del
portal

Mei[93]
del migrar (p. 61, ll. 69–72)

Vicuña draws the reader's attention to the space between the words and even the space between the letters so that, like a frontier, it can be recognised and then re-drawn and reformed.[94] The 'portal' for Vicuña, as mirrored in the stanzas above, allows for migration, even for the words themselves. The word 'migrar' most likely refers to Vicuña's own experience as an exile and migrant herself.

The individual, for Vicuña, is both the same person and the other at the same time, or, better said, exists between the same and the other, exists *with*. S/he is neither someone else, nor the same person, neither fully one nor the other. As Vicuña states in the third section:

Per haps, in di vi dual says
un divided dual attention
un divided dual belonging
to itself and the whole at once.

Dis solve into union it says.
You will always be longing (p. 73)

The between-state from which Vicuña writes and in which her poems (at least ideally) exist is both unique and shared, as she says in the third section: 'a uni verse wants to *con* verse'. Paradoxically, the individual must divide in order for it to form connections with others ('dual'), or become something inclusive ('con' instead of 'uni'), a process that also involves giving ('di'), speaking ('di' as imperative), and seeing ('vi'). In other words, poetry ('verse', as an act of giving, and requires language and vision), for Vicuña (and as we saw in PALABRAR*mas*), requires dissolution and reforming. However, the constant dissolving and division requires one to reach continually for something ungraspable. Because one will always be part individual and part collective, never fully one or the other, one 'will always be longing'.

93 Here, 'Mei' could be the translation of 'light' into Japanese (although the word has many definitions in Japanese), thus emphasising the light and energy that the space between words carries.
94 For Augé's definition of a frontier, see Augé, *Non-Places*, pp. xiv–xv.

As the title suggests and as a radical development from concretism, the visionary demands of the plastic 'non-place' in *Instan* have their temporal counterpart in what Vicuña calls 'ecstasy,' the affective experience of the instant. She explains in the third section, 'Time awakens inside words'. In particular, the 'time' of her poems is the instant, at once present and originary, at the beginning of time:

> Silence
> Turns the page
> The poem begins.
> Alba del habla, the dawn of speech [...]
>
> 'The soul co-authors the instant', Humberto Giannini says.
>
> Time undone by the instant!
>
> A continuum contradicted by name, time is 'tem': to cut.
>
> An instant is present,
> It 'stands',
> A filament of *sta*, a state of being, stamen,
> A thread in a warp,
> A web in ecstasy. (p. 69)

The poem, as an instant, according to Vicuña, exists both as an origin, as it exists on the page, and in the present because it is both continuous and ephemeral. Thus, time is 'undone by the instant!' Time is organised by past and future, beginning and end, but the instant of poetry is always in the present. As she says poetically, it is a 'web in ecstasy', 'ecstasy' coming from the Greek ékstasis, meaning displacement, away from (ec) stance (stasis), or out of oneself. We can now say that the word is instant *on the page*, instant is present, present is a web in ecstasy, and this web exists within a 'non-place' of a consciousness out of time.

The image of a web in 'ecstasy' mirrors many of the 'drawings' in section one (Figure 4.3). Each line, as a thread, crosses over and connects to make a web. Moreover, this thread is 'in a warp'. The thread seems to be spinning in a circular motion, as though someone were spinning it into yarn from wool (in other words, creating it). As she says in another part of the third section, the poem itself is a vortex: 'El poema se desvanece en el vórtice entre las dos'.[95] The energy from the spinning vortex disappears, or dissipates, in the space between the two 'lenguas'. To form the 'web in ecstasy', the poem's words (or the threads) 'dissipate' like 'dissolving particles' in a space between. Because the 'threads' of space between the words, moreover, draw the reader away from the signifieds of the words, the act of moulding, that is, of plasticity, in *Instan* occurs as 'ecstasy'; the reader engages with the space beside the subjective word.

For Vicuña, connections in such a web gain strength in the instant. The instant, for her is a cord, like the string of a quipu:

95 The image of the poem as vortex is reminiscent twentieth-century Vorticism, such as the pre-WWI works of Ezra Pound and Wyndham Lewis, in which they attempted to create a spiralling energy that spun into a culminating point.

el instante
es la cuerda
vital (p. 66, ll. 82–84, Figure 4.5)

The instant in which the poem originates is the vital string that forms connections.[96] Moreover, the relationship between the quipu-like poem, in which words precariously hang down the page and the drawings, that take apart the threaded quipu-threads and weave them across the page, emphasises the vitality of strings as bonding material.

These bonds recall an origin, in fact, the beginning of life: infancy, that is, the time without speech.[97] For Vicuña, the poem similarly begins without language; her extremely short lines and the drawings of the dismantled words suggest the beginnings of language out of silence. She alludes (see below) to the imagery of milk to indicate a necessary state for poetic language. During infancy, one needs to drink breast milk (or some substitute formula) in order to survive. Vicuña emphasises that words themselves carry a similar, vital milk of infancy. Such a state of infancy can imply the involvement of a motherly figure, and here Vicuña yet again conveys a feminist vision of a language of a place between. In the second and third sections, the woman's body to which Vicuña refers is and creates the time and space of between-ness through words; words are the location and time of the 'non-place', and these words are possessed by and embody the motherly figure. Firstly, the woman is the creator of both time and speech:

madre
de habla

imán
del gen

palabra
estrella

mother
of time (p. 59, ll. 9–16)

From the first page, the female figure seems to be the force (both 'imán' and

96 The originating instant, however, does not stay in the past, but continuously recurs in the present. Unlike Deleuze and Guattari's rhizome, in which its shoots can always break off and recreate, Vicuña's poems in *Instan*, however, may recur, but they do not explicitly reshape every time they are read — a reader might become lost when following the lines or might take a while to find where to begin following the lines of a drawing and thus might not read the drawing in a unique fashion, but eventually each reader can find the same logical reading (especially with the help of the poem of the second section) of the drawing. Because the lines connecting the letters and words in many of the 'drawings' are already drawn for the reader and have already been solidified, this book, furthermore, does not fully realise a rhizomatic poetry where the lines can be broken, reformed, renewed, or 'deterritorialised' and 'reterritorialised' by the reader. Deleuze and Guattari, *A Thousand Plateaus*, pp. 9–15. While Deleuze and Guattari's rhizome cannot be captured in any particular instance for fear that it will solidify and come to represent itself, rather than be its constantly moulding self, the 'drawings' are nonetheless, I suggest, *instan*ces of a rhizomatic poetry, or, more precisely, they are like photographs taken of a rhizome at a specific point in time.

97 The word etymologically means 'not able to speak'.

'magnet') of the word, which occurs in time, in an 'instant'. The instant of speech originates with the motherly figure that provides sustenance (words and images, 'imá/gen'). She also provides the genetic code ('gen'); the genes she passes on to the infant could be undeveloped words that, as the infant grows and is provided sustenance (milk), develop into a full language.

The motherly figure creates words on the page not only temporally, but also materially and spatially. Through translating words and parts of words, Vicuña finds the word milk within the words in the following excerpt from the poem:

carry back
el re late
la justicia
de la relación
de volver
el juguito
vital
¿adónde
la leche
de una
teta
común?
a com mon
teat?
milk
del trans
late?
[...]
a suckling
of musical
ink?

la her
mandad
de los rhythm
s (pp. 62–63, ll. 98–125, Figure 4.5)

Mother's milk, according to Vicuña, comes from both the act of translating and the word itself: trans*late* (it sounds like words from Romance languages: latte, leite, lait, leche, etc.). In order to arrive at this meaning of the word, one has first to cut up the word and cross over to other languages. This milk can also be found in the word 'relate'. Vicuña takes the word apart to form the word 're-late', which could be interpreted as 'milk again/back', or 'carry back' (go back to the origin). Vicuña thus connects the words relate, translate, and milk; translation allows for relation because both of the words *carry* the milk that allows for life. The 'non-place' of translation is therefore the space of relation, which is a 'milky' female space.[98]

By breaking up the word 'hermandad', Vicuña also proposes that the space of relationships, this space *between* people, is female. Not only does Vicuña tell us

98 While this could be read as the space of Deleuze and Guattari's 'becoming-woman', it risks essentialising 'woman' as a motherly figure. See Deleuze and Guattari, *A Thousand Plateaus*.

that the word is feminine, but, and more importantly, she separates the English word 'her' from the rest of the word 'mandad'. Vicuña emphasises that fraternal relationships include the feminine other ('her'). One could also read this in two other opposing ways: Vicuña could be separating the 'her' from the rest of the word, meaning 'command' or be 'in charge of', to separate the feminine from the masculine and paternal power (within the Spanish word 'mandad' we find the English word 'man' and the word 'dad'). Moreover, 'mandad', could be read as the plural second person imperative of the infinitive 'mandar', meaning 'to command'. One could also read the word 'her' as a possessive adjective, thus reading the stanza as (more or less) 'her command of rhythms'. 'Her command of rhythms' could thus imply that she (woman) is in command of language. Through the ambiguity of the meaning of this phrase, Vicuña attempts to take away the power of any one signified and away from a male-dominated space to allow the female to 're-territorialise' the space. Feminising the space, however, does not mean a transfer of power from one set of hands to another, but instead a transfer of power from one to many.[99]

In sum, *Instan* is a plastic work, in that the book, like concrete poems, has to be physically manipulated or moulded to be read. The connections Vicuña desires people to recognise and strengthen are not just mental or metaphorical, but physical. Vicuña exaggerates the concretist emphasis on the relationship between reader, text and other potential readers. However, unlike the concrete poets, Vicuña responds to and expresses her temporal and spatial context as an exile of the late twentieth century into the twenty-first. In the age of the Internet, a time in which physical relationships tend to be pushed aside in favour of virtual ones, Vicuña urges us to understand the importance of these relationships, despite the ephemeral and precarious nature that the contemporary world grants them. She evokes on the page the 'non-place' of a pre-symbolic language and the 'ecstasy' of encounter, with it as the vital and transformative occasion for a response to exile. The 'non-place' of the in-between can continuously be moulded and restructured (plasticity) because it doesn't exist as something static, but rather can move to and from its poles. The force that moulds is the translator, the one who 'mirrors' but then 'carries over'. In *Instan*, the translator is feminine, mother, because the space of the between exists not fully belonging to any phallocentric society. The translator is also both poet and reader (or at least leans towards being the reader); Vicuña lays out the translations for the reader to translate. It is through the poetry of this feminine 'non-place' that one can combat the destructive nature of a space without connections. Vicuña attempts to change her situation of exile from one of solitude to one of solidarity and invites others to do so as well. In other words, the page becomes the poetic site for the recovery of relationships.

99 Vicuña here, does not use an essentialist approach, but recognises that the subject of 'woman' is multiple. Although her feminist position is unclear at points, instead of solely essentialising or completely deterritorialising 'woman', she might be attempting, like many contemporary feminists, to reconcile the multiplicity of difference of women without completely deterritorialising subjectivities or falling into the trap of failing to recognise his/her own position into which Rosi Braidotti claims Deleuze falls. Rosi Braidotti, 'Nomadism with a Difference: Deleuze's Legacy in a Feminist Perspective', *Man and World*, 29 (1996), 305–14 (pp. 308–14).

The Book

In comparison to what she achieves in *Instan*, in which the unit of poetry, like that of the Noigandres group, is the page (that, when read, forms its own ephemeral instant), in *cloud-net*, Vicuña, like the neoconcrete poets in some of their poetry, makes the unit the entire book. In fact, Vicuña moves beyond the covers of a book; the book presents references to and stands in conjunction with previous performances and installations similarly titled *cloud-net*.[100] Published in 1999, the book includes essays, poems and photographs that are placed in relation to multiple forms of the project, *cloud-net*, in its entirety. The project began as a dance performance in a New York City pier in 1999. The performance was then the focus of a video, also called *cloud-net*. The video, along with other performances and found objects, was presented at three unique (yet similar) installations in Buffalo, New York (1998), Houston, Texas (1999), and New York City, New York (1999).

Vicuña has described *cloud-net* in its entirety as a poem; the poem thus consists of all four parts: the performance, the installations, the video and the book/catalogue.[101] It is easy to think of *cloud-net* simply as a miscellany of prose and verse statements about Vicuña's art, presented alongside a collection of poems and a catalogue of her visual art and performances. But the book in its very essence presents a range of possibilities for individuals to assert their rights in response to political oppression and the necessarily active role that the reader of her art plays in that assertion. The book becomes an experiment in egalitarian art that differs from that offered in her poetry of the word (in PALABRAR*mas*) and the page (in *Instan*) as it extends from the page connecting with events and performances out of the book, even though elements of the previous books can be found in this work. *Cloud-net* uses and extends the concrete and plastic poetics of the word and the page. However, while concrete poems exist as permanent objects that promote ephemeral readings, *cloud-net* attempts to make permanent the immediacy and ephemerality of events as well as objects, performance and installation art, while simultaneously attempting the apparent opposite, to keep alive the immediacy of participation.

The book of *cloud-net*, as an amalgamation of media and relationships to past events and as a woven message, brings into question the permanence of our world. Vicuña complicates the nature of the poem, as the book becomes a larger manifestation of the poem: the book-as-poem supposes that a poem can have the same effect as a book, but also that a book may be a manifestation of the effects of a poem (weaving and readerly participation, for example), but made permanent. Individual poems within the book draw on concrete poetics like those used in PALABRAR*mas* and *Instan*, but the plasticity of the book brings concretist readerly participation and object creation into new, three-dimensional spaces. While concrete poems are

100 Many concrete poems also move beyond the page into musical performances and videos, a movement that emphasises the process of their creation and the various forms their readings can take. See, for example, the various forms of Ronaldo Azeredo's 'Velocidade', such as in Christian Caseli (director), *Cinco Poemas Concretos* (Rio de Janeiro, 2007), <https://www.youtube.com/watch?v=yC3e7rmSYM4> [accessed 10 May 2015].

101 Vicuña, 'Re: *cloud-net* and other question'.

objects that require active readers/viewers, *cloud-net* strays from the concretist goal of objectivity by placing in conversation specific events of the past with the present and future. Vicuña makes objects out of ephemeral performances and installations as a means of bringing them into the future with their readings.

As Vicuña explains in the magazine *Naked Punch*, her project emerged from the fact that she was asked by three curators to create a travelling installation that would at once 'change from place to place, and yet, always be the same'.[102] After meditating on this idea, as she says, she came upon the image of a 'cloud-basket protecting the Earth from our violence, the heat we create which is warming the atmosphere' and then, after reading a poem by the Indian poet and philosopher Sri Aurobindo, came up with the title 'cloud-net.'[103] A 'cloud-net,' for Vicuña (and those who have engaged with the project), allows the poet and reader to look at the vulnerable state of the current world in a new way in the hope of saving it from further destruction, for example, from global warming.[104] Vicuña reclaims the idea of the net or web, one used so often for capitalist endeavours (such as the Inter*net*, the World Wide *Web* and *net*working), by focusing on an aspect of the net or web that emphasises the 'web of life', that is, the strength of connections that form the net (those between people, past and present, cultures, people and earth, etc.). In an interview with David Levi Strauss (which is included in the book of *cloud-net*), she explains what she means by 'net' and 'web' today:

> That's why I began the poem of cloud-net with the line "hanging by a thread, the web says..." — to play again with the forgotten association between the World Wide Web and the web of life. For someone like me, "www" is "weaving, weaving, weaving." Other fragments of the poem continue to play with certain capitalist ideas such as "net worth," proposing a new form of reading it, as the worth of the net itself. (p. 19)

Part of this 'new form of reading' was manifested in performance. A few days after she titled the project in 1998, she invited some friends to an unannounced event at the Finger Pier on the Hudson River. The three women who attended danced with threads, weaving them together and unweaving them into a large net as roller-bladers, runners and bikers passed through. These skaters and bikers, as Vicuña describes, 'rode under or above [the net], becoming for an instant, the images of a living loom.'[105] The video titled *cloud-net* is of this performance. It is set with the World Trade Center in the background, and, towards the end, includes words and phrases in white writing, which fade in and out on top of the performance. The installations — all unique performances — included videos, readings and songs by Vicuña herself as she held threads of wool that she encouraged the audience to touch and move around, and tables (in the book, called the 'Poet's Table') with what she calls 'precarios', or found, thrown away objects (that are both precarious

102 Vicuña, 'On Cloud Net', *Naked Punch*, 9 (2007).

103 Ibid.

104 Vicuña's warnings of the destruction of the Earth due to global warming are particularly prominent in the poems 'sweatshop' and 'dheu', and are further explained in the 'Notes to the Poems' (p. 95).

105 Vicuña, 'On Cloud Net'.

and prayers, as discussed above), on them. In this form that blends together various media from distinct past events, Vicuña brings together time and space and attempts to make the ephemeral permanent. Moreover, she fuses media together because, as she explains in the interview with Strauss:

> I am a mixed person, a person of two cultures. So I don't trust either [textile or word as medium] — that is the reality. I use everything because I want to ask them all to remember. I write, I sing, I weave at the same time, because I'm at the moment of emergency, at the moment of danger, when you actually feel that all of this could go away. Life itself could go away. The web can disappear. (p. 20)

In *cloud-net*, Vicuña includes concretist poetics of the page, but blends it with practices of the ephemeral performance. In the same interview, she explains that the world is precarious and in need of prayer, with many aspects of it, particularly the importance of relationships, fading from people's memories. In this forgetting, I argue, is the failure to remember the connections we need to maintain the 'web of life'. Vicuña defamiliarises the webs so familiar to us in contemporary technology and creates new ones in multiple forms. She does so in order to allow the viewer/reader/listener to experience them in new ways that remind us of their simultaneous importance and vulnerability. She carries the performance and installations into the book in an attempt to combat this forgetfulness.

The attempt to create something permanent (the book) is what distinguishes *cloud-net* from PALABRAR*mas* (the word) and *Instan* (the page). Making the project into a book, that is, making something fleeting into something stable, is not one-sided. There is a trade-off: the project can survive, but is now something stable and more difficult to change. The ephemerality through which relationships can be continuously woven and unwoven crystallises (to an extent). Moreover, the project moves from the (relatively) non-commercial performance and installations to a book to be sold. In other words, it becomes a product of the very thing she attempts to oppose, that is, consumer society.[106] Through readerly participation, the relational and ephemeral aspects that characterise the performances and installations still (paradoxically) exist, albeit subtly, even though they reside in the stable and permanent book.

The book must be considered in its entirety, but not as the sole catalogue of the project's performances, videos and installations, but rather as one form of it. Not only a collection of poems, it is a collection of interconnected parts (each section and page are connected to each other) and intra-connected parts (not only are the pages and sections connected to the other parts of the project, they also are connected to the reader) that form a whole, a 'many in one'. Because the text requires collaboration with the reader, it moves towards a non-hierarchical authorship. While most concrete poets (particularly those of the Noigandres group) use the spatial arrangement on the page to allow the reader to create his/her own

106 As the poet Guillermo Boido explains, 'La poesía no se vende porque la poesía no se vende'. Mario Arteca and others, *¿Quién habla en el poema?* (Buenos Aires: Dock, 2012), p. 29. However, Vicuña's book is now in a product-form that potentially can be sold.

path through the text, Vicuña extends the unit for participation to the entire book. What particularly distinguishes it from her other books that promote active readerly engagement and concrete poems is its particular relationship to past events; while the concrete poets aim to create ahistorical objects devoid of any context, Vicuña brings ephemeral happenings from the historical past into the book. With such relationships in mind, she attempts to produce similar events in the future through the medium of the book. In *cloud-net*, Vicuña aims to create readers who engage critically with the text and then, she hopes, the world, in order to save it from destruction. While the sections of the book are to be read linearly in a chronological progression, the poems, photographs, and the book's relationship with the previous performance, video and installations complicate the conventional linear reading practices confined and defined by a beginning and an end, and instead emphasise what occurs in between. The non-linear reading of the book can mimic or become the unpredictable 'reading' of the real world; it is connected to real events that have occurred outside the book. If the explications that follow tend to dwell upon 'the word' or 'the page', it is because it is there that the dynamic process of reading takes place, only to extend outward to the larger structure of the book. As I argue, the immediacy of imaginative encounters with word and page becomes, in the context of the stability of the structure of the book, a vision of a reader and community that also can become stabilised in its manifestation of positive human relationships.

In order to explore the book as a whole, I will first describe and analyse *cloud-net* as a book in its complexity and then look at three poems within it. Each of these poems shows how the intentions of the book are realised on a smaller scale. Books, as I have said, typically offer a sense of permanence and stability. Yet, *cloud-net*, in its title, in all the heterogeneous materials within it, in the fact that parts of it are directly performance-and installation-based, and in its driving images of fragility and precariousness, suggests the opposite. This juxtaposition resembles that of the performance of a concretist object-poem with the ephemerality of the readings that it promotes. However, unlike concrete poems, *cloud-net* engages with this paradox in relation to specific contexts. Like the image of the World Trade Center in Vicuña's video, which is a stable image of capitalism and consists of two stable buildings, but is also (as Vicuña argues) on the brink of destruction, the book exists in limbo between immortality and destruction. The image of the World Trade Center in the video is set up against the words: 'We will all go away un less [*sic*] a new net worth is born'.[107] The book is a tool for reconstruction; Vicuña blurs the distinction between the book as artefact and the larger world, and *cloud-net* seems to exist as a *part* of the world, not solely a metaphor for it.

The book of *cloud-net* consists of two main sections: the first part consists of 'Introductions' and 'Essays,' which includes introductions by the curators of each installation, and the essays, 'The Vision', by Laura Hoptman (a curator at the Museum of Modern Art in New York) 'Hilumbres at the Crossroads', by Surpik Angelini (an independent curator and writer), and an interview of Vicuña conducted by David Levi Strauss (a writer and critic). The second part is called

107 Vicuña, 'On Cloud Net'.

'Basket Book', which includes poems and letters written by and photographs by and of Vicuña. The introductions and essays, while they do 'introduce' the 'Basket Book', are an integral part of the book as a whole. Vicuña seems to have included them to signal to the reader that the act of reading the rest of *cloud-net* will require critical and creative engagement. Including others' expressions of their experiences in introductory essays not only orients the reader to think critically about the upcoming poems, it also gives the reader an idea of what to expect and what the past parts of the project were like. These essays, moreover, are images of the project's plasticity: the essayists' reactions embody the collaborative process of the book.

After the essays, *cloud-net* turns to work by Vicuña, photographers (including Vicuña herself) and workshop participants, thus extending its collaborative feature to creative projects. This second section, 'Basket Book', consists mainly of photographs, poems, and notes. It opens with what looks like a picture of a blackboard with criss-crossing threads drawn in chalk that form a loose net. The next pages present one poem in a long, thin line of hand-written Spanish and English words. Following the poem is a quote from Sri Aurobindo (which contains the word 'cloud-net'), and then, on the next page, is a black and white photograph of Vicuña covered in white threads and wearing a white, cone-shaped hat covering her face (Figure 4.6). The next pages of 'Basket Book' include black and white photographs of the installations and stills from the video of the performance at the pier accompanied by poems, including 'Er', which alludes to the performance at the pier.[108]

On the following pages, Vicuña includes two photographs of herself in 1969, one with a loosely woven net over her head, and the other with a loosely-knitted vest, followed by a poem 'Red cabezal' and its translation 'Head net'. The next twenty pages consist of poems in either string-like forms (vertical lines made of short stanzas with short lines) or woven shapes (short stanzas spaced out on the page as though they were threads woven together) accompanied by photographs of 'nets' found on the streets of New York City. Next follow four pages of coloured photographs that provide a surprising flood of colour for the reader. The photographs are of the poet's tables of 'precarios' that were exhibited in the installations. She provides three lists of the items on each installation table. Following these poem-lists, are two photographs of large threads woven across the rooms in which the Houston and New York City installations took place. The next section consists of poems accompanied by more photographs of spots on New York buildings, streets with criss-crossing lines, and clouds of steam.[109] As this summary indicates, 'Basket Book' resembles a filled basket because of its contents, containing a jumble of heterogeneous materials that not only recall performances and installations, but various material poem-objects, all of which invite the reader to pick and choose and make sense of the whole.

108 The photographs that accompany the poem 'Er', while from the same footage, come from two separate films: *cloud-net* and *pulsar*.

109 These poems explicitly address global warming and post-industrial working conditions.

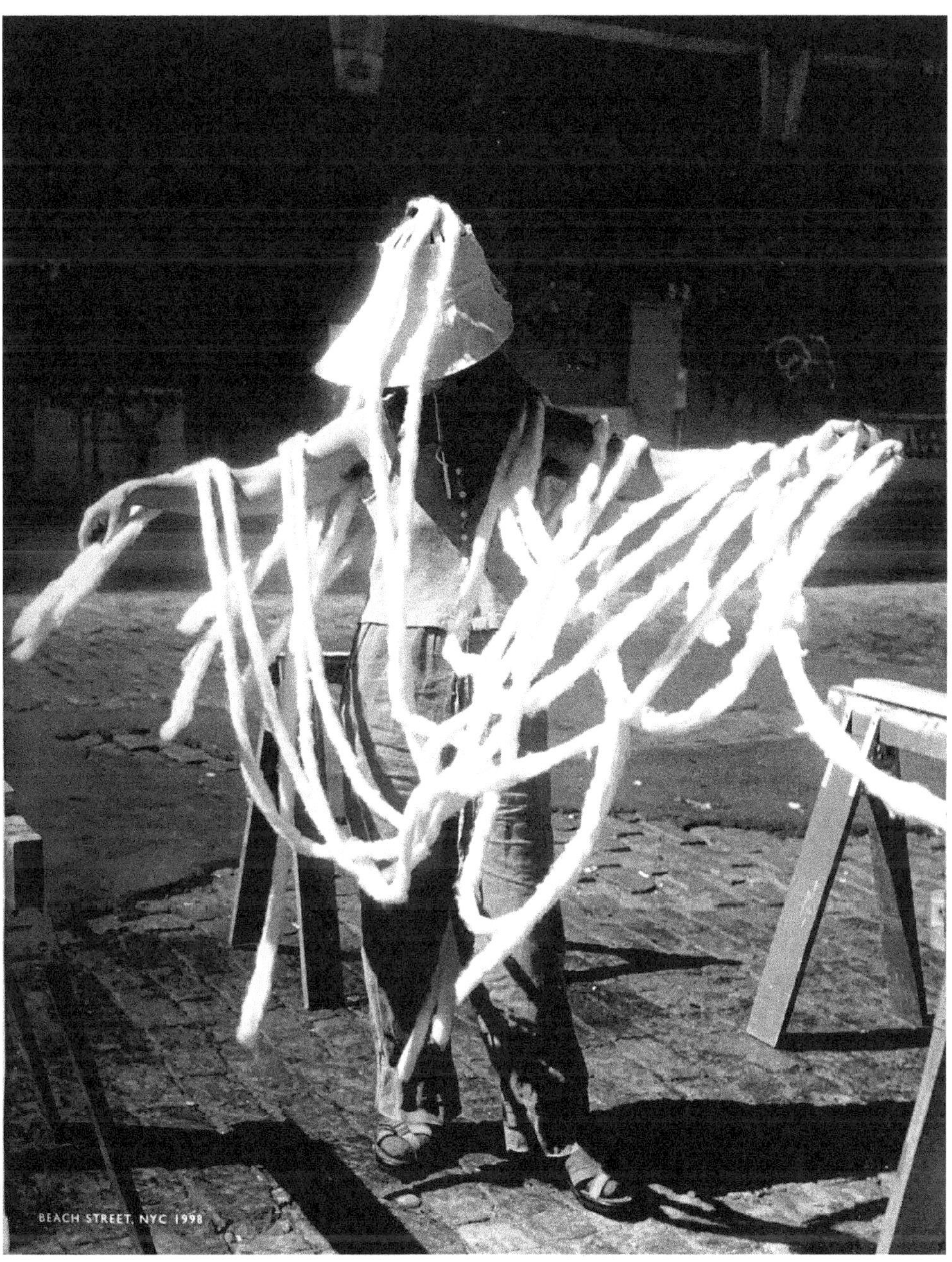

Fig. 4.6. Vicuña, *cloud-net* (1999): Photograph of Vicuña. Courtesy of Cecilia Vicuña.

'Basket Book' concludes with direct addresses to the readers of and participants in *cloud-net.* Vicuña presents a letter to the reader (which includes quotes and anecdotes), a letter to the workshop participants (in which Vicuña encourages the participants to write poems about the installations and includes two examples of these poems in the book) and a page of 'notes' on the poems. These letters and notes invite the reader to reflect again on the poems and photographs s/he has just read and seen. The book thus begins and ends with critical reflections, which explicitly encourage the reader to contemplate the text continuously throughout the book. At least formally, the heterogeneity of the parts, each equally important in creating the whole, helps break down potential for an authoritarian text.

This book, for Vicuña, is a 'woven message' (p. 13). In *cloud-net* and in her other works, Vicuña wants the reader to think that its instants (the moments of the installations and performances) become permanent when they become part of a web created by readers and text. Such a 'web' is what Vicuña seems to mean by a 'book'. She thinks of the book as three-dimensional. The relationship that Vicuña, as the Brazilian concretists do with their individual poems, desires between reader and text is similar to that required of a person's engagement with a three-dimensional object of the plastic arts in that the reader, in 'moulding' the text, has to consider it from a variety of perspectives. The book form of *cloud-net* is no longer contingent upon a place and time the way that the installations are, but instead will continue to exist regardless of the time and place of interaction; the book can last forever (at least until it disintegrates), whereas the installations had temporal beginnings and ends.

The first poem I discuss, that begins 'Hanging by a thread' (p. 30, Figure 4.7), is representative of the book as a whole. In this poem, Vicuña creates an object-like plastic poem that, in its call for collaborations between the text and reader, can be continuously moulded. Like a spider that hangs on a thread waiting for a breeze to carry it to another place in order to form its web, the words, in the manner of a calligramme, look as though they are suspended on the page, precariously waiting for the reader to weave its web. Vicuña urges the reader to be like a spider and like a human weaver, and to be aware of and participate in the creation of a web of connections. Without this collaboration, the individual threads that make connections between substances and between people might break. By urgently inviting the reader into the conversation ('we will weave', 'web up/web on', for example), Vicuña insists that the poem by itself threatens to fall apart. In the 'Notes to the Poems,' she argues that contemporary society and the earth it inhabits are in a similarly precarious position, and thus require a conscious re-evaluation of their current state (p. 95). The poem is precarious both as instability and prayer. It seems to be a prayer for the strengthening of these bonds. Like a prayer, which might be a plea or a cry for help, so this poem in its precariousness conveys an urgent need for change. The book acts to maintain, at least on a small scale, the precarious state of human community.

The poem's web can be seen visually. The calligramme of the images of threads that form a web converts the poem into (at least virtually) a three-dimensional

h
a
n
g
i
n
g
by a thread
the
web
says: www
we will weave

una puerta llorosa
y piedras en los pies

a weeping door
and stones on your feet

web up
web on

re a lida des
a linea das

weaving clouds
against death

Fig. 4.7. Vicuña, *cloud-net* (1999): 'Hanging by a thread...'.
Courtesy of Cecilia Vicuña.

object and illustrates how the precariousness of individual words can be momentarily stabilised when they come together to form a poem. For example, Vicuña spells the first word, 'hanging', one letter at a time going down the page to give the sense that the word itself is hanging like a thread.[110] As the poem develops, it spatially acts out what the poem discusses: a loosely woven text(ile). The words start at the left margin, move diagonally towards the right, then move back to the middle and towards the right again. They themselves become the smaller threads that are spun into the larger thread of the poem, and in turn woven together into a web; the reader connects the words as s/he moves across the page, just as one would weave threads together by moving left to right, right to left, over and under the other strings. By inviting the reader to participate in this way, Vicuña creates an active reading practice similar to that of concrete poetry, except that she draws out from that practice what is at best latent in concretism, the precariousness of community building. Rather than making webs of abstract lines that, as some might argue, create impersonal relationships, she weaves webs that bring back the personal. Near the beginning of the poem, she translates 'www' from the known 'World Wide Web' to 'we will weave', thus defamiliarising a large, impersonal technological web into one of personalised (or even humanised) collaboration. The woven web that Vicuña, with the help of the reader, creates with the calligramme strengthens the larger web of the poem.

Vicuña attributes agency to this newly oriented web: 'the/web/says: www/we will weave' (ll. 9–12). The personified web first articulates sounds, then words; the poem moves horizontally through the preverbal to the verbal, just as the word moves from threads into a web. However, Vicuña's web says 'we will weave' before the web of the poem has been completed, or 'woven' by the reader. The reader must then participate in the weaving of the poem by using the sounds of the word 'web' to thread through the poem, a weaving enhanced by the alliteration of 'w'. Like a *verbivocovisual* poem, the letter 'w' communicates visually, aurally and semantically; the sound of the 'w' and the visual repetition of the letter make connections. Not only is the letter repeated, but also its very components are internally repetitive since the 'w' itself is a letter that consists of two letters, two 'v's.[111] Vicuña's use of prepositions emphasises the need for this spatial movement: 'web up/web on' (ll. 17–18). She directs the reader to 'web' in not one, but multiple directions. The reader also weaves different parts of speech together: is 'web' a verb, a noun, or both? If 'web' is read as a noun, 'web up' and 'web on' suggest directions, a kind of map, or even a pattern for weaving a particular textile.

While the construction of the phrasal verb is impossible in Spanish, the words nonetheless connect to a particularly colloquial Chilean Spanish: 'web up' sounds like 'wuea' and 'web on' like 'wuevon', which are idioms derived from the word for 'dude' or 'idiot' (they are used often in colloquial Chilean Spanish, almost as

110 The hanging word is similar to Lira's calligrammatic lines, in which the word 'colgando' is hanging on the page (See Chapter 3).

111 The Spanish and English words for the letter 'w' explain precisely this: 'doble uve/b' and 'double u'.

'filler' words).[112] Vicuña thus expresses her position between two worlds through the sound, meaning, register and appearance of the two phrases. This particular combination of languages and parts of speech into one phrase encourages, as I have discussed above, the reader ultimately to combat authoritarian, hierarchical societies. As Rachel Blau DuPlessis explains, the goal of a contemporary polylingual work is to create plurality, rather than to establish authority.[113] By writing in both Spanish and English, Vicuña achieves such plurality in this poem. While one may consider polylingualism as potentially alienating for speakers of one language, or even alienating for a speaker who does not feel fully integrated in either language, I argue that, like Martínez and Lira, Vicuña uses multiple languages as a means to enhance collaboration. In order to combat potential alienation, Vicuña includes translations and/or explanations of particular words at the end of the book, and, in some cases, puts English and Spanish side by side. In many of the string-like poems of *cloud-net*, Vicuña includes a non-literal translation (even the spatial arrangements of some lines change between translations) on the facing page that was translated in collaboration with Rosa Alcalá. Unlike Martínez and Lira, who tend not to translate the multiple languages they use and thus create the possibility of alienating their readers, Vicuña provides translations, albeit not always literal ones, seeking to eliminate a single authoritative language in the work.

For Vicuña, a collaborative, concretist creative process is urgent because the poem by itself is not enough to stabilise the web. The poem needs to be renewed continuously by the reader's weaving as soon as possible. This active reading practice can then in turn be directed toward the world. As one moves through the poem, the verb tenses change accordingly, indicating a movement from a future goal or vision when the words have yet to be woven together, 'we will weave' (l. 12), to action now with the imperative, 'web up/web on' (ll. 17–18), and then to the progressive: 'weaving clouds' (l. 21). Finally, by the end of the poem, the weaving is actually taking place (though, like 'web up', 'weaving' here could be seen as an adjective). The web demands (via the imperative) a future of weaving that will be realised when the reader (the recipient of the imperative prayer) weaves.

Such different weavings give life to the book. In 'Hanging by a thread', the web of words that Vicuña insists that the reader create is what keeps the poem 'alive'. Despite their living qualities, the web is fragile. Ultimately, it is created out of only loosely formed material (water vapour), for we are in the act of 'weaving clouds/ against death' (ll. 21–22). In its etymology (coming from Old English 'clod' or 'clud', meaning clump of earth), 'cloud' becomes more solid and easier to hold as it connects earth and sky.[114] The clouds might have the potential to fight 'against death'. This fight, as implied formally throughout the book, and more explicitly in some of the other poems, could be the fight against the death of the Earth and the elimination of personal relationships between people. She thus urges us to

112 'Wuevon' also has origins in 'huevo', meaning egg or testicle.

113 Rachel Blau DuPlessis, 'Agency, Social Authorship, and the Political Aura of Contemporary Poetry', *Textual Practice*, 30.7 (2009), 987–99, p. 94.

114 Interestingly, the etymology of 'nube', from Latin 'nubes', might be the Greek word 'nephos', with one meaning being 'bird-net'.

weave together: 'we will weave'. The word 'against', however, might have another meaning, that is, looking at the positioning of the words on the page, one can interpret the word 'against' in the sense of 'up against' or 'next to', so that these clouds also exist in relation to death:

> weaving clouds
> against death (ll. 21–22)

This image of the clouds in opposition to or even next to death illustrates the transformation of something thread-like and precarious into something woven. The cloud exists in a place between earth and sky, and on the edge of life and death. The cloud, if condensed into a web by the reader, will become immortal: it will not have an end (death), but will exist (and remain) as an entity in-between. In 'Hanging by a thread,' the weaving and its precariousness is a small instance of what the book as a whole invites.

Through an illumination of the divine energy that emerges from precariousness, the poem 'Illapa' (p. 64–65, Figure 4.8) provides another example of the book's web-like connections between reader, text and the divine. Vicuña illustrates the dual nature of the precarious poem: the fragile words that have not yet been read allow for one to re-create repeatedly the world around him/her. Like the poem in *Instan*, this calligrammatic poem, as something to be manipulated manually, looks like a quipu.[115] Just as a quipu is formed by knotted string, the poem resembles a long string with knots tied on it. The words and their squiggling letters appear like threads tied together into stanzas (knots) of one or two short lines. Like one string of a quipu, an invisible thread that the reader forms as s/he looks at the page seems to connect the stanzas of the poem.

Because these lines are very short, they seem to be either produced out of nothing or swallowed up by nothing. Just as a single thread can in itself fray or, when joined with other threads, be woven into a web, the very short lines are either close to disappearing altogether or they are positioned to form a larger, more stable verbal structure. Vicuña attempts to show a beginning (or a possible end) by using such small lines. There is not yet any action or gesture ('no el acto/ni el gesto' [ll. 5–6]), but only the possibility for them.[116] The poem's reference to Illapa, the Andean god of thunder and lightning, can be explained because this god uses his energy of transformation and disruption to produce a larger, complete quipu.

In this poem, Vicuña demonstrates how divine energy comes from the interaction of the words themselves with a reader. Energy is created when one looks closely at a word and takes apart words. Indeed, in this poem (as well as in her other work), Vicuña wants to provoke a release of energy in a reader. She cuts up the word 'transforma' by expanding it into a phrase: 'trans/de la forma' (ll. 9–10). The prefix

115 Collaborative authorship was literally tangible during the performance and the installations, as participants manipulated threads of loosely spun yarn.

116 In her English version of the poem, Vicuña translates 'poder' to 'possibility', another Deleuzean image of changing power, to potential or possibility ('the capacity to affect or be affected'). See Deleuze, *Spinoza: Practical Philosophy*, trans. by Robert Hurley (San Francisco: City Lights Books, 1988), p. 125.

Illapa

El brillo
remoto

del primer
poder

no el acto
ni el gesto

si no
su doblez

trans
de la forma

mundo
al envés

ni truenos
ni rayos

ni relam
paguear

si no

trás
tocar

el uno en tres

el ruido
en luz

la luz
en ruidal

Fig. 4.8. Vicuña, *cloud-net* (1999): 'Illapa'.
Courtesy of Cecilia Vicuña.

Illapa

the remote
shine

of first
possibility

neither act
nor gesture

its crease

trance
of the form

world
inside-out

Illapa

not
thunder

nor rays

nor lightening

touch
in transit

one in three

light
in noise

noise
in light

'trans' is placed on its own line. Separated from the rest of the word, one thinks of its meaning as a prefix: through, across, beyond. Not only does this prefix suggest an idea important to weaving, that is, crossing through, but it also carries the reader somewhere beyond the meaning of the word to which it might be connected. She translates 'trans' to 'trance', which adds to its sense of being beyond: when one is in a trance, that is, not fully conscious, one is *beyond* consciousness. Her translation is not literal, and thus does not privilege one language over the other. Instead, her poetry moves towards the possibility of a language free of hierarchy. In addition, the translation demonstrates that the words are not stuck to one meaning, but instead are free to move around.

When thought of together, the prefix 'trans' with the root 'forma', the word denotes a change of form. However, the reader has to make this 'formation' of the word 'transforma' on his/her own because this 'trans' is not completely attached to its root, but instead is of ('de') it ('forma'). The word 'form' itself contains the crossing through-ness and beyond-ness of the prefix. Moreover, in a concretist way, Vicuña 'deforms' the words 'transforma' and 'deform' ('*de* la *form*a'). Illapa's 'divine' energy thus emerges through transformation and deformation, particularly of words; just as Lira concludes (see Chapter 3), Vicuña demonstrates that its divinity does not come from its power of *creatio ex nihilo*, but from the re/deformation of words. It is in the word itself (as a thread) where the possibility for the world begins and formation (and deformation) occurs, and within the collaboration with the reader the energy of the words is *becoming*, never fully *being*.[117]

It is within the word itself that the divine nature, the overwhelming transformative energy of Illapa exists. In particular, Illapa exists as one in three: 'el uno en tres' (l. 20). This line could refer to the Andean god's name, 'Illapa' or 'Illapantac', who, as Vicuña explains in the 'Notes to the poems' section, 'condenses thunder, lightning, and thunderbolt' (p. 95). The three-in-one is also a powerful image in other cultures: it could refer to the Christian trinity, or to Plato's division of the soul: for Plato, the soul, being one, consists of reason (the guardians), spirit (principle), and appetite (hunger, pain, etc.).[118] Whether intentional or not, this phrase highlights the similarities between different ancient religions and philosophies; in other words, Vicuña blends together international philosophies on the page.

The reader can experience the three parts of Illapa (thunder, lightning, and thunderbolt) not solely semantically, but also visually and aurally; energy bursts through meaning onto the reader's senses and thus into the poem's present. For example, the harsh sounds of the alliteration of 't' throughout the poem (but also in bursts of alliteration at the beginning and towards the end) gives the poem a sense of thunder, and, combined with the light, open 'i' sounds throughout the poem, create an aural image of a thunder and lightening storm. Vicuña forms another connection between senses through sonic and semantic synaesthesia, i.e. blending the words pertaining to different senses, as a sort of palindrome: 'el ruido/en luz// la luz/en ruidal' (ll. 21–24). Light can be found in noise and vice-versa. Light and

117 Deleuze and Guattari, *A Thousand Plateaus*, pp. 7–25.

118 Plato, *The Republic*, trans. by Desmond Lee, 2nd edn (London: Penguin Books, 1974), Book IV.

sound, however, are not tangible substances and they precede words, just as the threads of a web precede the web. Thus, something more must be added to bring this originary moment into full being and to weave the thread into a web.

How does the book function in relation to *cloud-net*'s other manifestations as performances and installations? The poem 'Er' (pp. 34–41, Figure 4.9) particularly demonstrates the dynamic between book and performance. It describes the performance at the New York City pier and is accompanied by photographs taken from the video of that performance. Here, in order to maintain the possibility for continuous formation and re-formation, Vicuña attempts to condense the past of the performance, the present of the book and the video, and the possible future web created by readers of *cloud-net*. She blends these timelines together with an even more distant past, weaving together a mythical past of Er, the time of Plato and his translators, and the time of Vicuña's 'translation' of the myth into performance and back into writing. Vicuña's (ironic) allusions to Plato, specifically Book X of *The Republic*, throughout the 'Basket Book' question the nature of mortality, immortality and eternity posed by the book and exhibits.[119]

Vicuña moves beyond the concretist focus on the page and even beyond the book by connecting the poem to actions that have occurred in the past. She describes the performance-event of 'Er' through the story of the three Fates — Clotho, Lachesis and Atropos. In this poem, spread over three pages, each page accompanied by three photographs of the performance, she brings events (performances and installations) onto the pages of the book and exemplifies the performative, eventful nature of *cloud-net*. She therefore attempts to bring together past, present and future into one moment and one place.[120] Like a fertility rite/ritual that makes the plants grow, a death ritual that makes contact with the dead, a medicinal ritual that cures disease (what Jerome Rothenberg would call a 'language event'), the events of *cloud-net* are performances that attempt to get something done in the real world.[121]

In the spirit of the 'language event', Vicuña in this poem urges that free will existing in poetry is available to all and should be used to transform the precarious state of the world; the state of the world is not fixed or determined, but instead can be changed if we choose to change it. The poem begins (and the event began) by chance (although not wholly by chance, as Vicuña invited the dancers):

119 Vicuña's decision to allude to Plato's version of this myth must be ironic because of Plato's belief that the poets moved us away from the Forms. See Plato, *The Republic*.

120 The 'poet's tables' also demonstrate this blending of time. The five coloured photographs of objects on tables (supposedly what Vicuña calls the 'Poet's tables' of each exhibit) precede three poems, titled 'The poet's table (Buffalo)', 'The poet's table (Houston)', and 'The poet's table (New York)'. Each poem is a list of 'objects' (some are more abstract or unlikely to fit on a table) that correspond in some ways to the previous photographs.

121 See Jerome Rothenberg, *Technicians of the Sacred*, 2nd edn (Berkeley: University of California Press, 1985), pp. 113–46 and 512–21. In addition, when describing PALABRAR*mas*, Méndez-Ramírez explains that 'Vicuña is not interested in the prophetic power of the word, but rather the ACTIVE POWER of the word'. Thus, her poetry is not supposed to be consumed passively, but instead to be taken and used actively. Méndez-Ramírez, 'Cryptic Weaving', in *The Precarious*, p. 67.

Er

I invited a group of dancers to join me in an unannounced event. Entirely by chance, only three girls came, Rosa, Luisa and Alicia.

They were late and the place became dusk
the darkness becoming light as they danced and wove.

I thought of the three *Mocrae: Clotho, Lachesis & Atropos*
s
p
i
n
n
i
n
g
life and death
the *Moerae* or Fates
but fate is not
the force that predetermines events
as the dictionary says
fate is to speak
and you fate yourself
as you speak

a turn of phrase becoming blood
your destiny,
to *hit the mark*

and they came to a mysterious place, at which
there were two chasms
the myth says
two heavenly openings
and two earthly openings

by one of each pair souls departed
and by the other they came back
and there
in that intermediate space

Fig. 4.9. Vicuña, *cloud-net* (1999): 'Er'.
Courtesy of Cecilia Vicuña.

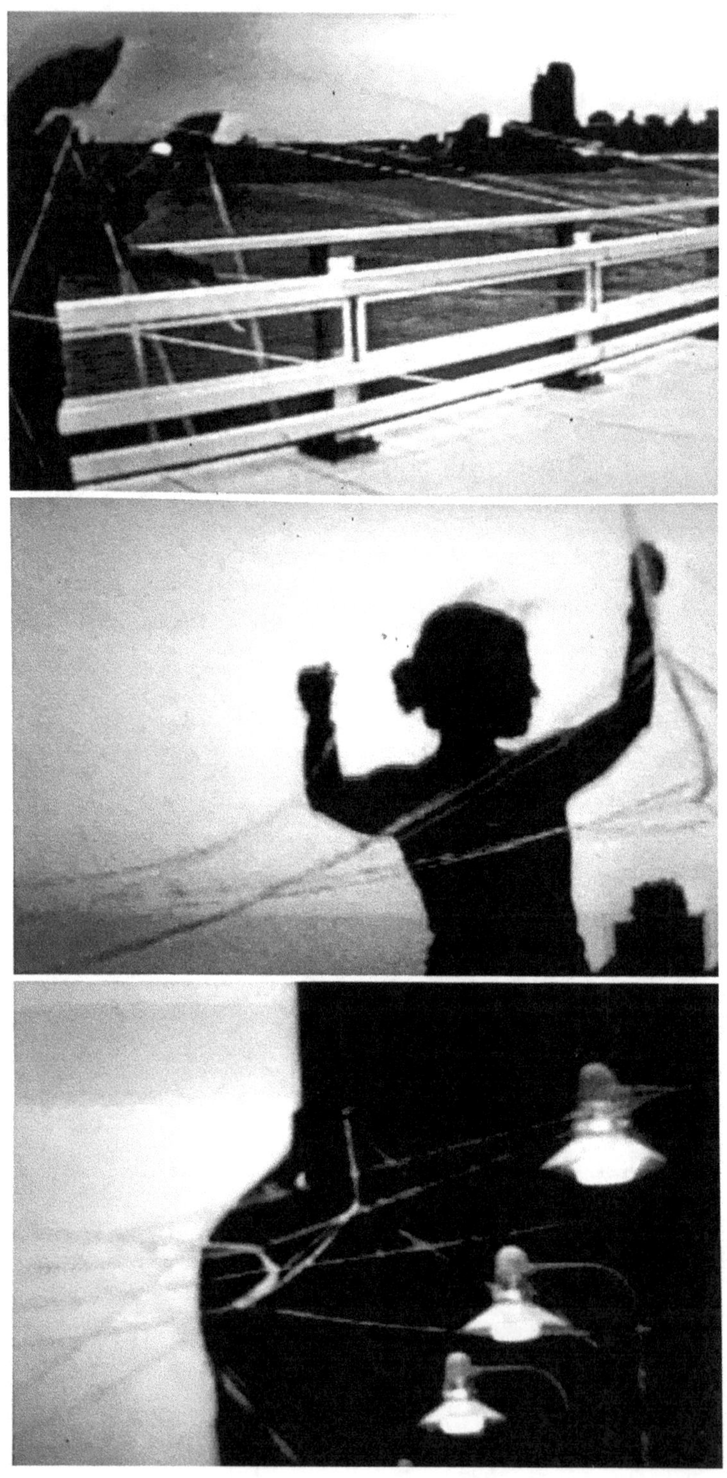

(it was the South Finger pier in lower Manhattan
a cool summer night)
in that between ness
they were told:
you will be the messenger
of what you see
dancing and balancing
the thread in the air

bladers passed by
waving their blades
weavers waving
their waves

after seven days they came to a shaft of light
like a column extending through
the whole Heaven and Earth
a beam of light
like a child dancing in the dust
and here,
translators disagree:

a series of circles surrounded the shaft, eight of them,
the whorl of the spindle and in each of them a siren
hummed a note

el tono es la cuerda, el hilo de voz

all notes creating one harmony
all notes turning a sound
on which revolutions turn
"depend," I read

harmos
being
"a joining"
harmony
an agreement

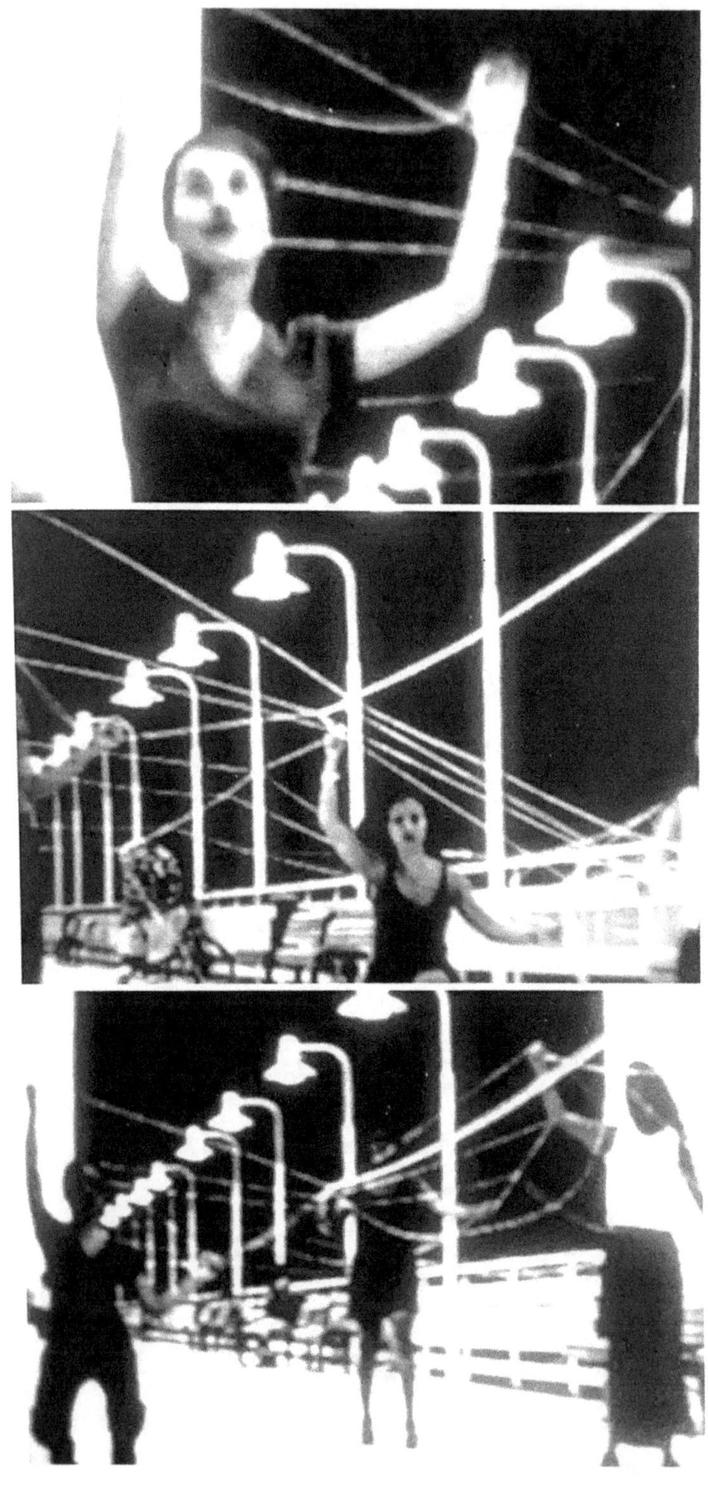

a woman, angry at a thread
caught in her bike said:
"is this a booby trap?"
"only in your mind"
the girls thought
as she threw the web into the river
dark as the sea

the thread pulsating and throbbing
a heart in the sea

and in the extremities of it three girls

pushed to the edge
by the force of the spin
spinning of Necessity

three girls singing
at once
of the present
the future and the past

spinner
allotment
and neverturnback
each one a portion,
a fragment of ourselves
the shaft of light
the thread of life
sobbing in the sea.

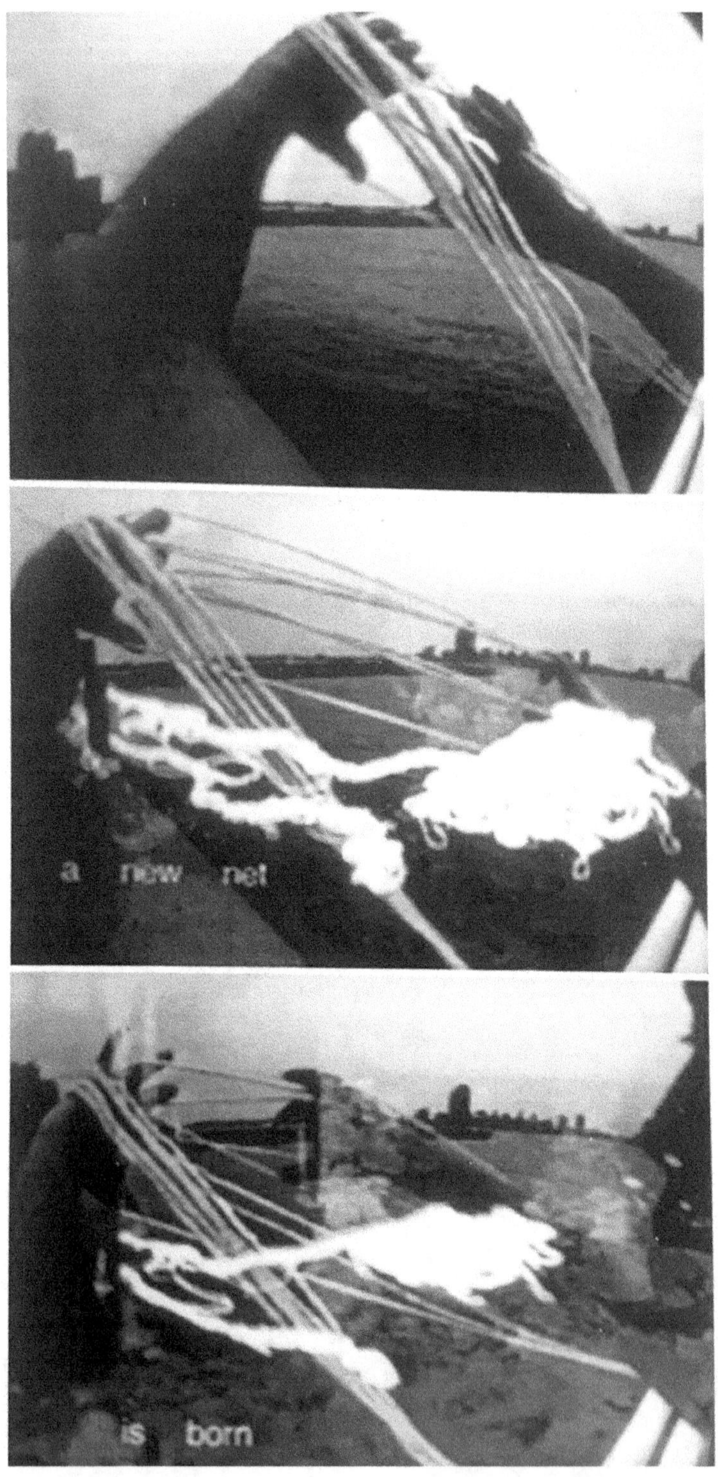
a new net
is born

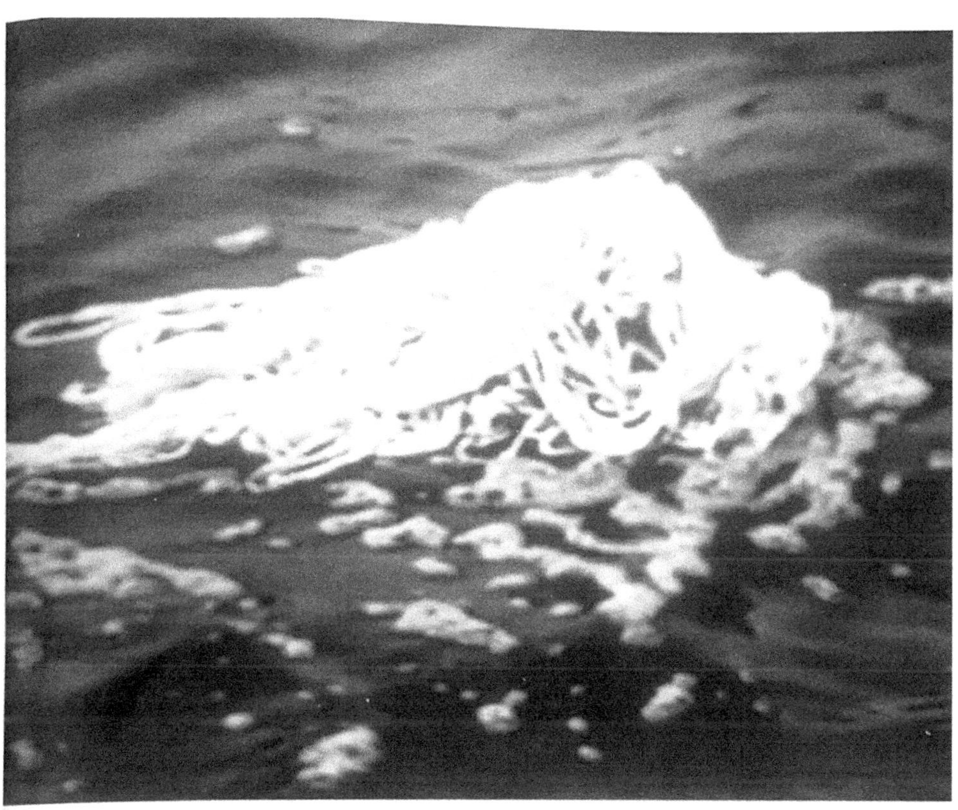

> I invited a group of dancers to join me in an unannounced event. Entirely by chance, only three girls came, Rosa, Luisa and Alicia.
>
> They were late and the place became dusk
> the darkness becoming light as they dance and wove. (p. 34, ll. 1–4)

However, this chance does not mean that people do not have any control over the event:

> the Moerae or Fates
> but fate is not
> *the force that predetermines events*
> as the dictionary says
> fate is to speak
> and you fate yourself
> as you speak (p. 34, ll. 15–21)

As Plato explains in Book X of *The Republic*, souls have an initial decision to choose their fate, and, thus, they do not act purely passively through their destinies, but have an active voice.[122] Similarly, the dancers in this poem — although three, as opposed to more or fewer, of them showed up by chance — created their fate by accepting the invitation. The dance also requires words because, as Vicuña claims, one's fate is created through voiced words.[123] Vicuña therefore positions the performance in relation to the words on the page (as well as the words on the video).

The creation of fate, as Vicuña describes in 'Er', occurs in a specific location in the middle of heaven and earth. As she explains, paraphrasing Plato's myth of Er:

> and they came to a mysterious place, at which
> *there were two chasms*
> the myth says
> *two heavenly openings*
> *and two earthly openings*
>
> *by one of each pair souls departed*
> *and by the other they came back*
> and there
> in that intermediate space
> (it was the South Finger pier in lower Manhattan
> a cool summer night)
> in that between ness
> they were told:
> you will be the messenger
> *of what you see*
> dancing and balancing
> the thread in the air (pp. 34–36, ll. 25–41)

This 'intermediate space' is one not of beginning or end, or of heaven or hell, but one in the middle where one's free will comes into play. As Anna Reckin says,

122 We are free to choose what we do, but we have no freedom, in the sense of control, over what happens after we act. It is the consequences of our freely chosen actions that are in the hands of (the) fate(s).

123 The etymology of 'fate' is 'fatum', meaning 'speech'.

cloud-net as a whole is 'dwelling in in-betweenness, one language is transforming itself into the next [...] like dwelling in the trans, transformation of the language'.[124] And this free will occurs through expression, expression through speech, but also through dance, weaving and thus poetry. The words themselves weave together:

bladers passed by
waving their blades
weavers waving
their waves (p. 36, ll. 42–45)

The placement of the lines mirrors the criss-crossing of a weaving. And as the words are woven, they blend (or 'cross-over') into new words: 'bladers' to 'blades' to 'waves', 'waving' to 'weavers', back to 'waving' and then 'waves'. The roller-bladers similarly weave and wave through the threads, criss-crossing their blades and each other. Vicuña 'weaves' together the metaphors and performance through the visual and aural characteristics of the words and their placement on the page.[125]

The place in which translation occurs in 'Er' is full of energy. Vicuña describes the place in which the girls weave as one that moves towards the edges of the string:

the thread pulsating and throbbing
a heart in the sea

and in the extremities of it three girls

pushed to the edge
by the force of the spin (p. 38, ll. 73–77)

The centrifugal force of spinning drives the girls outwards away from a centre. Although one could read 'the extremities' as the sides of a place between, one could also read it as on the border between the outside and the inside, in other words, the space of exile and 'non-place'. Specifically, this performance occurred at a post industrial pier, a place that exists on the edge of water and land, and thus a 'non-place' of capitalism.

As the place where the threads cross over and that the dancers weave together, the in-between place of free will is the place where souls 'cross over', that is, are translated, to different worlds. She crosses between the direct quotes, which are in English, but italicised, to her account of the performance, which is in English, to reflections on the previous two, which are in Spanish. She uses the languages and typography to switch between the far, mythical past, to the past of the performance, to the present:

a beam of light
like a child dancing in the dust
and here,
translators disagree:

124 Anna Reckin, 'Cecilia Vicuña's *cloud-net*', *How2*, 1.5 (2001), <http://www.asu.edu/pipercwcenter/how2journal/archive/online_archive/v1_5_2001/current/alerts/reckin.html> [accessed 15 May 2015].

125 Another example of 'weaving' is that of bringing together different social domains: roller blades belong to a contemporary urban society, and weaving to a 'traditional' one.

a series of circles surrounded the shaft, eight of them,
the whorl of the spindle and in each of them a siren
hummed a note

el tono es la cuerda, el hilo de voz

all notes creating one harmony
all notes turning a sound
on which revolutions turn
"depend," I read
harmos
being
"a joining"
harmony
an agreement (p. 36, ll. 49–65)

As I discussed above, such a place of in-betweenness is one of translation and ultimately one of poetry; as Joris explains, translators can be considered poets and poets can be considered translators.[126] The translators (or poets) at first disagree seemingly about the following translation of Plato, but once the strings of the voice ('el hilo de voz') come together, agreement occurs. The agreement (or 'harmony', as its etymology — another way of bringing the past into the present — 'joins' the two words together), furthermore, occurs as 'a joining'. It is translation that brings the words together, and thus harmony, where relationships form and tighten, has occurred in this place.

Vicuña blends together the myth of Er and the event she planned and carried out in New York by paraphrasing and quoting Plato's account of the myth and recounting her event through poetry and photography. She therefore blends together the past, present and future of *cloud-net.*[127] In the poem, she explains that this place is not only one in which souls join, but also one in which aspects of time (past, present and future) converge through song:

three girls singing
at once
of the present
the future and the past (p. 38, ll. 79–82)

The image of bringing together past, present and future, as the Fates do in the myth of Er, emphasises what Vicuña has created by moving the ephemeral and location-contingent event/installation into a (relatively) immortal book which can be read anywhere in the present.

To sum up, Vicuña makes past events permanent in order to bring them into action for the present and future. Unlike Martínez, who deconstructs the notion of the conventional and experimental novel by including a plethora of references and media, and Lira, who *detourns* Chilean poetry, Vicuña relates her book to specific actions that she and other participants have carried out; she makes a permanent

126 Joris, *A Nomad Poetics*, pp. 111–12.

127 Her quotes come from *Dialogues of Plato: Translated into English, with Analyses and Introduction*, ed. by Benjamin Jowett (Cambridge: Cambridge University Press, 2010).

object, whose individual pages in many cases evoke three-dimensionality, out of instants that required the full engagement of the bodies and minds of the participants. As a departure from typical concrete poetry, the book, for Vicuña, allows the ephemeral collective actions to be, to an extent, recreated when read in the present.

Cloud-net is a call for a re-evaluation of the current state of our society and earth. In particular, Vicuña urges the reader not only to recognise how we are destroying the earth and weakening our relationships with other people, but to attempt to reverse destruction and to find new ways to strengthen our interactions. The cloud-net, for Vicuña, reflects the current state of the world, manifested in city steam clouds, metonymies for the exploitation of immigrants and the lower classes, or the 'contamination' of oppression (as illustrated in the photographs of steam and industrial buildings in New York City and particularly in the poem 'Sweatshop'), and in the World Wide Web, a net of relationships of quick, non-physical communication. However, the cloud-net also has the potential to save the world and its relationships from destruction; it is the mist-cloud of the rain forest: as Vicuña writes near the end of the book of *cloud-net*, 'Cesta de nubes/cloud basket of thoughts/we are the union/they are the thread' (p. 91). In other words, if we recognise and look at these webs we have created in a new way, we might see earth and society's worth differently and will be encouraged to save it. Julie Phillips Brown describes the binary nature of the *cloud-net* as a duality of 'manifestation' and '*manifestación*':

> As an antidote to such widespread danger, *cloud-net* proposes a perpetual movement between two opposite but complementary modes of poiesis: manifestation and *manifestación*. Manifestation refers to the physical transformation that occurs when the poet's words take on a material, tactile form in and beyond the page of the book, such that the poetic vision and the material world meet and co-create one another. But for Vicuña, the process of manifestation also necessitates its complementary counter-force, *manifestación*. Taken from the Spanish for "demonstration" or "protest," *manifestación* describes a poetic rewriting of the world not through progress, but through encumbrance, obstacle, protest, and stoppage.[128]

Manifestación, in this sense, could also (or better) be called defamiliarisation; Vicuña wants the reader to slow down, contemplate and see the world and its precariousness in a new, unfamiliar light. It is the manifestation of concretism that Vicuña takes and combines with manifestación. Like Rothenberg's 'language events', the web's creation by the reader is also a sort of ritual performance (although the performance is changed and renewed each time it is read) with the aim to change the world outside of the book itself. In other words, *cloud-net*, through its plasticity, is a prayer of/for both manifestation and manifestación.

128 Brown, '"Touch in Transit"', pp. 210–11.

Conclusion

The basis of Vicuña's vision, like that of concrete poets, is one of poetry's etymological root, *poiesis*. As she herself has explained, 'Para mí, poesía es una visión de mundo, es creación, es la idea que estamos aquí para crear'.[129] In this chapter, I have argued that Vicuña's work invites us to make (*poiesis*) something new, or to create, that is, to become engaged as plastic artists. PALABRAR*mas*, *Instan*, and *cloud-net* exemplify Vicuña's desire that *everyone* create, that art's readers represent a democracy; the author is no longer the sole creator, but the readers and participants also engage in the process of making. Vicuña's poetry, along with concrete poetry, is an example of plastic poetry, the precariousness of which Vicuña's poetry emphatically explains and performs.

In PALABRAR*mas*, Vicuña demonstrates a concretist plasticity of words. Here, the reader can form, reform and deform a virtual rhizomatic web as s/he paths his/her way through the word-poems. The words, on their own, act as three-dimensional objects shaped according to the perspective of the viewer/reader. In *Instan*, Vicuña expands the poetry's plasticity to the page; the poetic unit is no longer the word, but the space between the letters and words on the page. Through word-drawings and the related poem, she creates her own version of quipus: just as a quipu could be read according to the position of the knot on the thread in relation to the other knots, her poems require a reading of the relationships between the words, of the space in which these words 'cross over' or translate. It is from this 'non-place' that one can continuously mould and remould; because the 'non-place' is not attached to any and only exists between signifieds, the risk for solidification and 'territorialisation' diminishes.

What particularly distinguishes her from the concrete poets is her movement off the page through the integration of past and future poetic and artistic actions. Plasticity in *cloud-net* occurs in the wider scale of the book, and even pushes the boundaries to include performances, videos and installations as part of the textual object. In this project, the book helps to make permanent the ephemerality, but also the immediacy, of the performances and installations, attempting to bring that immediacy into the realm of the written word. The availability of the word to deformations, deconstructions and re-interpretations suggests a certain reverence for it, from the concretists to Vicuña, one that she judges in all of its manifestations in her work divine. Her project in its entirety and the translation between its parts allows for the reading process to become an event in which the reader *acts* (carries out an action) to redefine continuously the world around. The texts I have analysed are only three examples of the plethora of work that Vicuña and her readers have produced and continue to produce and mould in innovative ways today.

As someone who perceives herself between cultures, Vicuña attempts to write a democratic, communal poetry about, for and with others who exist in-between. Instead of suffering with this struggle, Vicuña attempts to use it as a platform for multiplicity to exist; it is in the tension *between* cultures and languages that her

129 Bianchi, *La memoria*, p. 176.

poetry thrives. From this space between, Vicuña wants her readers to engage the world affectively; she wants the reader/participant of her work to experience both 'affecting' and 'being affected' and to understand that as humans we can experience both.[130] She thus urges that we use our capacities to change and be changed to re-evaluate our identities and how we interact and to improve continuously the precarious world in which we live. Vicuña does not want the world to stabilise, however, but wants us to use its fragility to create a world of multiplicity and equality.

130 Vicuña has placed her work in relationship to the science of ethology. Ethology, founded by Jakob von Uexküll, is the study of animal behaviour, described by Deleuze as 'the study [...] of the capacities for affecting and being affected'. Vicuña, 'Re: cloud net and other questions', and Deleuze, *Spinoza, Practical Philosophy*, p. 125.

CONCLUSION

We have seen how the Chilean poets Juan Luis Martínez, Rodrigo Lira and Cecilia Vicuña develop and expand upon Brazilian concretist poetics, entering into a long line of experimental poetry within and outside of Latin America. As I discussed in Chapter 1, first, both the Chilean poets and the Brazilian concretists can be categorised generally as neo-avant-garde poets because they respond to the successes and failures of the historical avant-garde by experimenting with new forms of poetry. Second, they all embody a particularly Latin American trait of 'antropofagia', that is, they perform the 'cannibalisation' of European, African, Asian and indigenous American cultures and literature. Thirdly, they all contribute to the literary history of visual poetry that has its (known) origins in Ancient Greece as poetry that is *made* to be seen.

In the 1950s, the Brazilian concrete poets synthesised visual and experimental techniques, especially those seen in the poetic experiments of the early twentieth century, into object-like poems that both utilised the forms and techniques of and criticised the consumerist and capitalist societies that were beginning to thrive in Latin America and the world in general. For them, object-poems brought to the fore the materiality of language, especially its aural and visual qualities; in their terms, they created *verbivocovisual* poems. For the concretists, the reader's appreciation of the essential materiality of language necessitates a preoccupation with the constitutive parts of the word and the spatial relationships between them and other words. Moreover, concrete poems, in order to be objective, often are asyntactic and devoid of the subjective, lyric 'I' (with the exception of the author's name attached to the work). This objectivity allows the reader to step in as a temporary subject making his/her way through the work.

As we have seen, the three Chilean poets form unique experimental poems that expand upon concretist poetics. The Chilean poets particularly develop the object-like characteristics of concrete poetry, that is: 1) they emphasise the materiality of language by using the page (or beyond) as their principal poetic unit; 2) they stretch signifiers away from their conventional signifieds in order to foreground the sensuous characteristics of language; and 3) they dismantle the conventional authorial subject to allow for more 'objectivity'. These qualities in the poems that the Chilean poets expand upon from the concretists make room for the reader to engage actively, using multiple senses as well as their intellect to form their own readings.[1] However, the poets stray away

1 It is worth noting that contemporary poets in Chile have continued to draw directly on the Brazilian concretists. For example, the Orquesta de Poetas (which has included the poets Federico

from typical concretist poetics to express particularly Chilean political and social concerns.

In his assemblage of materials and discourses from multiple disciplines and a variety of sources, the first of the poets I consider, Juan Luis Martínez, questions traditional and accepted notions of language, authorship and national context in relation to literature. In *La nueva novela*, he emphasises the 'verbivocovisual' aspects of poetry through experiments with nonsense language, musical scores and meditations, and attempting (but failing) to strip the poem to its primary concretist unit of the page. In these poems, he demonstrates that the aural and visual aspects of poetry, while they can be highlighted, cannot ultimately be drained of all meaning (that is, the semantic aspect) without the work losing its status as poem. Like the concretists, Martínez also questions his relationship to the text as author by working towards an anonymous text. He dismantles his status as sole authority in the text by meditating on his biographical relation to the text, the physical nature of his signature on the page in relationship to himself as person and ultimately by opening up space for the reader to participate in the text. Unlike the concrete poets, however, he does not eliminate his role from the text completely, but allows author and reader to meet as (more or less) equals on the page. Through his myriad international references and explorations of universal truths, Martínez moves towards the creation of an objective book; the wide scope of his (both literary and disciplinary) allusions contribute to the non-subjective and international elements, thereby expanding upon the concretist goal. Ultimately, however, he inserts enough references to Chile to direct his criticisms toward the local expressions of dictatorship. In particular, after the military coup, he added a Chilean flag to the book, provocatively suggesting that the book itself refers to and occupies the nation, with all of its heterogeneous elements, thereby dismantling the present vision of an autocracy.

The second poet studied here, Rodrigo Lira, develops concretist poetics as an extension of Chilean 'antipoetry'. Through his *détournement* of Chilean literature,

Eisner, Fernando Pérez, Pablo Fante, José Burdiles, Marcela Parra and Felipe Cussen) has not only clearly stated the influence the Brazilian concretists have had on their work (see Fernando Pérez Villalón, '"Todos instrumentos": Crónica de una orquesta', *Revista transas* (14 Nov 2019), <https://www.revistatransas.com/2019/11/14/todosintrumentos_perezvillalon/> [accessed 20 March 2021]) but even collaborated with Augusto de Campos in an audiovisual project (see Orquesta de Poetas, *Registro de poetas* (2020), <https://www.orquestadepoetas.cl/videosregistrodepoetas> [accessed 20 March 2021]). The poet Martín Gubbins, as Ernesto González Barnet points out, also has clear concretist tendencies (although he draws particularly from the Anglophone concretists). (See Ernesto González Barnet, 'Martín Gubbins', *Proyecto patrimonio* (2007), <http://www.letras.mysite.com/egb190607.htm> [accessed 20 March 2021). Just as Felipe Cussen (who also has recognised the concretist influence on his work; see above), Andrés Anwandter has written concrete poems, particularly those that appeared in the Writers' Forum in 2002 (Cussen, 'Andrés Andwandter: La apertura continua', *Estudios Filológicos*, 40 (2005), pp. 65–78). Another contemporary poet who has clear concretist tendencies is Pía Sommer. See, for example, Pía Sommer, *Cuadernillo* (Málaga: Ediciones Imperdonables, 2018). As this list, along with the plethora of critical texts that I have cited throughout this book, implies, Martínez, Lira and Vicuña's development of Brazilian concrete poetry has continued and perhaps even allowed for a more receptive atmosphere to experimental poetics in Chile today.

Lira takes from the concretists their preoccupation with language as material and emphasises the materiality of a specifically Chilean poetic tradition; his *détournement* extends to replacing one (given) word with his own or with disassembling that word. However, Lira does not praise this material, but disassembles it (and even the works of those poets who have already attempted to do so, that is, those who created and developed antipoetics) to such an extreme that one can no longer consider it part of the Chilean canon. Lira not only uses Chilean literary material for this dismantlement, but also, like the concrete poets, 'steals' and reworks materials and forms from quotidian life in order to criticise that society. His 'committed' poems, while not directly attacking the regime under which he wrote, re-form conventional (and even so-called experimental) literary and non-literary forms into implicit criticisms of the dictatorship.

The final poet studied here, Cecilia Vicuña, expands upon concretist preoccupations with the materiality of language and the dismantlement of the authorial subject through her plastic poetry of the word, page and book. In PALABRAR*mas*, her most explicitly concretist work, she opens up the resonances of words by revealing their visual characteristics and etymologies, a process that invites the reader to enter further into this opening up and to form various combinations of phonemes and words. Each time the poem is read, a new path connecting phonemes, words and ideas is temporarily created. This rich 'sculpting' of language in the hands of poet and reader creates a new form of community and instantiates the plasticity of her work. The paths between the words are solidified and extended into plotted constellations and webs in *Instan*. In this book, the reader plastically engages with the entire page. The relationship between the written words, the drawn lines and the white space in between allows Vicuña not only to express her condition as an exile, but also to mould her precarious position into one from which infinite connections with and by readers can be made. These connections redirect the loneliness one may feel in such a position into the creation of ephemeral, yet resilient virtual communities. In *cloud-net*, she places these ephemeral connections in relation to performances and installations in which webs have been previously spun by her and other participants. Her book allows these instances to be accessed and recreated in new ways each time they are read. Vicuña's development of concrete poetics into a poetry of plasticity in all these instances both expresses her condition as an exile and reformulates it (metaphorically and sometimes literally) into one in which relationships can remain or become strong, yet detached from propagandistic roots.

While all the poets above share many concretist characteristics, the Chilean poets are ultimately distinct from the Brazilian ones. A running thread that distinguishes the Chileans from the main Brazilian concretist movement is their deliberate incorporation of subjectivity into their otherwise object-like poetry. I propose that a principal reason for this difference is the poets' artistic reactions to the political and social contexts in which they live. Their use of 'subjectivity', in this instance, indicates the necessary affective need to acknowledge and then to challenge specific social conditions.

The Noigandres group in Brazil, in contrast, was not responding to such obvious oppression, but rather writing under general political stability and relative economic prosperity. It is possible that this relative stability could have allowed them to use an object-like poetry to generally criticise the consumerism and commercialism that came in tandem with the Brazilian president Juscelino Kubitschek's agenda of rapid modernisation and industrialisation (his motto being 'fifty years [of progress] in five'). When Brazil was controlled by dictatorship beginning in 1964, the Brazilian concretists at least theoretically attempted to incorporate and build upon subjective responses to society in their object-like poems. (We see this attempt in the neoconcrete, semiotic and progress poems of the 1960s and 1970s). Nonetheless, the oppression and censorship was not as apparent as it was in Chile under Pinochet and the differences between these new concretist experiments and the initial ones are not drastic.[2] It is thereby possible that the need to comment critically on the local social and political situation was perhaps not as urgent for the Brazilian concretists. Martínez, Lira and Vicuña, on the other hand, all create committed poetry that addresses and criticises their local, subject-dependent contexts of living under or exiled as a consequence of a brutal dictatorship.

Despite their many differences, the Brazilian and Chilean experiments share an important feature: they are all manifestations of a search for objectivity, that is, for object-like expressions.[3] As we saw in the third chapter, this striving allows the poets to express criticism without falling into the trap of propaganda. In the Adornian sense, they all to an extent create 'committed' poems that use form as a means of criticism (see Chapter 3); it is through active bodily and intellectual interactions between reader and poem-as-object that these poems avoid becoming propaganda yet remain committed. This type of commitment provides space for non-authoritarian and non-ideological critique and change. By considering thoughts and ideas as things to be manipulated and moulded, the poets of these object-like poems allow them to escape fixed ontologies, identities and ideologies, and to enable the reader to engage with them productively. In other words, object-poems require and allow for active readerly participation that is not subordinate to the author or his/her words; the more the reader's path through the work is contingent on that reader and his/her position in relation to and movements with and around the text, the less didactic and dictatorial the text becomes. In turn, these mouldable texts can affect us readers not forcefully or without our input, but with us guiding the way, and become intersubjective creations mediated through the material artefact of the poem; they perform and encourage democracy.

Instead of considering a poem as someone's ideas, thoughts or emotions expressed through the semantics of language, sometimes supported by or brought out through musical patterns, the poem-as-object allows one to engage kinaesthetically the whole body, that is, the senses and mind. This emphasis on materiality also forces

2 Robert Schwarz argues that in 1964–1969 in Brazil, even though a right-wing military dictatorship was in power politically, the leftist cultural hegemony remained more or less intact. Robert Schwarz, *Misplaced Ideas: Essays on Brazilian Culture* (London: Verso, 1992), p. 127.

3 An interesting comparison to draw in a future project would be to the objectivists who emerged in the 1930s in the United States (such as Louis Zukofsky, Charles Reznikoff and Lorine Niedecker) and at the beginning of the 1980s in Argentina (such as Daniel García Helder, Martín Prieto and Daniel Freidemberg).

us to consider the media through which poetry can be expressed and the potential limits or possibilities one can achieve through different forms. The poets studied in this book have taken the use of the page to its limits, but their experiments anticipate how new forms, such as digital and internet spaces, can bring poetry to exciting and important new levels today and also how apparently 'intangible' material (such as the internet) can in fact be used to form tangible, strong connections between people.

If we treat poems as things in this world to be valued not as mere consumerist tools, there is no reason not to treat other things in this world with the respect and care that we have for things that cannot be passively consumed. So much of our surroundings (including people) in today's society are treated solely as consumer goods (things to be consumed) or instrumental tools (things to be used), which in turn has allowed us to destroy the world and people around us. However, if we begin to consider objects as carrying their own histories, their own 'subjectivities', and their own ability to affect positively our development as humans, we can develop new, creative ways of constructing strong relationships with each other and our world. As Pablo Neruda says:

> Es muy conveniente, en ciertas horas del día o de la noche, observar profundamente los objetos en descanso: las ruedas que han recorrido largas, polvorientas distancias, soportando grandes cargas vegetales o minerales, lo sacos de las carbonerías, los barriles, las cestas, los mangos y asas de los instrumentos del carpintero[...]Las superficies usadas, el gasto que las manos han infligido a las cosas, la atmósfera a menudo trágica y siempre patética de estos objetos, infunde unas especiales de atracción no despreciable hacia la realidad del mundo. La confusa impureza de los seres humanos se percibe en ellos, la agrupación, uso y desuso de los materiales, las huellas del pie y de los dedos, la constancia de una atmósfera humana inundando las cosas desde lo interno y lo externo. Así sea la poesía que buscamos.[4]

This appreciation for our world is what poetry can achieve.

4 Pablo Neruda, *Para nacer he nacido* (Barcelona: Editorial Seix Barral, 1978), pp. 140–41.

BIBLIOGRAPHY

Adams, Jacqueline, *Art Against Dictatorship: Making and Exporting Arpilleras Under Pinochet* (Austin: University of Texas Press, 2013)

Adorno, Theodor W., *Notes to Literature*, ed. by Rolf Tiedemann, vol 1 (New York: Columbia University Press, 1991)

——, *Notes to Literature*, ed. by Shierry Weber Nicholson, vol 2 (New York: Columbia University Press, 1992)

——, 'On the Fetish-Character in Music and the Regression of Listening', *Essays on Music*, ed. by Richard Leppert (Berkeley: University of California Press, 2002), pp. 288–318

Agamben, Giorgio, *The End of the Poem* (Stanford: Stanford University Press, 1999)

Aguilar, Julio César, 'Rodrigo Lira: Una aproximación neobarroca a su poética de genial esquizofrénica', *Crítica.cl* (2016), 1–14

Aliaga Rovira, Alejandro, 'Rodrigo Lira, poeta chileno: Muerto en Navidad...vivo en el papel', *El Mercurio de Antofagasta*, 21 April 2001, p. 5

Amich, Candice, 'From Precarity to Planetarity: Cecilia Vicuña's Kon Kon', *The Global South*, 7.2 (2013), 134–52

de Andrade, Oswald, 'Manifesto Antropófago', *Nuevo Texto Crítico*, 7.23 (1999), 25–31

Anwandter, Andrés, 'Nota sobre Guillermo Deisler', *Cyber Humanitatis*, 21 (2002), <http://web.uchile.cl/vignette/cyberhumanitatis-aaa/CDA/vida_sub_simple3/0,1250,PRID%253D1093%2526SCID%253D1096%2526ISID%253D5,00.html> [accessed 27 November 2020]

Alvarez, Mariola, *Neoconcretism and the Making of Brazilian National Culture, 1954–1961* (Unpublished doctoral thesis, University of California-San Diego, 2012)

Apollinaire, Guillaume, *Selected Writings*, ed. by Roger Shattuck (New York: New Directions, 1950)

Arendt, Hannah, *The Human Condition*, 2nd edn (Chicago: University of Chicago Press, 1958)

Ariz Castillo, Yenny Karen, 'Ecología y literatura en la poesía chilena contemporánea: *Semi ya*, de Cecilia Vicuña, y "Cardosanto", de Soledad Fariña', *Mitologías Hoy*, 12 (2015), 294–311

——,'Los animales en la *Wik'uña* de Cecilia Vicuña: Figuras opuestas y complementarias', *La Palabra*, 23 (2013), 51–62

——, 'La red espiritual de Ollantaytambo en *La Wik'uña*, de Cecilia Vicuña: Agua, piedra y luz', *Revista Humanidades*, 5.2 (2015), 1–28

Arteca, Mario and others, *¿Quién habla en el poema?* (Buenos Aires: Dock, 2012)

Augé, Marc, *Non-Places: An Introduction to Supermodernity*, trans. by John Howe, 2nd edn (London: Verso, 2008)

Ávila, Carlos, *Aqui y Agora* (Belo Horizonte: Dubolso, 1981)

Ayala, Matías, *Lugar incómodo: Poesía y sociedad en Parra, Lihn y Martínez* (Santiago: Ediciones Alberto Hurtado, 2010)

——, 'Teatralidad, sujeto y poesía en Enrique Lihn', *Alpha*, 38 (2014), 255–68

Azeredo, Ronaldo, *Lá Bis os Dois* (São Paulo: O Autor, 2002)

BAKHTIN, MIKHAIL, 'Discourse in the Novel', *The Dialogic Imagination: Four Essays* (Austin: University of Texas Press, 1981), pp. 259–422

BARTHES, ROLAND, 'The Death of the Author', *Image, Music, Text* (London: Fontana, 1977), pp. 142–48

BATTISTA, KATHY, 'WACK! Art and the Feminist Revolution', *Third Text*, 21 (2007), 463–72

BEARDSLEY, M. C. and W.K WIMSATT JR, 'The Intentional Fallacy', *The Sewanee Review*, 54.3 (1946), 468–88

BECKER, JESSICA, *Poetics of Materiality: Medium, Embodiment, Sense, and Sensation in 20th- and 21st-Century Latin America* (doctoral thesis, University of California, Berkeley, 2014)

BENJAMIN, WALTER, *The Work of Art in the Age of Mechanical Reproduction*, trans. by J. A. Underwood (London: Penguin Books, 2008)

BERNSTEIN, CHARLES, *Content's Dream: Essays 1975–1984* (Evanston: Northwestern University Press, 2001)

——, and JAY SANDERS, *Poetry Plastique* (New York: Granary Books, 2000)

BERTRAND, LOÏC, 'The Language of Things: An Archaeology of Musique Concrète', *Organised Sound*, 22.3 (2017), 354–61

BIANCHI, SOLEDAD, 'Agrupaciones literarias de la década del sesenta,' *Revista Chilena de Literatura*, 33 (1989), 103–20

——, *La memoria: Modelo para armar* (Santiago: Dirección de Bibliotecas, Archivos y Museos, 1995)

——, 'Notar y anotar márgenes: Poesía chilena: 1960–1990', *Simpson*, 7 (1992), 88–101

——, *Poesía chilena: Miradas, enfoques, apuntes* (Santiago: Ediciones Documentas CESOC, 1990)

BISHOP, ELIZABETH (ed.), *An Anthology of Twentieth-Century Brazilian Poetry* (Middletown: Wesleyan University Press, 1972)

BLUME SÁNCHEZ, JAIME, 'Rodrigo Lira, poeta posmoderno', *El Instituto*, 7 (1994), 145–59

BOHN, WILLARD, *The Aesthetics of Visual Poetry, 1914–1928* (Cambridge: Cambridge University Press, 1986)

——, *Reading Visual Poetry* (Madison: Fairleigh Dickinson University Press, 2011)

BOLLIG, BEN, 'Exiles and Nomads: Perlongher in Brazil', *Hispanic Research Journal*, 7.4 (2006), 337–51

——, *Néstor Perlongher: The Poetic Search for an Argentine Marginal Voice* (University of Wales Press, 2008)

——, 'Tie Me Up, Tie Me Down: On the Neobarroco, Masochist Suspension and Class Tension in the Work of Néstor Perlongher', *Romance Studies*, 22.2 (2004), 165–82

BORGES, JORGE LUIS, *Ficciones* (Buenos Aires: Emecé, 1956)

——, *Textos recobrados 1919–1929* (Buenos Aires: Emecé, 1997)

BOURRIAUD, NICOLAS, *Relational Aesthetics*, trans. by Simon Pleasance and Fronza Woods (Dijon: Les Presses du Réel, 2002)

——, *The Radicant*, trans. by James Gussen and Lili Porten (New York: Lukas & Sternberg, 2009)

BRAIDOTTI, ROSI, 'Nomadism with a Difference: Deleuze's Legacy in a Feminist Perspective', *Man and World*, 29 (1996), 305–14

BRAGA, EDGARD, *Tatuagens: Poemas* (São Paulo: Invenção, 1976)

BRASIL, EMANUEL and WILLIAM JAY SMITH (eds.), *Brazilian Poetry 1950–1980* (Middleton, CT: Wesleyan University Press, 1983)

BRAVO, EDUARDO, 'El caos tras la poesía', *El Centro*, 9 April 2000, p. 11

BROWN, JULIE PHILLIPS, '"Touch in Transit": Manifestation/*Manifestación* in Cecilia Vicuña's *cloud-net*', *Contemporary Women's Writing*, 5 (2011), 208–31

BÜRGER, PETER, *Theory of the Avant-Garde* (Manchester: Manchester University Press, 1984)

——, and OTHERS, 'Avant-Garde and Neo-Avant-Garde: An Attempt to Answer Certain Critics of Theory of the Avant-Garde', *New Literary History*, 41.4 (2010), 695–715

CAMNITZER, LUIS, *Conceptualism in Latin American Art: Didactics of Liberation* (Austin: University of Texas Press, 2007)

DE CAMPOS, AUGUSTO, *Balanço da Bossa e outras Bossas*, 5th ed. (São Paulo: Editora Perspectiva, 2005)

——, *Despoesia* (São Paulo: Perspectiva, 1994)

——, *Equivocábulos* (São Paulo: Invenção, 1970)

——, *Poemas* (Buenos Aires: de Buenos Aires, 1974)

——, *Poesia* (São Paulo: Editora Brasiliense, 1986)

——, *Poetamenos*, 2ª edn (São Paulo: Invenção, 1973)

——, *Verso, Reverso, Controverso* (São Paulo: Perspectiva, 1978)

——, *Viva Vaia: Poesia 1949–1979* (São Paulo: Brasiliense, 1986)

——, and OTHERS, *Mallarmé*, 3ª edn (São Paulo: Perspectiva, 1991)

——, and OTHERS, *Teoria da Poesia Concreta: Textos, Críticos e Manifestos, 1950–1960* (São Paulo: Invenção, 1965)

DE CAMPOS, HAROLDO, *A Arte no Horizonte do Provável: E outros Ensaios* (São Paulo: Perspectiva, 1969)

——, *Depoimentos de Oficina* (São Paulo: Unimarco Editora, 2002)

——, *Haroldo de Campos 1962/63* (São Paulo: Edições Noigandres, 1964)

——, *A Máquina do Mundo Repensada* (São Paulo: Ateliê Editorial, 2000)

——, *Melhores Poemas*, 3ª edn (São Paulo: Global, 2000)

——, *Metalinguagem e outras Metas: Ensaios de Teoria e Crítica Literaria*, 4th edn (São Paulo: Editora Perspectiva, 1992)

——, *A Operação do Texto* (São Paulo: Editora Perspectiva, 1976)

——, *A ReOperação do Texto*, 2nd edn (São Paulo: Editora Perspectiva, 2013)

——, *Ruptura dos Gêneros na Literatura Latino-americana* (São Paulo: Editora Perspectiva, 1977)

——, *Xadrez de Estrelas: Percurso Textual, 1949–1974* (São Paulo: Editora Perspectiva, 1976)

CAREAGA, ROBERTO, *La poesía terminó conmigo* (Santiago: Ediciones Universidad Diego Portales, 2017)

CARRASCO, IVAN, 'Antipoemas de la antipoesía', *Anales de Literatura Chilena*, 3 (2002), 53–62

——, 'La antipoesía: Manifestación política heterogénea', *Atenea (Concepción)*, 510 (2014), 95–109

——, 'Antipoesía y neovanguardia,' *Estudios Filológicos*, 23 (1988), 35–53

——, 'Poesía chilena de la última década (1977–1987)', *Revista Chilena de Literatura*, 33 (1989), 31–46

——, 'Las voces étnicas en la poesía chilena actual', *Revista Chilena de Literatura*, (1995), 57–70

CAWS, MARY A., *The Poetry of Dada and Surrealism: Aragon, Breton, Tzara, Éluard and Desnos* (Princeton: Princeton University Press, 1970)

CARROLL, LEWIS, *Alice's Adventures in Wonderland* (London: Vintage, 2007)

——, *Jaguadarte*, trans. by Augusto de Campos (São Paulo: Nhambiquara Editora, 2014)

CASELLI, CHRISTIAN (director), *Cinco poemas concretos* (Rio de Janeiro, 2007), <https://www.youtube.com/watch?v=yC3e7rmSYM4> [accessed 10 May 2015]

CID, ALBA and ISAAC LOURIDO (eds.), *La poesía actual en el espacio público* (Binges: Éditions Orbis Tertius, 2015)

CIXOUS, HÉLÈNE, 'The Laugh of the Medusa', *Signs*, trans. by Keith Cohen and Paula Cohen, 1.4 (1976), 875–93

CLARK, MEREDITH G., 'Warping the Word: The Technology of Weaving in the Poetry of Jorge Eduardo Eielson and Cecilia Vicuña', *Textile*, 10.3 (2012), 312–27

COBBING, BOB and PETER MEYER (eds.), *Concerning Concrete Poetry* (London: Writers Forum, 1978)

COLEMAN, VERA, 'Emergent Rhizomes: Posthumanist Environmental Ethics in the Participatory Art of Ala Plástica', *Confluencia*, 31.2 (2016), 85–98

——, 'El huso en el centro del universo: El entrelazamiento cuántico en la poesía visual de Cecilia Vicuña', *Letras femeninas*, 42.1 (2016), 179–93

COLERIDGE, SAMUEL T. and WILLIAM WORDSWORTH, *Lyrical Ballads* (Grandview: Coradella Collegiate Bookshelp Editions, 2007)

COROMINAS, JOAN, *Breve diccionario etimológico de la lengua castellana* (Madrid: Editorial Gredos, 1987)

CORTÁZAR, JULIO, *Rayuela*, ed. by Andrés Amorós, 26th edn (Madrid: Ediciones Cátedra, 2014)

COYLE, JOHN, and OTHERS, *The Midnight Letterbox: Selected Correspondence, 1950–2010* (Manchester: Carcanet Press, 2015)

CROW, JOANNA, 'Mapuche Poetry in Post-Dictatorship Chile: Confronting the Dilemmas of Neoliberal Multiculturalism', *Journal of Latin American Cultural Studies*, 17 (2008), 221–40

CUSSEN, FELIPE, 'Andrés Andwandter: la apertura continua', *Estudios Filológicos*, 40 (2005), 65–78

——, 'Del pajarístico al lenguaje de los pájaros', *Acta Literaria*, 39 (2009), 91–103

——, 'El constructor de cajitas', *Revista Laboratorio* (2009), 1–6

——, 'De la fotocopia al pdf: Juan Luis Martínez y Tan Lin', *Estudios Filológicos*, 57 (2016), 25–41

——, 'Versos sueltos, lugares comunes, poemas encontrados', *Acta Literaria*, 46 (2013), 9–19

DAYDI-TOLSON, SANTIAGO, 'La obra de Juan Luis Martínez: Un ejemplo de poética actual', *Romance Languages Annual*, 3 (1991), 406–10

DEBORD, GUY and KEN KNABB (eds.), *Situationist International Anthology*, trans. by Guy Debord and Ken Knabb (Berkeley: Bureau of Public Secrets, 2006)

DELEUZE, GILLES, *The Fold: Leibniz and the Baroque*, trans. by Tom Conley (London: The Athlone Press, 1993)

——, *Pure Immanence: Essays on a Life*, trans. by Anne Boyan (New York: Zone Books, 2001)

——, *Spinoza: Practical Philosophy*, trans. by Robert Hurley (San Francisco: City Lights Books, 1988)

——, and FÉLIX GUATTARI, *A Thousand Plateaus*, trans. by Brian Massumi (Minneapolis: University of Minnesota Press, 1987)

DERRIDA, JACQUES, *Of Grammatology* (Baltimore: Johns Hopkins University Press, 1974)

——, *Margins of Philosophy* (London: The Harvester Press, 1982)

DRAPER, R. P., 'Concrete Poetry', *New Literary History*, 2 (1971), 329–40

DONOSO, CLAUDIA, 'Lo precario, el canto y el rito', *Revista Apsi*, 218 (1987), 44–46

DRUCKER, JOHANNA, *The Visible Word: Experimental Typography and Modern Art, 1909–1923* (Chicago: University of Chicago Press, 1994)

——, and OTHERS (eds.), *Experimental-Visual-Concrete: Avant-Garde Poetry since the 1960s*, (Amsterdam: Rodopi, 1996)

DOUGLAS-FAIRHURST, ROBERT, *The Story of Alice* (London: Harvill Secker, 2015)

DUPLESSIS, RACHEL BLAU, 'Agency, Social Authorship, and the Political Aura of Contemporary Poetry', *Textual Practice*, 30.7 (2009), 987–99

ECHAVARREN, ROBERTO and OTHERS (eds.), *Medusario: Muestra de poesía latinoamericana* (México, D.F.: Fondo de Cultura Económica, 1996)

ELIOT, T.S., 'Burnt Norton', *Collected Poems of T. S. Eliot: 1909–1935* (New York: Harcourt, Brace and Company, 1936), pp. 213–20

EMERSON, RALPH WALDO, *Emerson's Essays [First and Second Series]* (London: Dutton, 1955)

Erber, Pedro, 'The Word as Object: Concrete Poetry, Ideogram, and the Materialization of Language', *Luso-Brazilian Review*, 49.2 (2012), 72–101

Erdman, David V. (ed.), *The Illuminated Blake: William Blake's Complete Illuminated Works with a Plate-by-Plate Commentary* (New York: Dover, 1992)

Falck, Robert, 'Parody and Contrafactum: A Terminological Clarification', *The Musical Quarterly*, 65.1 (1979), 1–21

Fariña, Soledad and Elvira Hernández (eds.), *Merodeos en torno a la obra poética de Juan Luis Martínez* (Santiago: RIL Editores, 2001)

Folch Mass, Nicolas, 'Rodrigo Lira revisitado', *Cyber Humanitatis*, 44 (2007), 1–8

Fondos Cultura: Libro y lectura, *Juan Luis Martínez*, <http://juanluismartinez.cl/jlm/juan-luis-martinez/biografia/> [accessed 10 December 2016]

Foster, Hal, 'What's Neo about the Neo-Avant-Garde?', *October*, 70 (1994), 5–32

Forster, Merlin and David Jackson, *Vanguardism in Latin American Literature: An Annotated Bibiliographical Guide* (New York: Greenwood, 1990)

Foucault, Michel, 'What is an Author?', *Essential Works of Foucault 1954–1984: Aesthetics, Method, and Epistemology*, vol 2 (New York: The New Press, 1998)

——, *This is Not a Pipe* (Berkeley: University of California Press, 1983)

Franchetti, Paulo, 'Poetry and Technique: Concrete Poetry in Brazil', *Portuguese Studies*, 24 (2008), 56–66

Franco, Jean, *An Introduction to Spanish-American Literature*, 3rd edn (Cambridge: Cambridge University Press, 1994)

Fuentes, Carlos, *La nueva novela hispanoamericana* (México, D.F.: Editorial Joaquín Mortiz, 1969)

Fuentes Leal, Mariela and Juan Zapata Gacitúa, 'La escritura del lenguaje en Enrique Lihn y Germán Marín', *Universum*, 31 (2016), 45–66

Galindo, Oscar, 'El alfabestiario universal de *La nueva novela* de Juan Luis Martínez', *Revista Chilena de Literatura*, 57 (2000), 21–40

——, 'Áreas verdes de la realidad: Martínez y Zurita en el contexto de la poesía neovanguardista hispanoamericana', *Revista de Crítica Literaria Latinoamericana*, 38.76 (2012), 364–65

——, 'Neovanguardias hipervitalistas en la poesía hispanoamericana (1958–1976): Nihilistas, revolucionarios, solidarios y amorosos', *Taller de Letras*, 52 (2013), 11–37

——, 'Palabras e imágenes, objetos y acciones en la postvanguardia chilena', *Estudios Filológicos*, 42 (2007), 109–21

Gardel, Carlos, *Silencio* (YouTube), <https://www.youtube.com/watch?v=rO3ytWP9i78> [accessed 10 July 2017]

Genette, Gérard, *Palimpsests: Literature in the Second Degree*, trans. by Channa Newman and Claude Doubinsky (Lincoln: University of Nebraska Press, 1997)

——, *Paratexts: Thresholds of Interpretation*, trans. by Jane E. Lewin (Cambridge: Cambridge University Press, 1997)

Goldsmith, Kenneth, *From (Command) Line to (Iconic) Constellation*, <http://www.ubu.com/papers/goldsmith_command.html> [accessed 15 April 2016]

——, *Uncreative Writing: Managing Language in the Digital Age* (New York: Columbia University Press, 2011)

Gonzalez, Mike and David Treece, *The Gathering of Voices: The Twentieth-Century Poetry of Latin America* (London: Verso, 1992)

González, Yanko, 'El rasguñón letal del poeta Rodrigo Lira', *El Llanquihue*, 6 de mayo de 1997

Gordon, Kelly, 'Weaving Sight-Weaving Life: Threading the Sacred and Seeking the Meaning of Photography in Cecilia Vicuña's Works', *Hipertexto*, 11 (2010), 93–102

GOTTLIEB, MARLENE and ENRIQUE LIHN, 'Enrique Lihn', *Hispamérica*, 36 (1983), 35–44

GREENBERG, CLEMENT, *Art and Culture* (London: Thames and Hudson, 1961)

GRÜNEWALD, JOSÉ LINO, *Escreviver* (Rio de Janeiro: Nova Fronteira, 1987)

GUARDIOLA-RIVERA, OSCAR, *What if Latin America Ruled the World?: How the South Will Take the North into the 22nd Century* (London: Bloomsbury, 2010)

GUILLORY, JOHN, *Cultural Capital: The Problem of Literary Canon Formation* (Chicago: The University of Chicago Press, 1993)

GULLAR, FERREIRA, 'An Overview of Brazilian Art', *Diogenes*, 191 (2000), 109–14

——, *Crime na Flora, ou, Ordem e Progresso* (Rio de Janeiro: José Olympio, 1986)

——, *Em Alguma Parte Alguma* (Rio de Janeiro: José Olympio, 2010)

——, *Livro-poema* (Rio de Janeiro: Frauenfeld, 1965)

——, *Poemas* (Rio de Janeiro: Coleção Espaço, 1958)

——, *Toda Poesia (1950–1980)*, 3rd edn (Rio de Janeiro: Civilização Brasileira, 1983)

——, and ALFREDO BOSI, *Os Melhores Poemas de Ferreira Gullar* (São Paulo: Global Editora, 1983)

——, *O Formiguero*, 2nd edn (Rio de Janeiro: Autêntica, 2015)

GOMRINGER, EUGEN, *Ideogramme = idéogrammes = ideograms = ideogramas* (São Paulo: Frauenfeld/Schweiz, n.d.)

GONZÁLEZ BARNET, ERNESTO, 'Martín Gubbins', *Proyecto patrimonio* (2007), <http://www.letras.mysite.com/egb190607.htm> [accessed 20 March 2021]

GUTMAN, PETER, 'The Sounds of Silence,' (Classical Notes: 1999), <http://www.classicalnotes.net/columns/silence.html> [accessed 10 May 2015]

GUZMÁN, JORGE, *Contra el secreto profesional: lectura mestiza de César Vallejo* (Santiago: Editorial Universitaria, 1991)

HEIDEGGER, MARTIN, *Poetry, Language, Thought* (New York: Harper & Row, 1971)

HERBERT, GEORGE, *The Temple* (London: Penguin Classics, 2017)

HERNÁNDEZ, FELISBERTO, *Los libros sin tapas* (Buenos Aires: El Cuenco de Plata, 2010)

HERRERA, JUAN, '*La nueva novela* de Juan Luis Martínez: Poesía protohipertextual en el contexto de la ideósfera', *Acta Literaria*, 35 (2007), 9–27

HOBSBAWM, ERIC, *Behind the Times: The Decline and Fall of the Twentieth-Century Avant-Gardes* (London: Thames and Hudson, 1998)

HOPKINS, BUDD, 'Modernism and the Collage Aesthetic', *New England Review*, 18 (1997), 5–12

HOPKINS, DAVID (ed.), *Neo-Avant-Garde* (Amsterdam: Rodopi, 2006)

HUIDOBRO, VICENTE, *El espejo de agua* y *Ecuatorial* (Buenos Aires: Pequeño Dios Editores, 2011)

Internationale Situationniste #1: Definitions, trans. by Ken Knabb (June 1958), <http://www.cddc.vt.edu/sionline/si/definitions.html> [accessed 5 July 2016]

IRIARTE, IGNACIO, 'Barroco, Modernismo, Neobarroco', *Orbis tertius*, 20.21 (2015), 106–14

IRIGARAY, LUCE, *Speculum of the Other Woman*, trans. by Gillian C. Gill (Ithaca: Cornell University Press, 1985)

JACKSON, K. DAVID (ed.), *Haroldo de Campos: A Dialogue with the Brazilian Concrete Poet* (Oxford: Centre for Brazilian Studies, 2005)

JACKSON, SCOTT, 'Juan Luis Martínez: The Novelist of Non-Existence', *Confluencia*, 12.1 (1996), 134–40

JAKOBSON, ROMAN, *Fundamentals of Language*, trans. by Morris Halle (Gravenhage: Mouton, 1956)

——, 'Linguistics and Poetics', in *Modern Criticism and Theory: A Reader*, ed. by David Lodge and Nigel Wood, 3rd edn (London: Pearson, 2008)

JARRY, ALFRED, *The Ubu Plays*, trans. by Lyril Connolly and Simon Watson Taylor (London: Methuen, 1968)

Joannon, Cristóbal, 'Un poeta hiperliterario, cómico y apaciguado', *Revista Universitaria*, 82 (2004), 68–69

Joris, Pierre, *A Nomad Poetics* (Middletown: Wesleyan University Press, 2003)

——, and Jerome Rothenberg (eds.), *Poems for the Millennium: From Post War to Millennium*, vol 2 (Berkeley: University of California Press, 1998)

Jowett, Benjamin (ed.), *Dialogues of Plato: Translated into English, with Analyses and Introduction* (Cambridge: Cambridge University Press, 2010)

Kircher, Athanasius, *Musurgia Universalis*, vol 1 (Rome: Ex Typograpia Haeredum F. Corbellitti, 1650)

Kirkpatrick, Gwen, 'Desapariciones y ausencias en *La nueva novela* de Juan Luis Martínez', *Revista de Crítica Literaria Latinoamericana,* 25 (1999), 225–34

Kosick, Rebecca, 'Assembling *La nueva novela*: Juan Luis Martínez and a Material Poetics of Relation', *Latin American Research Review*, 52.5 (2017), 854–73

Kostelanetz, Richard and Gertrude Stein, *The Yale Gertrude Stein: Selections* (New Haven: Yale University Press, 1980)

Kraft, David, *Birdsong in the Music of Olivier Messiaen* (Unpublished doctoral thesis, Middlesex University, 2000)

Lao-Tzu, *Tao Te Ching*, trans. by Stephen Addiss and Stanley Lombardo (Indianapolis: Hackett Publishing Company, 1993)

Lastra, Pedro and Enrique Lihn, *Señales de ruta de Juan Luis Martínez* (Santiago: Ediciones Archivo, 1987)

Lecercle, Jean-Jacques, *The Violence of Language* (London: Routledge, 1999)

Leong, Peter, 'Poetry Homework: Pedagogy, Memory, and Politics in the Visual Poetry of Juan Luis Martínez', *A Contracorriente*, 14.2 (2017), 162–88

Lessing, Gotthold Ephraim, *Laocoön: An Essay on the Limits of Painting and Poetry* (London: Longman, Brown, Green, and Longmans, 1853)

Lerner, Ben, *The Hatred of Poetry* (London: Fitzcarraldo Editions, 2016)

Levinson, Brett, *The Ends of Literature: The Latin American 'Boom' in the Neoliberal Marketplace* (Stanford: Stanford University Press, 2001)

Lihn, Enrique, *El paseo ahumada* (Barcelona: Minga, 1985)

Lira, Rodrigo, *Buelos barrios: Boladas boludas*, ed. by Marcelo Gatica (Santiago: Piélago, 2016).

——, *Cartapacio*, (Biblioteca Nacional de Chile) <http://www.memoriachilena.cl/602/w3-article-72711.html> [accessed 26 April 2018]

——, *Declaración jurada* (Santiago: Ediciones Universidad Diego Portales, 2006)

———, *Rodrigo Lira: Proyecto de obras completas*, edited by Milagros Abalo (Santiago: Ediciones Universidad Diego Portales, [1984] 2013)

Livon-Grosman, Ernesto and Cecilia Vicuña (eds.), *The Oxford Book of Latin American Poetry: A Bilingual Anthology* (Oxford: Oxford University Press, 2009)

Lolas, Jazmín, 'Mi trabajo ha sido censurado durante cuarenta años' (*Las Últimas Noticias*, 2006) <http://www.letras.s5.com/cv200106.htm> [accessed 20 January 2015]

Lynd, Juliet, 'Precarious Resistance: Weaving Opposition in the Poetry of Cecilia Vicuña', *PMLA*, 120 (2005), 1588–1607

——, 'Hondo es el pozo del tiempo: Memory and Violence in Raúl Zurita's *Las ciudades de agua*', *Mandorla*, 13 (2007), 405–20

Mackey, Carol, 'The Continuing Khipu Traditions: Principles and Practices', in *Narrative Threads*, ed. by Jeffrey Quilter and Gary Urton (Austin: University of Texas Press, 2002), pp. 320–47

Mallarmé, Stéphane, *Un Coup de dés jamais n'abolira le hazard* (Paris: Éditions Gallimard, 1914)

Martí, José, *Obras completas*, vol. 16 (Habana: Centro de Estudios Martinianos, 2001)
Martínez, Juan Luis, *Aproximación de un Principio de Incertidumbre a un proyecto poético* (Santiago de Chile: Editorial Nómade, 2010)
——, *La nueva novela* (Santiago: Ediciones Archivos, 1977)
——, *Poemas del otro: Poemas y diálogos dispersos* (Santiago: Universidad Diego Portales, 2003)
——, *La poesía chilena* (Santiago de Chile: Ediciones Archivo, 1978)
Martins, Sergio, '"The Pulp of Color": Toward a Notion of Expenditure in Ferreira Gullar's Neo-Concrete Writings', *October*, 152 (2015), 103–20
——, 'Phenomenological Openness', *Third Text*, 26.1 (2012), 79–90
Masiello, Francine, 'Oliverio Girondo: El carnaval del lenguaje', *Hispamérica*, 6.16 (1977), 3–17
Massumi, Brian, *A User's Guide to Capitalism and Schizophrenia: Deviations from Deleuze and Guattari* (Cambridge: Massachussetts Institute of Technology, 1992)
de Melo e Castro, E. M., *Visão Visual: 1961–1993* (Rio de Janeiro: Francisco Alves, 1994)
Mendes, Gilberto (YouTube), 'Nascemorre' (2010), <https://www.youtube.com/watch?v=O6JrRwuY7Kk> [accessed 10 May 2015]
Merino, Roberto, 'La llamada elíptica', *Talleres Gráficos,* 268 (1988), iv–v
Micharvergas, Martín (ed.), *Nueva poesía joven en Chile* (Buenos Aires: Ediciones Noé, 1972)
Milán, Eduardo. 'Parra en dos tiempos', *Revista de teoría y crítica de poesía latinoamericana*, 6 (2018), 108–19
Millán, Gonzalo, *La ciudad* (Quebec: Les Editions Maison Culturelle, 1979)
Milnes, Andrés Cáceres, 'Una lectura de *El gran vidrio* de Marcel Duchamp y *La nueva novela* de Juan Luis Martínez como una articulación meta-poética y autorreflexiva', *Aisthesis*, 55 (2014), 97–115
——, and others, 'Una lira desolada: Parodia y frustración en *Proyecto de obras completas y declaración jurada*', *Universum*, 31 (2016), 45–66
Mitchell, W. J. T., 'The Commitment to Form; Or, Still Crazy after All These Years', *PMLA*, 118.2 (2003), 321–25
Moi, Toril, *Sexual/Textual Politics* (Methuen: London, 1985)
Monarca, Patricia, *Juan Luis Martínez: El juego de las contradicciones* (Santiago: RIL, 1998)
Monelle, Raymond, 'Musica Significans: Proceedings of the 3rd International Congress on Musical Signification', *Contemporary Music Review*, 16 (1992)
Montes, Hugo, 'Rubén Darío y la antipoesía', *Revista Chilena de Literatura*, 30 (1987), 191–94
Morales, Andrés, 'Para una lectura interpretativa de *La poesía chilena* de Juan Luis Martínez', *Revista Chilena de Literatura*, 69 (2006), 107–12
——, 'Vicente Huidobro y la poesía chilena actual', *Anales de Literatura Chilena*, 9 (2008), 235–40
Morgan, Edwin and others, *The Midnight Letterbox: Selected Correspondence, 1950–2010* (Manchester: Carcanet Press, 2015)
Motte, Warren, 'First and Second Manifesto', *Oulipo: A Primer of Potential Literature* (Lincoln: University of Nebraska, 1986), pp. 26–29
Müller-Bergh, Klaus, 'Feijoada, Coke and the Urbanoid: Brazilian Poetry since 1945', *World Literature Today,* 53.1 (1979), 22–30
Neruda, Pablo, *Estravagario* (Buenos Aires: Losada, 1958)
——, *Libro de preguntas* (Buenos Aires: Losada, 1974)
——, *Odas elementales,* 4th edn (Buenos Aires: Editorial Losada, 1977)
——, *Para nacer he nacido* (Barcelona: Editorial Seix Barral, 1978)
'Nicanor Parra', *Memoria Chilena* (Santiago: Biblioteca Nacional de Chile) <http://www.memoriachilena.cl/602/w3-article-3629.html> [accessed 16 June 2017].

'Orquesta de poetas', *Registro de poetas* (2020), <https://www.orquestadepoetas.cl/videosregistrodepoetas> [accessed 20 March 2021]

Ortega y Gasset, José, *La deshumanización del arte y otros ensayos estéticos*, 4th edn (Madrid: Revista de Occidente, 1956)

Ortiz, Fernando, *Contrapunteo cubano del tabaco y el azúcar* (Havana: Consejo Nacional de Cultura, 1963)

Parra, Nicanor, *Artefactos visuales* (Concepción: Universidad de Concepción, 2002)

——, *Obra gruesa* (Santiago: Editorial Universitaria, 1969)

——, *The Stone and the Thread: Andean Roots of Abstract Art*, trans. by Esther Allen (Austin: Texas University Press, 1996)

Paternosto, Cesar, 'Cecilia Vicuña', *Review: Literature and Arts of the Americas*, 22.39 (1988), 14–15

Paz, Octavio, *Transblanco* (Rio de Janeiro: Editora Guanabara, 1986)

Pearsall, Judy (ed.), *The Concise Oxford Dictionary*, 10th edn (Oxford: Oxford University Press, 1999)

Pérez Villalón, Fernando, '"Todos instrumentos": Crónica de una orquesta', *Revista transas* (14 Nov 2019), <https://www.revistatransas.com/2019/11/14/todosintrumentos_perezvillalon/> [accessed 20 March 2021]

Perloff, Marjorie, 'Collage and Poetry', in *Encyclopedia of Aesthetics*, ed. by Michael Kelly (New York: Oxford University Press, 1998), pp. 384–87

——, '"Concrete Prose" in the Nineties: Haroldo de Campos's "Galáxias" and After,' *Contemporary Literature,* 42 (2001), 270–93

——, 'Marjorie Perloff: A Conversation with Kenneth Goldsmith,' *Jacket 21* (Feb. 2003)

——, 'Refiguring the Poundian Ideogram: from Octavio Paz's Blanco/Branco to Haroldo de Campos's Galáxias', *Modernist Cultures*, 7.1 (2012), 40–55

——, *Unoriginal Genius: Poetry by Other Means in the New Century* (Chicago: The University of Chicago Press, 2010)

Perlongher, Néstor, 'As Viagens da Vanguarda', *Leia Livros*, 62 (1983), p. 21

Perrone, Charles, 'From Noigandres to "Milagre da Alegria": The Concrete Poets and Contemporary Brazilian Popular Music', *Latin American Music Review*, 6.1 (1985), 58–79

Pignatari, Décio, 'Concrete Poetry: A Brief Structural-Historical Guideline', trans. by Jon Tolman, *Poetics Today,* 3 (1982), 189–95

——, *Exercício Findo* (São Paulo: Invenção, 1968)

——, *O organismo quer...* (São Paulo: S.C.P., 1960)

——, *Poesia Pois é Poesia: 1950–2000* (São Paulo: Ateliê Editorial, 2004)

——, *Vocogramas* (São Paulo: Dimip, 1985)

——, and others, *Noigandres 5: Antologia do Verso à Poesia Concreta (1949–1962)* (São Paulo: Massao Ohno, 1962)

Pineda, Victoria, 'Speaking about Genre: The Case of Concrete Poetry', *New Literary History*, 26 (1995), 379–93

Plato, *The Republic*, trans. by Desmond Lee, 2nd edn (London: Penguin Books, 1974)

Poblete, Ignacio, *Nicanor Parra, Jerome Rothenberg, Cecilia Vicuña* (YouTube, 2004), <https://www.youtube.com/watch?v=YV77uldGSUM> [accessed 14 May 2015]

Polanco, Jorge, *Pajarístico: Aproximaciones a la obra de Juan Luis Martínez* (Valparaíso: Ediciones Universitarias de Valparaíso, 2015)

Price, Rachel, 'Object, Non-Object, Transobject, Relational Object: From "Poesia concreta" to "A nova objetividade"', *Revista de Letras,* 47 (2007), 31–50

Quezada, Jaime, 'Juan Luis Martínez: El desórden de los sentidos', *Ercilla* (23 November 1977), 49–50

Rama, Ángel, *Transculturación narrativa en América Latina* (Mexico, D. F.: Siglo XXI Editores, 1982)

RANCIÈRE, JACQUES, *Aesthetics and its Discontents* (Cambridge: Polity Press, 2009)

Raúl Zurita habla sobre Juan Luis Martínez (YouTube), <https://www.youtube.com/watch?v=lUFBlbEvLZY> [accessed 24 January 2016]

RECKIN, ANNA, 'Cecilia Vicuña's *cloud-net*', *How2*, 1.5 (2001), <http://www.asu.edu/pipercwcenter/how2journal/archive/online_archive/v1_5_2001/current/alerts/reckin.html> [accessed 15 May 2015]

Research Planning Memorandum on Some Thoughts about New Brands of Cigarettes for the Youth Market, (Minnesota Documents, 1973) <https://www.industrydocumentslibrary.ucsf.edu/tobacco/docs/#id=gmnx0096> [accessed 1 February 2018]

REYES, ALFONSO, 'La jitanjáfora', in *Revista libra (1929)*, ed. by Rosa Corral (Mexico City: Colegio de México, 2003), pp. 1–22

RICHTER, EMMA, 'Tras los cambios en la poesía: J. L. Martínez', *Estudios Filológicos*, 51 (2013), 115–29

DE LOS RÍOS, VALERIA, 'La fotografía como clave de lectura de *La nueva novela*', *Estudios Filológicos*, 44 (2009), 53–65

RIOSECO, MARCELO, 'La escritura exasperada', *Hispamérica*, 108 (2007), 101–08

——, *Maquinarias reconstructivas: Poesía y juego en Juan Luis Martínez, Diego Maquieira y Rodrigo Lira* (Santiago: Editorial Cuarto Propio, 2013)

——, 'La poésia matemática de Juan Luis Martínez', *Revista Iberoamericana*, 232 (2010), 855–74

RIVKIN, JULIE and MICHAEL RYAN (eds.), *Literary Theory: An Anthology*, 2nd edn (Oxford: Blackwell, 2004)

ROBINSON, JEFFREY and JEROME ROTHENBERG (eds.), *Poems for the Millennium: Romantic and Postromantic Poetry*, vol 3 (Berkeley: University of California Press, 2009)

ROBINSON, RACHEL, 'Plastic Poetry of the Page: Cecilia Vicuña's *Instan*', *Latin American Literary Review*, 40.90 (2018), 33–43

ROTHENBERG, JEROME, *Technicians of the Sacred*, 2nd edn (Berkeley: University of California Press, 1985)

ROWE, WILLIAM, *Poets of Contemporary Latin America: History and the Inner Life* (Oxford: Oxford University Press, 2000)

——, 'Raúl Zurita: Language, madness and the social wound', *Travesia*, 2.2 (1993), 183–218

SANTIAGO, SILVIANO, *The Space In-Between* (Durham: Duke University Press, 2001)

DE SARMIENTO, OSCAR, 'Intersecting Reflections: Huidobro through Juan Luis Martínez's La nueva novela', *Hispanic Issues Online*, 5 (2010), 152–66

SARTRE, JEAN-PAUL, *What is Literature?*, trans. by Bernard Frechtman (Abingdon: Routledge Classics, 2001)

DE SAUSSURE, FERDINAND, *Course in General Linguistics*, trans. by Roy Harris (London: Gerald Duckworth and Co., 1983)

SCHEUNEMANN, DIETRICH (ed.), *Avant-Garde/Neo-Avant-Garde* (Amsterdam: Rodopi, 2005)

SCHWARZ, ROBERT, *Misplaced Ideas: Essays on Brazilian Culture* (London: Verso, 1992)

SEPÚLVEDA, JESÚS, *Poets on the Edge: Vicente Huidobro, César Vallejo, Juan Luis Martínez, and Néstor Perlongher* (Florida: Brown Walker, 2016).

——, 'Sólo tendrás piedras: Rodrigo Lira', *Memoria Chilena* <http://www.memoriachilena.cl/602/w3-article-3693.html> [accessed 20 September 2017]

SEPÚLVEDA, MAGDA, 'Cecilia Vicuña: La subjetividad poética como una operación contracanónica', *Revista Chilena de Literatura*, 57 (2000), 111–26

——, 'Para una entrada en la imaginación poética alimentaria chilena', *Revista chilena literaria*, 86 (2014), 119–213

SEPÚLVEDA ZELAYA, CARMEN G., *The Legal and Political Battles over the Distribution of Emergency Contraception in Chile under the Presidencies of Ricardo Lagos (2000–2005) and Michelle Bachelet (2006–2010)* (unpublished PhD thesis, UCL, 2014)

Sheppard, Robert, *When Bad Times Made for Good Poetry* (Exeter: Shearsman Books, 2011)

Sherwood, Kenneth, 'Elaborate: Versionings: Characteristics of Emergent Performance in Three Print/Oral/Aural Poets', *Oral Tradition*, 21 (2006), 119–47

da Silva, Renato Rodrigues, 'Ferreira Gullar's Non-Object, or How Neoconcrete Poetry Became One with the World', *Word and Image*, 29.3 (2013), 257–72

Small, Irene V, 'Exit and Impasse', *Third Text*, 26.1 (2012), 91–101

Smith, Jessica, 'The Plasticity of Poetry', *Literature Compass*, 3 (2006), 613–24

Solt, Mary Ellen (ed.), *Concrete Poetry: A World View* (Bloomington: Indiana University Press, 1968)

——, 'Concrete Poetry', *Books Abroad*, 44 (1970), 421–25

Sommer, Pía, *Cuadernillo* (Málaga: Ediciones Imperdonables, 2018)

Soo-Jie, Lee, 'La (in)comunicación en Artefactos de Nicanor Parra', *Espéculo: Revista de estudios literarios* (2006), <https://webs.ucm.es/info/especulo/numero34/parra.html> [accessed 15 October 2018]

Soros, Juan, 'Blurring the Boundaries between Land Art and Poetry in the Work of Raúl Zurita', *Review: Literature and Arts of the Americas*, 45.2 (2012), 227–35

Stein, Gertrude, *Lectures in America* (New York: Random House, 1935)

——, *The Yale Gertrude Stein* (New Haven: Yale University Press, 1980)

Sternberg, Ricardo da Silveira Lobo, 'Memory and History in Ferreira Gullar's *Poema Sujo*', *Revista Canadiense de Estudios Hispánicos*, 14.1 (1989), 131–43

Stoffel, Stephanie Lovett, *Lewis Carroll and Alice* (London: Thames and Hudson, 1997)

STP (Global Information Network about Drugs), <http://www.ginad.org/en/drugs/drugs/407/stp> [accessed 20 July 2017]

Sturrock, John, *The French New Novel* (Oxford: Oxford University Press, 1969)

Suárez, Zenaida M, 'Objetualismo en Juan Luis Martínez: el significante palpable', *Estudios Filológicos*, 51 (2013), 83–98

——, *Palabras ya escritas: Relecturas de* La nueva novela *de Juan Luis Martínez* (Santiago: RIL editores, 2019)

Sullivan, Lawrence, *Icanchu's Drum: An Orientation to Meaning in South American Religions* (New York: Macmillan, 1988)

Tayler, Irene, *Blake's Illustrations to the Poems of Gray* (Princeton: Princeton University Press, 1971)

Taylor, Carole Anne, *A Poetics of Seeing: The Implications of Visual Form in Modern Poetry* (New York: Garland, 1985)

Travis, Christopher, 'Beyond the Vanguardia: The Dialectical Voice of Enrique Lihn', *Romance Quarterly*, 49.1 (2002), 61–74

Trier, James (ed.), *Detournement as Pedagogical Praxis* (Boston: Sense Publishers, 2014)

Tedlock, Dennis, *Popol Vuh: The Mayan Book of the Dawn of Life*, rev. edn (New York: Simon & Schuster, 1996)

——, 'Ethnopoetics,' (n.d.), <http://epc.buffalo.edu/authors/tedlock/syllabi/ethnopoetics.html> [accessed 20 May 2015]

Teruggi, Daniel, 'Musique Concrète Today: Its Reach, Evolution of Conception and Role in Musical Thought', *Organised Sound*, 20.1 (2015), 51–59

——, 'The Context of a Vanguard: Toward a Definition of Concrete Poetry', *Poetics Today*, 3 (1982), 149–66

Unruh, Vicky, *Latin American Vanguards: The Art of Contentious Encounters* (Berkeley: University of California Press, 1994)

Urton, Gary, 'Writing the History of an Ancient Civilization without Writing: Reading the Inka Khipus as Primary Sounds', *Journal of Anthropological Research*, 73.1 (2017), 1–21

de Valdivia, Pedro, *Carta al Emperador Carlos V. 4 de Septiembre de 1545* (Universidad de Chile), <http://www.historia.uchile.cl/CDA/fh_article/0,1389,SCID%253D11303%2526

ISID%253D405%2526PRT%253D11300%2526JNID%253D12,00.html> [accessed 30 June 2017]

VALDIVIESO, JAIME, 'Juan Luis Marítnez: El contra-universo en las páginas de un libro', *La Época* (11 de septiembre, 1988)

VALLEJO, CÉSAR, *Trilce*, ed. by Julio Ortega (Madrid: Ediciones Cátedra, 1991)

VÁSQUEZ ROCCA, ADOLFO, 'Alteridad e identidad en *La nueva novela* de Juan Luis Martínez: La deconstrucción de la noción de autor', *Convergencias Literatura*, 6 (2007), 130–45

——, 'Nicanor Parra: antipoemas, parodias y lenguajes híbridos de la antipoesía al lenguaje del artefacto', *Nómadas* (2012), 1–20

——, 'La reconfiguración del concepto de autor: Alteridad e identidad en la poesía de Juan Luis Martínez', *Cyber Humanitatis*, 33 (2005)

VICUÑA, CECILIA, *Cloud-Net* (New York: Art in General, l999)

——, 'Cloud-net', *Knit Knit*, 6 (2005)

——, *Cloud-net* [video], (1998), <https://vimeo.com/home/myvideos> [accessed 15 May 2015]

——, and IGNACIO POBLETE, *Palabrarmas* (2006), <https://vimeo.com/67557355> [accessed 25 January 2015]

——, *Instan* (New York: Kelsey St Press, 2002)

——, *I tú* (Buenos Aires: Tsé~Tsé, 2004)

——, *Luxumei o el traspie de la doctrina: Poemas 1966–1972* (México: Editorial Oasis, 1983)

——, 'On Cloud Net', *Naked Punch*, 9 (2007)

——, *Palabra e hilo = Word & Thread* (Edinburgh: Morning Star Publications, 1996)

——, PALABRAR*mas* (Santiago: RIL editores, 2005)

——, *Precario/Precarious* (New York: Tanam Press, l983)

——, *QUIPOem*, ed. by Catherine de Zegher (Middletown: Wesleyan University Press, l997)

——, 'Re: cloud-net and other questions', email to Rachel Robinson, 30 March 2015

——, *Saborami* (Devon: Beau Geste Press, 1973)

——, 'Sobre Cecilia Vicuña', *Cecilia Vicuña* (n.d.), <http://www.ceciliavicuna.org/esp_sobre.htm> [accessed 4 December 2014]

——, *Split Temple*, trans. by Rosa Alcalá (New York: Ugly Duckling Press, 2012)

——, *El templo* (New York: Situations, 2001)

——, *Unravelling Words and the Weaving of Water* (St. Paul: Graywolf Press, 1992)

——, *V* (Lima: tRpode editors, 2009)

——, *La Wik'Uña* (Santiago: Atenea, 1990)

——, and EDWIN MORGAN, PALABRAR*mas*/WURDWAPPIN*schaw* (Edinburgh: Morning Star Publications, 1994)

VERA, ADOLFO, 'Rodrigo Lira o en cansancio del lenguaje [entrevista], *Letras*, 64 (1999)

VERISSIMO, ERICO, *Brazilian Literature: An Outline* (New York: The Macmillan Company, 1945)

WEBSTER, MICHAEL, *Reading Visual Poetry after Futurism: Marinetti, Apollinaire, Schwitters, Cummings* (New York: Lang, 1995)

WEINTRAUB, SCOTT, *Juan Luis Martínez's Philosophical Poetics* (Lewisburg: Bucknell University Press, 2015)

——, 'Mourning for the Future: Poetic Inheritance in Juan Luis Martínez's *La poesía chilena*', *Revista Canadiense de Estudios Hispánicos*, 37.2 (2013), 255–78

——, *La última broma de Juan Luis Martínez: No solo ser otro sino escribir la obra de otro* (Santiago: Cuarto Propio, 2014)

WEIZMAN, EYAL, 'Walking through Walls: Soldiers as Architects in the Israeli Palestinian Conflict', *Radical Philosophy*, 136 (2006), 8–22

WHITE, STEVEN, 'La traducción y la poesía chilena postgolpe: Historicidad e identidad de género', *Revista Chilena de Literatura*, 42 (1993), 275–79

WILLIAMS, EMMETT (ed.), *An Anthology of Concrete Poetry* (Brooklyn: Primary Information, 2013)

WILLIAMSON, EDWIN, *The Penguin History of Latin America*, rev. edn (London: Penguin, 2009)

WOOD, OLIVER NOBLE, '"Ensíllenme el asno rucio": Parody and Burlesque in A Contrafactum', in *A Poet for all Seasons: Eight Commentaries on Góngora*, ed. by Nigel Griffin and Oliver Noble Wood (New York: Hispanic Seminary of Medieval Studies, 2013), pp. 1–23

WORDSWORTH, WILLIAM, *Lyrical Ballads* (Grandview: Coradella Collegiate Bookshelf Editions, 2007)

XISTO, PEDRO, *Logogramas: Concreções do Logos* (São Paulo: Invenção, 1967)

YÉPEZ, HERIBERTO, 'The Dialectic of Romantic and Postromantic Ethopoetics (after Certain Hispano-American Visual Poetries)', in *Active Romanticism*, ed. by Julie Carr and Jeffrey C. Robinson (Tuscaloosa: The University of Alabama Press, 2015), pp. 197–211

ZALDÍVAR, MARÍA INÉS, 'El contexto de Guillermo Desiler en Chile y la generación poética de los 60', *Taller de letras*, 41 (2007),109–20

DE ZEGHER, CATHERINE (ed.), *The Precarious: The Art and Poetry of Cecilia Vicuña* (Hanover: Wesleyan University Press, 1997)

ZURITA, RAÚL, *Mi mejilla es el cielo estrellado* (Coahuila: Aldus, 2004)

INDEX

www.ingramcontent.com/pod-product-compliance
Lightning Source LLC
LaVergne TN
LVHW081258100826
845148LV00005B/910

* 9 7 8 1 8 3 9 5 4 0 2 9 5 *